プロジェクトアームズ

PROJECT ARMS

The Fourth Revelation : Meltdown

vol. 17

PROJECT ARMS
The Fourth Revelation: Meltdown
Vol. 17

Created by Ryoji Minagawa and Kyoichi Nanatsuki

English Adaptation/Lance Caselman
Translation/Katy Bridges
Touch-up Art & Lettering/Kathryn Renta
Cover & Interior Design/Mark Schumann
Editor/Jonathan Tarbox

Editor in Chief, Books/Alvin Lu
Editor in Chief, Magazines/Marc Weidenbaum
VP of Publishing Licensing/Rika Inouye
VP of Sales/Gonzalo Ferreya
Sr. VP of Marketing/Liza Coppola
Publisher/Hyoe Narita

Printed in the U.S.A.

Published by VIZ Media, LLC
P.O. Box 77010
San Francisco, CA 94107

10 9 8 7 6 5 4 3 2 1
First printing, September 2007

CONTENTS

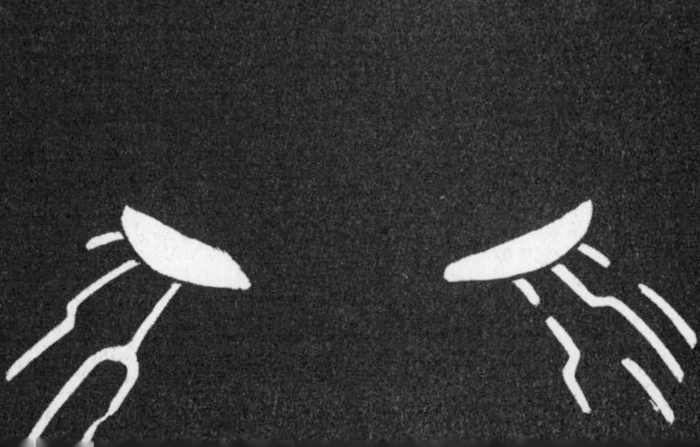

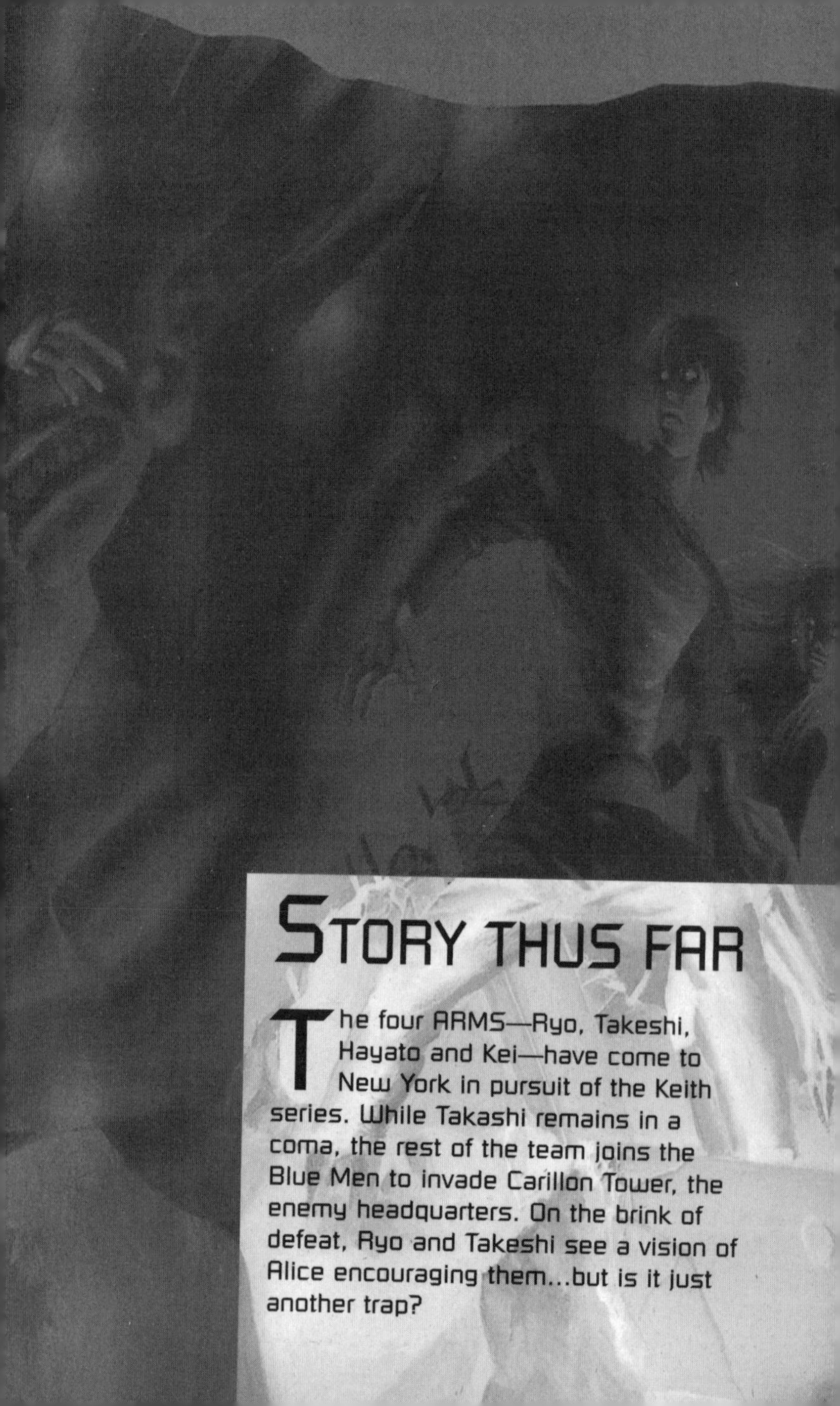

STORY THUS FAR

The four ARMS—Ryo, Takeshi, Hayato and Kei—have come to New York in pursuit of the Keith series. While Takashi remains in a coma, the rest of the team joins the Blue Men to invade Carillon Tower, the enemy headquarters. On the brink of defeat, Ryo and Takeshi see a vision of Alice encouraging them...but is it just another trap?

No. 1 BREAKDOWN

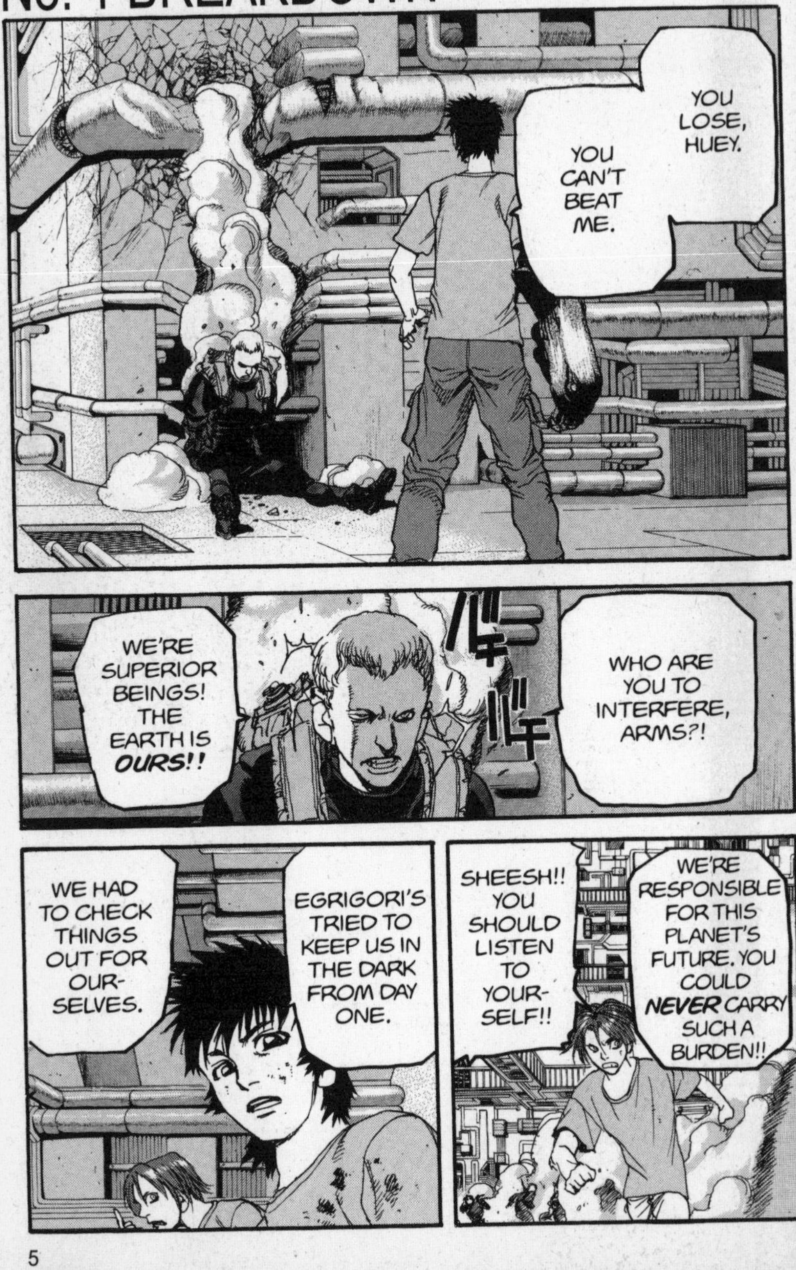
YOU LOSE, HUEY.
YOU CAN'T BEAT ME.
WHO ARE YOU TO INTERFERE, ARMS?!
WE'RE SUPERIOR BEINGS! THE EARTH IS ***OURS!!***
WE'RE RESPONSIBLE FOR THIS PLANET'S FUTURE. YOU COULD ***NEVER*** CARRY SUCH A BURDEN!!
SHEESH!! YOU SHOULD LISTEN TO YOUR-SELF!!
EGRIGORI'S TRIED TO KEEP US IN THE DARK FROM DAY ONE.
WE HAD TO CHECK THINGS OUT FOR OUR-SELVES.

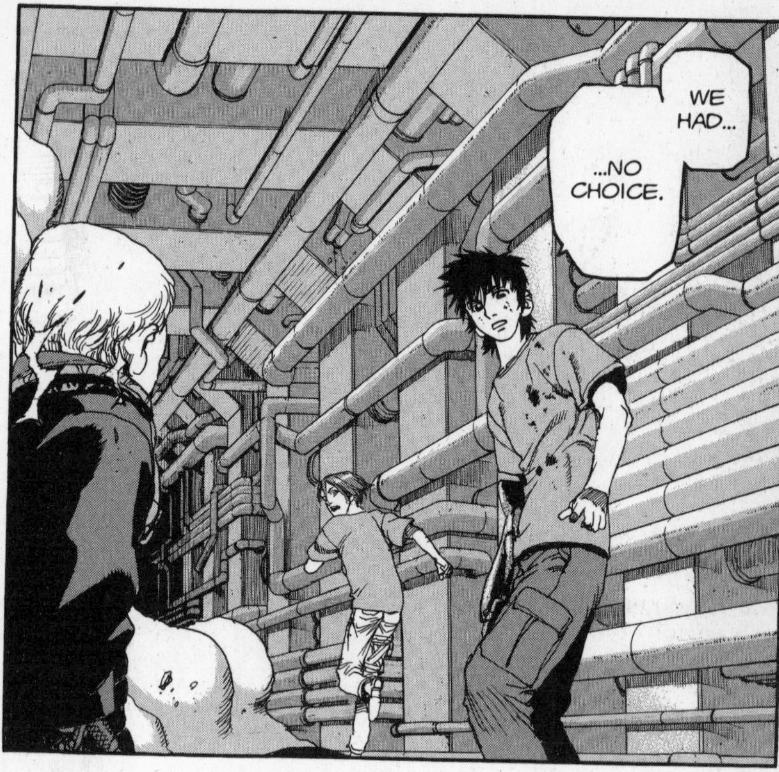
WE HAD...
...NO CHOICE.

No. 1 BREAKDOWN

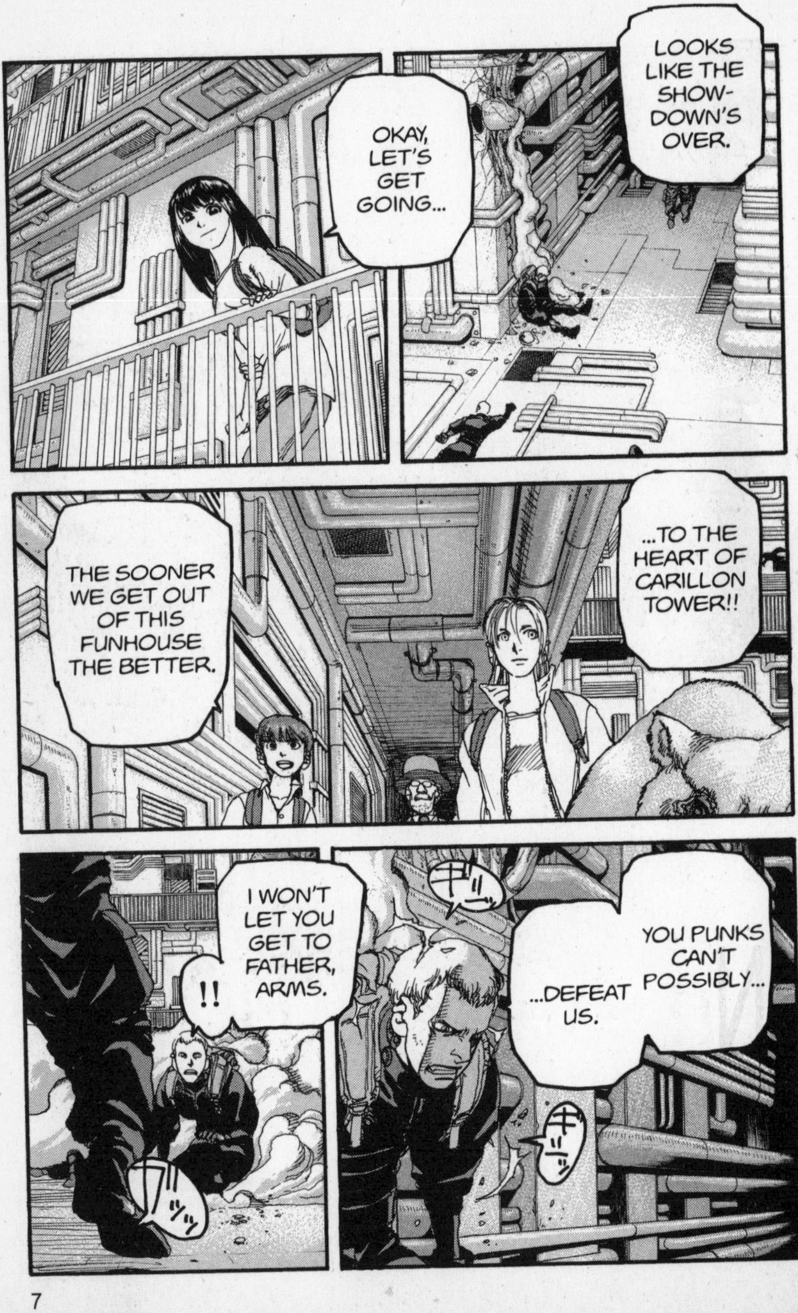
LOOKS LIKE THE SHOW-DOWN'S OVER.
OKAY, LET'S GET GOING...
...TO THE HEART OF CARILLON TOWER!!
THE SOONER WE GET OUT OF THIS FUNHOUSE THE BETTER.
YOU PUNKS CAN'T POSSIBLY...
...DEFEAT US.
I WON'T LET YOU GET TO FATHER, ARMS.
!!

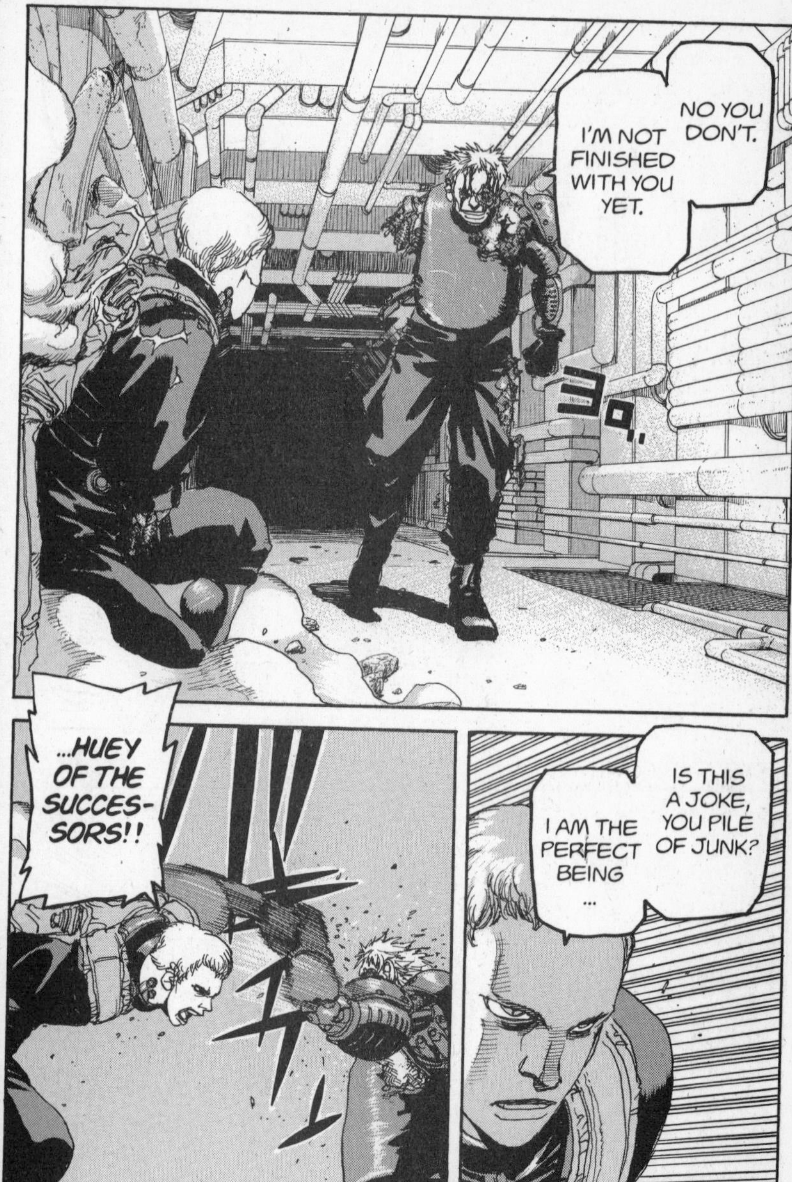
NO YOU DON'T.
I'M NOT FINISHED WITH YOU YET.
ヨロ
IS THIS A JOKE, YOU PILE OF JUNK?
I AM THE PERFECT BEING ...
...HUEY OF THE SUCCES-SORS!!

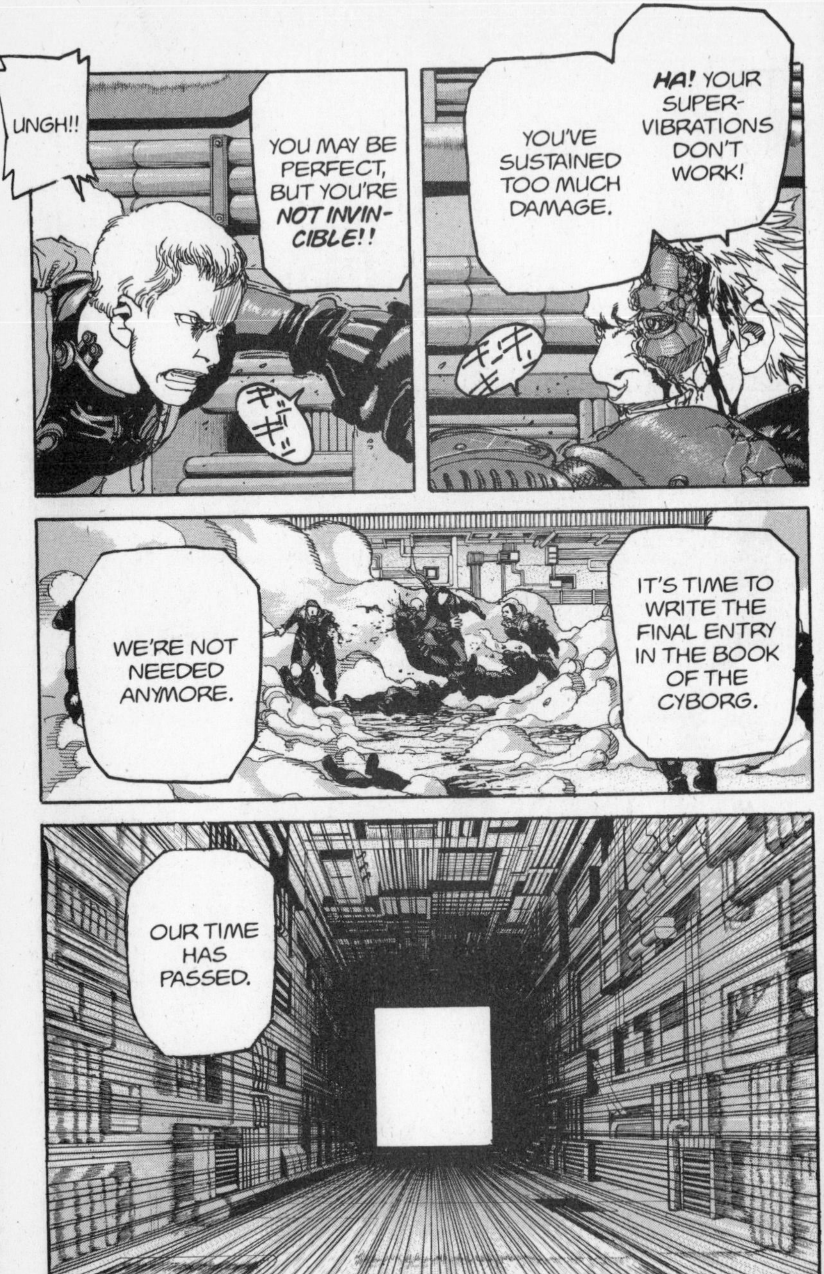
HA! YOUR SUPER-VIBRATIONS DON'T WORK!
YOU'VE SUSTAINED TOO MUCH DAMAGE.
YOU MAY BE PERFECT, BUT YOU'RE NOT INVINCIBLE!!
UNGH!!
IT'S TIME TO WRITE THE FINAL ENTRY IN THE BOOK OF THE CYBORG.
WE'RE NOT NEEDED ANYMORE.
OUR TIME HAS PASSED.

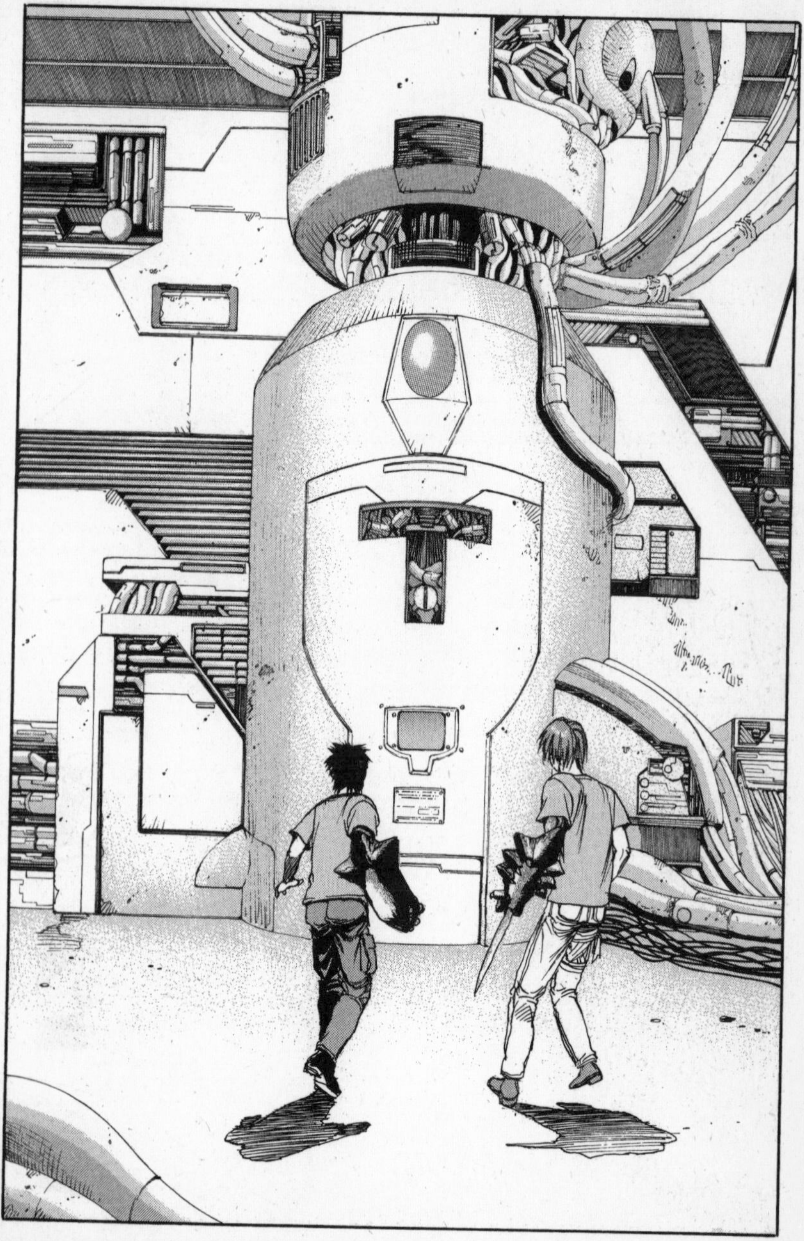

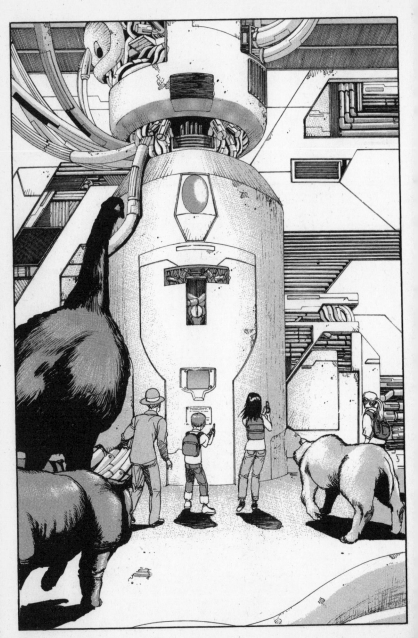

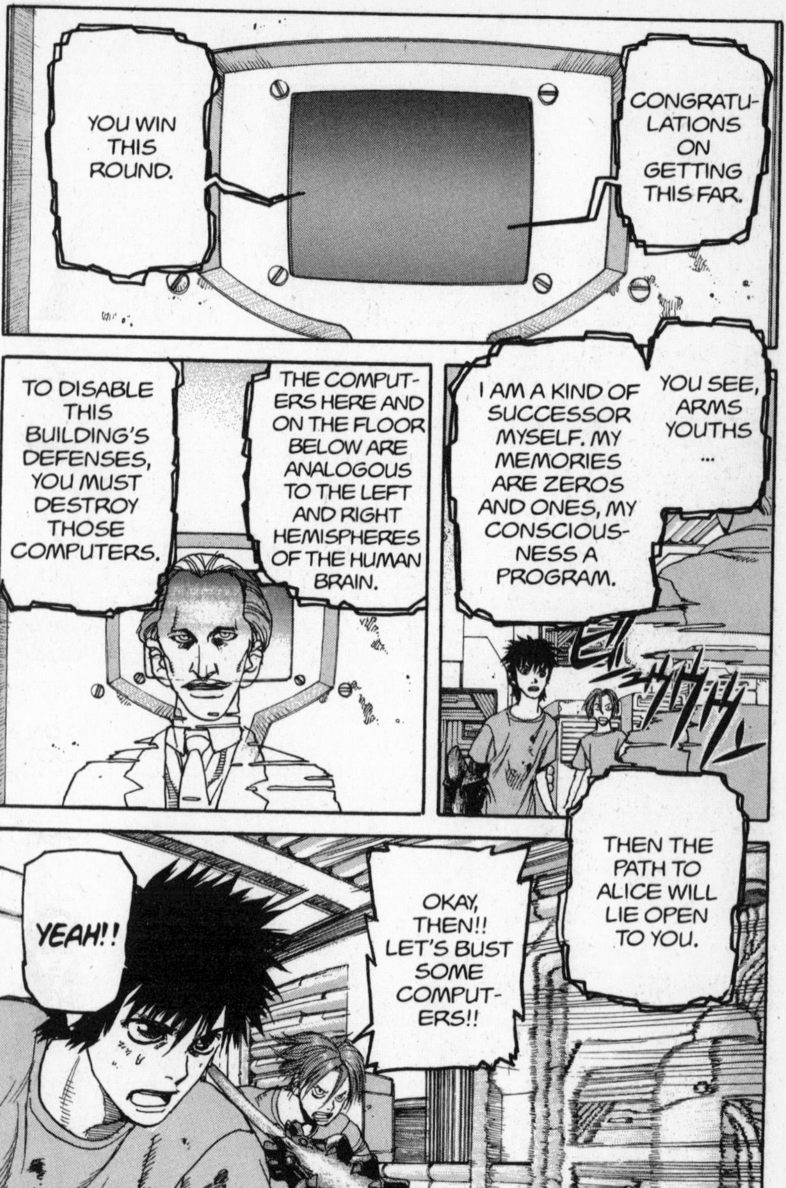
CONGRATULATIONS ON GETTING THIS FAR.
YOU WIN THIS ROUND.
YOU SEE, ARMS YOUTHS ...
I AM A KIND OF SUCCESSOR MYSELF. MY MEMORIES ARE ZEROS AND ONES, MY CONSCIOUSNESS A PROGRAM.
THE COMPUTERS HERE AND ON THE FLOOR BELOW ARE ANALOGOUS TO THE LEFT AND RIGHT HEMISPHERES OF THE HUMAN BRAIN.
TO DISABLE THIS BUILDING'S DEFENSES, YOU MUST DESTROY THOSE COMPUTERS.
THEN THE PATH TO ALICE WILL LIE OPEN TO YOU.
OKAY, THEN!! LET'S BUST SOME COMPUTERS!!
YEAH!!

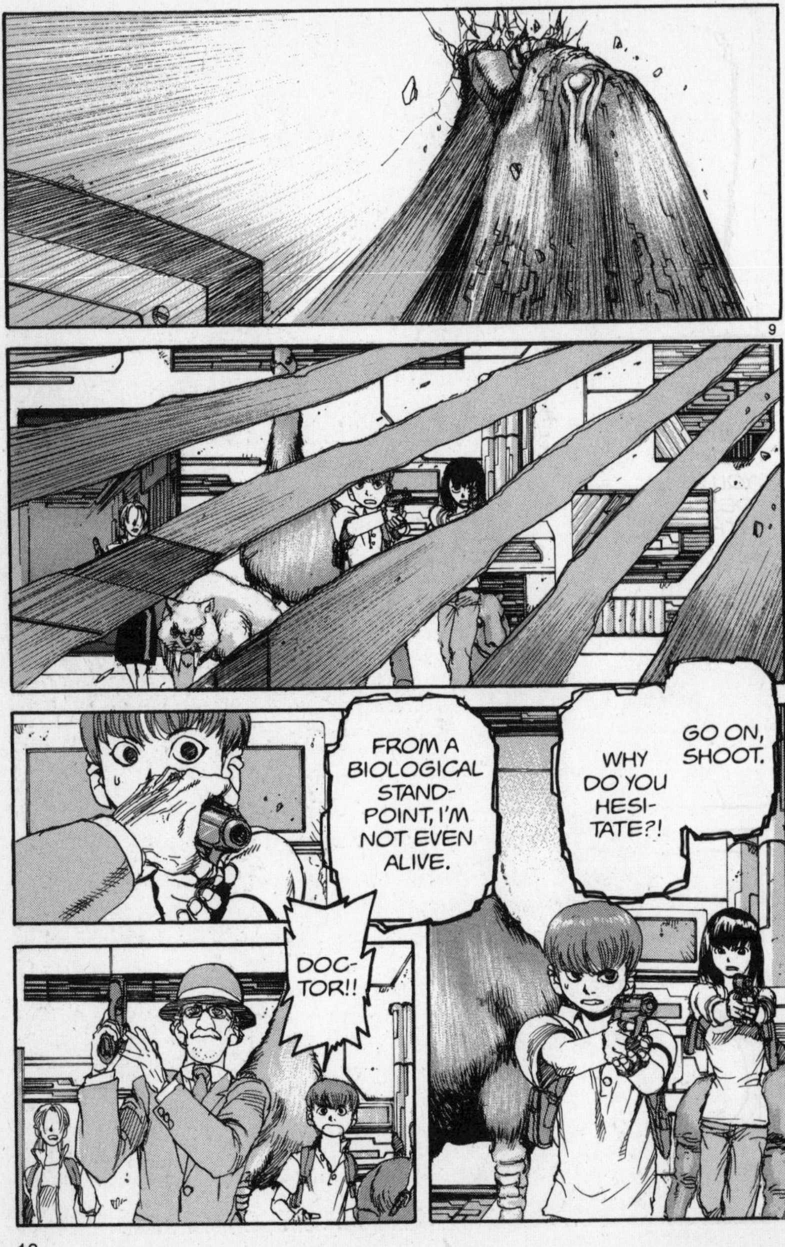
GO ON, SHOOT.
WHY DO YOU HESI-TATE?!
FROM A BIOLOGICAL STAND-POINT, I'M NOT EVEN ALIVE.
DOC-TOR!!

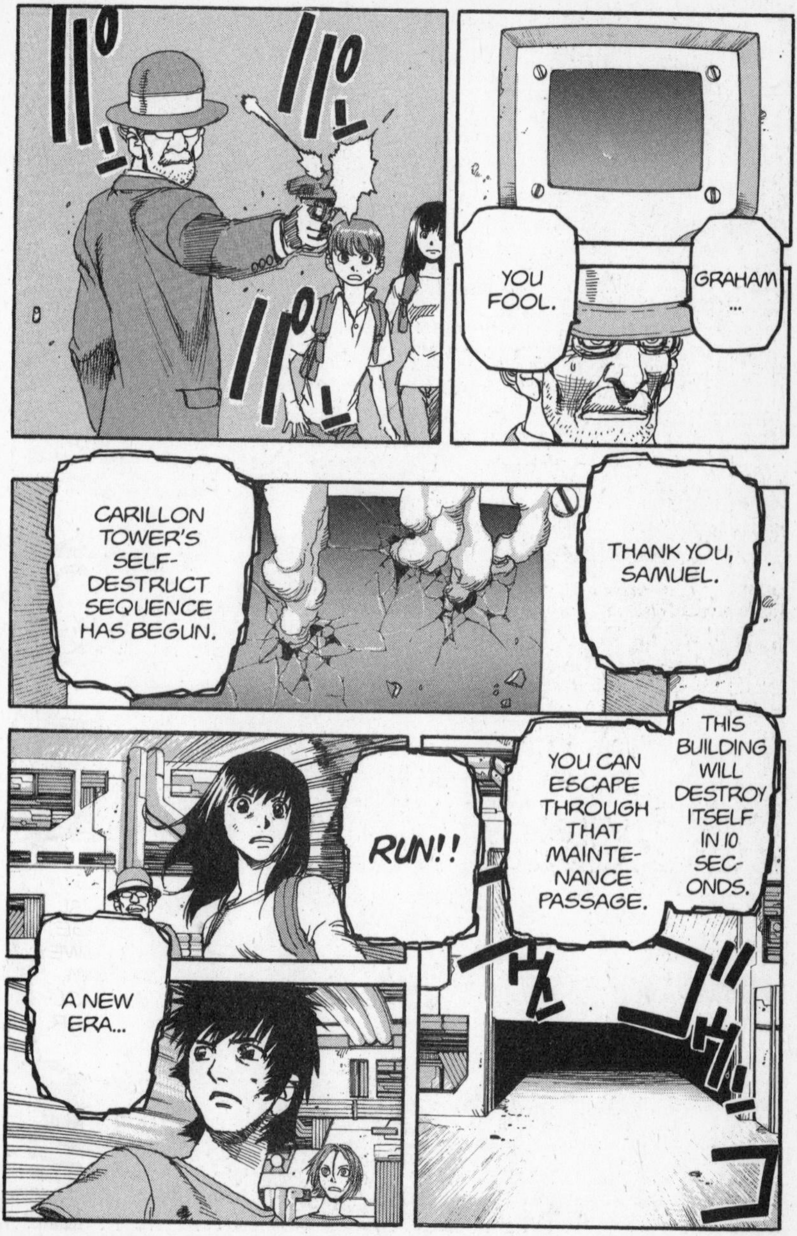
GRAHAM ...
YOU FOOL.
THANK YOU, SAMUEL.
CARILLON TOWER'S SELF-DESTRUCT SEQUENCE HAS BEGUN.
THIS BUILDING WILL DESTROY ITSELF IN 10 SECONDS.
YOU CAN ESCAPE THROUGH THAT MAINTENANCE PASSAGE.
RUN!!
A NEW ERA...

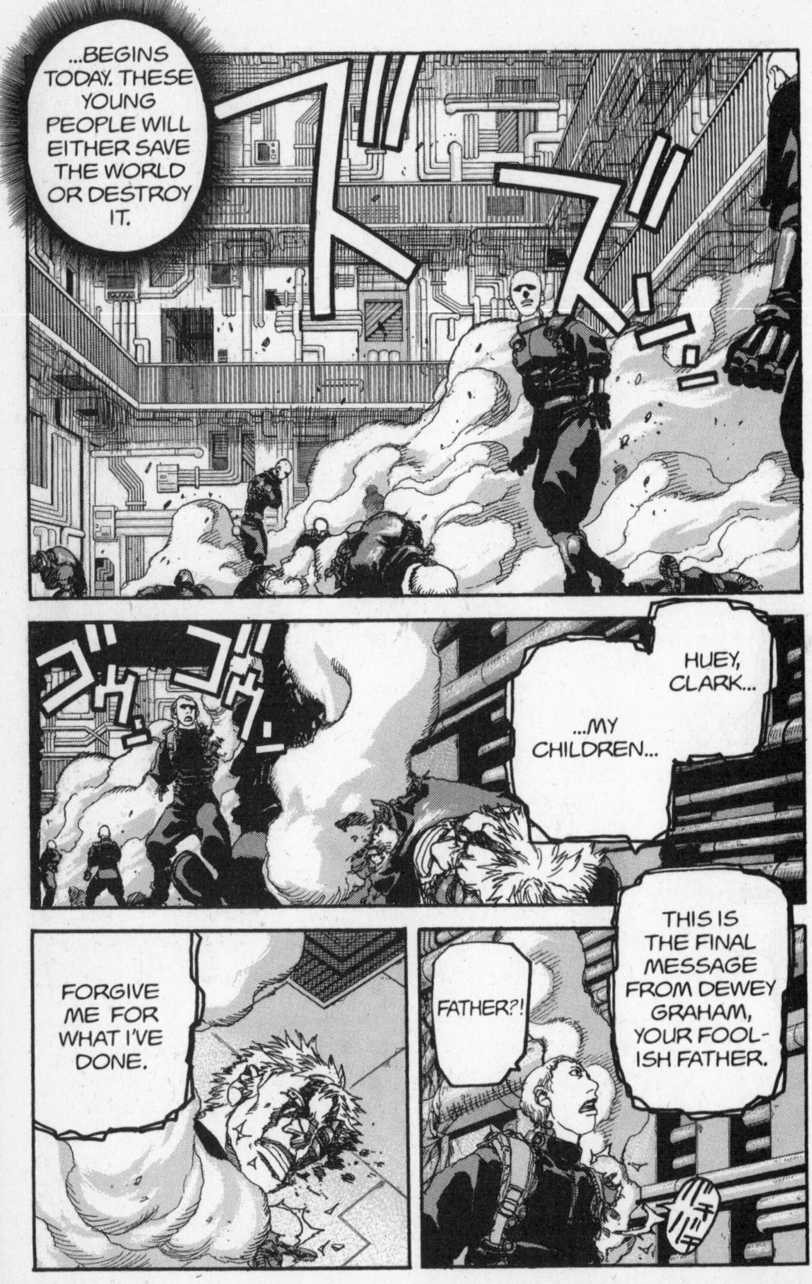
...BEGINS TODAY. THESE YOUNG PEOPLE WILL EITHER SAVE THE WORLD OR DESTROY IT.
HUEY, CLARK...
...MY CHILDREN...
THIS IS THE FINAL MESSAGE FROM DEWEY GRAHAM, YOUR FOOL-ISH FATHER.
FATHER?!
FORGIVE ME FOR WHAT I'VE DONE.

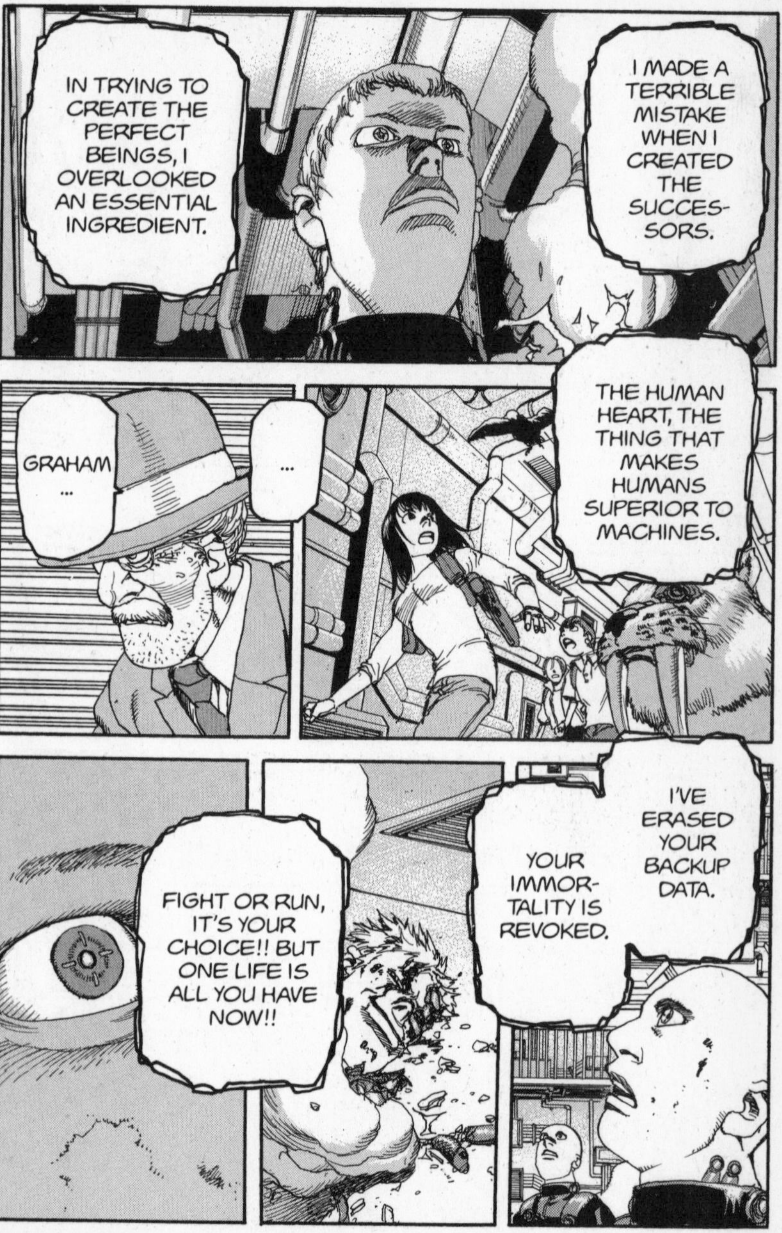
I MADE A TERRIBLE MISTAKE WHEN I CREATED THE SUCCESSORS.
IN TRYING TO CREATE THE PERFECT BEINGS, I OVERLOOKED AN ESSENTIAL INGREDIENT.
THE HUMAN HEART, THE THING THAT MAKES HUMANS SUPERIOR TO MACHINES.
...
GRAHAM ...
I'VE ERASED YOUR BACKUP DATA.
YOUR IMMORTALITY IS REVOKED.
FIGHT OR RUN, IT'S YOUR CHOICE!! BUT ONE LIFE IS ALL YOU HAVE NOW!!

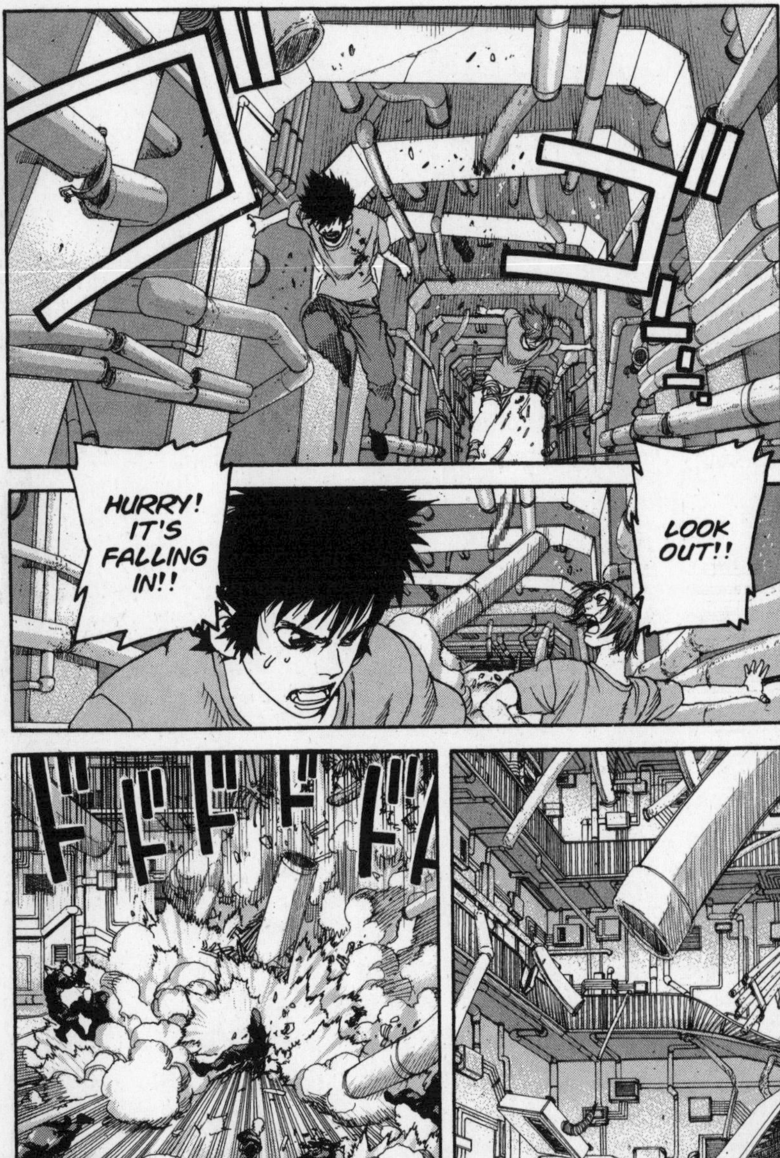
LOOK OUT!!
HURRY! IT'S FALLING IN!!

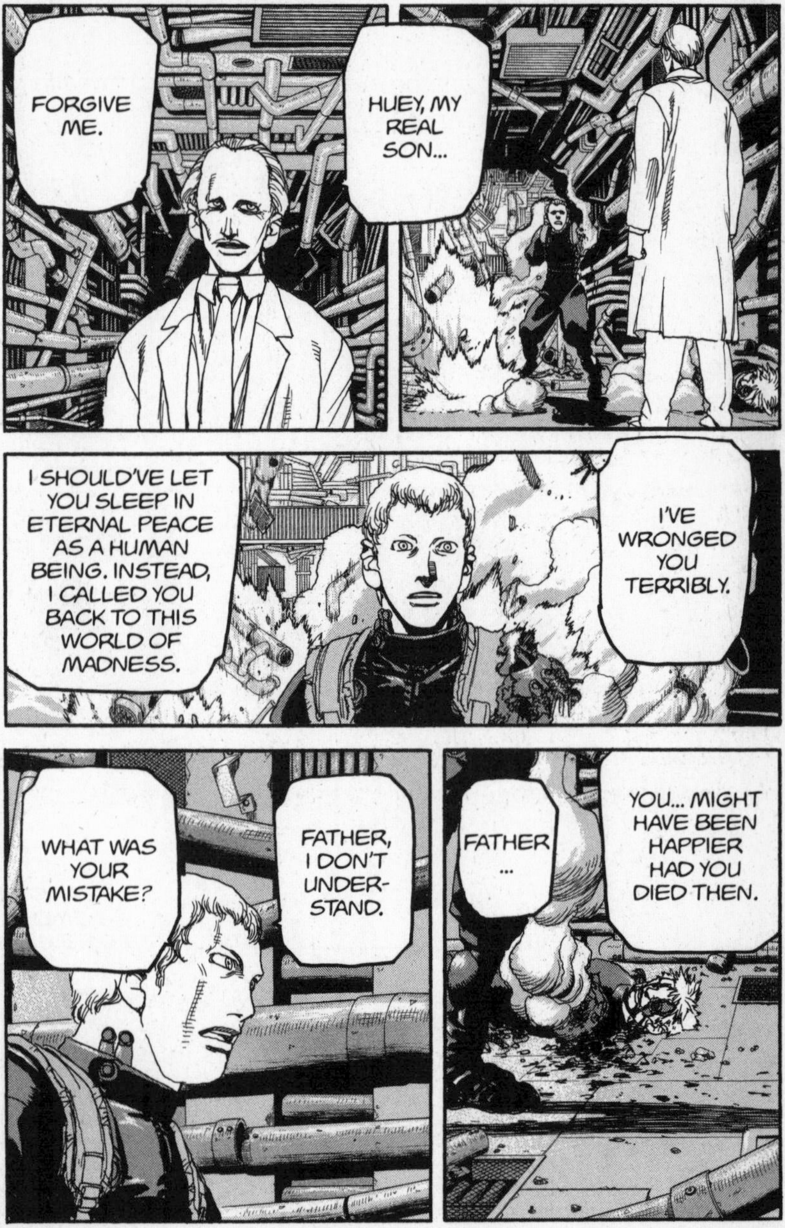
HUEY, MY REAL SON...
FORGIVE ME.
I'VE WRONGED YOU TERRIBLY.
I SHOULD'VE LET YOU SLEEP IN ETERNAL PEACE AS A HUMAN BEING. INSTEAD, I CALLED YOU BACK TO THIS WORLD OF MADNESS.
YOU... MIGHT HAVE BEEN HAPPIER HAD YOU DIED THEN.
FATHER ...
FATHER, I DON'T UNDER-STAND.
WHAT WAS YOUR MISTAKE?

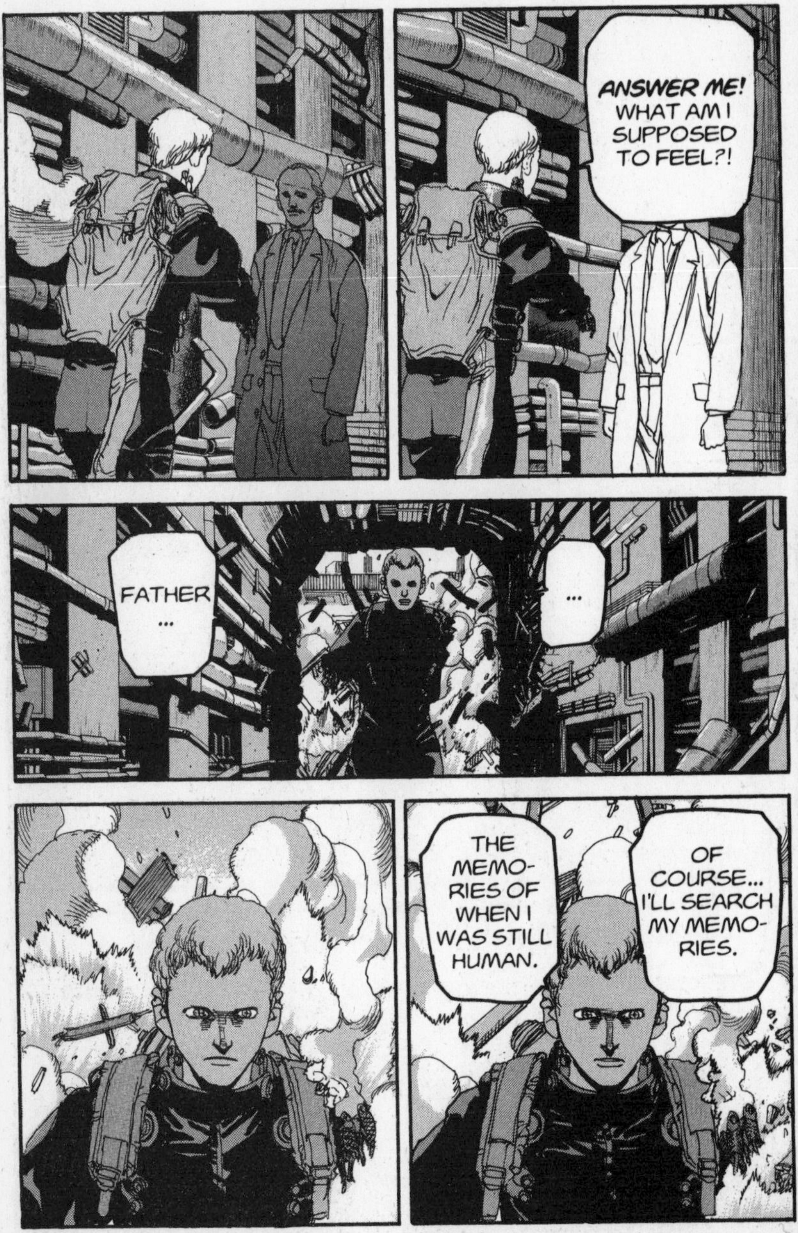
ANSWER ME! WHAT AM I SUPPOSED TO FEEL?!
...
FATHER ...
OF COURSE... I'LL SEARCH MY MEMORIES.
THE MEMORIES OF WHEN I WAS STILL HUMAN.

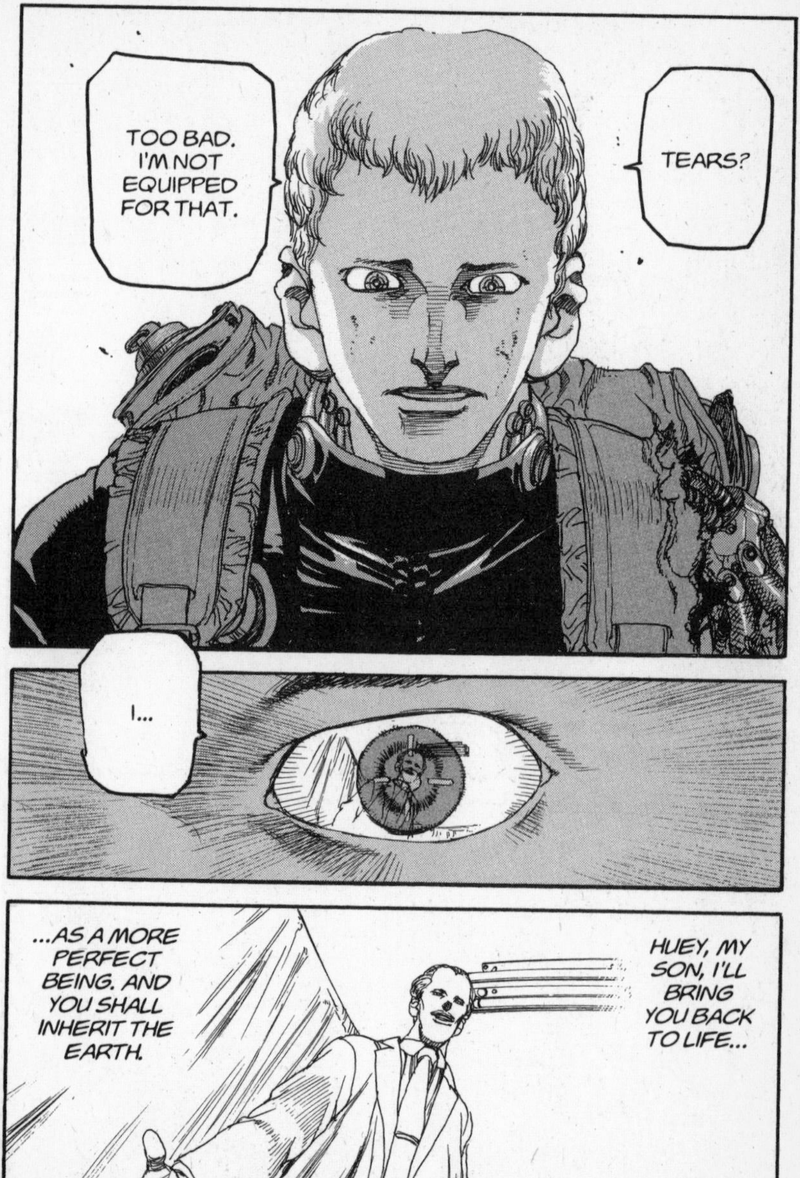
TEARS?
TOO BAD. I'M NOT EQUIPPED FOR THAT.
I...
HUEY, MY SON, I'LL BRING YOU BACK TO LIFE...
...AS A MORE PERFECT BEING. AND YOU SHALL INHERIT THE EARTH.

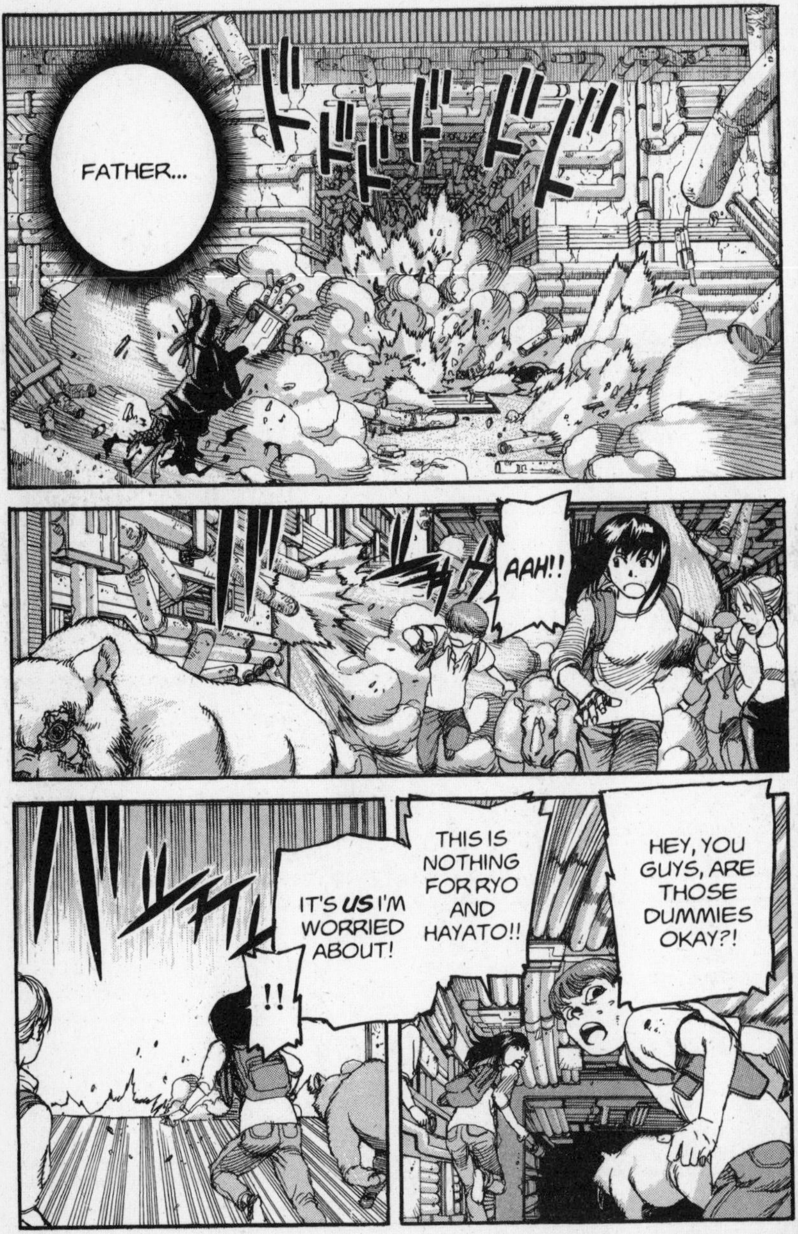

FATHER...
AAH!!
HEY, YOU GUYS, ARE THOSE DUMMIES OKAY?!
THIS IS NOTHING FOR RYO AND HAYATO!!
IT'S **US** I'M WORRIED ABOUT!
!!

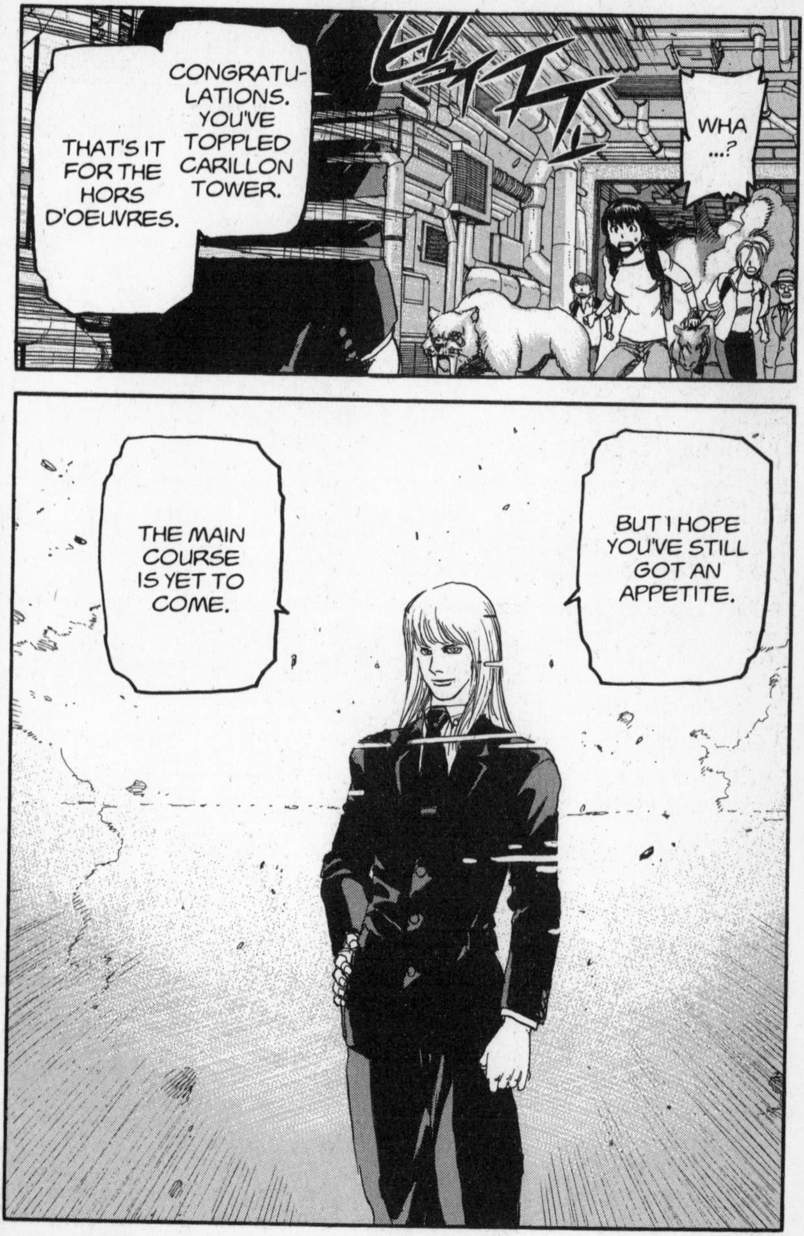
WHA ...?
CONGRATULATIONS. YOU'VE TOPPLED CARILLON TOWER.
THAT'S IT FOR THE HORS D'OEUVRES.
BUT I HOPE YOU'VE STILL GOT AN APPETITE.
THE MAIN COURSE IS YET TO COME.

No. 2 DEAD OR ALIVE

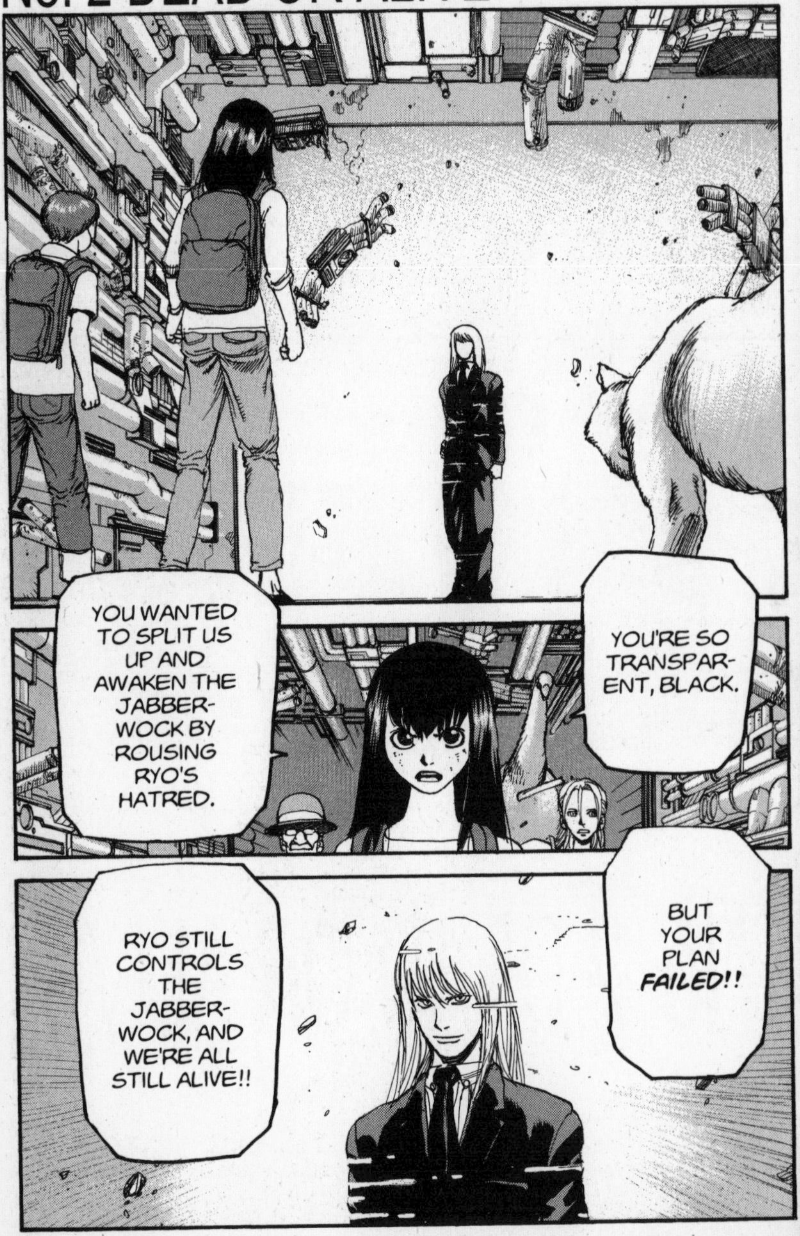

YOU'RE SO TRANSPARENT, BLACK.
YOU WANTED TO SPLIT US UP AND AWAKEN THE JABBERWOCK BY ROUSING RYO'S HATRED.
BUT YOUR PLAN ***FAILED!!***
RYO STILL CONTROLS THE JABBERWOCK, AND WE'RE ALL STILL ALIVE!!

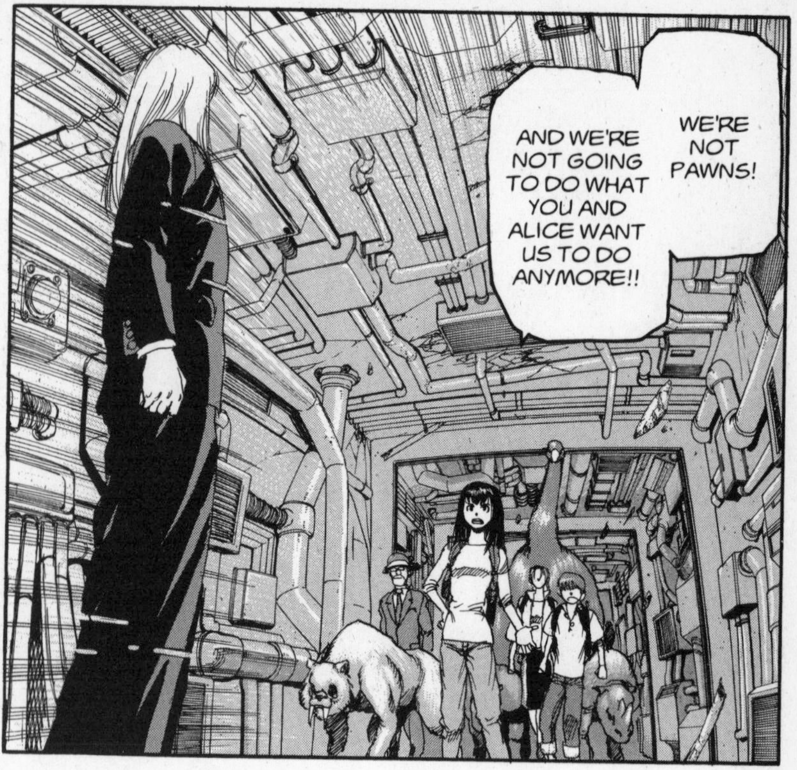
WE'RE NOT PAWNS!
AND WE'RE NOT GOING TO DO WHAT YOU AND ALICE WANT US TO DO ANYMORE!!

No. 2 DEAD OR ALIVE

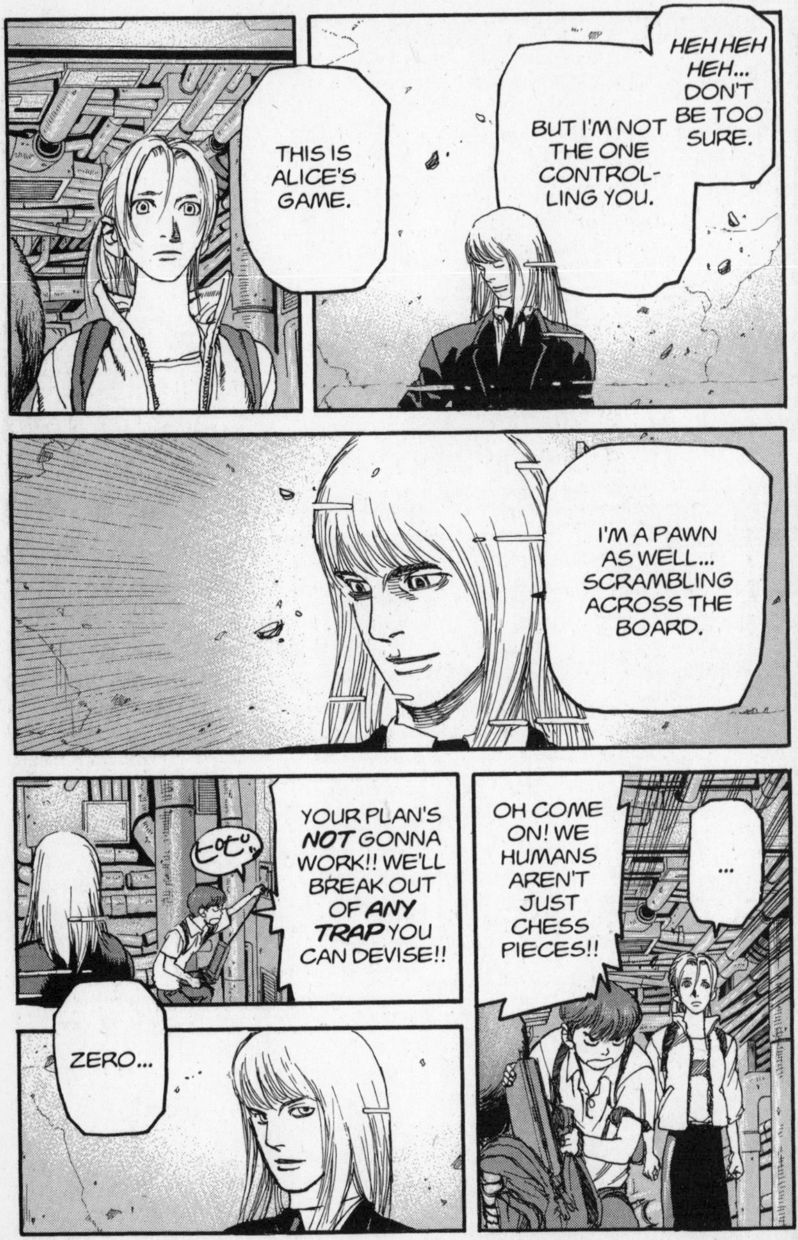
HEH HEH HEH... DON'T BE TOO SURE.
BUT I'M NOT THE ONE CONTROLLING YOU.
THIS IS ALICE'S GAME.
I'M A PAWN AS WELL... SCRAMBLING ACROSS THE BOARD.
...
OH COME ON! WE HUMANS AREN'T JUST CHESS PIECES!!
YOUR PLAN'S **NOT** GONNA WORK!! WE'LL BREAK OUT OF ***ANY TRAP*** YOU CAN DEVISE!!
ZERO...

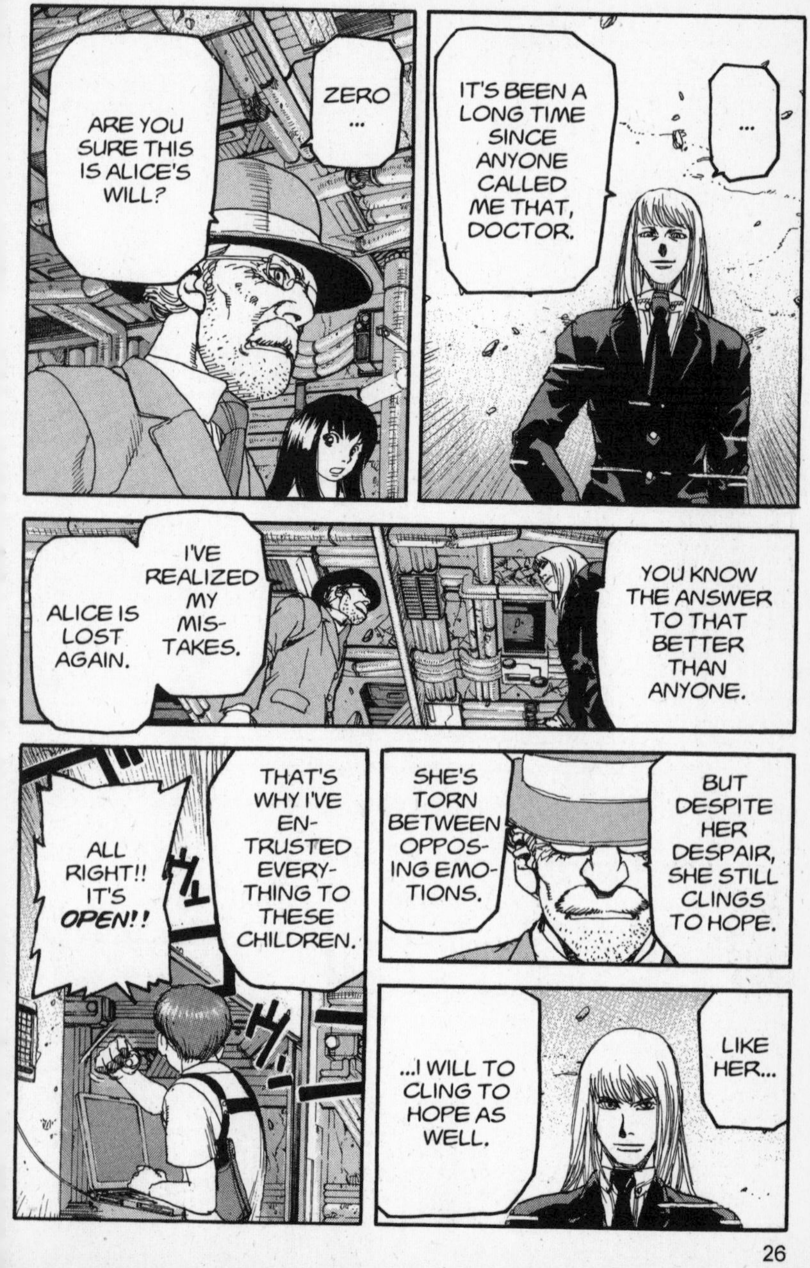
...
IT'S BEEN A LONG TIME SINCE ANYONE CALLED ME THAT, DOCTOR.
ZERO ...
ARE YOU SURE THIS IS ALICE'S WILL?
YOU KNOW THE ANSWER TO THAT BETTER THAN ANYONE.
I'VE REALIZED MY MIS-TAKES.
ALICE IS LOST AGAIN.
BUT DESPITE HER DESPAIR, SHE STILL CLINGS TO HOPE.
SHE'S TORN BETWEEN OPPOS-ING EMO-TIONS.
LIKE HER...
...I WILL TO CLING TO HOPE AS WELL.
THAT'S WHY I'VE EN-TRUSTED EVERY-THING TO THESE CHILDREN.
ALL RIGHT!! IT'S *OPEN!!*

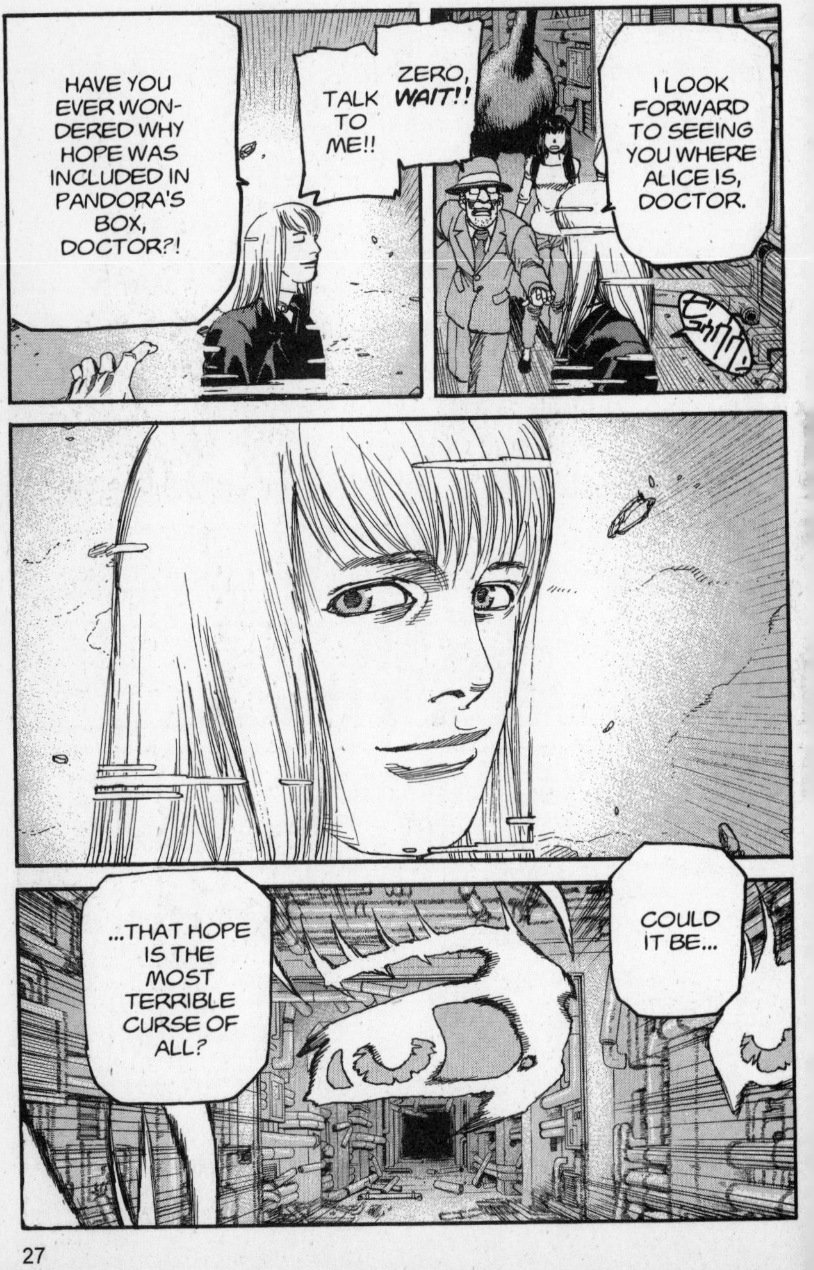

I LOOK FORWARD TO SEEING YOU WHERE ALICE IS, DOCTOR.
ZERO, WAIT!! TALK TO ME!!
HAVE YOU EVER WON-DERED WHY HOPE WAS INCLUDED IN PANDORA'S BOX, DOCTOR?!
COULD IT BE...
...THAT HOPE IS THE MOST TERRIBLE CURSE OF ALL?

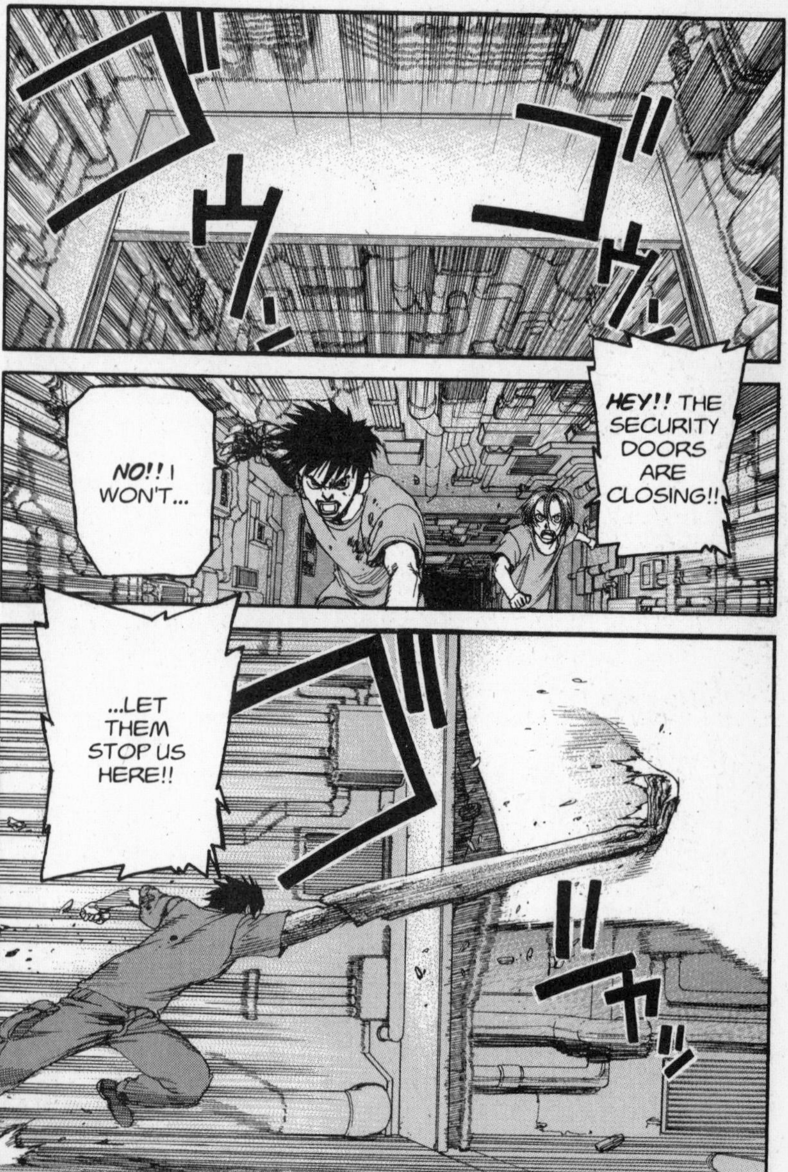
HEY!! THE SECURITY DOORS ARE CLOSING!!
NO!! I WON'T...
...LET THEM STOP US HERE!!

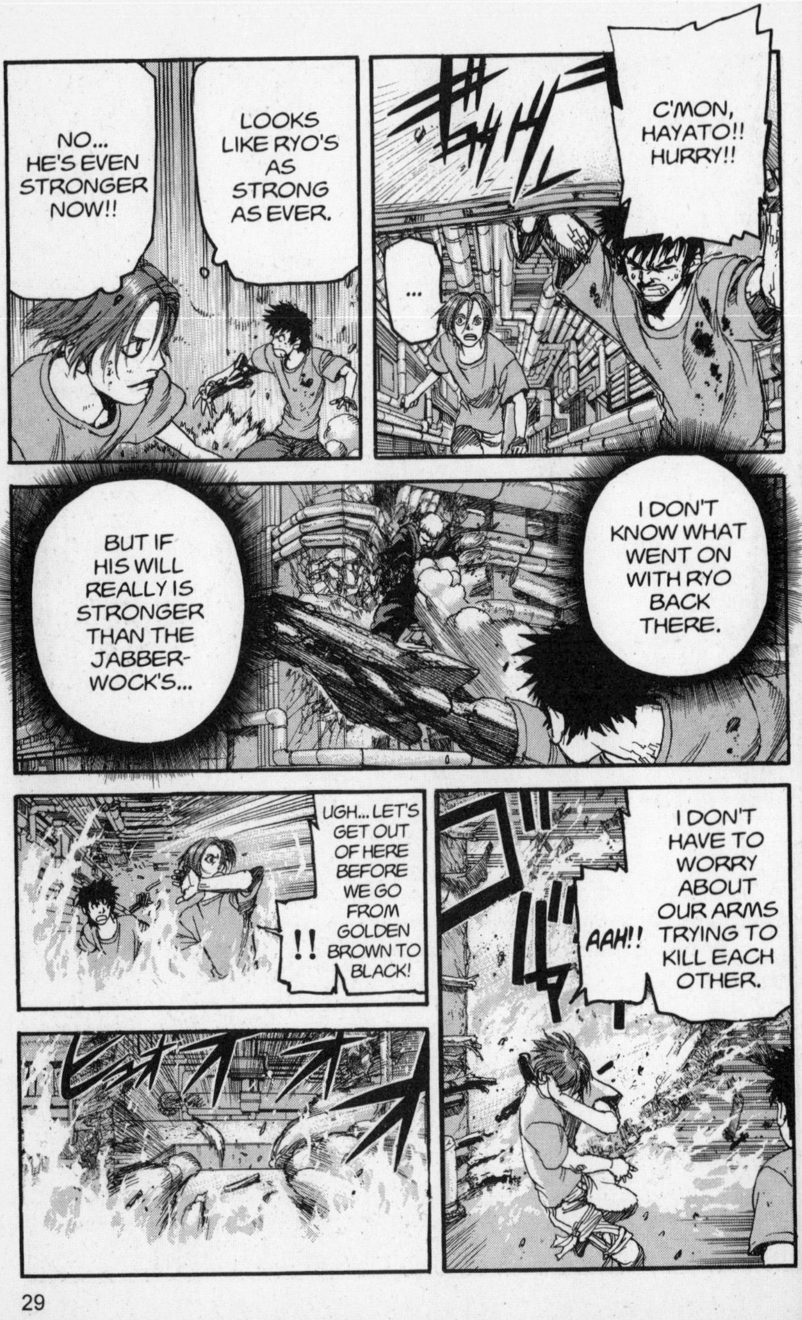
C'MON, HAYATO!! HURRY!!
...
LOOKS LIKE RYO'S AS STRONG AS EVER.
NO... HE'S EVEN STRONGER NOW!!
I DON'T KNOW WHAT WENT ON WITH RYO BACK THERE.
BUT IF HIS WILL REALLY IS STRONGER THAN THE JABBER-WOCK'S...
I DON'T HAVE TO WORRY ABOUT OUR ARMS TRYING TO KILL EACH OTHER.
AAH!!
UGH... LET'S GET OUT OF HERE BEFORE WE GO FROM GOLDEN BROWN TO BLACK!
!!

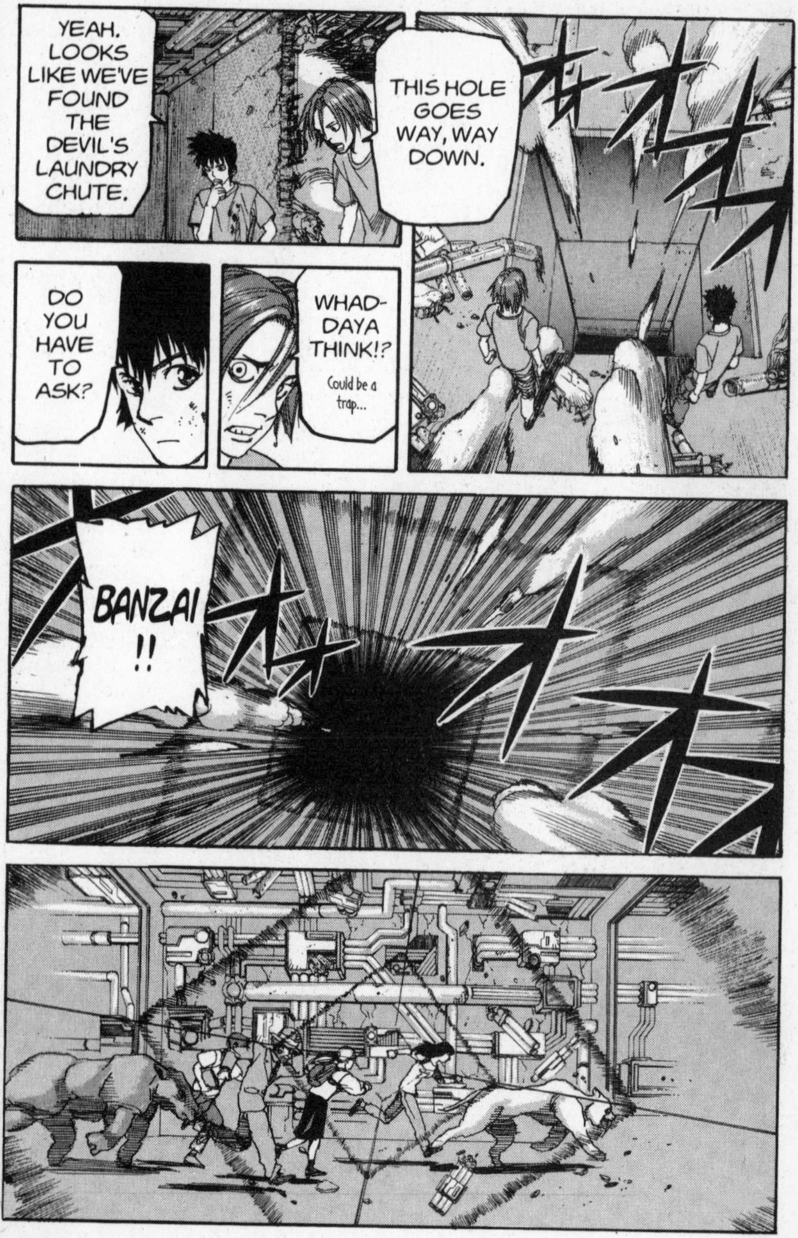
THIS HOLE GOES WAY, WAY DOWN.
YEAH. LOOKS LIKE WE'VE FOUND THE DEVIL'S LAUNDRY CHUTE.
WHAD-DAYA THINK!?
Could be a trap...
DO YOU HAVE TO ASK?
BANZAI !!

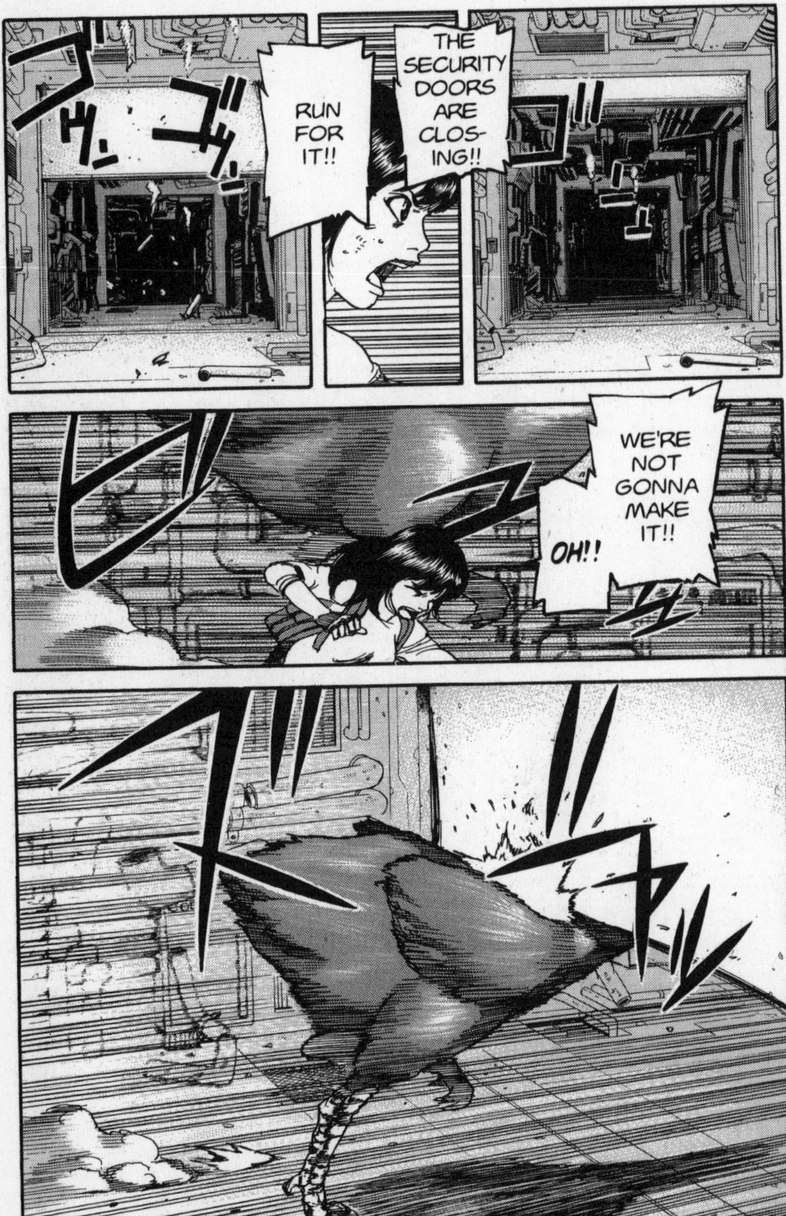
THE SECURITY DOORS ARE CLOSING!!
RUN FOR IT!!
WE'RE NOT GONNA MAKE IT!!
OH!!

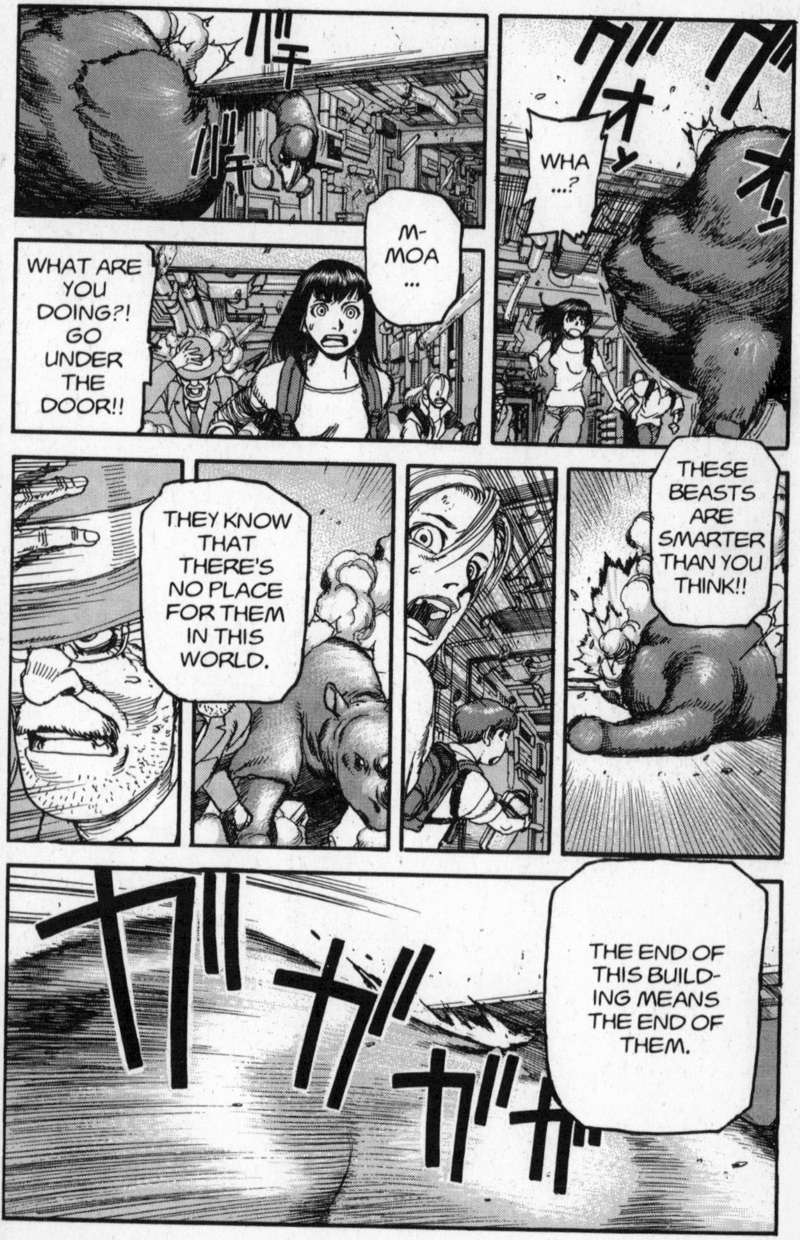
WHA ...?
M-MOA ...
WHAT ARE YOU DOING?! GO UNDER THE DOOR!!
THESE BEASTS ARE SMARTER THAN YOU THINK!!
THEY KNOW THAT THERE'S NO PLACE FOR THEM IN THIS WORLD.
THE END OF THIS BUILD-ING MEANS THE END OF THEM.

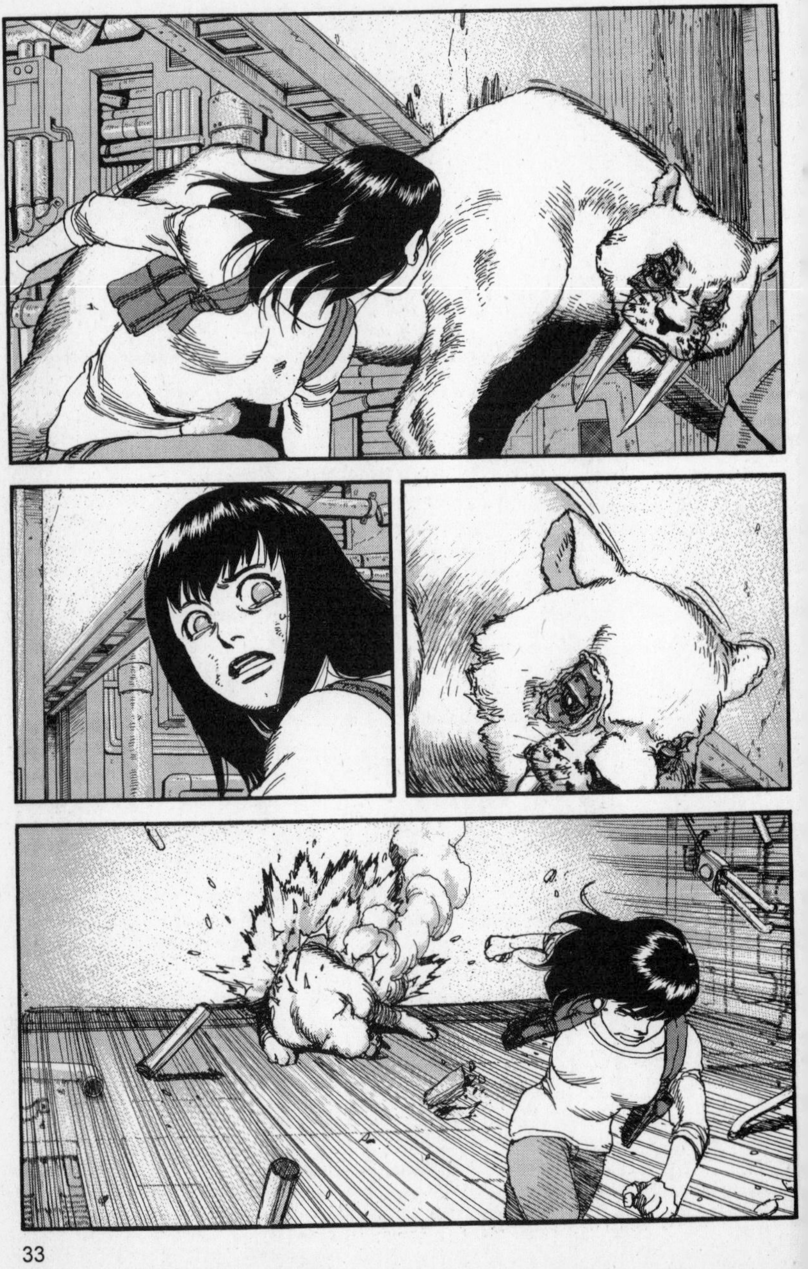

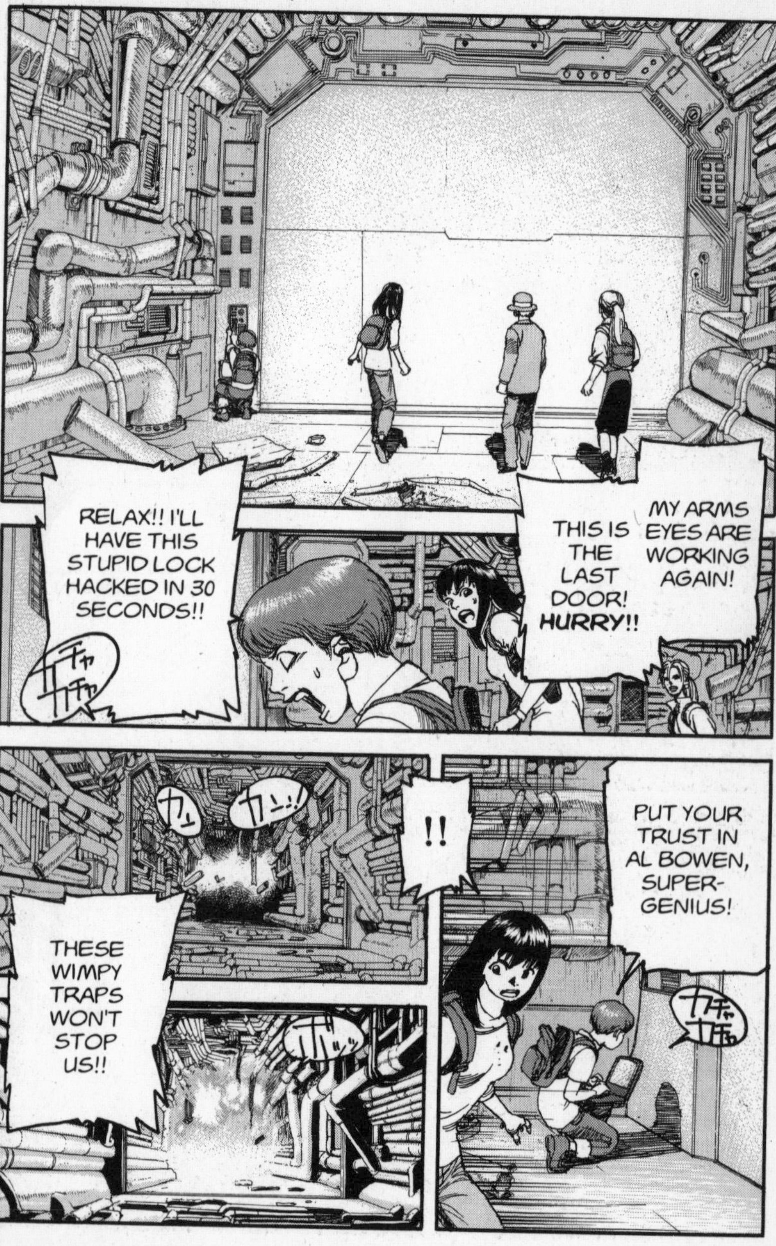
MY ARMS EYES ARE WORKING AGAIN!
THIS IS THE LAST DOOR! **HURRY!!**
RELAX!! I'LL HAVE THIS STUPID LOCK HACKED IN 30 SECONDS!!
カチャカチャ
PUT YOUR TRUST IN AL BOWEN, SUPER-GENIUS!
カチャカチャ
!!
カッ
カーッ!
THESE WIMPY TRAPS WON'T STOP US!!
ボッ

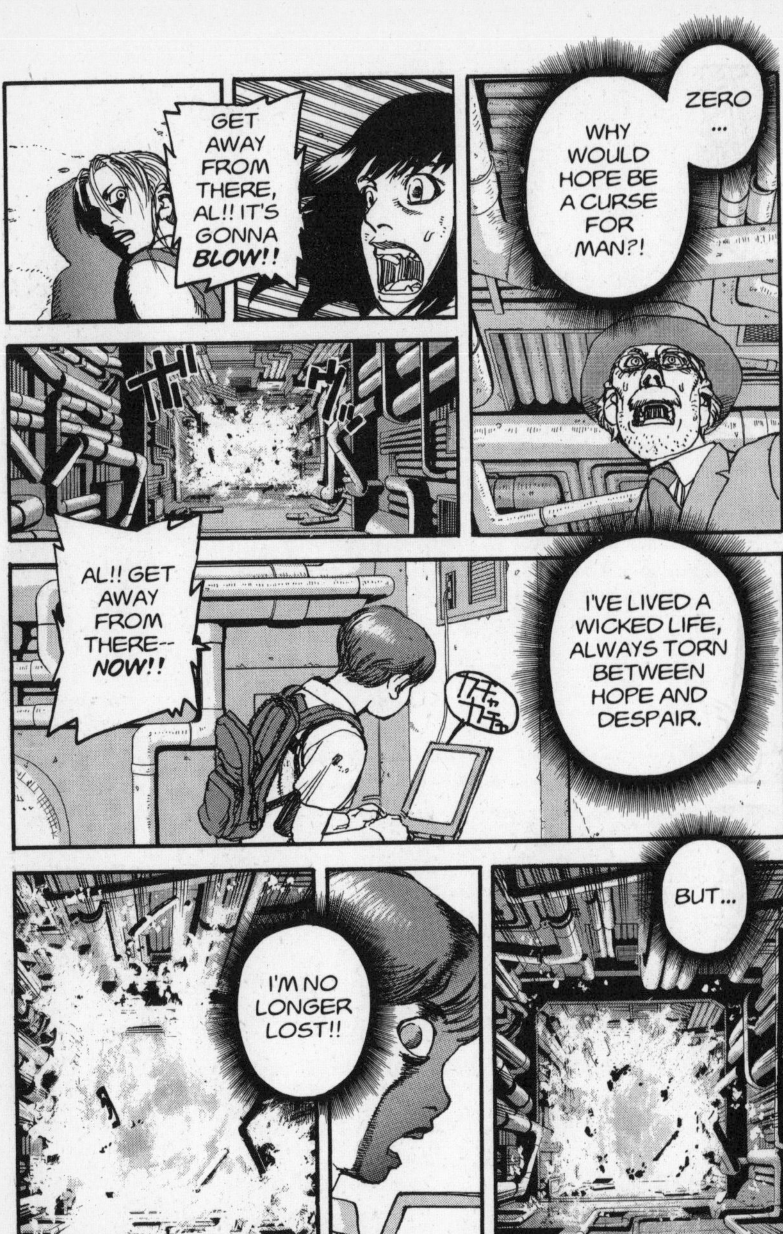
ZERO ...
WHY WOULD HOPE BE A CURSE FOR MAN?!
GET AWAY FROM THERE, AL!! IT'S GONNA BLOW!!
I'VE LIVED A WICKED LIFE, ALWAYS TORN BETWEEN HOPE AND DESPAIR.
AL!! GET AWAY FROM THERE-- NOW!!
BUT...
I'M NO LONGER LOST!!

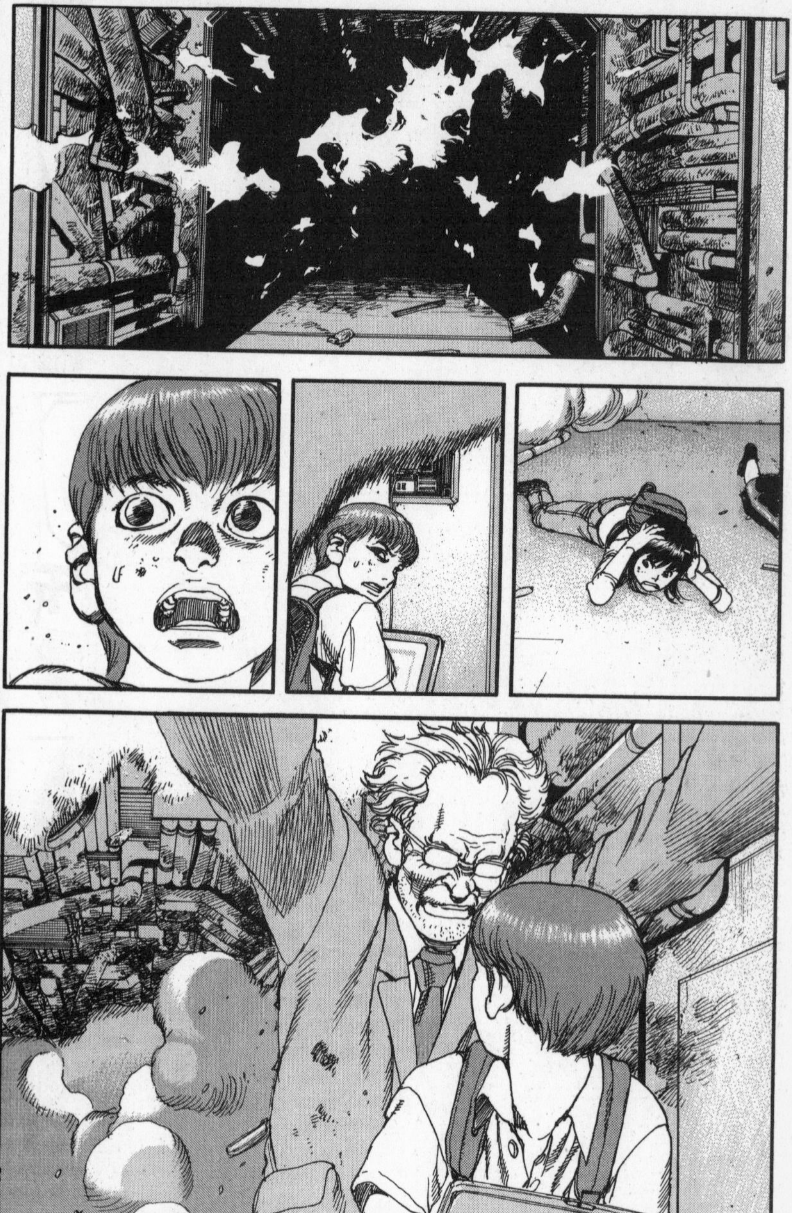

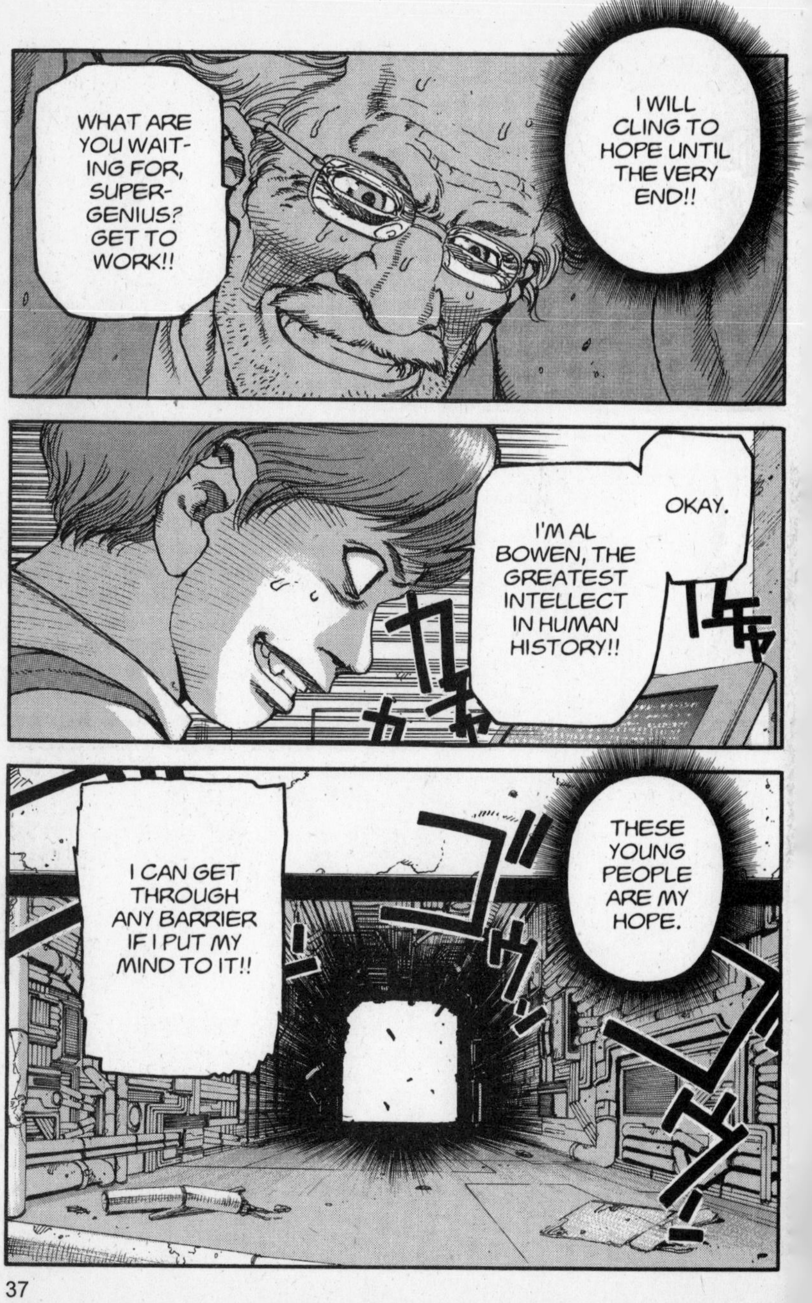
I WILL CLING TO HOPE UNTIL THE VERY END!!
WHAT ARE YOU WAIT-ING FOR, SUPER-GENIUS? GET TO WORK!!
OKAY.
I'M AL BOWEN, THE GREATEST INTELLECT IN HUMAN HISTORY!!
THESE YOUNG PEOPLE ARE MY HOPE.
I CAN GET THROUGH ANY BARRIER IF I PUT MY MIND TO IT!!

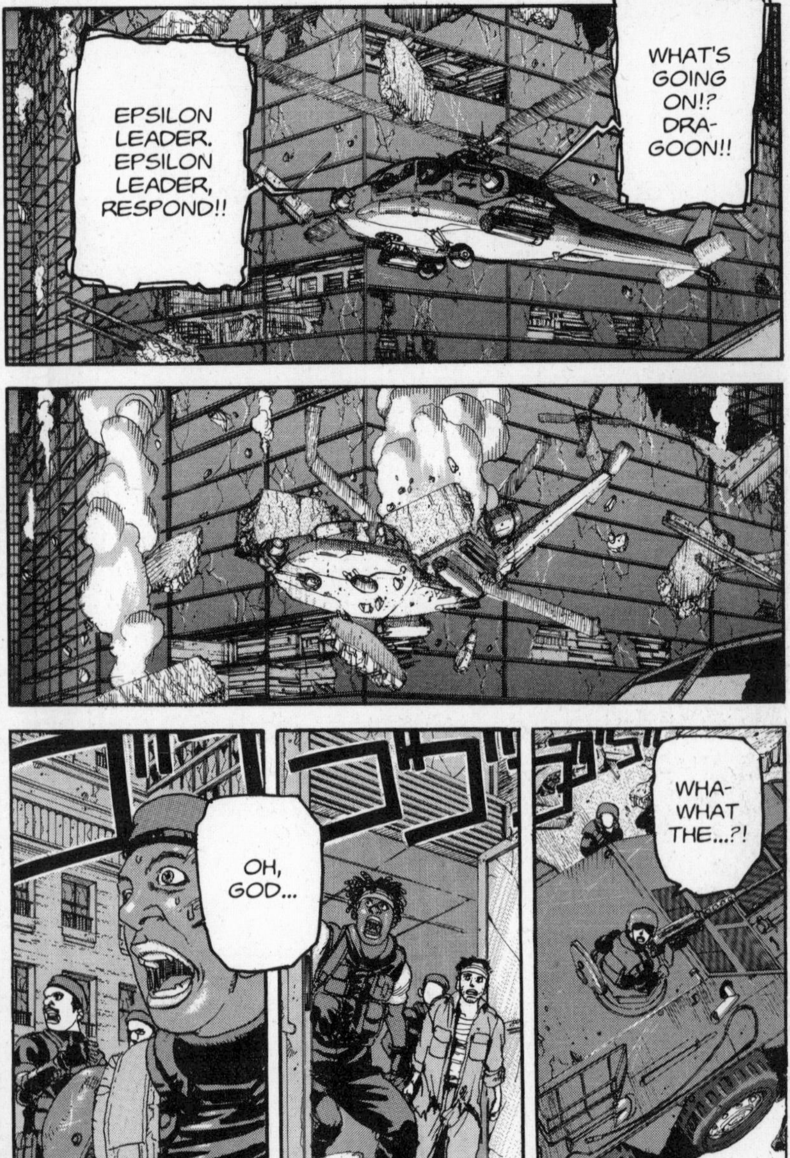
WHAT'S GOING ON!? DRA-GOON!!
EPSILON LEADER. EPSILON LEADER, RESPOND!!
WHA-WHAT THE...?!
OH, GOD...

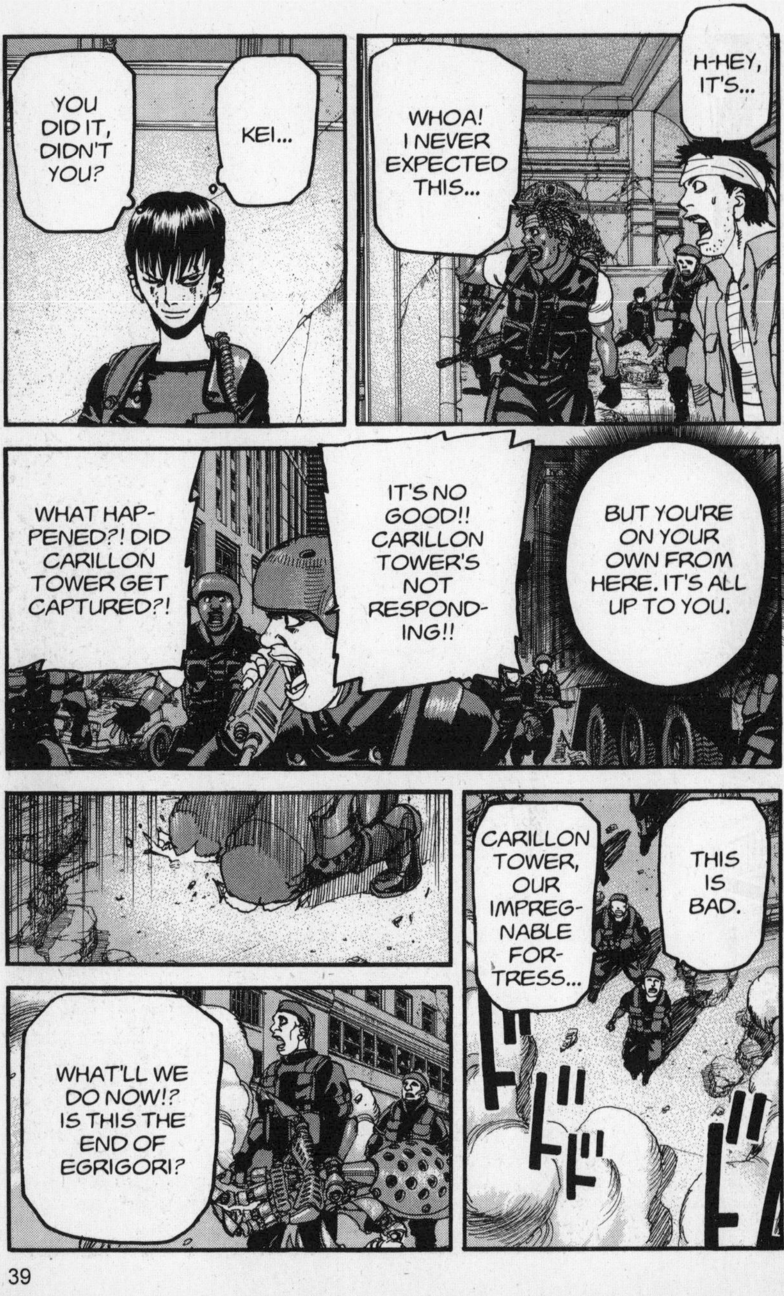
H-HEY, IT'S...
WHOA! I NEVER EXPECTED THIS...
KEI...
YOU DID IT, DIDN'T YOU?
BUT YOU'RE ON YOUR OWN FROM HERE. IT'S ALL UP TO YOU.
IT'S NO GOOD!! CARILLON TOWER'S NOT RESPOND-ING!!
WHAT HAP-PENED?! DID CARILLON TOWER GET CAPTURED?!
THIS IS BAD.
CARILLON TOWER, OUR IMPREG-NABLE FOR-TRESS...
ドドド
WHAT'LL WE DO NOW!? IS THIS THE END OF EGRIGORI?

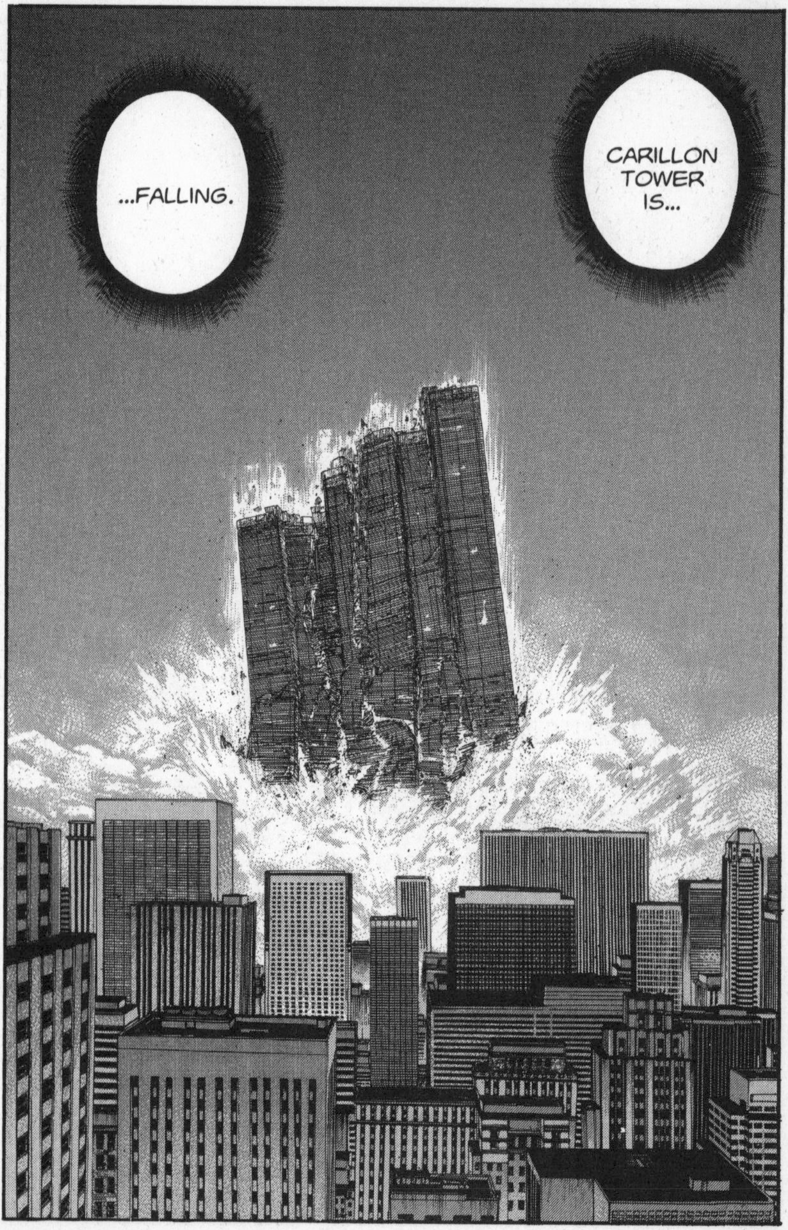
CARILLON TOWER IS...
...FALLING.

No. 3 PULSE

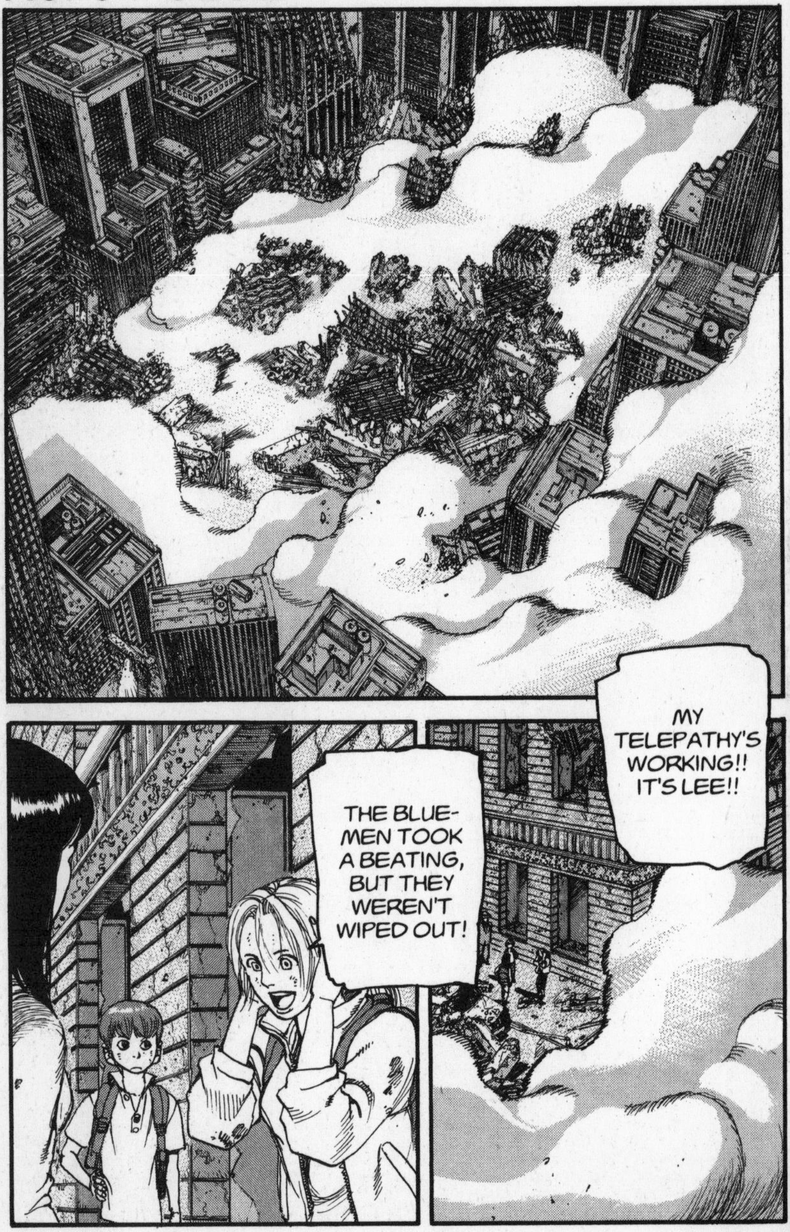

MY TELEPATHY'S WORKING!! IT'S LEE!!
THE BLUE-MEN TOOK A BEATING, BUT THEY WEREN'T WIPED OUT!

IS EVERY-ONE OKAY IN THERE?
THOSE OF US THAT ARE LEFT ARE RE-GROUPING!
BUT YOU REAL-IZE, KEI...
FOR YOU ARMS, THE REAL BATTLE BEGINS NOW.
I KNOW. RYO AND HAYATO ARE ALREADY INSIDE... I HOPE.
WE'VE GOT TO GET MOVING TOO!!
コオオオ
WE'RE GOING INTO THE RUINS OF CARIL-LON TOWER...
オオオオ

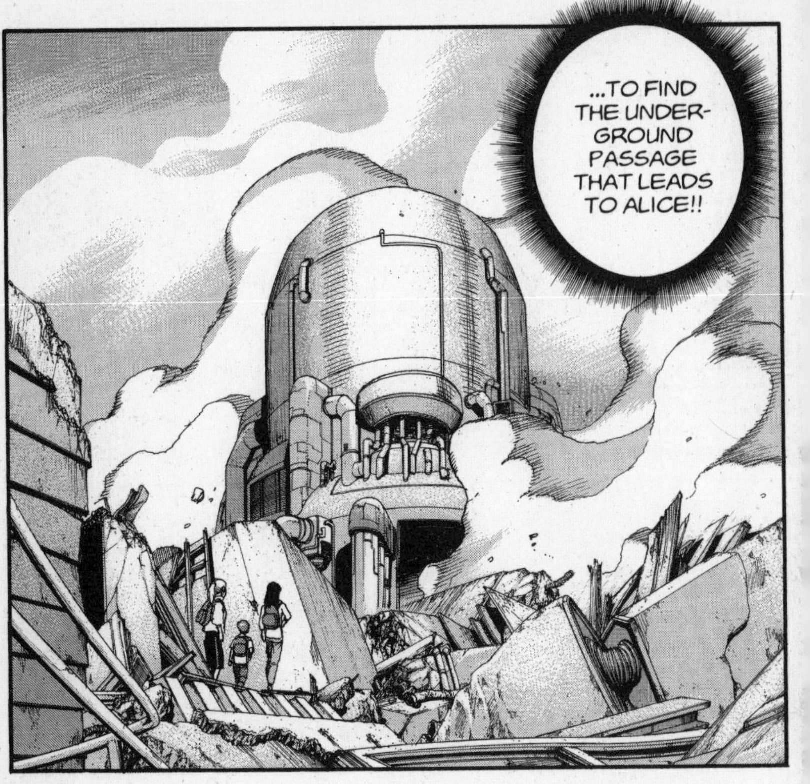
...TO FIND THE UNDER-GROUND PASSAGE THAT LEADS TO ALICE!!

NO. 3 PULSE

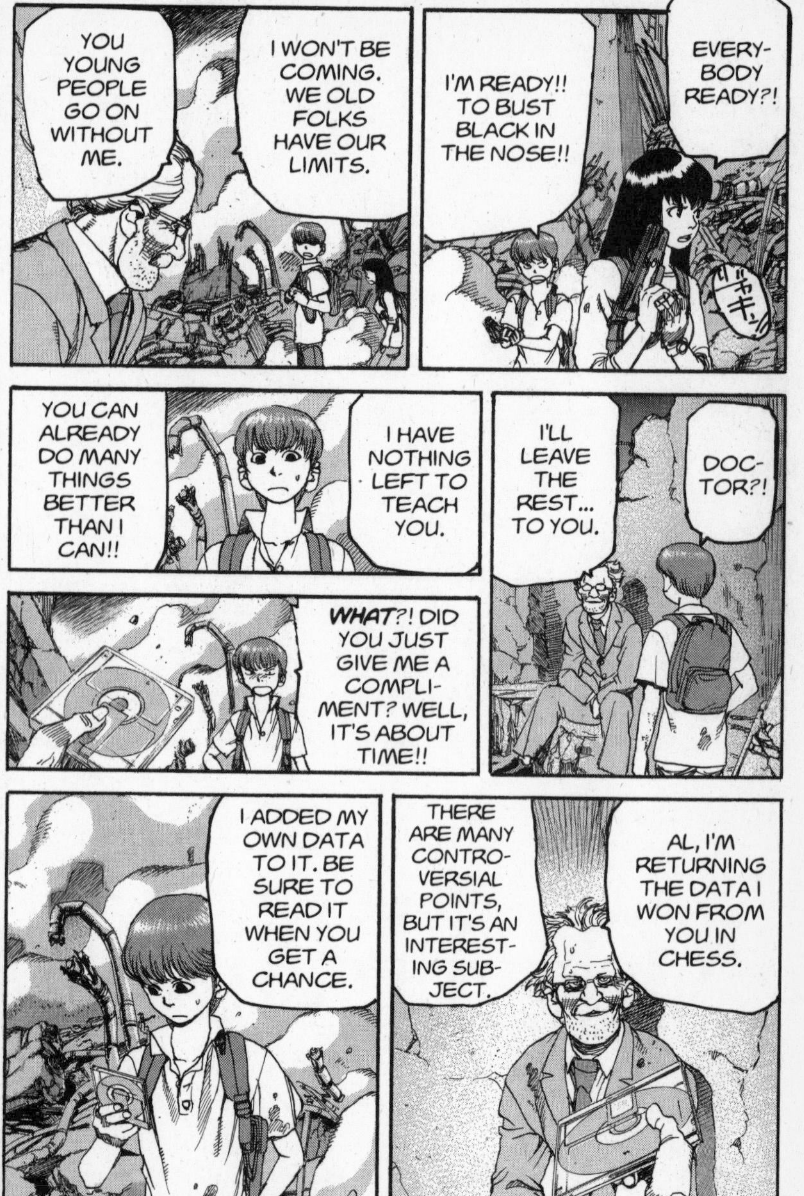
EVERYBODY READY?!
I'M READY!! TO BUST BLACK IN THE NOSE!!
I WON'T BE COMING. WE OLD FOLKS HAVE OUR LIMITS.
YOU YOUNG PEOPLE GO ON WITHOUT ME.
DOCTOR?!
I'LL LEAVE THE REST... TO YOU.
I HAVE NOTHING LEFT TO TEACH YOU.
YOU CAN ALREADY DO MANY THINGS BETTER THAN I CAN!!
WHAT?! DID YOU JUST GIVE ME A COMPLIMENT? WELL, IT'S ABOUT TIME!!
AL, I'M RETURNING THE DATA I WON FROM YOU IN CHESS.
THERE ARE MANY CONTROVERSIAL POINTS, BUT IT'S AN INTERESTING SUBJECT.
I ADDED MY OWN DATA TO IT. BE SURE TO READ IT WHEN YOU GET A CHANCE.

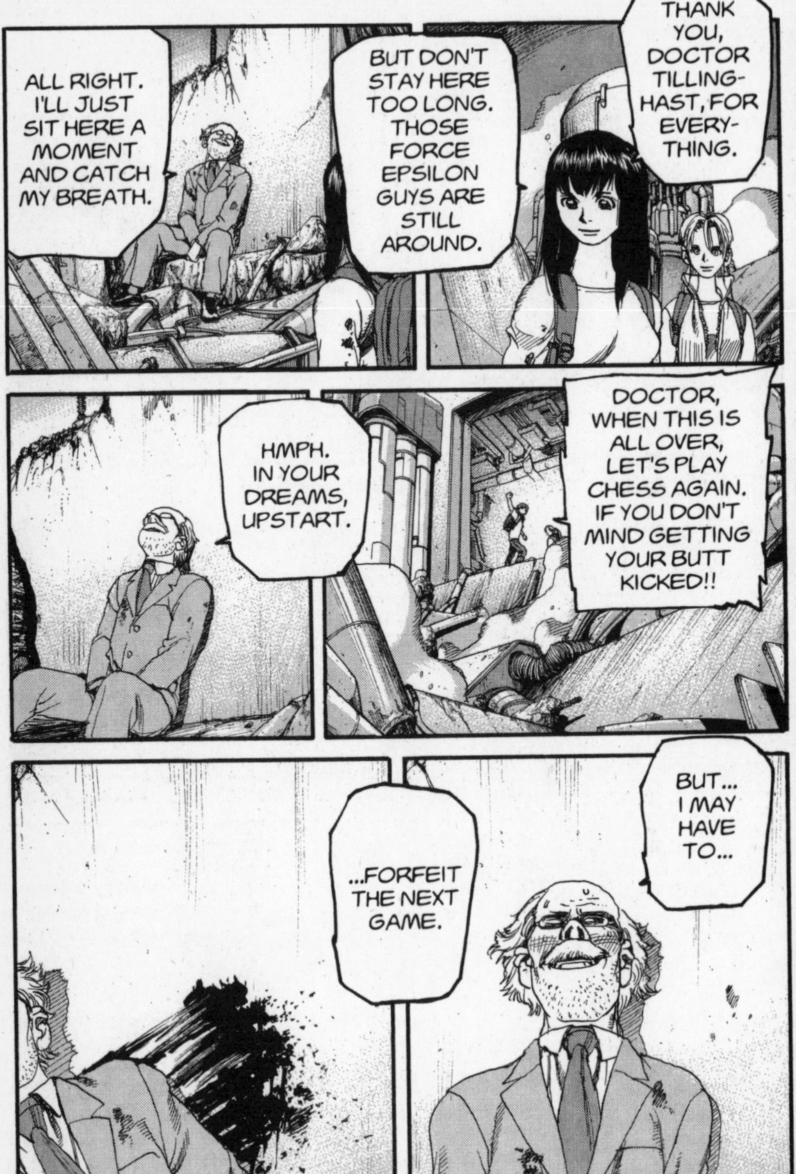
THANK YOU, DOCTOR TILLING-HAST, FOR EVERY-THING.
BUT DON'T STAY HERE TOO LONG. THOSE FORCE EPSILON GUYS ARE STILL AROUND.
ALL RIGHT. I'LL JUST SIT HERE A MOMENT AND CATCH MY BREATH.
DOCTOR, WHEN THIS IS ALL OVER, LET'S PLAY CHESS AGAIN. IF YOU DON'T MIND GETTING YOUR BUTT KICKED!!
HMPH. IN YOUR DREAMS, UPSTART.
BUT... I MAY HAVE TO...
...FORFEIT THE NEXT GAME.

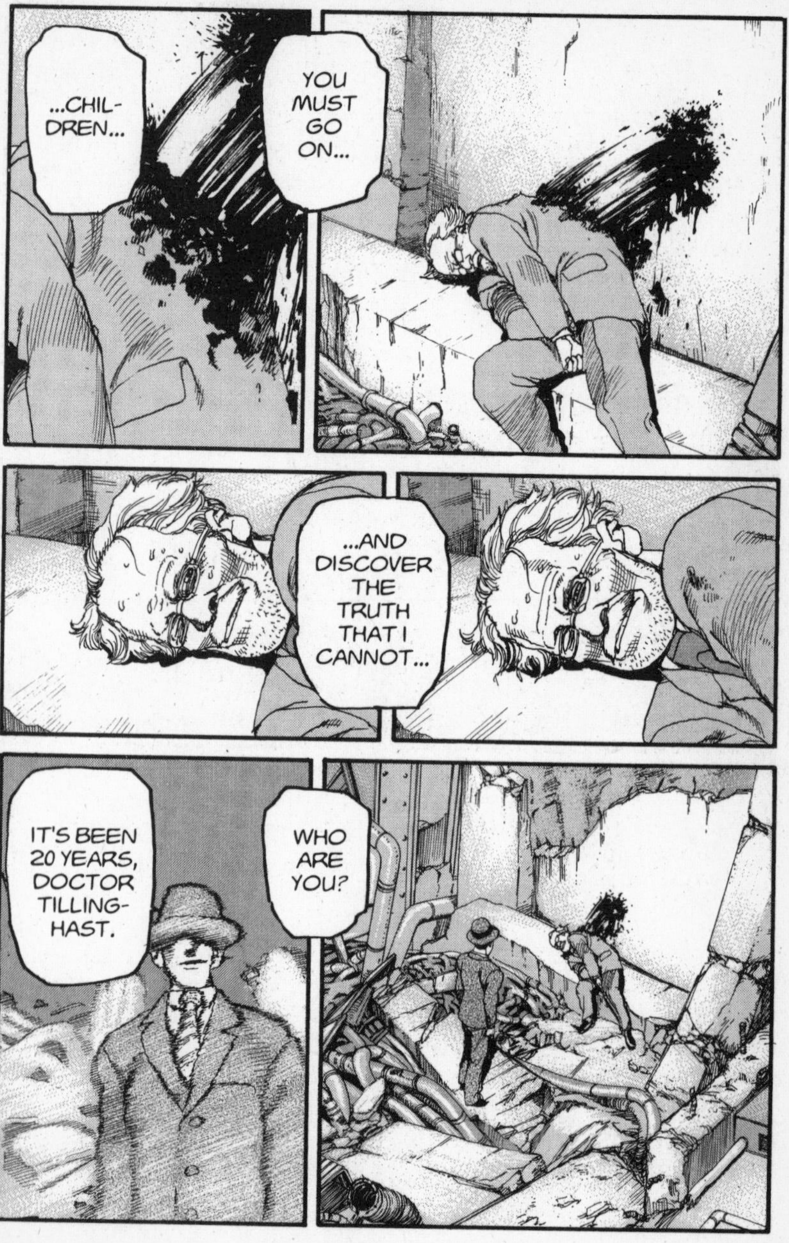
YOU MUST GO ON...
...CHIL-DREN...
...AND DISCOVER THE TRUTH THAT I CANNOT...
WHO ARE YOU?
IT'S BEEN 20 YEARS, DOCTOR TILLING-HAST.

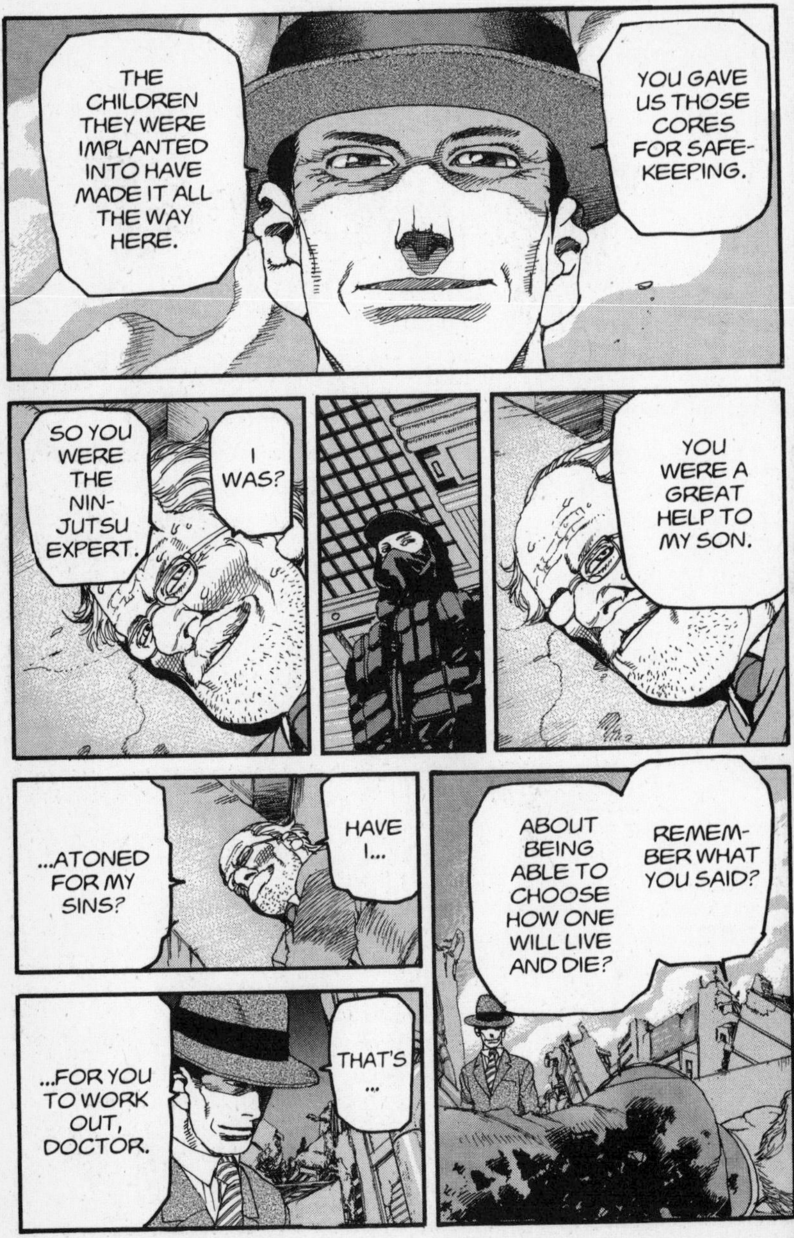
YOU GAVE US THOSE CORES FOR SAFE-KEEPING.
THE CHILDREN THEY WERE IMPLANTED INTO HAVE MADE IT ALL THE WAY HERE.
YOU WERE A GREAT HELP TO MY SON.
I WAS?
SO YOU WERE THE NIN-JUTSU EXPERT.
REMEM-BER WHAT YOU SAID?
ABOUT BEING ABLE TO CHOOSE HOW ONE WILL LIVE AND DIE?
HAVE I...
...ATONED FOR MY SINS?
THAT'S...
...FOR YOU TO WORK OUT, DOCTOR.

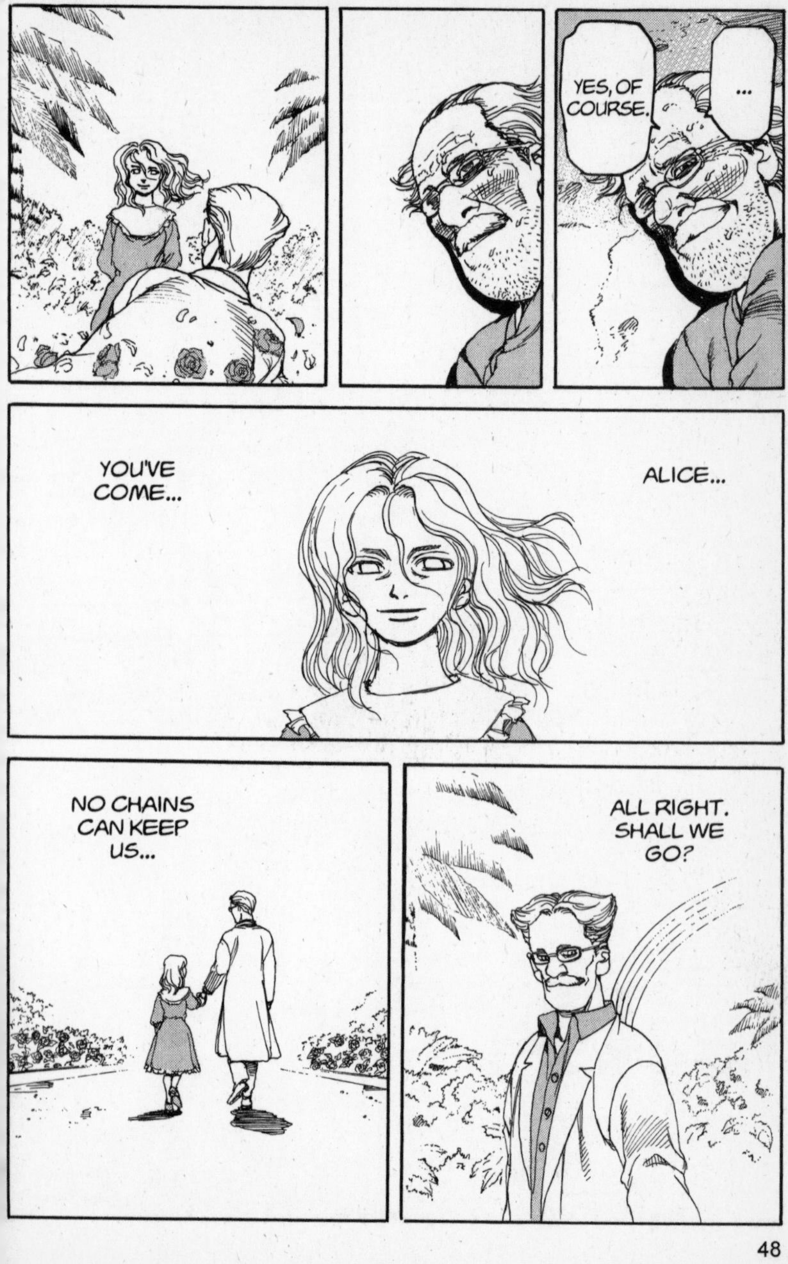
...
YES, OF COURSE.
ALICE...
YOU'VE COME...
ALL RIGHT. SHALL WE GO?
NO CHAINS CAN KEEP US...

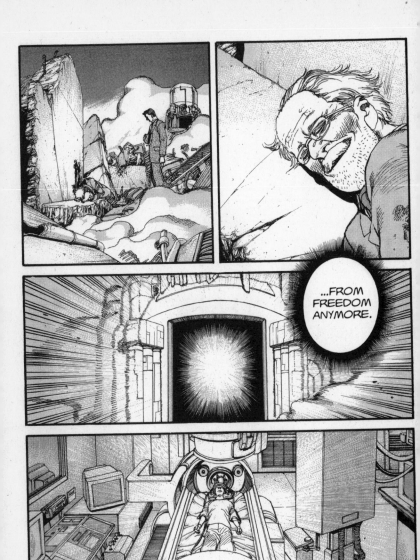

...FROM FREEDOM ANYMORE.

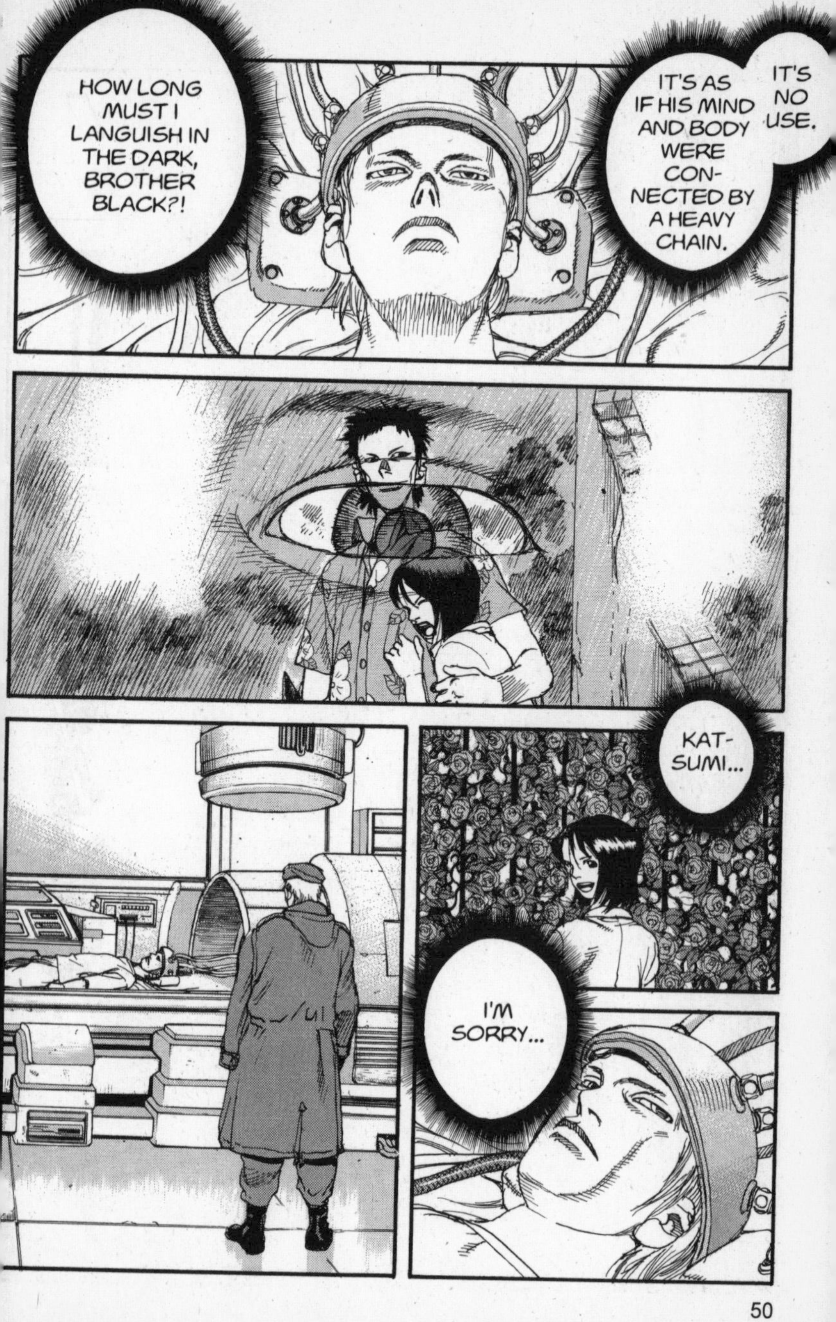
IT'S NO USE.
IT'S AS IF HIS MIND AND BODY WERE CON-NECTED BY A HEAVY CHAIN.
HOW LONG MUST I LANGUISH IN THE DARK, BROTHER BLACK?!
KAT-SUMI...
I'M SORRY...

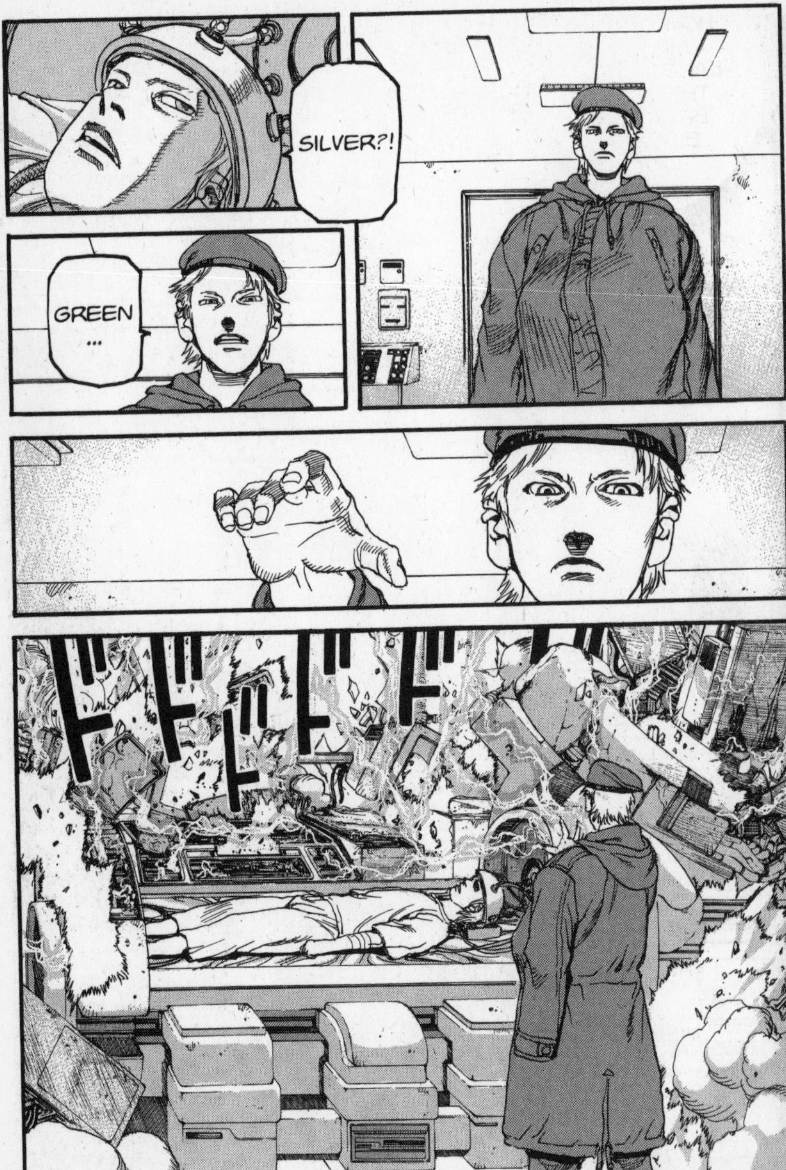
SILVER?!
GREEN ...

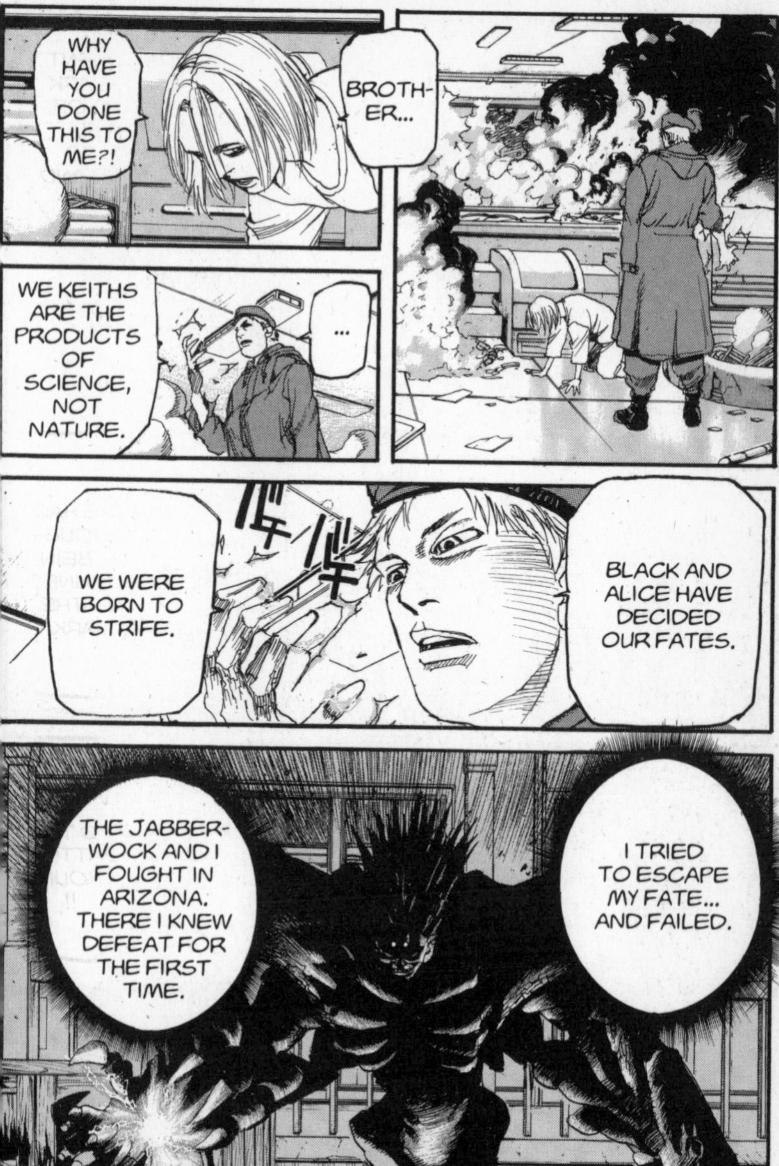
BROTH-ER...
WHY HAVE YOU DONE THIS TO ME?!
...
WE KEITHS ARE THE PRODUCTS OF SCIENCE, NOT NATURE.
BLACK AND ALICE HAVE DECIDED OUR FATES.
WE WERE BORN TO STRIFE.
I TRIED TO ESCAPE MY FATE... AND FAILED.
THE JABBER-WOCK AND I FOUGHT IN ARIZONA. THERE I KNEW DEFEAT FOR THE FIRST TIME.

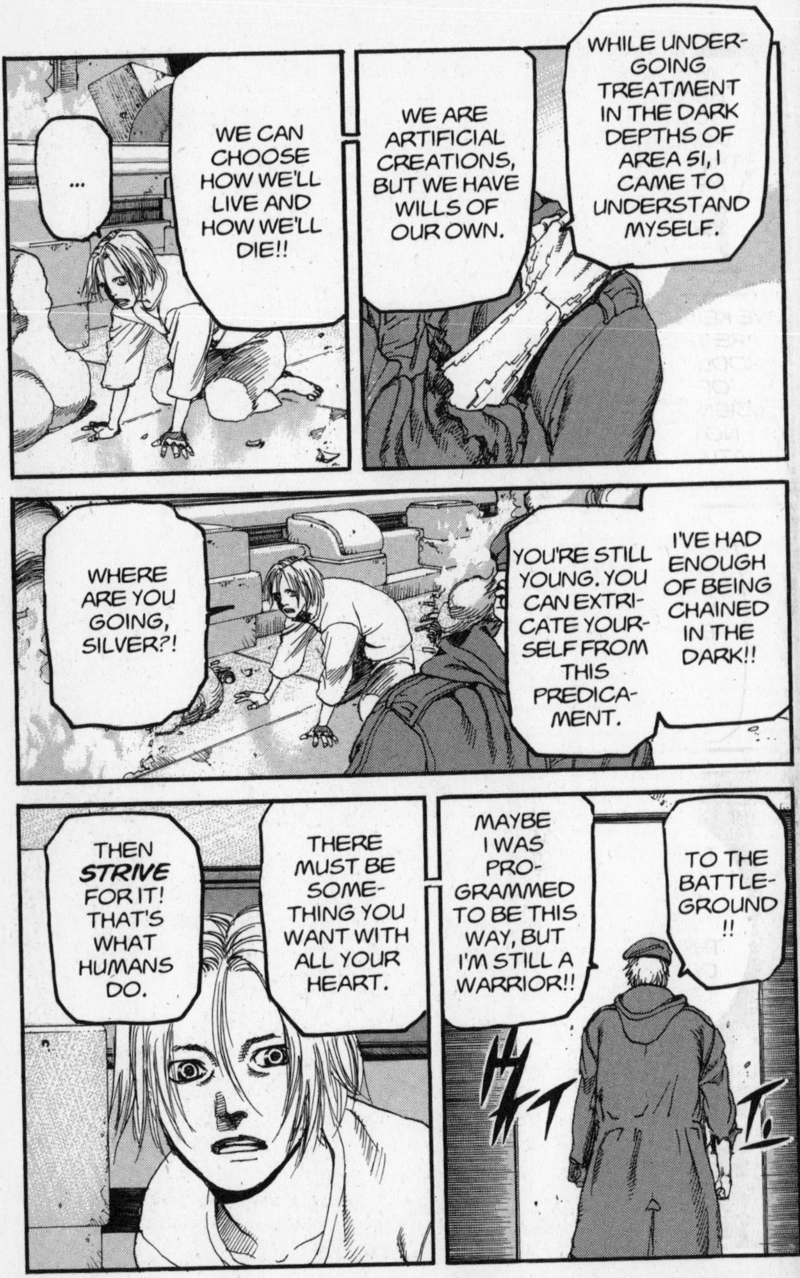
WHILE UNDER-GOING TREATMENT IN THE DARK DEPTHS OF AREA 51, I CAME TO UNDERSTAND MYSELF.
WE ARE ARTIFICIAL CREATIONS, BUT WE HAVE WILLS OF OUR OWN.
WE CAN CHOOSE HOW WE'LL LIVE AND HOW WE'LL DIE!!
...
I'VE HAD ENOUGH OF BEING CHAINED IN THE DARK!!
YOU'RE STILL YOUNG. YOU CAN EXTRI-CATE YOUR-SELF FROM THIS PREDICA-MENT.
WHERE ARE YOU GOING, SILVER?!
TO THE BATTLE-GROUND !!
MAYBE I WAS PRO-GRAMMED TO BE THIS WAY, BUT I'M STILL A WARRIOR!!
THERE MUST BE SOME-THING YOU WANT WITH ALL YOUR HEART.
THEN ***STRIVE*** FOR IT! THAT'S WHAT HUMANS DO.

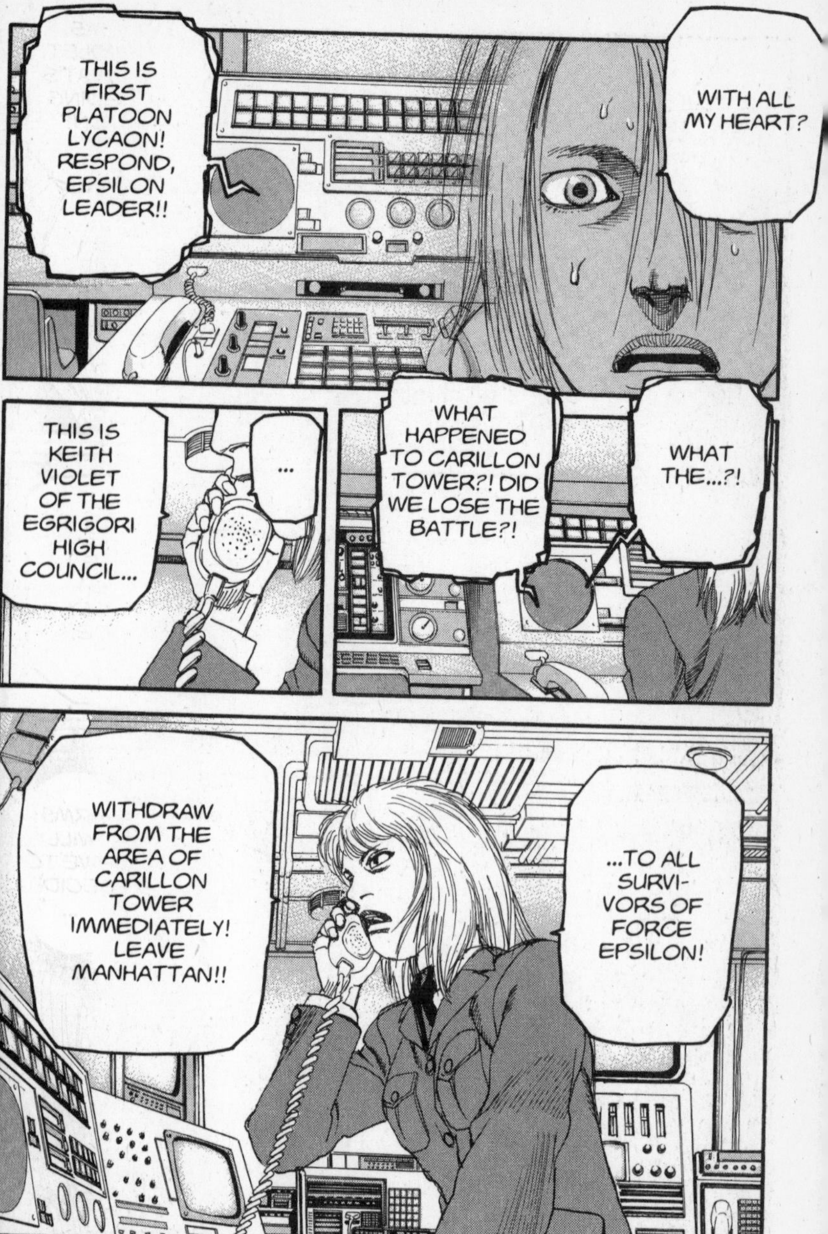

WITH ALL MY HEART?
THIS IS FIRST PLATOON LYCAON! RESPOND, EPSILON LEADER!!
WHAT THE...?!
WHAT HAPPENED TO CARILLON TOWER?! DID WE LOSE THE BATTLE?!
...
THIS IS KEITH VIOLET OF THE EGRIGORI HIGH COUNCIL...
...TO ALL SURVIVORS OF FORCE EPSILON!
WITHDRAW FROM THE AREA OF CARILLON TOWER IMMEDIATELY! LEAVE MANHATTAN!!

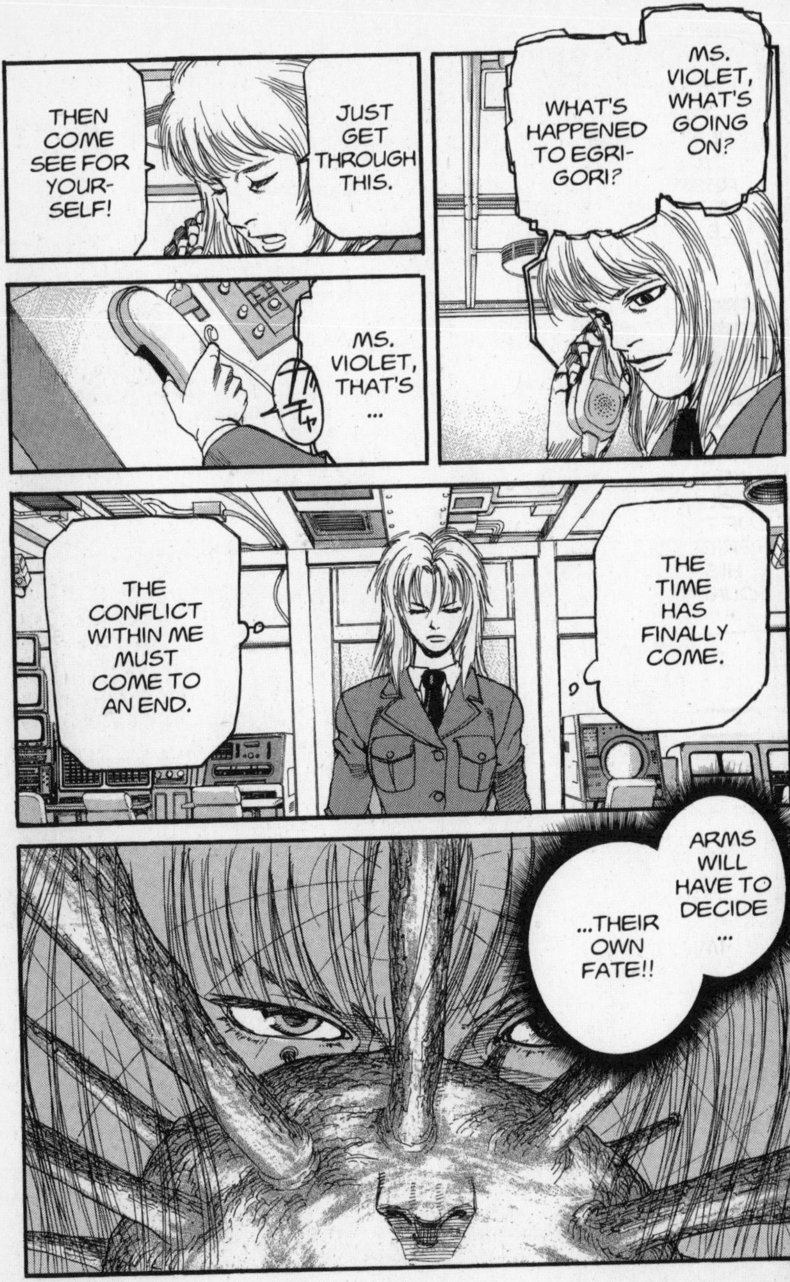
MS. VIOLET, WHAT'S GOING ON?
WHAT'S HAPPENED TO EGRI-GORI?
JUST GET THROUGH THIS.
THEN COME SEE FOR YOUR-SELF!
MS. VIOLET, THAT'S ...
THE TIME HAS FINALLY COME.
THE CONFLICT WITHIN ME MUST COME TO AN END.
ARMS WILL HAVE TO DECIDE ...
...THEIR OWN FATE!!

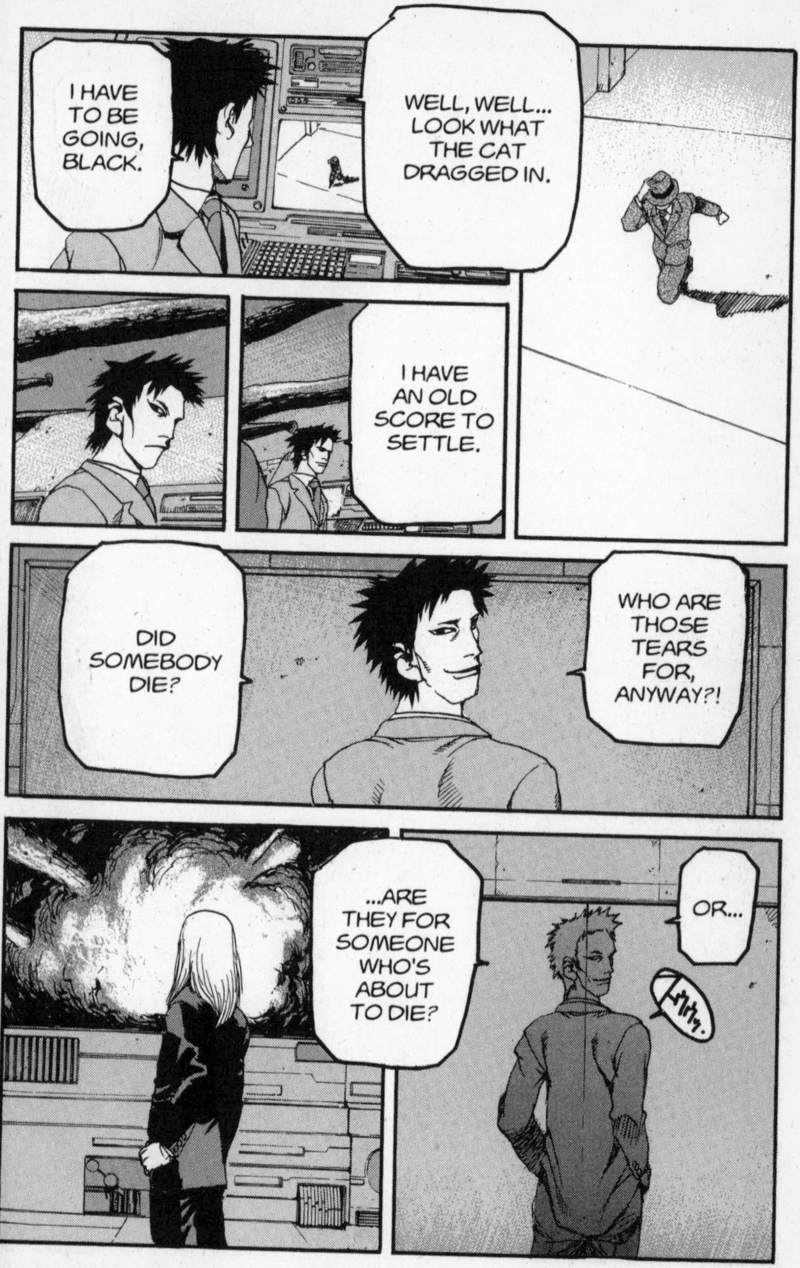
WELL, WELL... LOOK WHAT THE CAT DRAGGED IN.
I HAVE TO BE GOING, BLACK.
I HAVE AN OLD SCORE TO SETTLE.
WHO ARE THOSE TEARS FOR, ANYWAY?!
DID SOMEBODY DIE?
OR...
...ARE THEY FOR SOMEONE WHO'S ABOUT TO DIE?

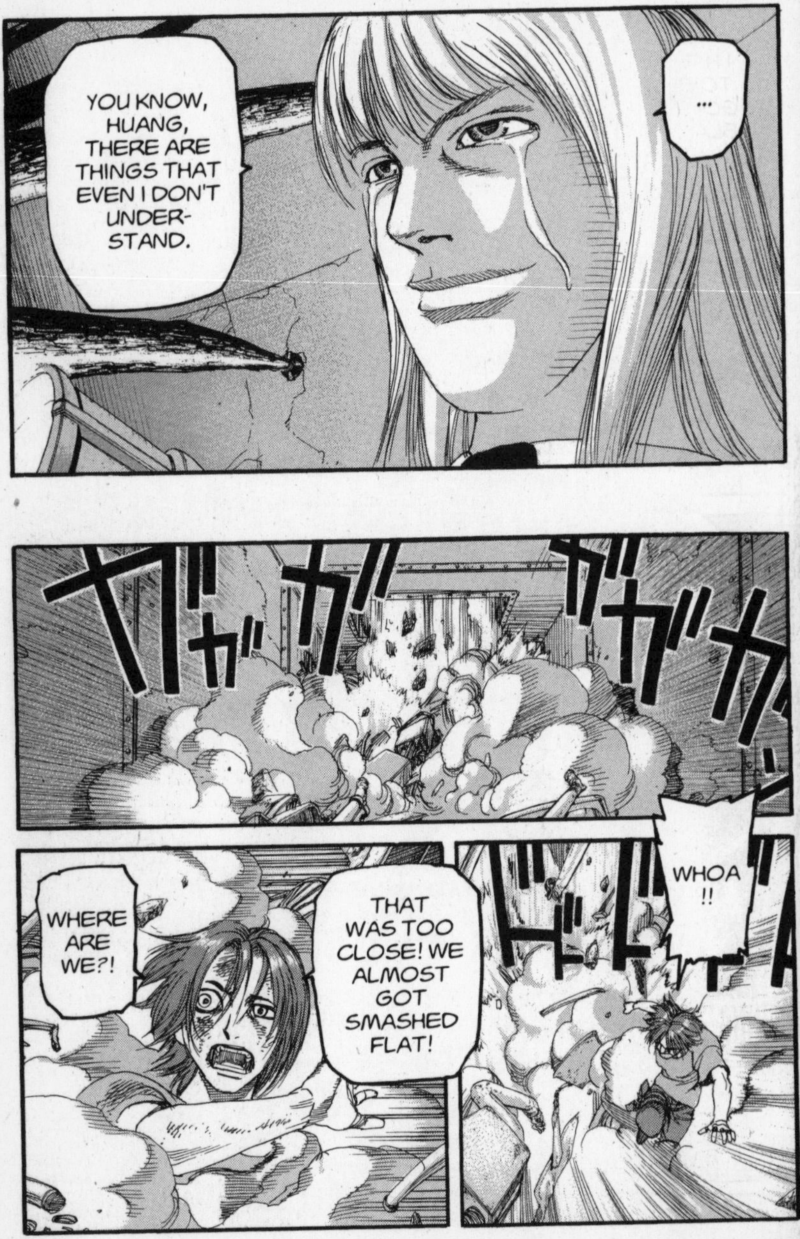
...
YOU KNOW, HUANG, THERE ARE THINGS THAT EVEN I DON'T UNDER-STAND.
WHOA !!
THAT WAS TOO CLOSE! WE ALMOST GOT SMASHED FLAT!
WHERE ARE WE?!

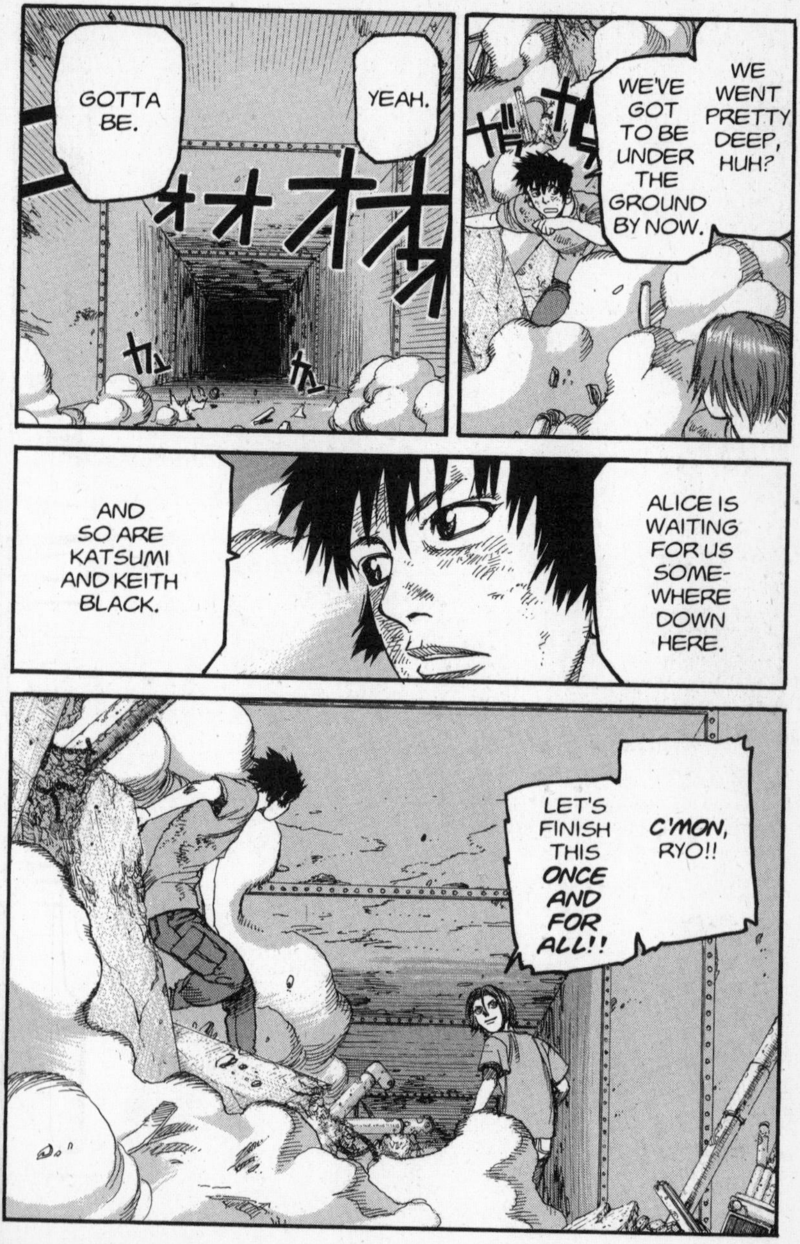
WE WENT PRETTY DEEP, HUH?
WE'VE GOT TO BE UNDER THE GROUND BY NOW.
YEAH.
GOTTA BE.
ALICE IS WAITING FOR US SOMEWHERE DOWN HERE.
AND SO ARE KATSUMI AND KEITH BLACK.
C'MON, RYO!!
LET'S FINISH THIS ONCE AND FOR ALL!!

No. 4 SILVER LIGHT

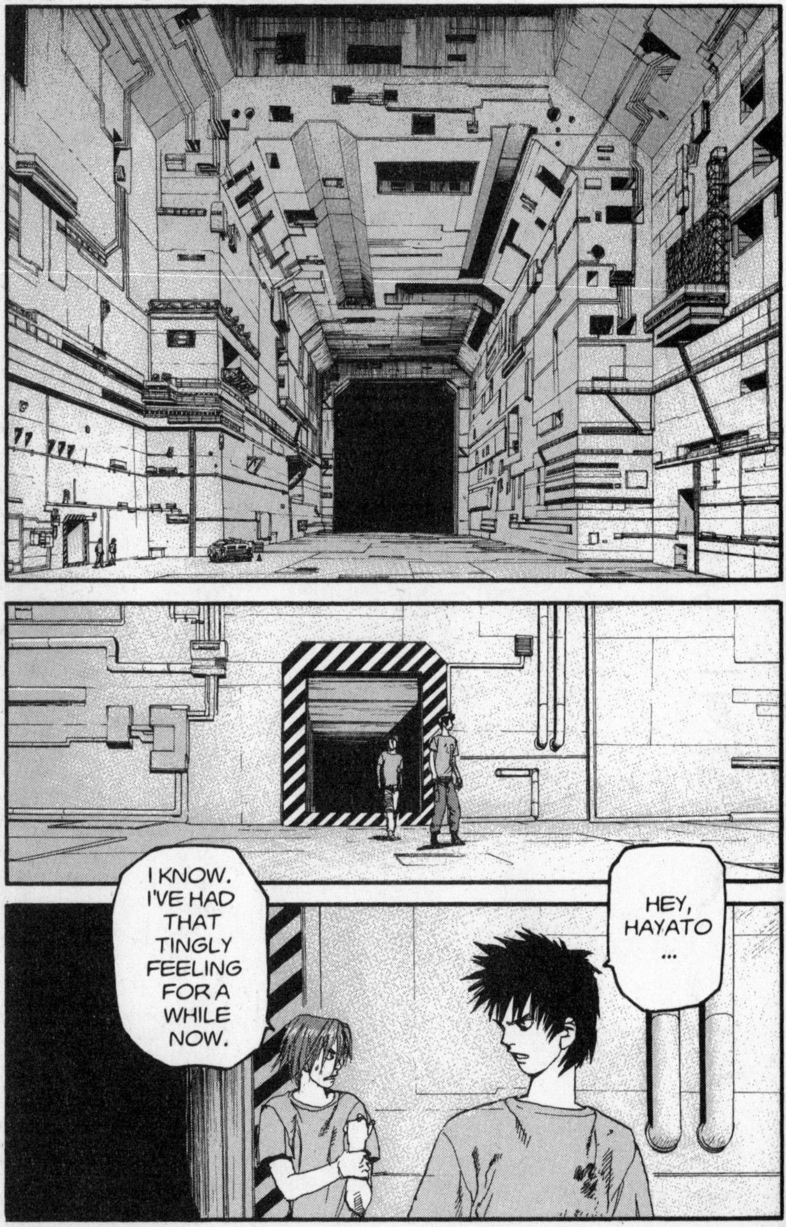
HEY, HAYATO ...
I KNOW. I'VE HAD THAT TINGLY FEELING FOR A WHILE NOW.

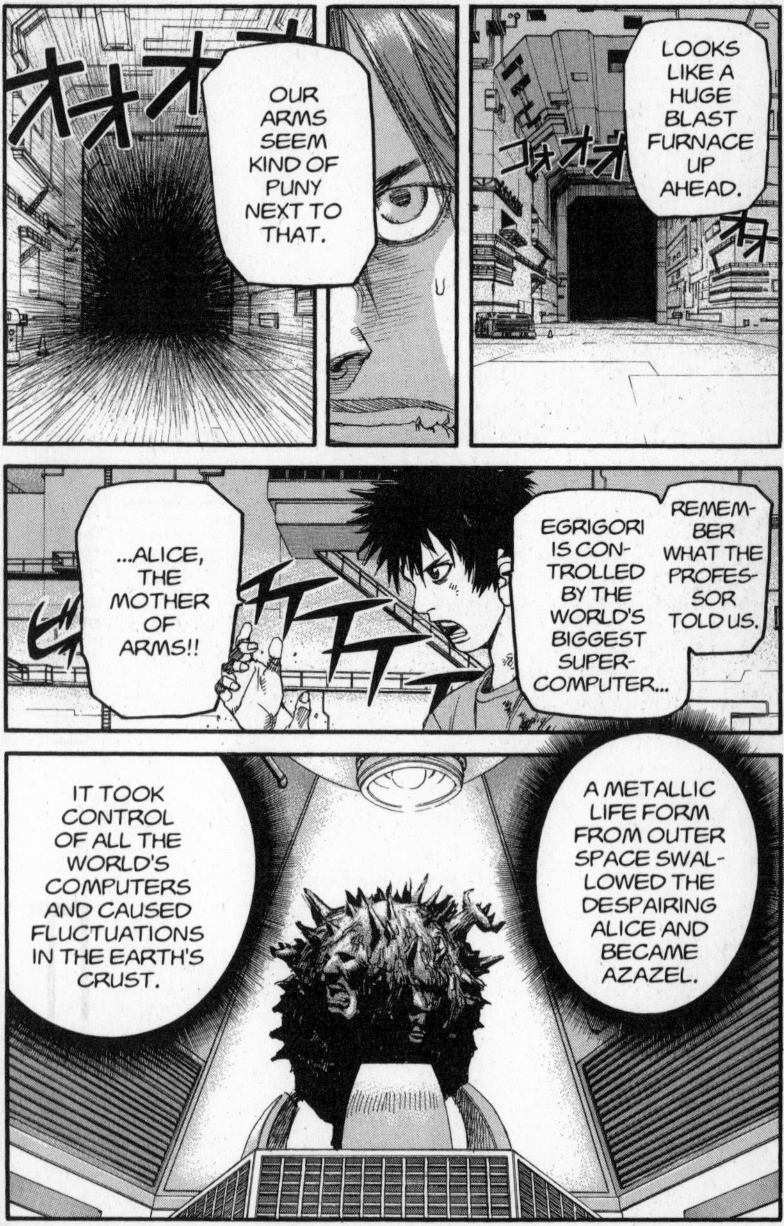
LOOKS LIKE A HUGE BLAST FURNACE UP AHEAD.
OUR ARMS SEEM KIND OF PUNY NEXT TO THAT.
REMEMBER WHAT THE PROFESSOR TOLD US.
EGRIGORI IS CONTROLLED BY THE WORLD'S BIGGEST SUPERCOMPUTER...
...ALICE, THE MOTHER OF ARMS!!
A METALLIC LIFE FORM FROM OUTER SPACE SWALLOWED THE DESPAIRING ALICE AND BECAME AZAZEL.
IT TOOK CONTROL OF ALL THE WORLD'S COMPUTERS AND CAUSED FLUCTUATIONS IN THE EARTH'S CRUST.

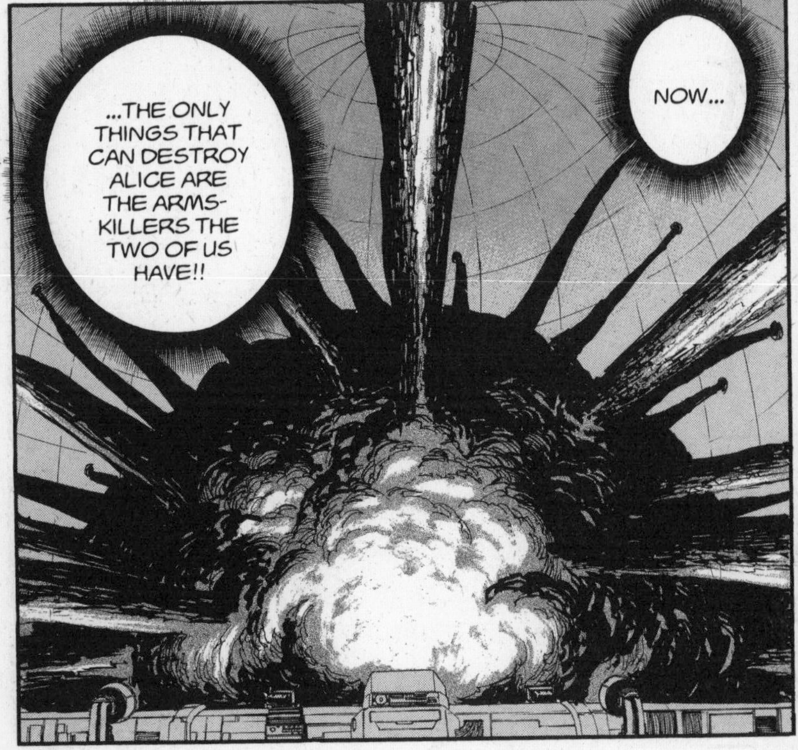
NOW...
...THE ONLY THINGS THAT CAN DESTROY ALICE ARE THE ARMS-KILLERS THE TWO OF US HAVE!!

No. 4 SILVER LIGHT

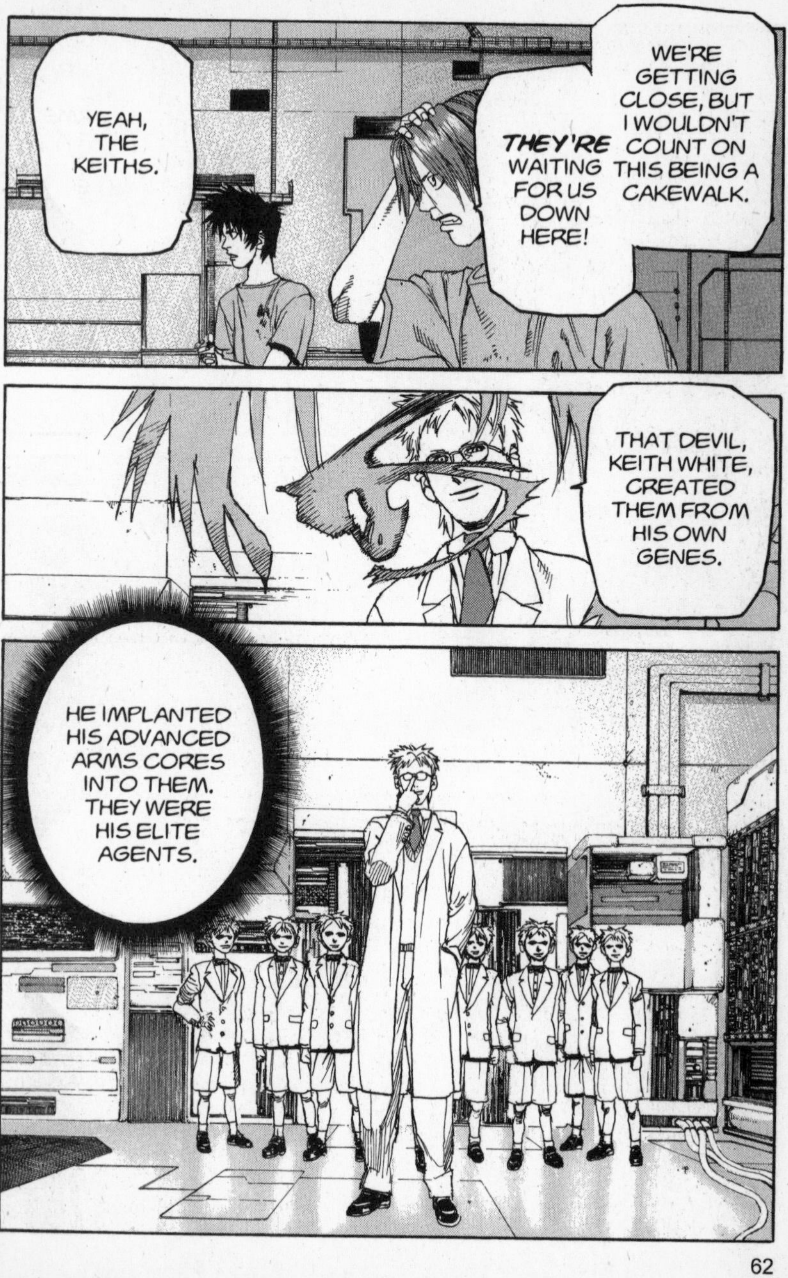
WE'RE GETTING CLOSE, BUT I WOULDN'T COUNT ON THIS BEING A CAKEWALK.
THEY'RE WAITING FOR US DOWN HERE!
YEAH, THE KEITHS.
THAT DEVIL, KEITH WHITE, CREATED THEM FROM HIS OWN GENES.
HE IMPLANTED HIS ADVANCED ARMS CORES INTO THEM. THEY WERE HIS ELITE AGENTS.

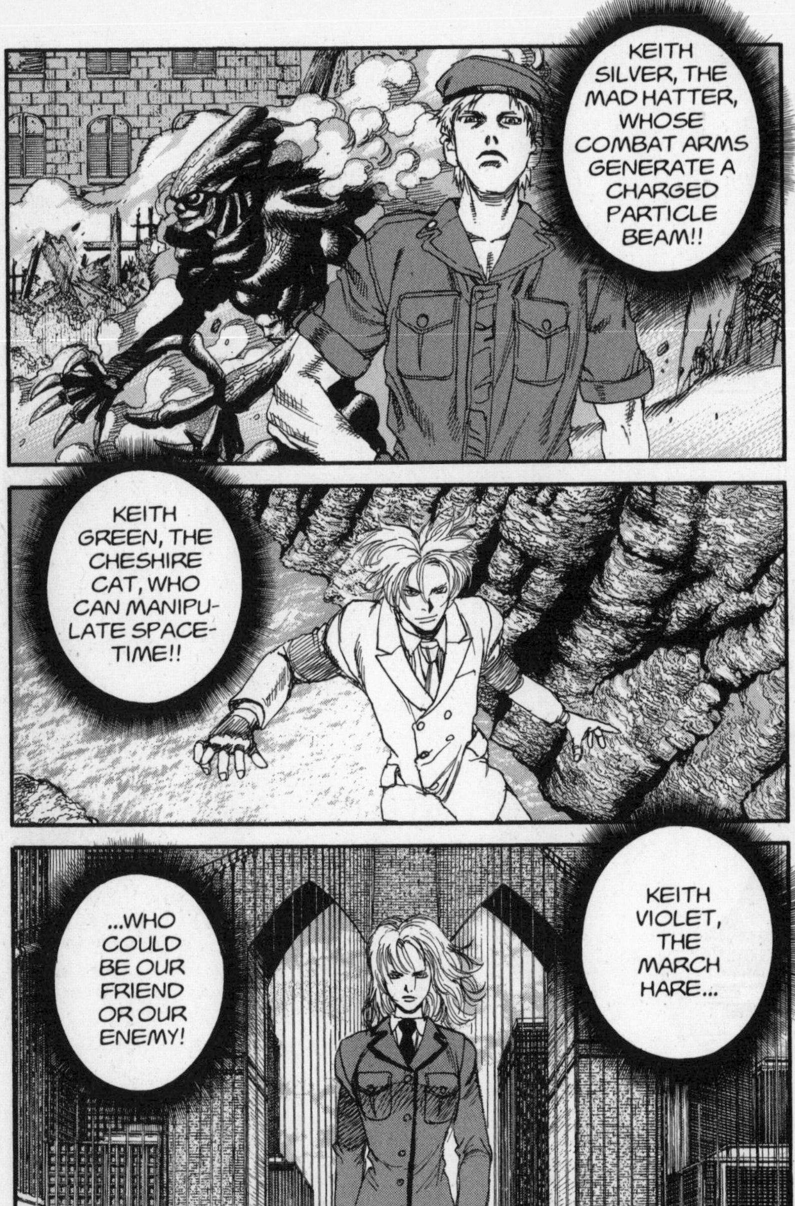
KEITH SILVER, THE MAD HATTER, WHOSE COMBAT ARMS GENERATE A CHARGED PARTICLE BEAM!!
KEITH GREEN, THE CHESHIRE CAT, WHO CAN MANIPU-LATE SPACE-TIME!!
KEITH VIOLET, THE MARCH HARE...
...WHO COULD BE OUR FRIEND OR OUR ENEMY!

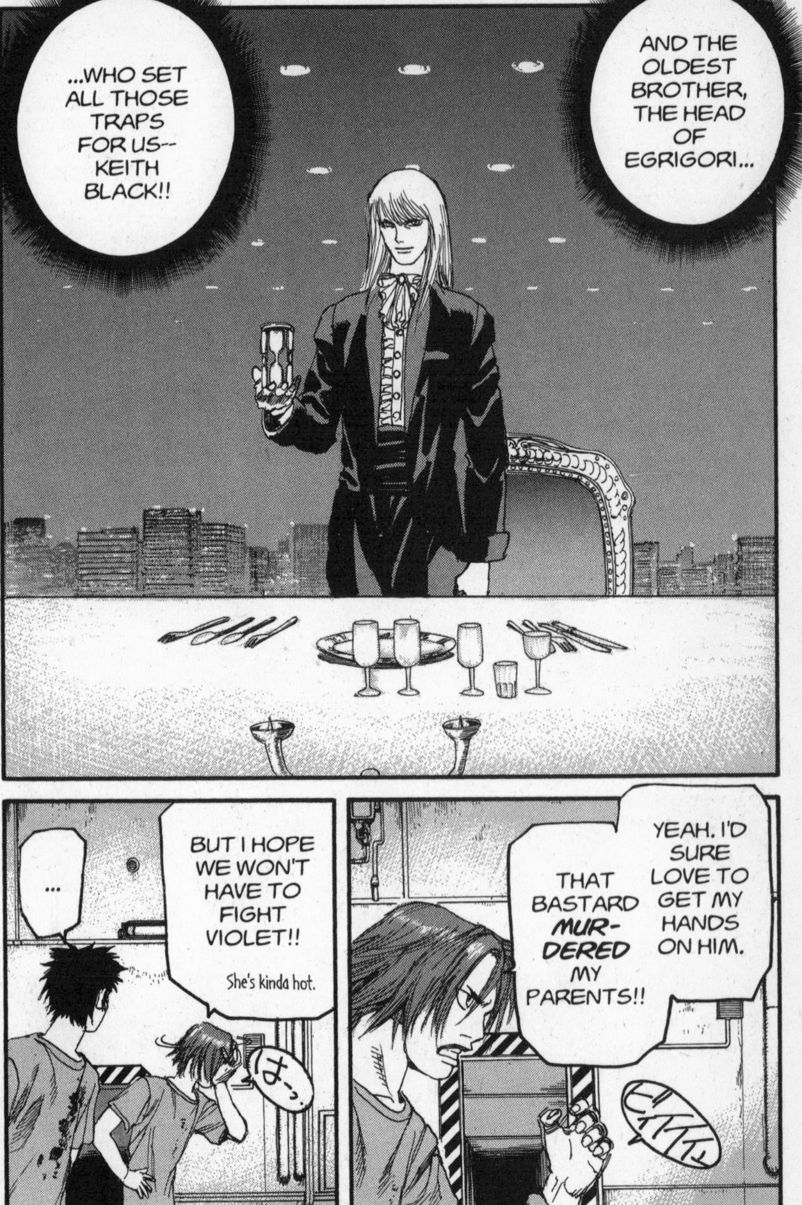
AND THE OLDEST BROTHER, THE HEAD OF EGRIGORI...
...WHO SET ALL THOSE TRAPS FOR US-- KEITH BLACK!!
YEAH. I'D SURE LOVE TO GET MY HANDS ON HIM.
THAT BASTARD MURDERED MY PARENTS!!
BUT I HOPE WE WON'T HAVE TO FIGHT VIOLET!!
She's kinda hot.
...
はーっ

WHEN WE FIND KATSUMI AND ALICE, WE'LL FIND KEITH BLACK.
SO QUIT COM-PLAINING!!
RIGHT. WE'VE GOT AN APPOINT-MENT TO KEEP.
Anyway, you're the one complaining.
C'MON, HAYATO!!
TO THE FINAL BATTLE!!

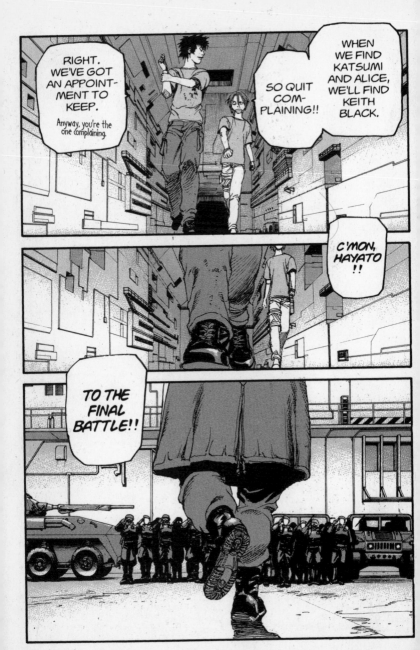

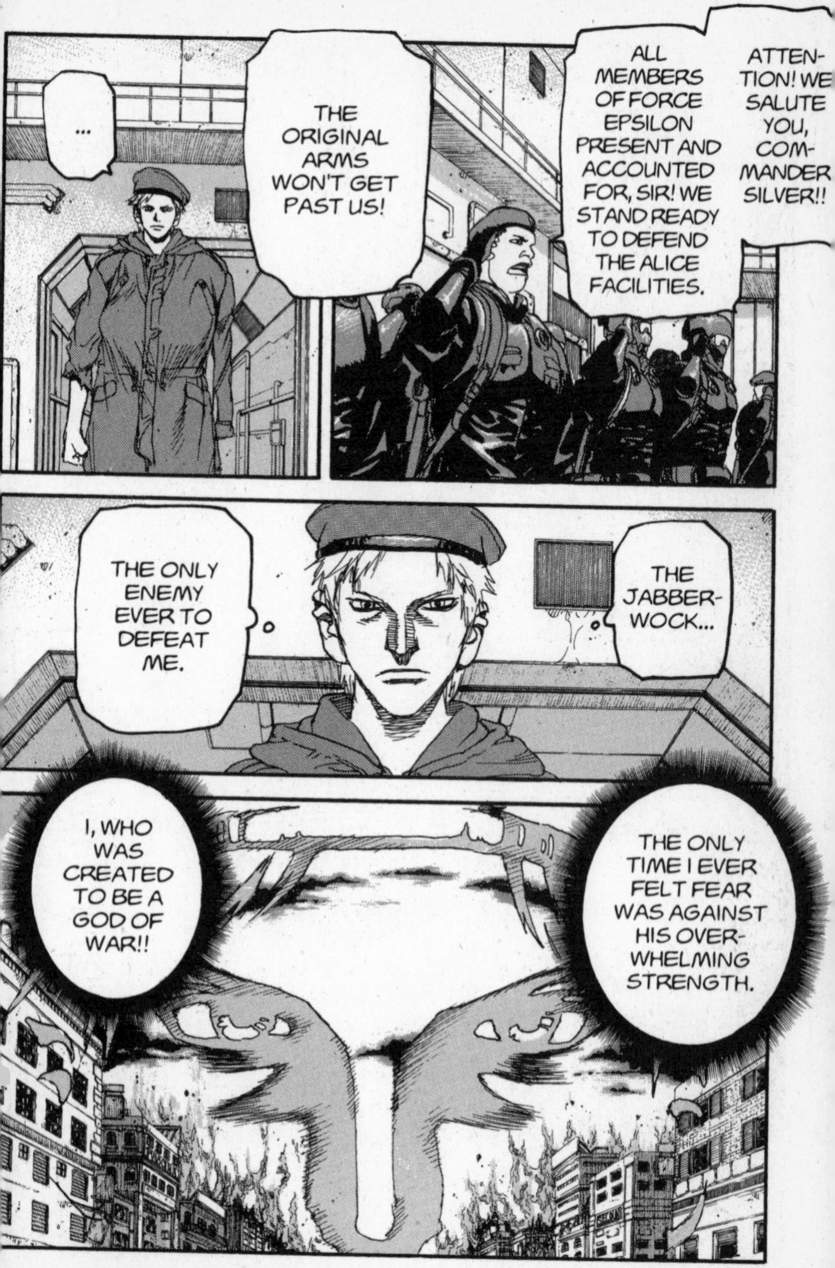
ATTENTION! WE SALUTE YOU, COMMANDER SILVER!!
ALL MEMBERS OF FORCE EPSILON PRESENT AND ACCOUNTED FOR, SIR! WE STAND READY TO DEFEND THE ALICE FACILITIES.
THE ORIGINAL ARMS WON'T GET PAST US!
...
THE JABBERWOCK...
THE ONLY ENEMY EVER TO DEFEAT ME.
THE ONLY TIME I EVER FELT FEAR WAS AGAINST HIS OVERWHELMING STRENGTH.
I, WHO WAS CREATED TO BE A GOD OF WAR!!

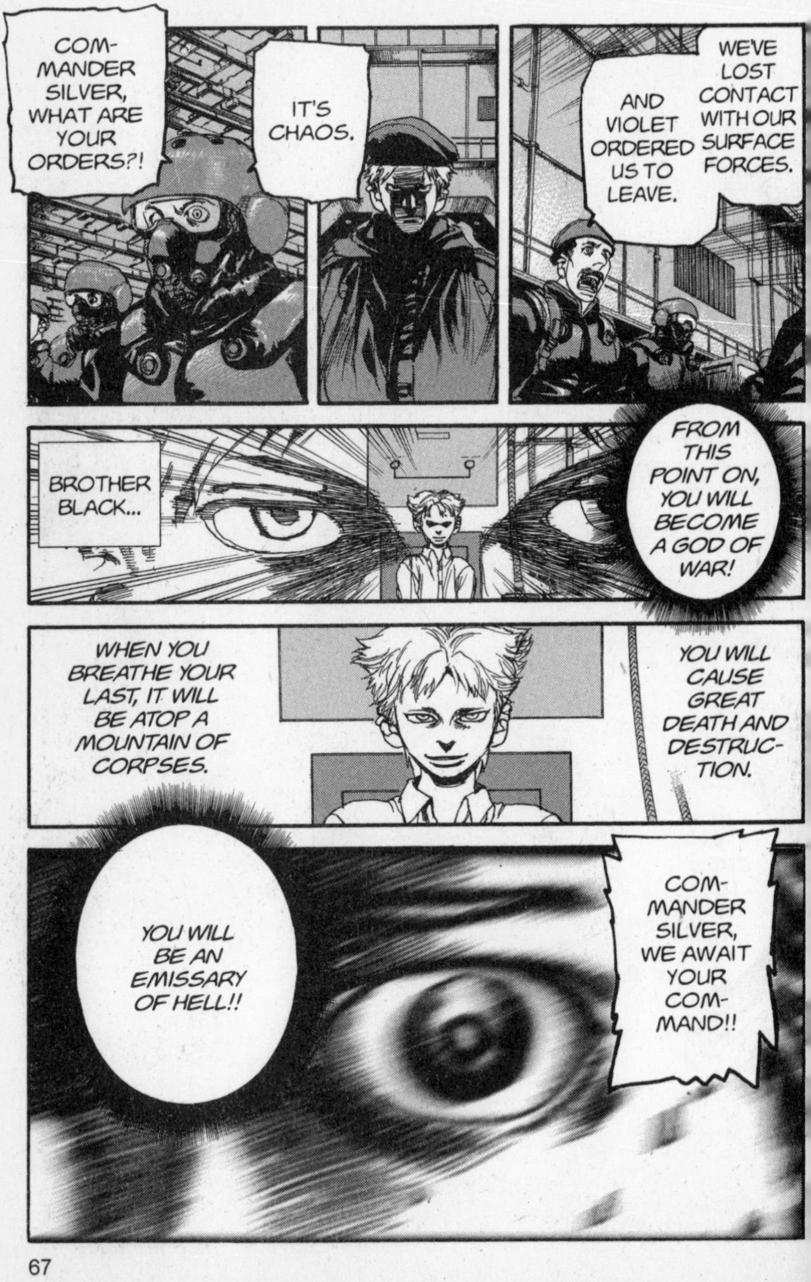
WE'VE LOST CONTACT WITH OUR SURFACE FORCES.
AND VIOLET ORDERED US TO LEAVE.
IT'S CHAOS.
COMMANDER SILVER, WHAT ARE YOUR ORDERS?!
FROM THIS POINT ON, YOU WILL BECOME A GOD OF WAR!
BROTHER BLACK...
YOU WILL CAUSE GREAT DEATH AND DESTRUCTION.
WHEN YOU BREATHE YOUR LAST, IT WILL BE ATOP A MOUNTAIN OF CORPSES.
COMMANDER SILVER, WE AWAIT YOUR COMMAND!!
YOU WILL BE AN EMISSARY OF HELL!!

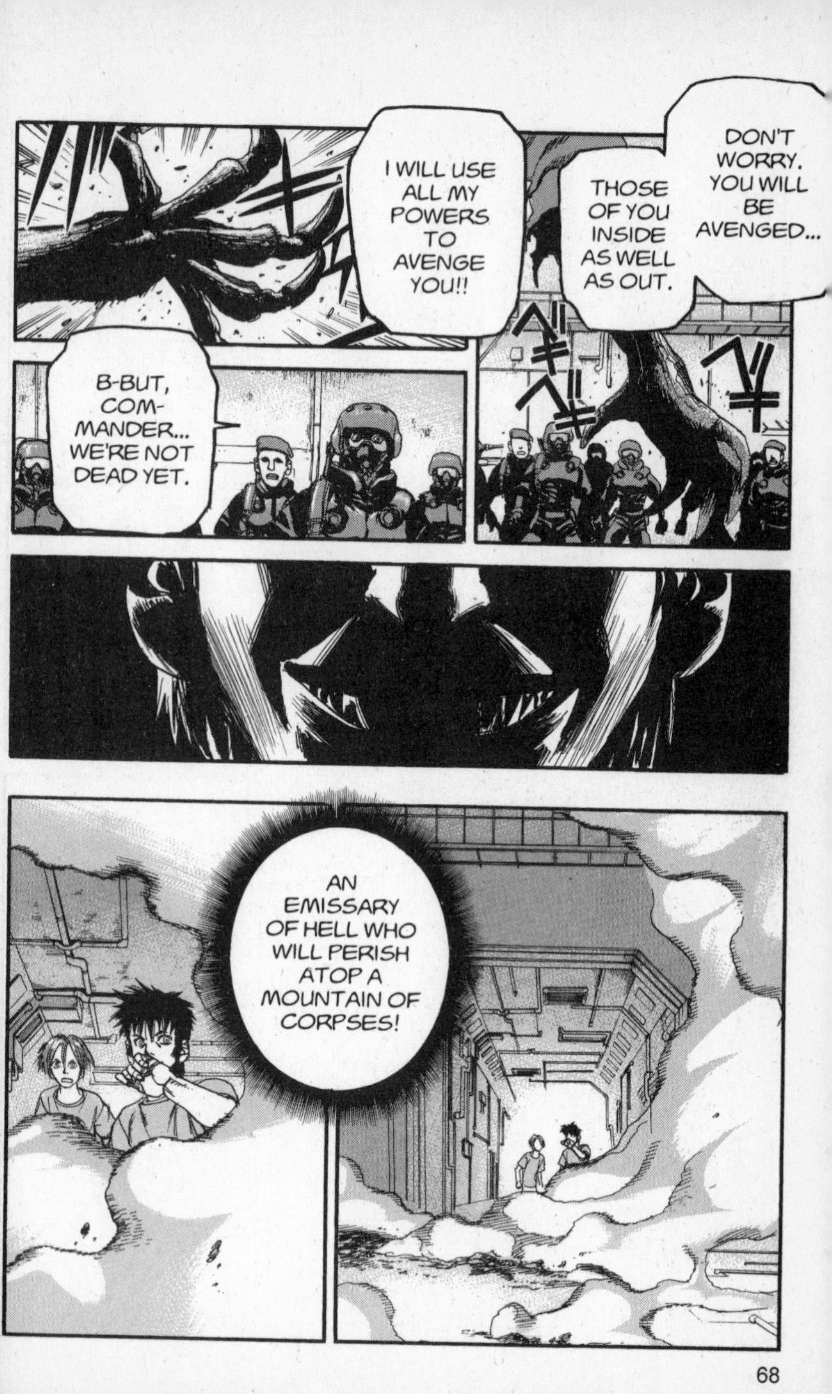
DON'T WORRY. YOU WILL BE AVENGED...
THOSE OF YOU INSIDE AS WELL AS OUT.
I WILL USE ALL MY POWERS TO AVENGE YOU!!
B-BUT, COM-MANDER... WE'RE NOT DEAD YET.
AN EMISSARY OF HELL WHO WILL PERISH ATOP A MOUNTAIN OF CORPSES!

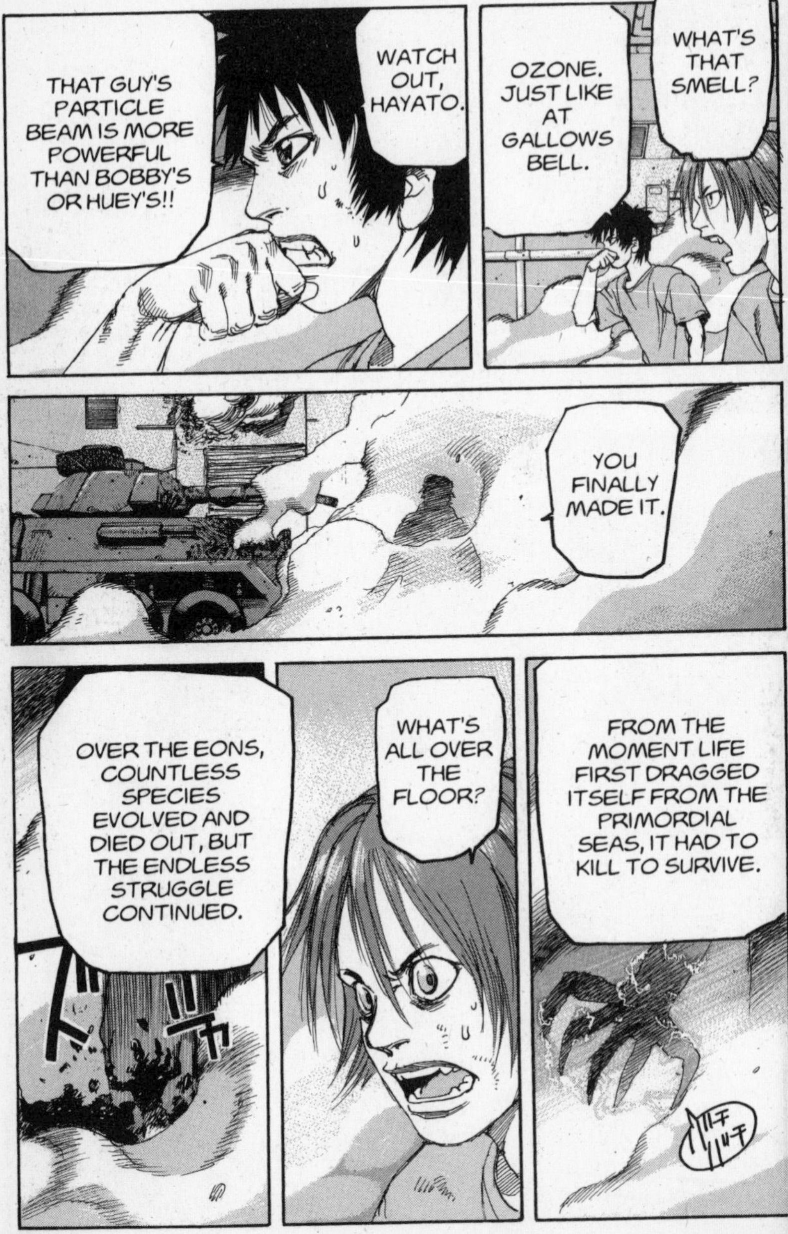
WHAT'S THAT SMELL?
OZONE. JUST LIKE AT GALLOWS BELL.
WATCH OUT, HAYATO.
THAT GUY'S PARTICLE BEAM IS MORE POWERFUL THAN BOBBY'S OR HUEY'S!!
YOU FINALLY MADE IT.
FROM THE MOMENT LIFE FIRST DRAGGED ITSELF FROM THE PRIMORDIAL SEAS, IT HAD TO KILL TO SURVIVE.
WHAT'S ALL OVER THE FLOOR?
OVER THE EONS, COUNTLESS SPECIES EVOLVED AND DIED OUT, BUT THE ENDLESS STRUGGLE CONTINUED.

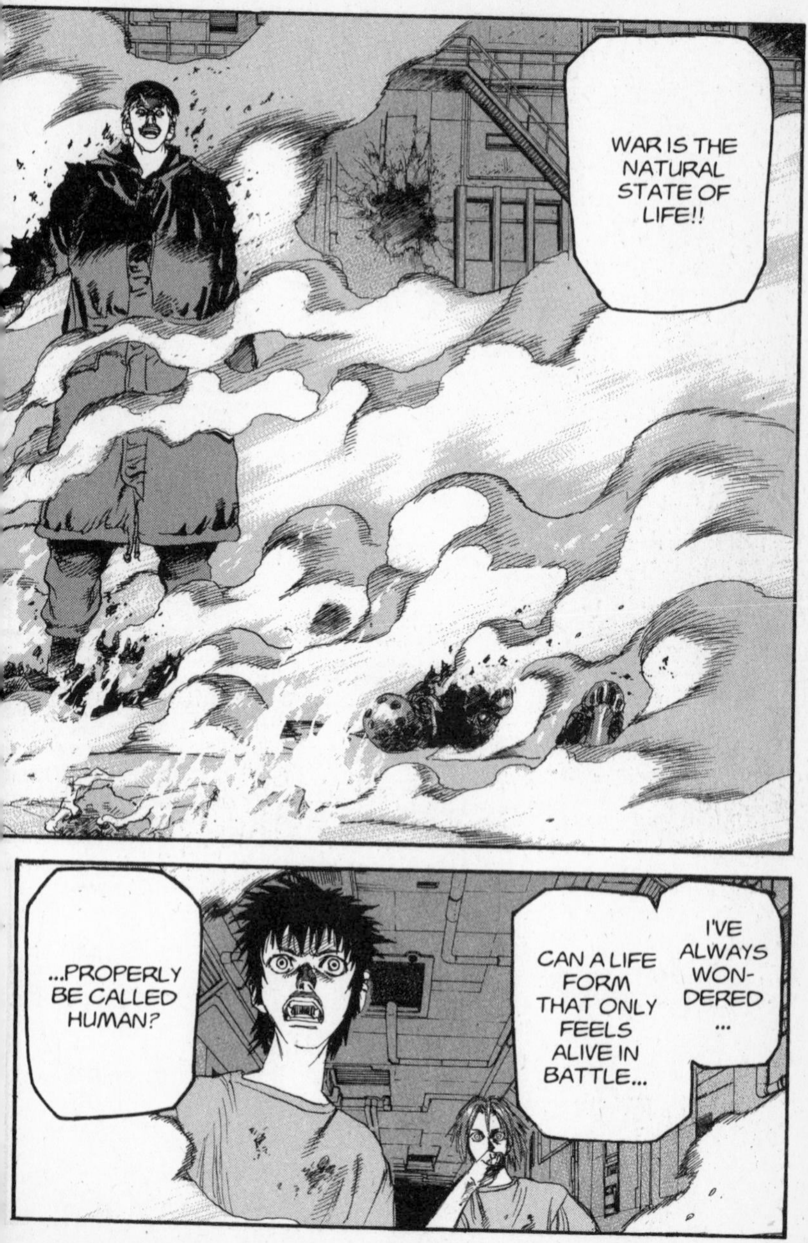
WAR IS THE NATURAL STATE OF LIFE!!
I'VE ALWAYS WON-DERED ...
CAN A LIFE FORM THAT ONLY FEELS ALIVE IN BATTLE...
...PROPERLY BE CALLED HUMAN?

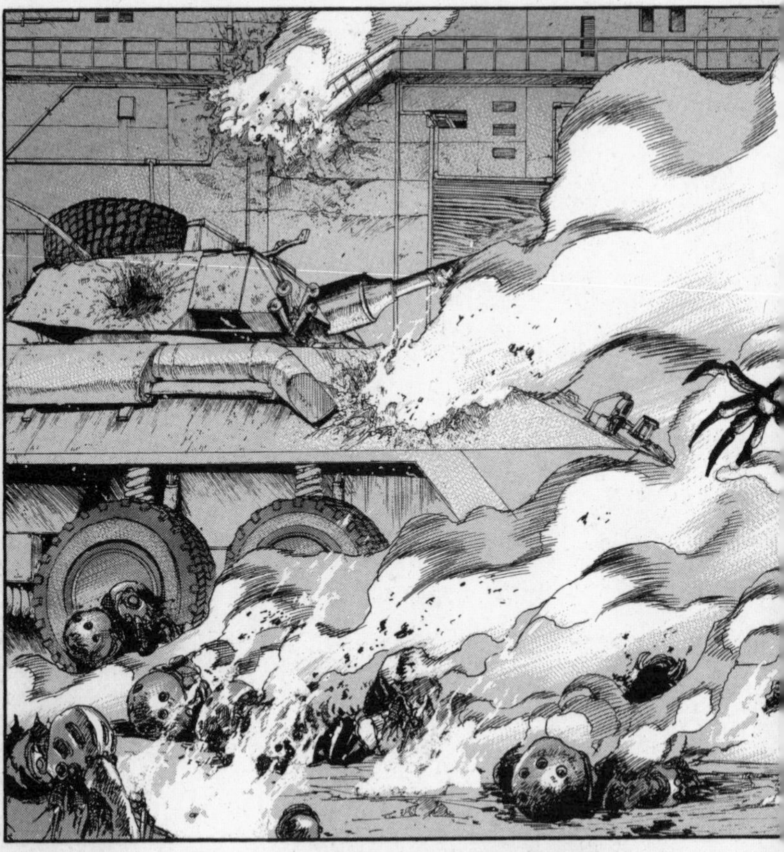

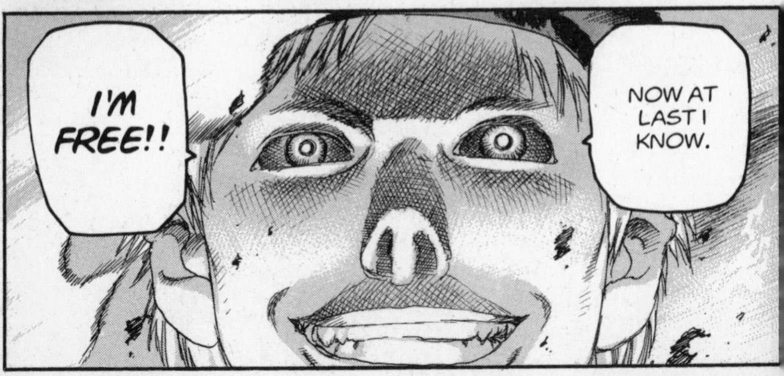
NOW AT LAST I KNOW.
I'M FREE!!

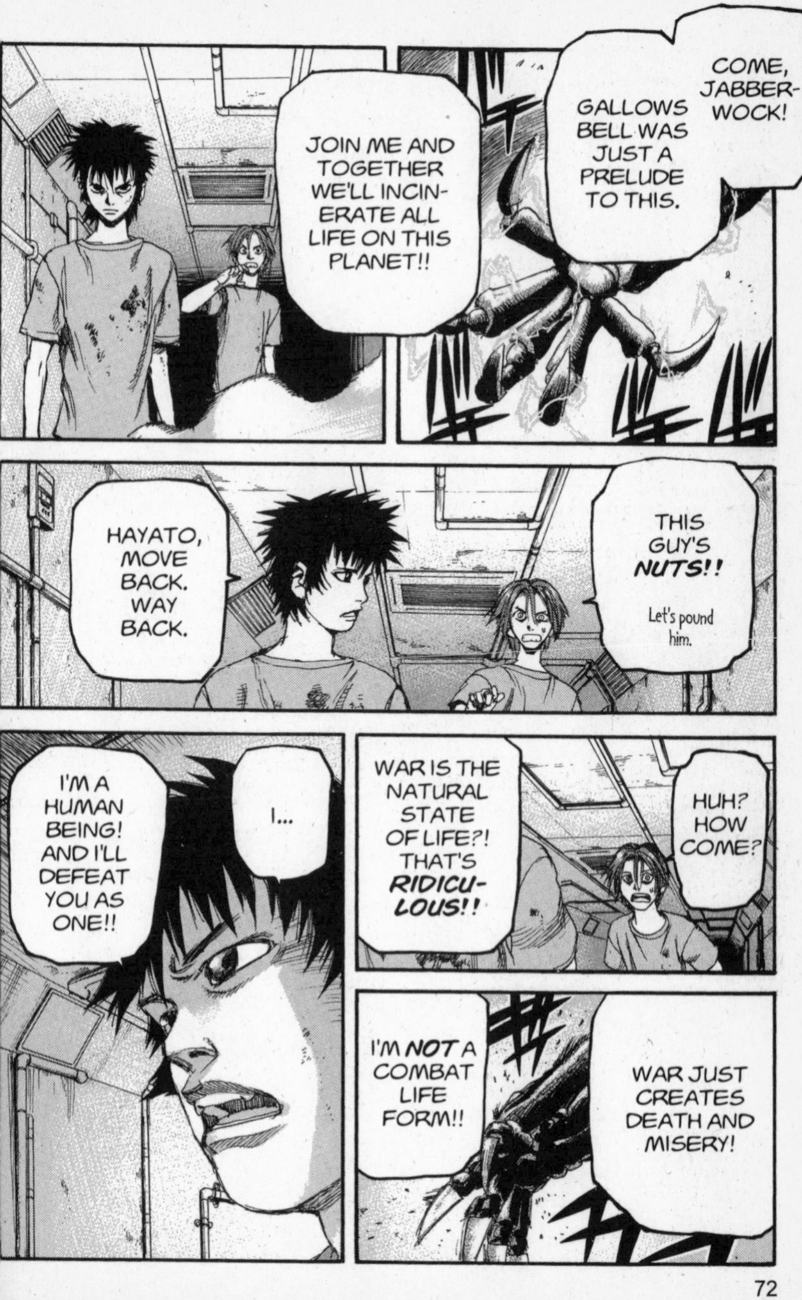
COME, JABBERWOCK!
GALLOWS BELL WAS JUST A PRELUDE TO THIS.
JOIN ME AND TOGETHER WE'LL INCINERATE ALL LIFE ON THIS PLANET!!
THIS GUY'S **NUTS!!**
Let's pound him.
HAYATO, MOVE BACK. WAY BACK.
HUH? HOW COME?
WAR IS THE NATURAL STATE OF LIFE?! THAT'S **RIDICULOUS!!**
WAR JUST CREATES DEATH AND MISERY!
I'M **NOT** A COMBAT LIFE FORM!!
I...
I'M A HUMAN BEING! AND I'LL DEFEAT YOU AS ONE!!

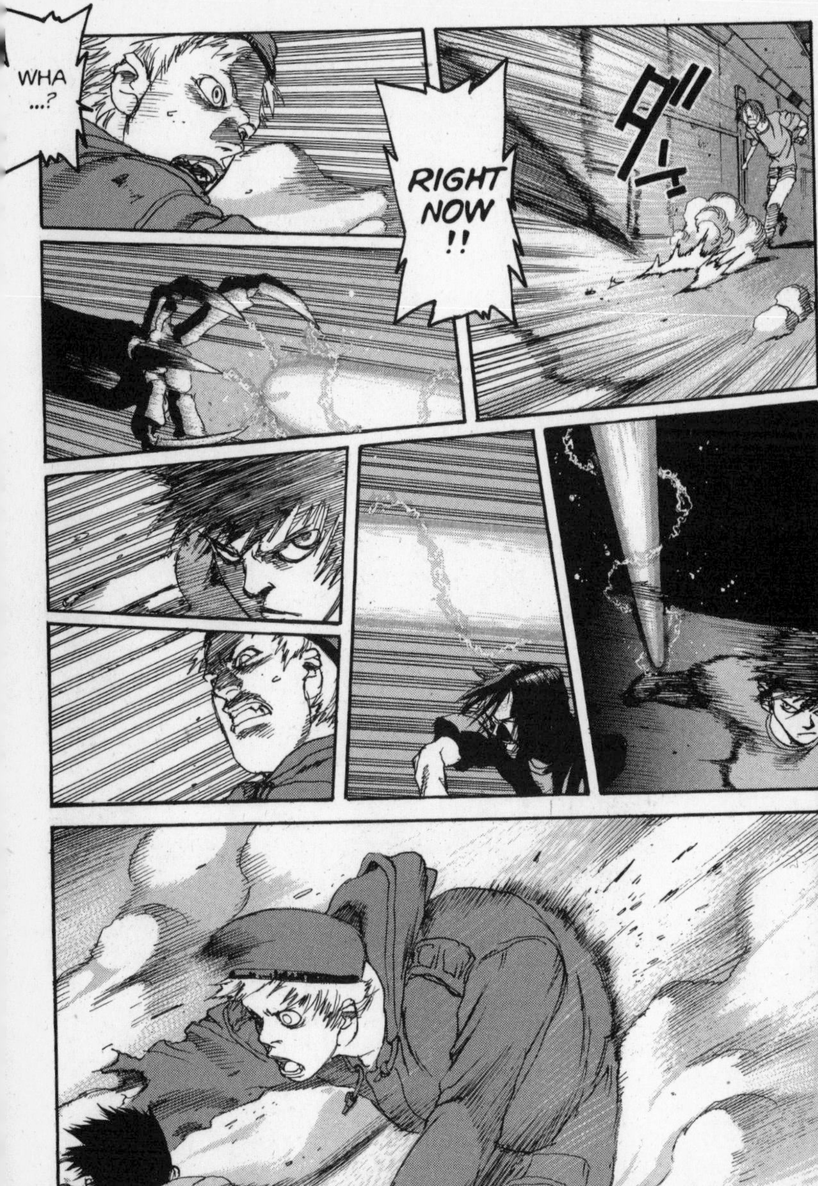

RIGHT NOW !!
ダーッ
WHA ...?

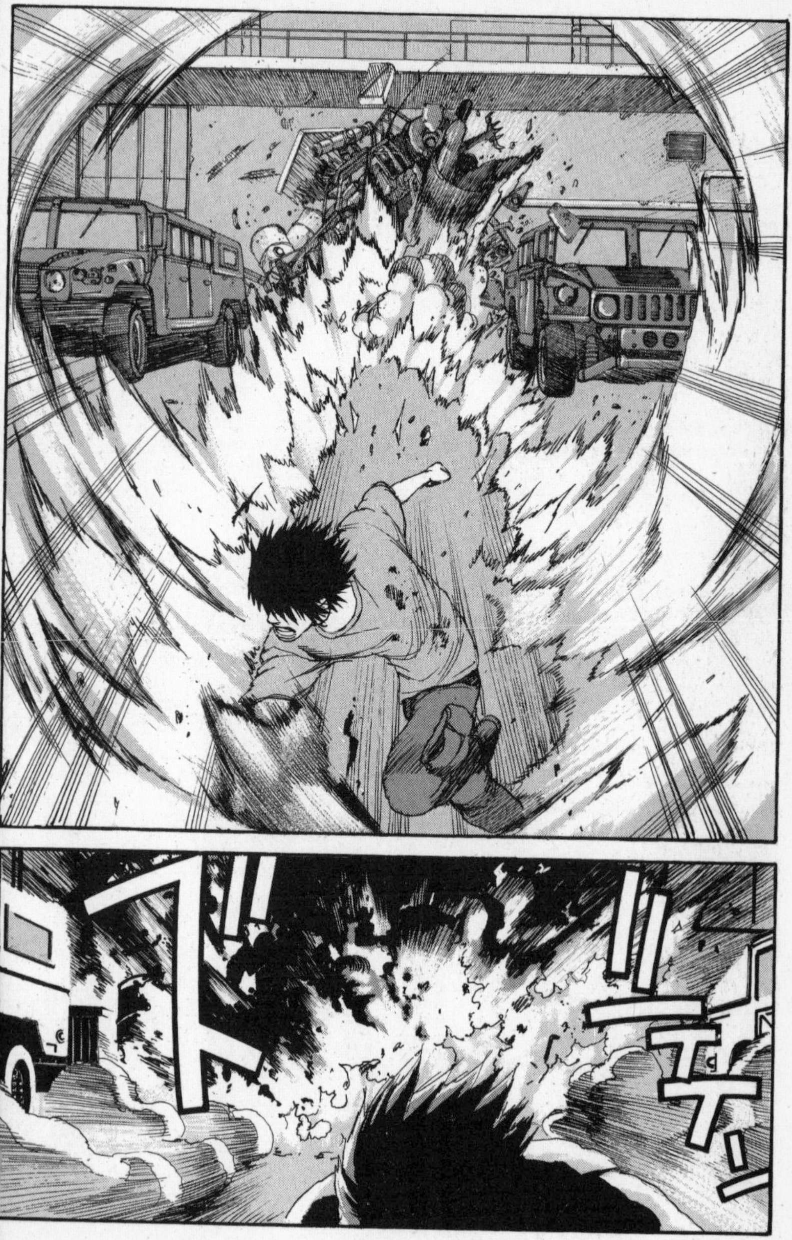

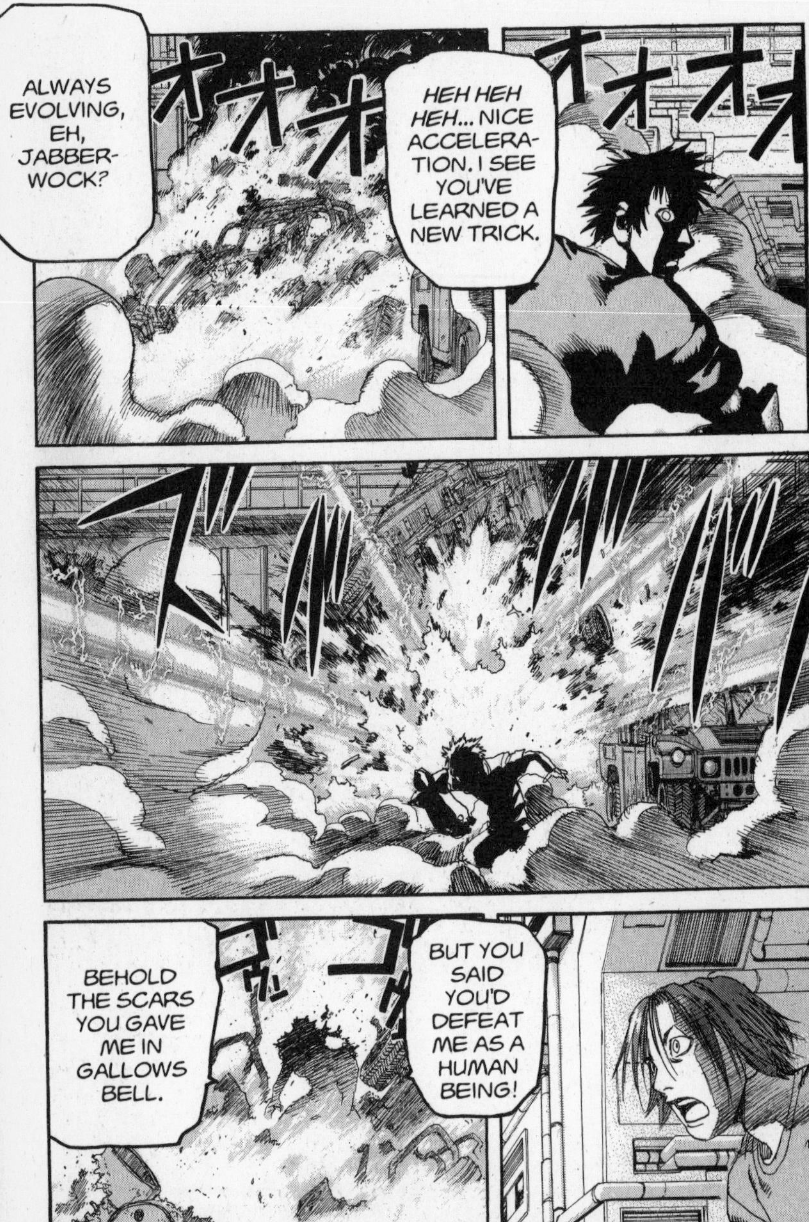
HEH HEH HEH... NICE ACCELERATION. I SEE YOU'VE LEARNED A NEW TRICK.
ALWAYS EVOLVING, EH, JABBERWOCK?
BUT YOU SAID YOU'D DEFEAT ME AS A HUMAN BEING!
BEHOLD THE SCARS YOU GAVE ME IN GALLOWS BELL.

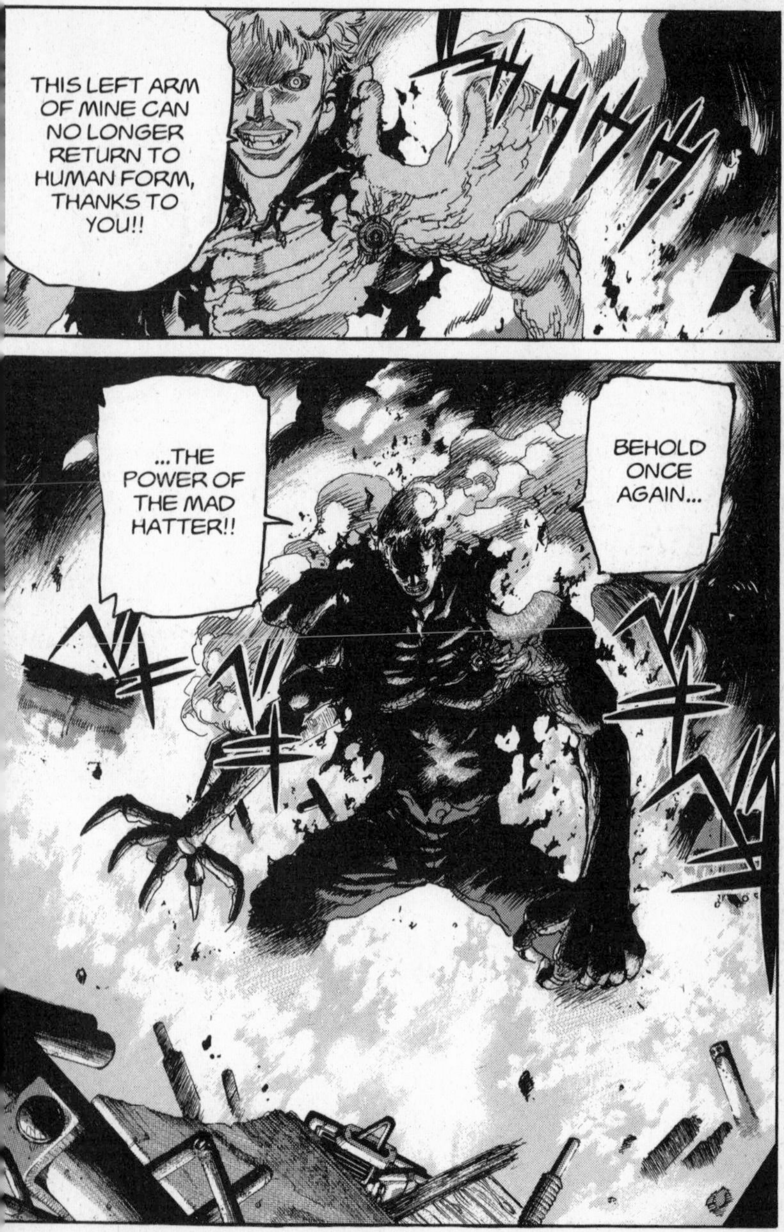
THIS LEFT ARM OF MINE CAN NO LONGER RETURN TO HUMAN FORM, THANKS TO YOU!!
BEHOLD ONCE AGAIN...
...THE POWER OF THE MAD HATTER!!

No. 5 MAD HATTER

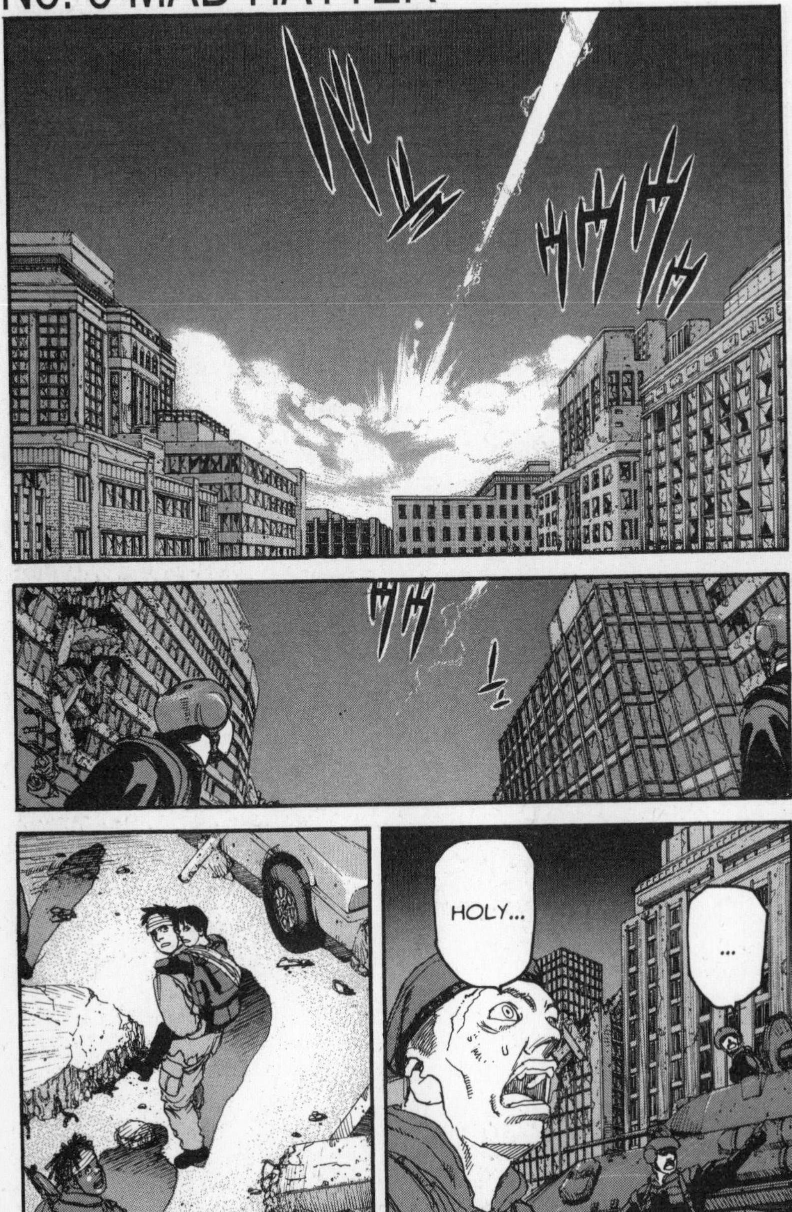
...
HOLY...

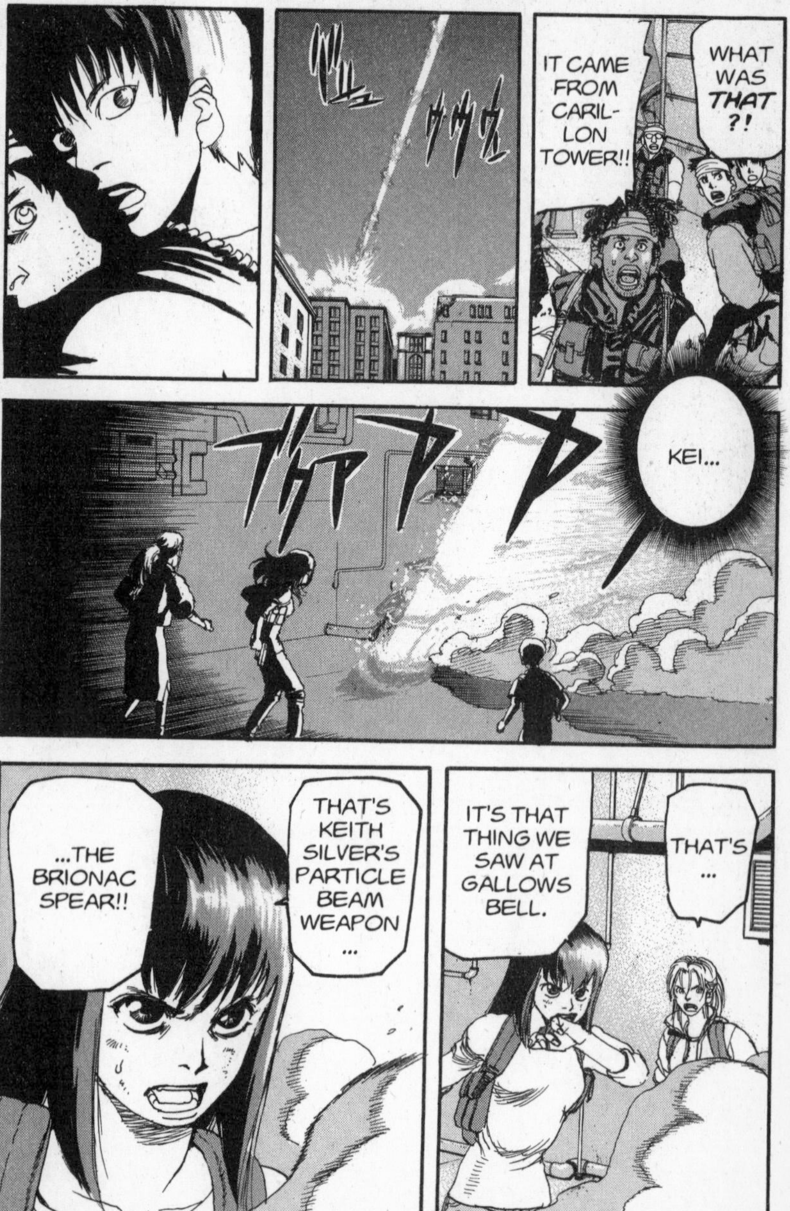
WHAT WAS THAT?!
IT CAME FROM CARIL-LON TOWER!!
KEI...
THAT'S ...
IT'S THAT THING WE SAW AT GALLOWS BELL.
THAT'S KEITH SILVER'S PARTICLE BEAM WEAPON ...
...THE BRIONAC SPEAR!!

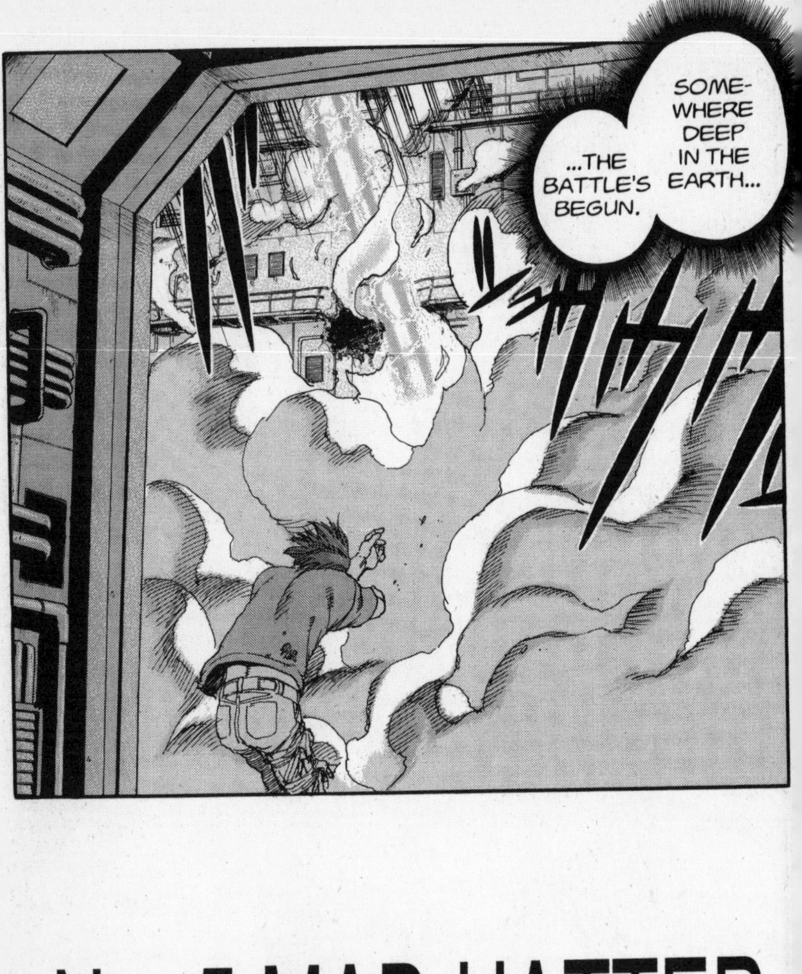
SOME-
WHERE
DEEP
IN THE
EARTH...
...THE
BATTLE'S
BEGUN.

No. 5 MAD HATTER

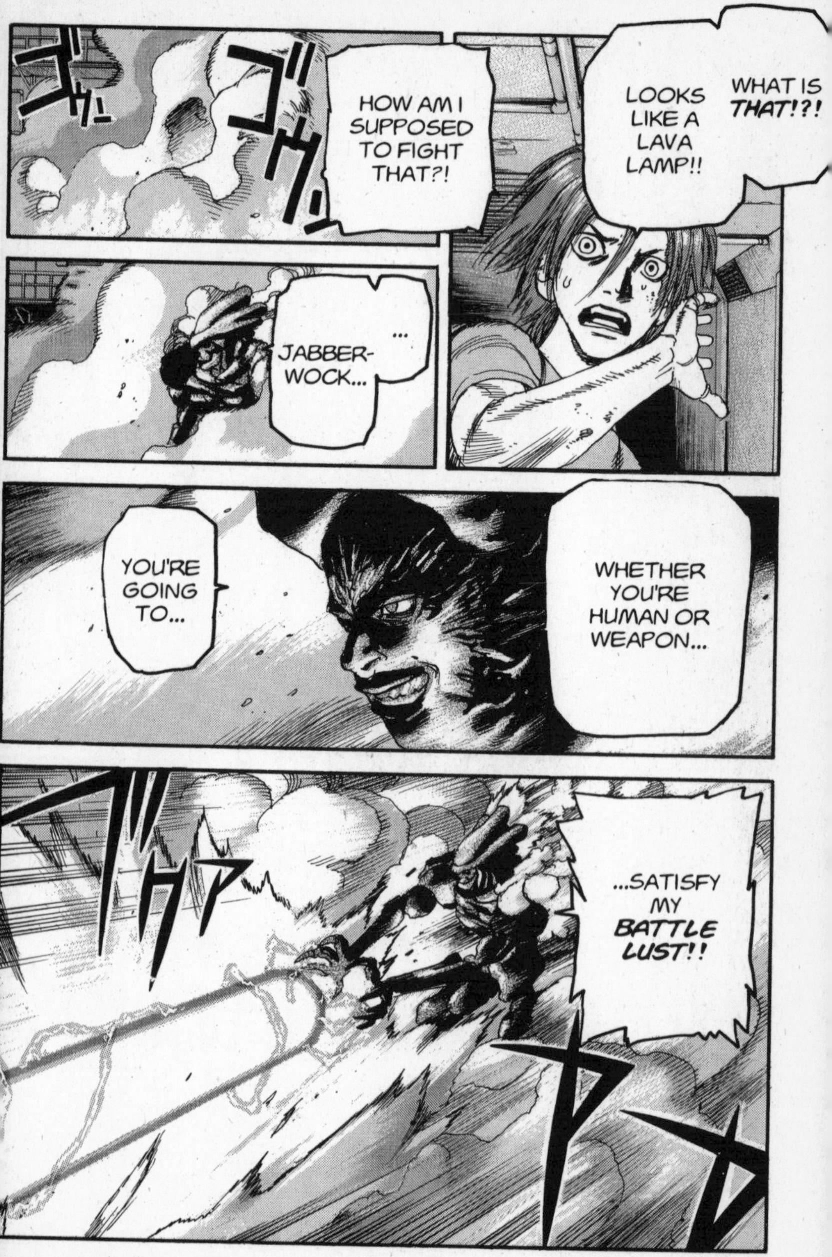
WHAT IS THAT!?!
LOOKS LIKE A LAVA LAMP!!
HOW AM I SUPPOSED TO FIGHT THAT?!
...
JABBER-WOCK...
WHETHER YOU'RE HUMAN OR WEAPON...
YOU'RE GOING TO...
...SATISFY MY BATTLE LUST!!

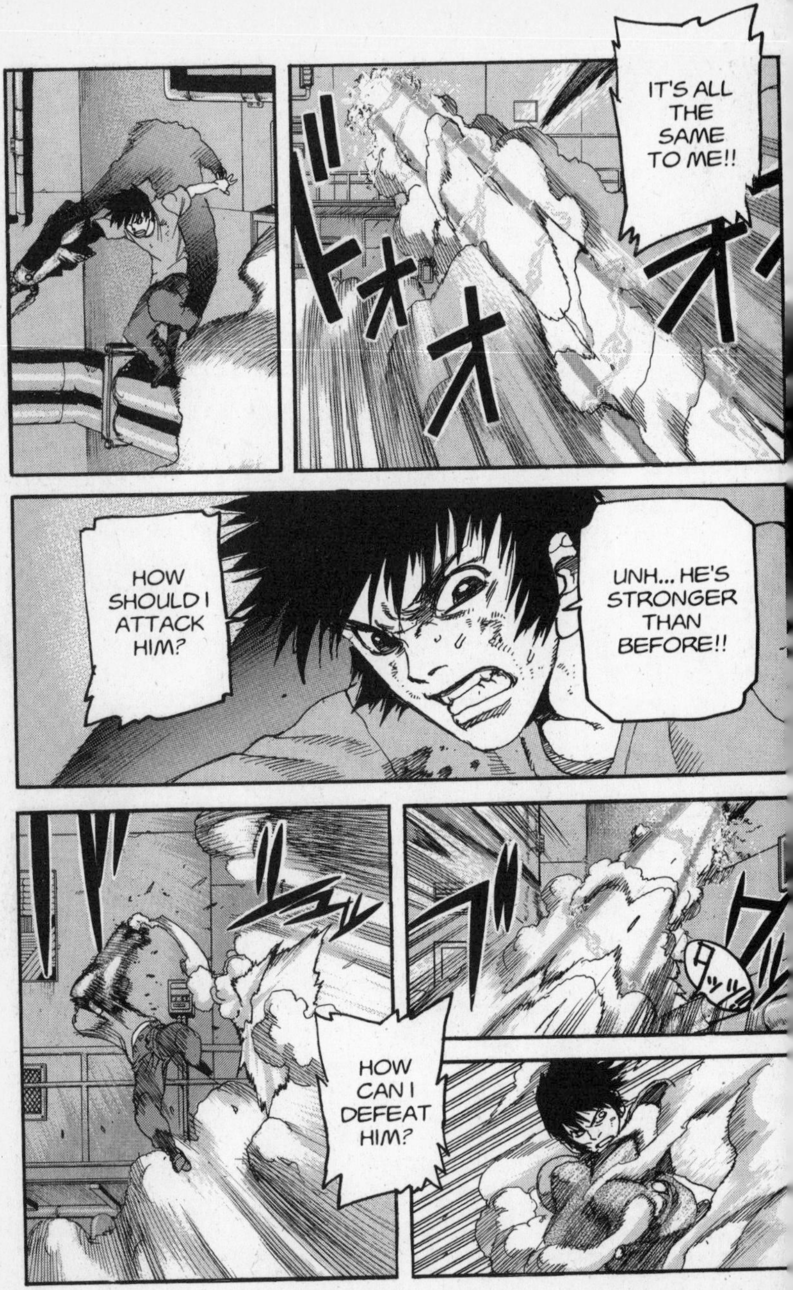
IT'S ALL THE SAME TO ME!!
UNH... HE'S STRONGER THAN BEFORE!!
HOW SHOULD I ATTACK HIM?
HOW CAN I DEFEAT HIM?

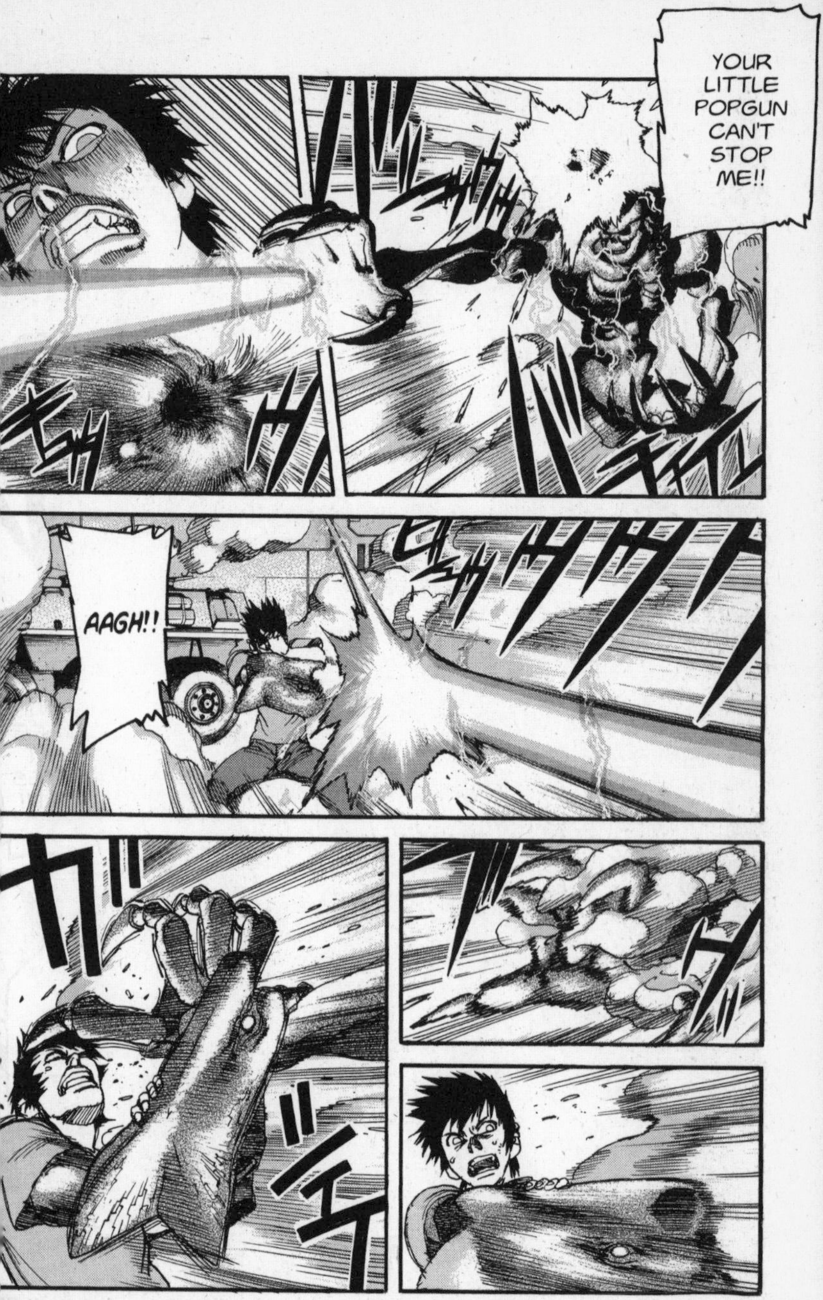
YOUR LITTLE POPGUN CAN'T STOP ME!!
AAGH!!

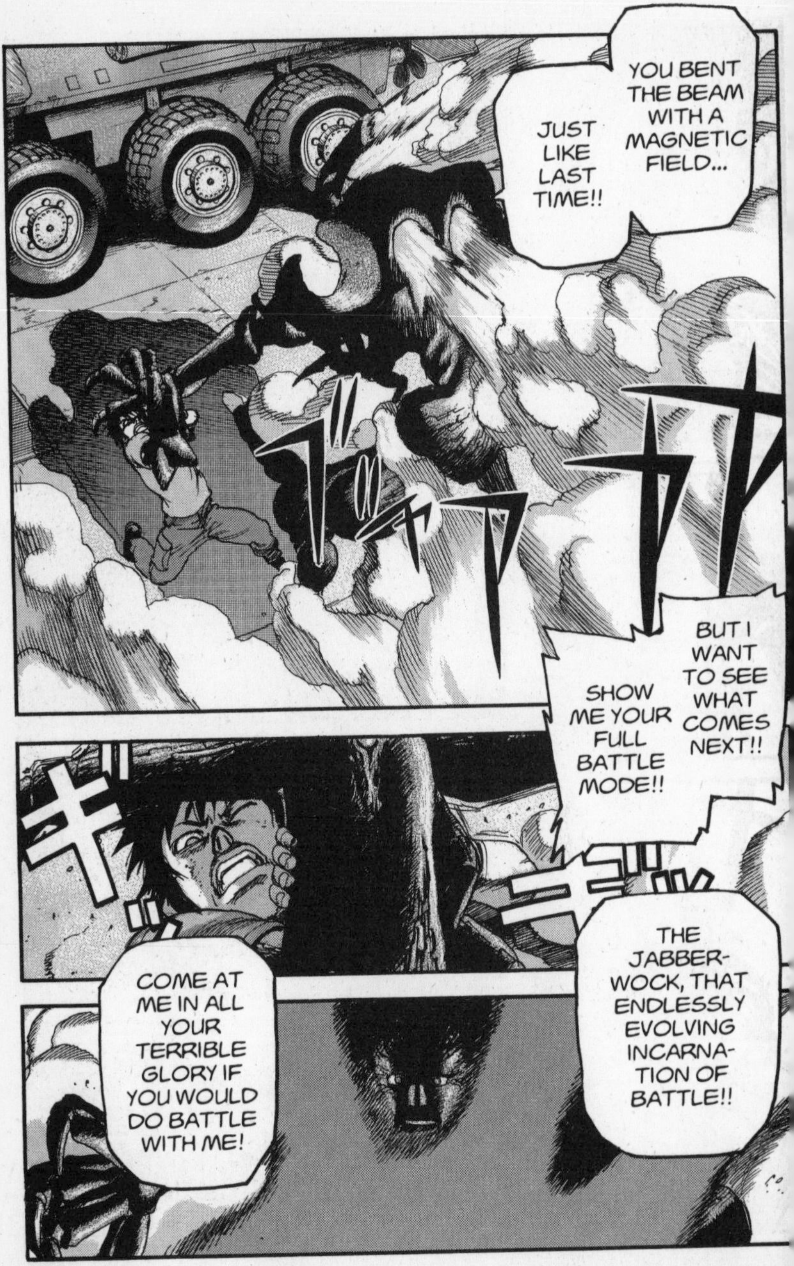
YOU BENT THE BEAM WITH A MAGNETIC FIELD...
JUST LIKE LAST TIME!!
BUT I WANT TO SEE WHAT COMES NEXT!!
SHOW ME YOUR FULL BATTLE MODE!!
THE JABBER-WOCK, THAT ENDLESSLY EVOLVING INCARNA-TION OF BATTLE!!
COME AT ME IN ALL YOUR TERRIBLE GLORY IF YOU WOULD DO BATTLE WITH ME!

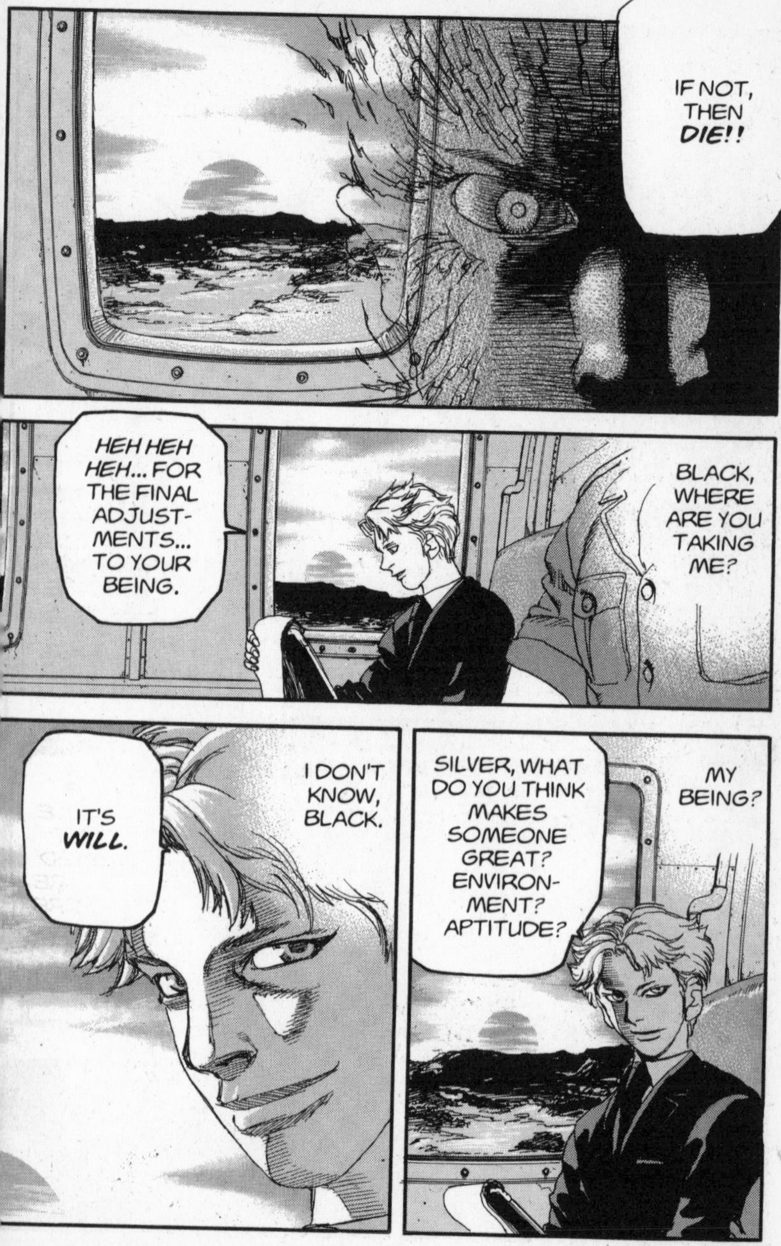
IF NOT, THEN DIE!!
BLACK, WHERE ARE YOU TAKING ME?
HEH HEH HEH... FOR THE FINAL ADJUSTMENTS... TO YOUR BEING.
MY BEING?
SILVER, WHAT DO YOU THINK MAKES SOMEONE GREAT? ENVIRONMENT? APTITUDE?
I DON'T KNOW, BLACK.
IT'S WILL.

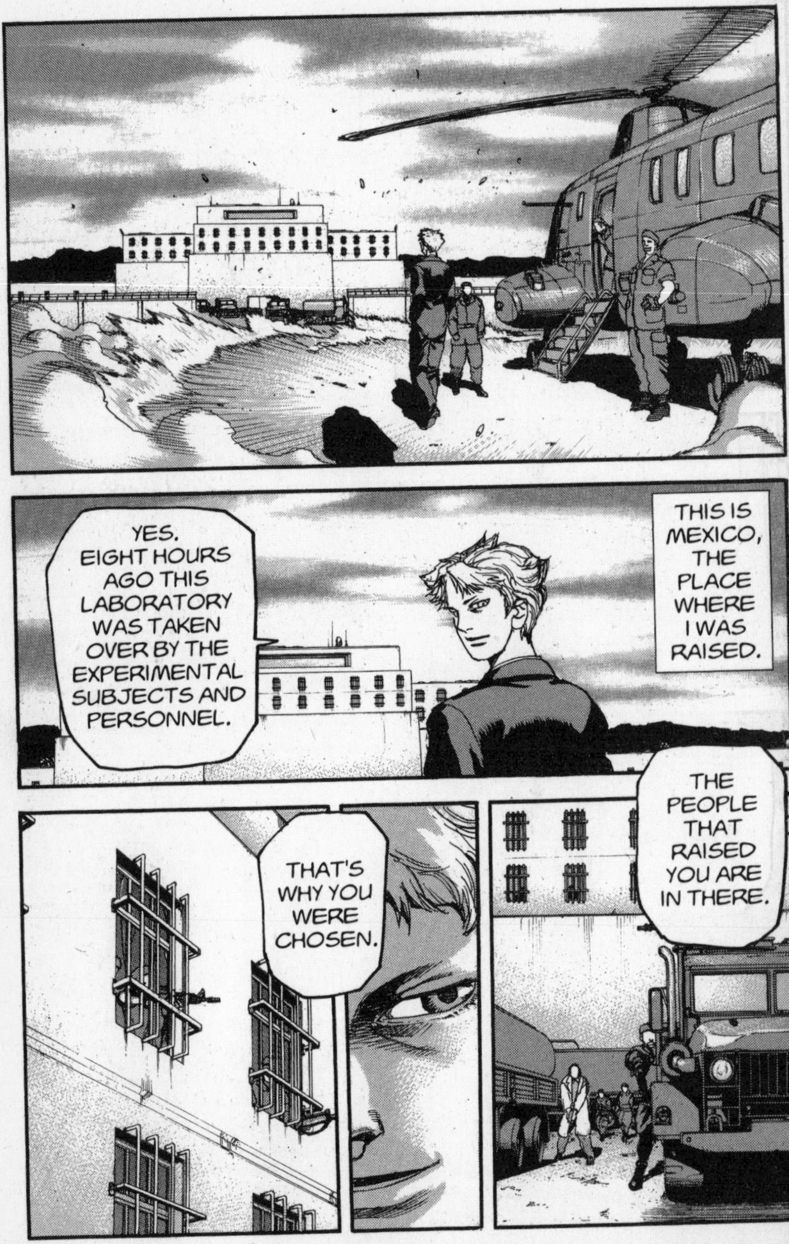
THIS IS MEXICO, THE PLACE WHERE I WAS RAISED.
YES. EIGHT HOURS AGO THIS LABORATORY WAS TAKEN OVER BY THE EXPERIMENTAL SUBJECTS AND PERSONNEL.
THE PEOPLE THAT RAISED YOU ARE IN THERE.
THAT'S WHY YOU WERE CHOSEN.

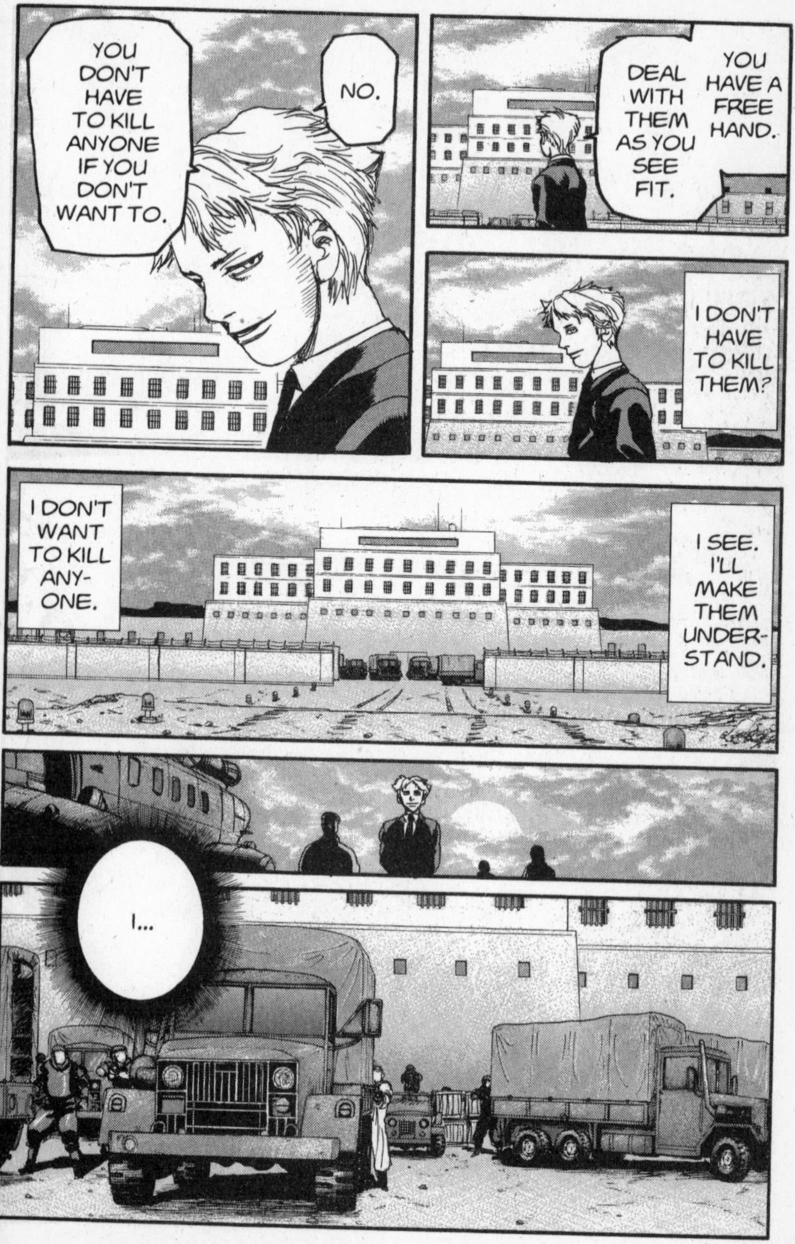
YOU HAVE A FREE HAND.
DEAL WITH THEM AS YOU SEE FIT.
I DON'T HAVE TO KILL THEM?
NO.
YOU DON'T HAVE TO KILL ANYONE IF YOU DON'T WANT TO.
I SEE. I'LL MAKE THEM UNDER-STAND.
I DON'T WANT TO KILL ANY-ONE.
I...

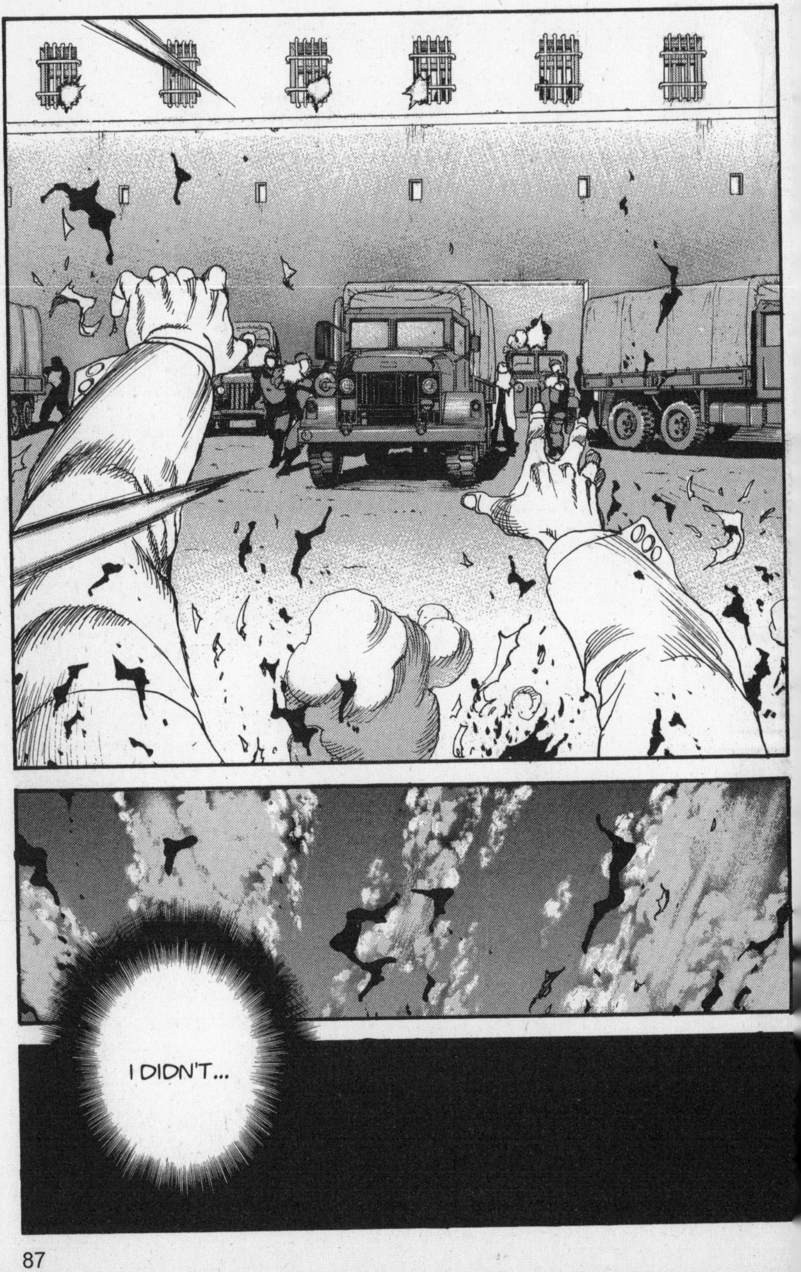
I DIDN'T...

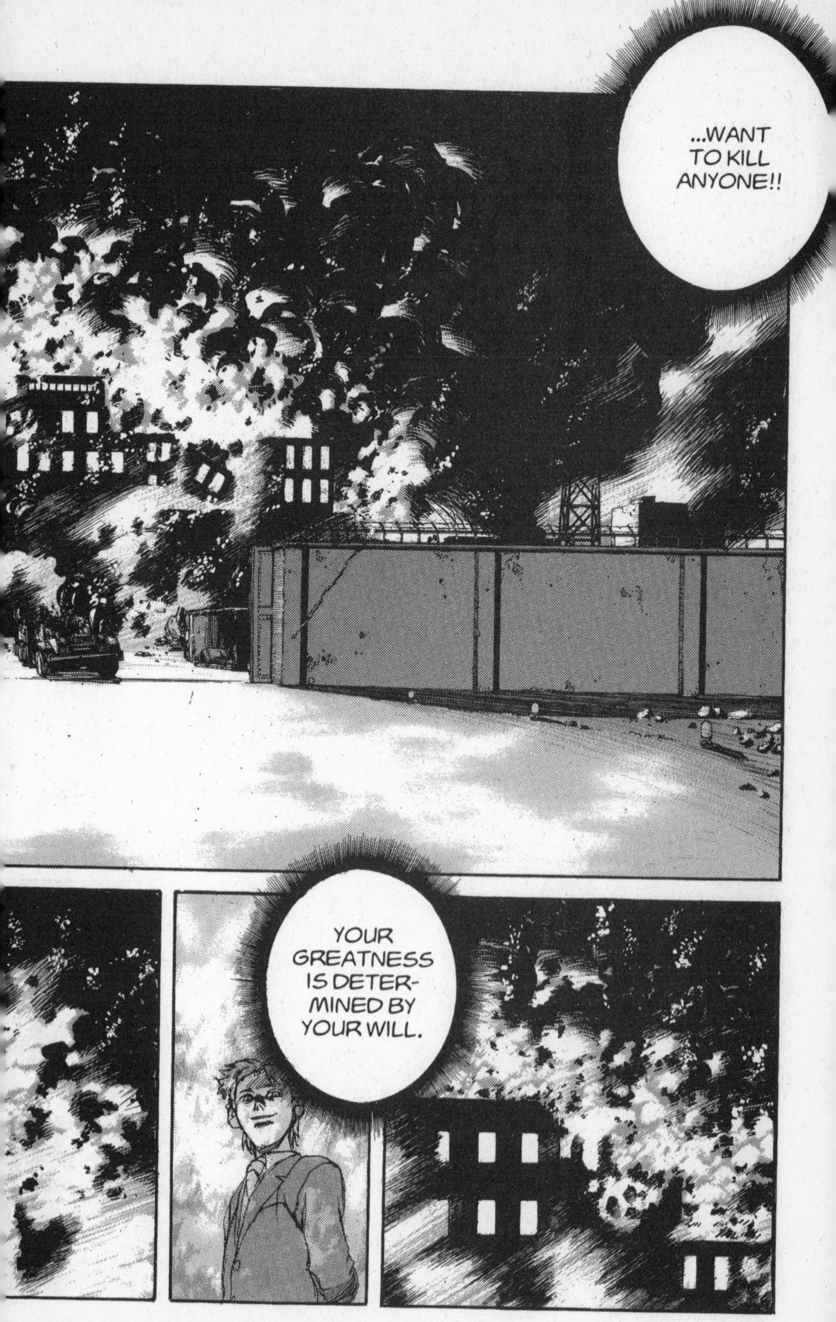
...WANT TO KILL ANYONE!!
YOUR GREATNESS IS DETER-MINED BY YOUR WILL.

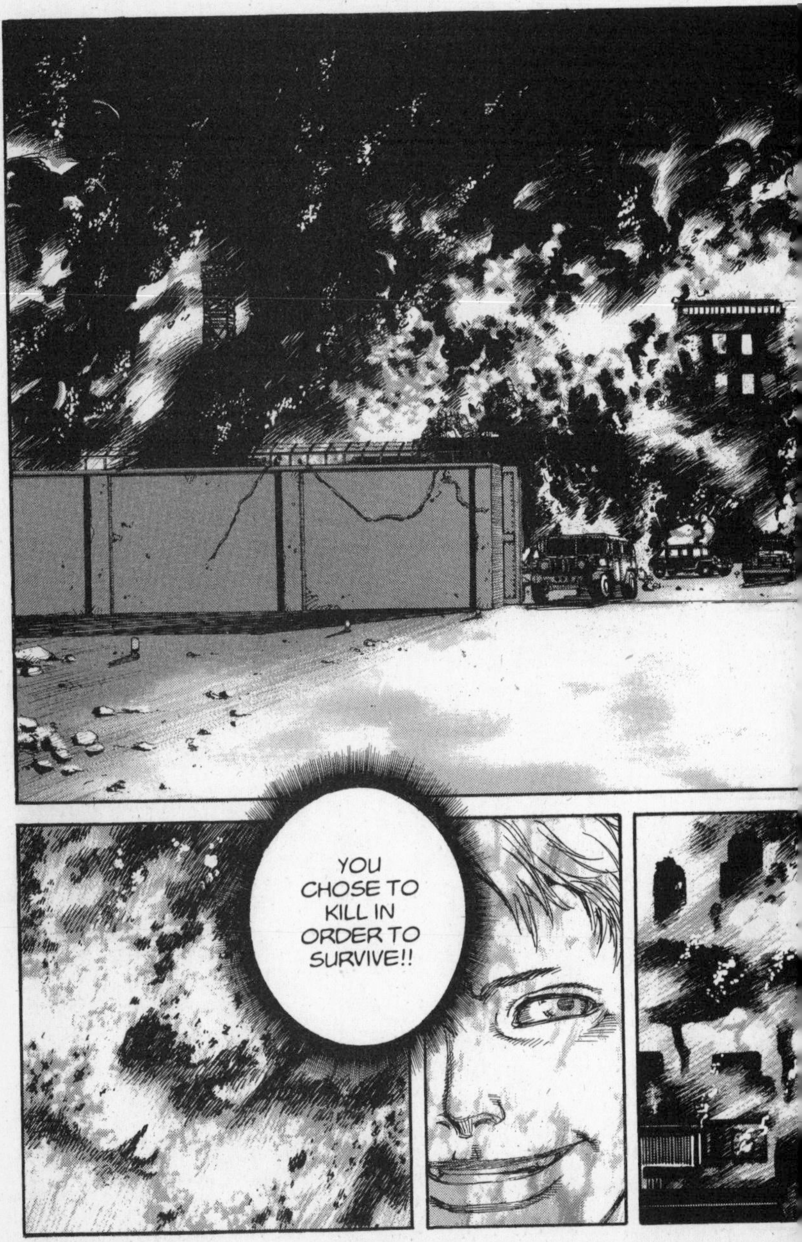
YOU CHOSE TO KILL IN ORDER TO SURVIVE!!

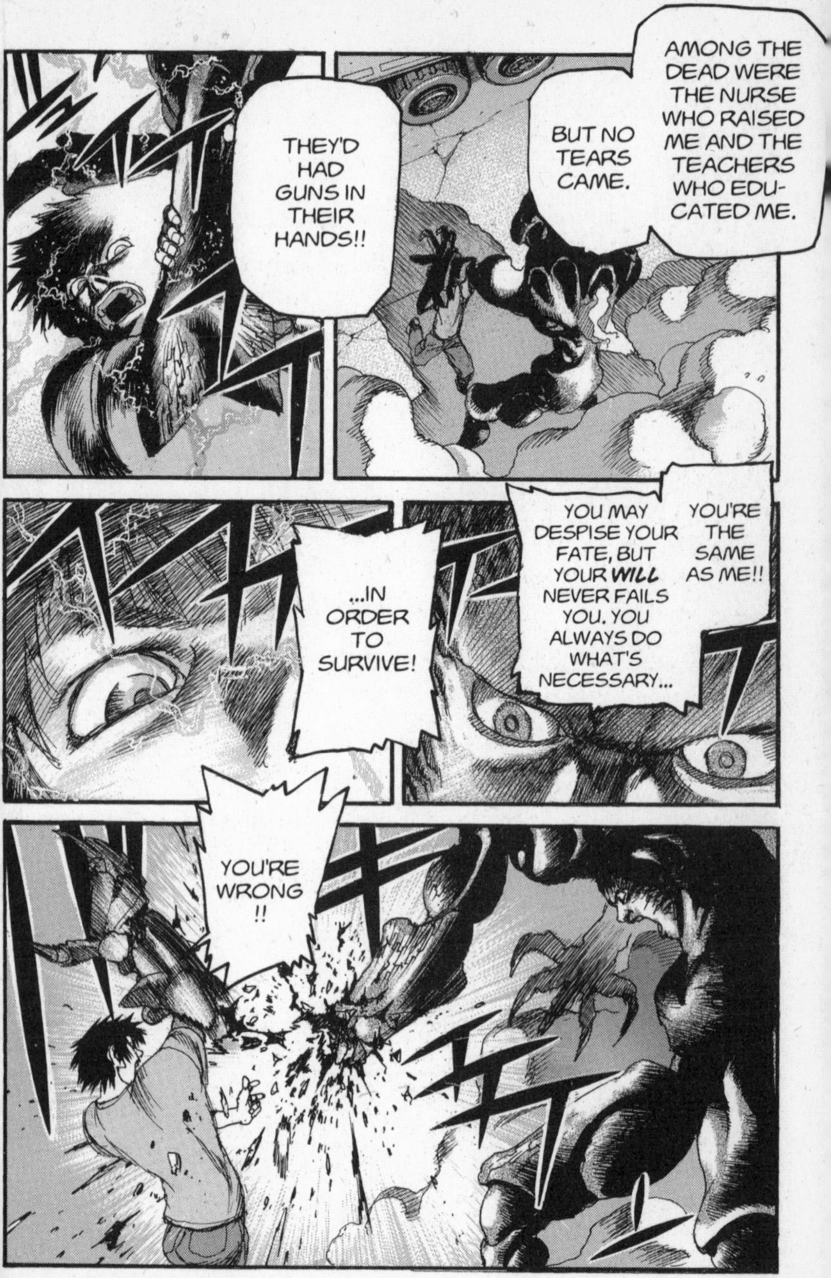
AMONG THE DEAD WERE THE NURSE WHO RAISED ME AND THE TEACHERS WHO EDUCATED ME.
BUT NO TEARS CAME.
THEY'D HAD GUNS IN THEIR HANDS!!
YOU'RE THE SAME AS ME!!
YOU MAY DESPISE YOUR FATE, BUT YOUR ***WILL*** NEVER FAILS YOU. YOU ALWAYS DO WHAT'S NECESSARY...
...IN ORDER TO SURVIVE!
YOU'RE WRONG !!

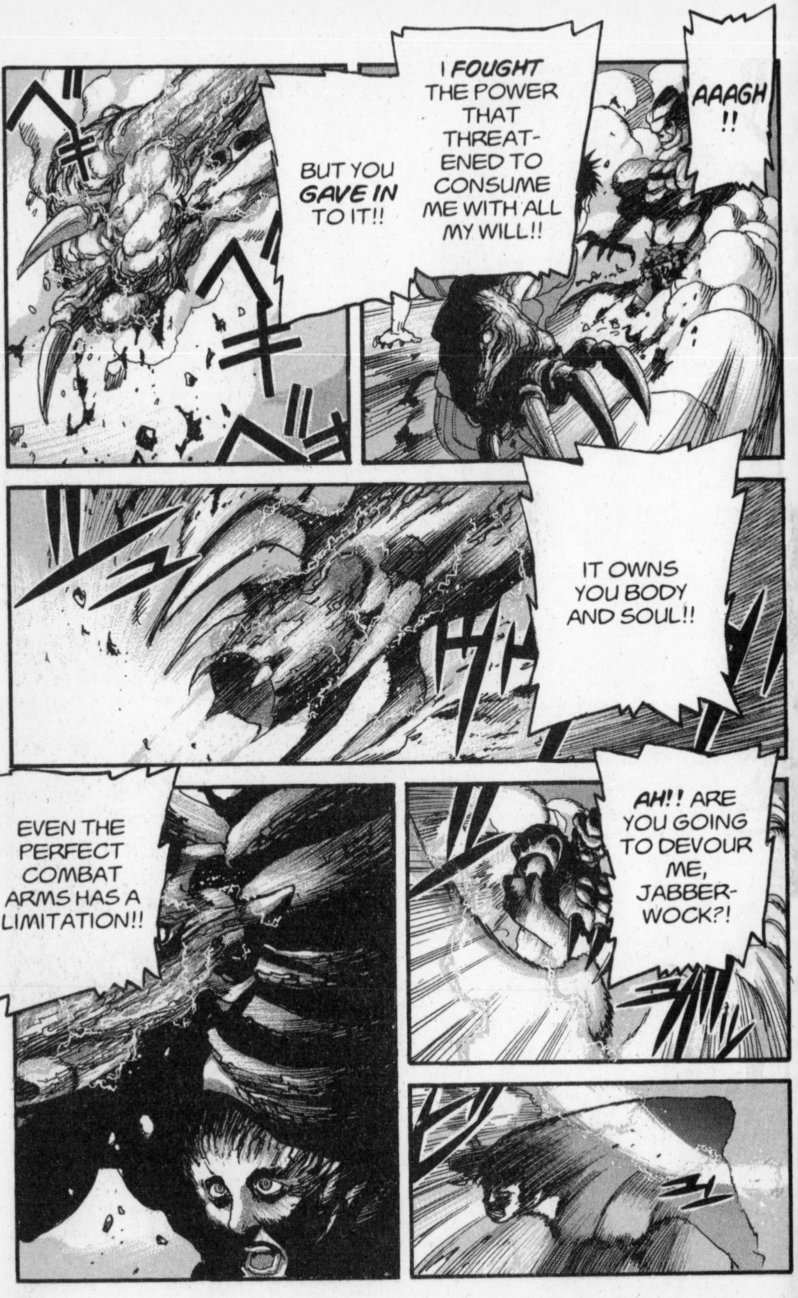
AAAGH!!
I FOUGHT THE POWER THAT THREAT-ENED TO CONSUME ME WITH ALL MY WILL!!
BUT YOU GAVE IN TO IT!!
IT OWNS YOU BODY AND SOUL!!
AH!! ARE YOU GOING TO DEVOUR ME, JABBER-WOCK?!
EVEN THE PERFECT COMBAT ARMS HAS A LIMITATION!!

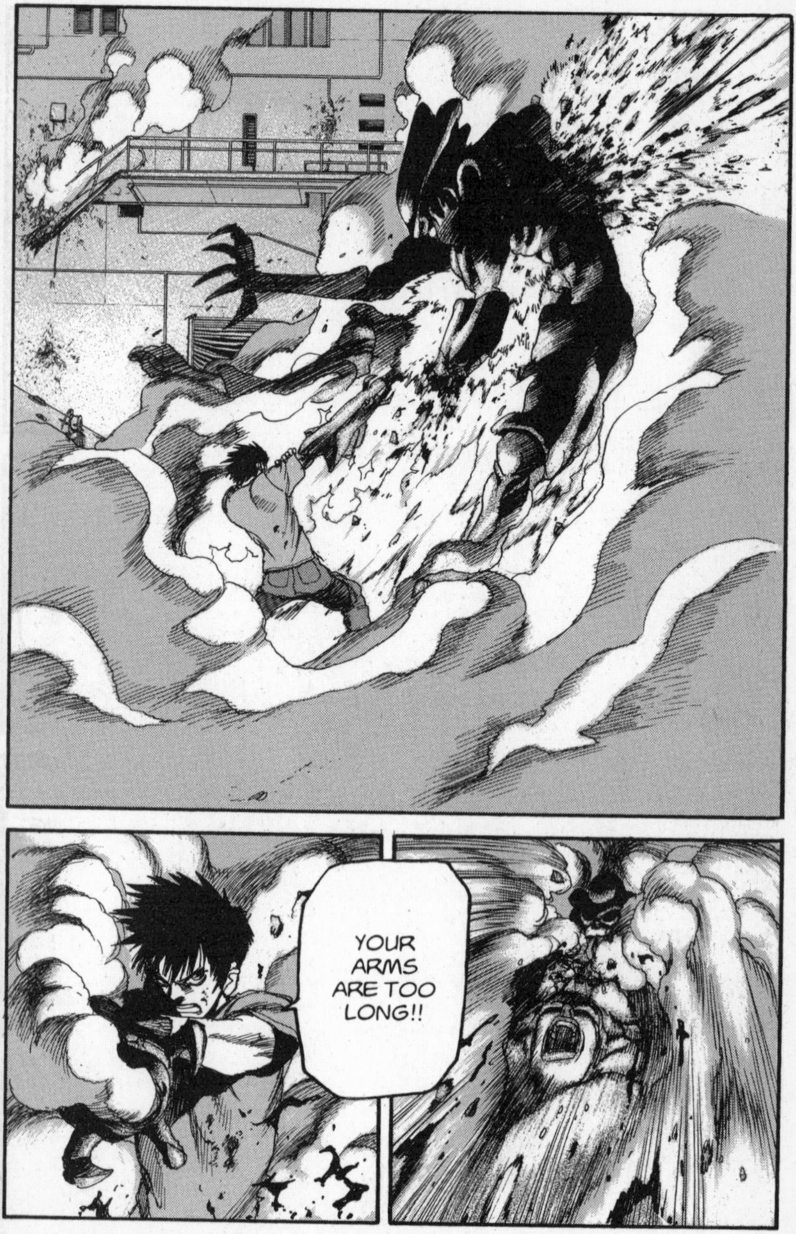
YOUR ARMS ARE TOO LONG!!

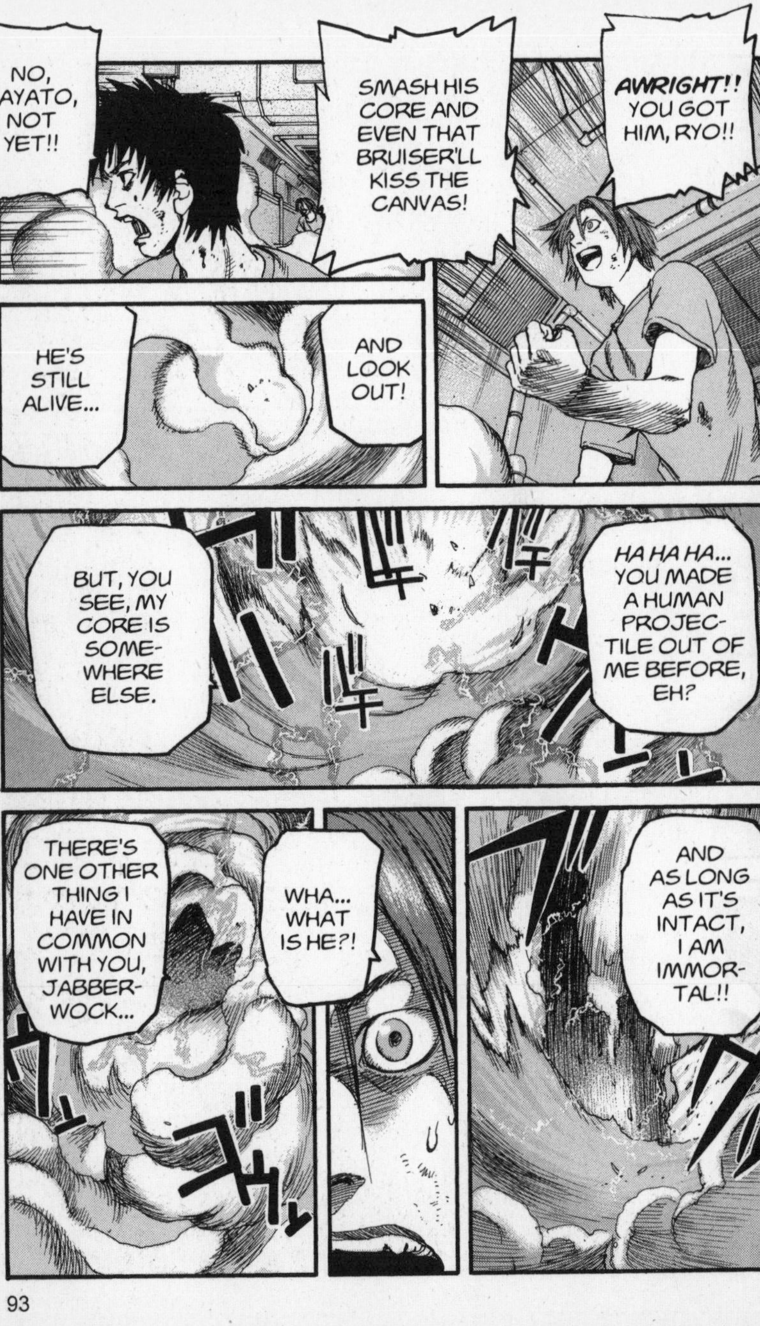
AWRIGHT!! YOU GOT HIM, RYO!!
SMASH HIS CORE AND EVEN THAT BRUISER'LL KISS THE CANVAS!
NO, HAYATO, NOT YET!!
HE'S STILL ALIVE...
AND LOOK OUT!
HA HA HA... YOU MADE A HUMAN PROJEC-TILE OUT OF ME BEFORE, EH?
BUT, YOU SEE, MY CORE IS SOME-WHERE ELSE.
AND AS LONG AS IT'S INTACT, I AM IMMOR-TAL!!
WHA... WHAT IS HE?!
THERE'S ONE OTHER THING I HAVE IN COMMON WITH YOU, JABBER-WOCK...

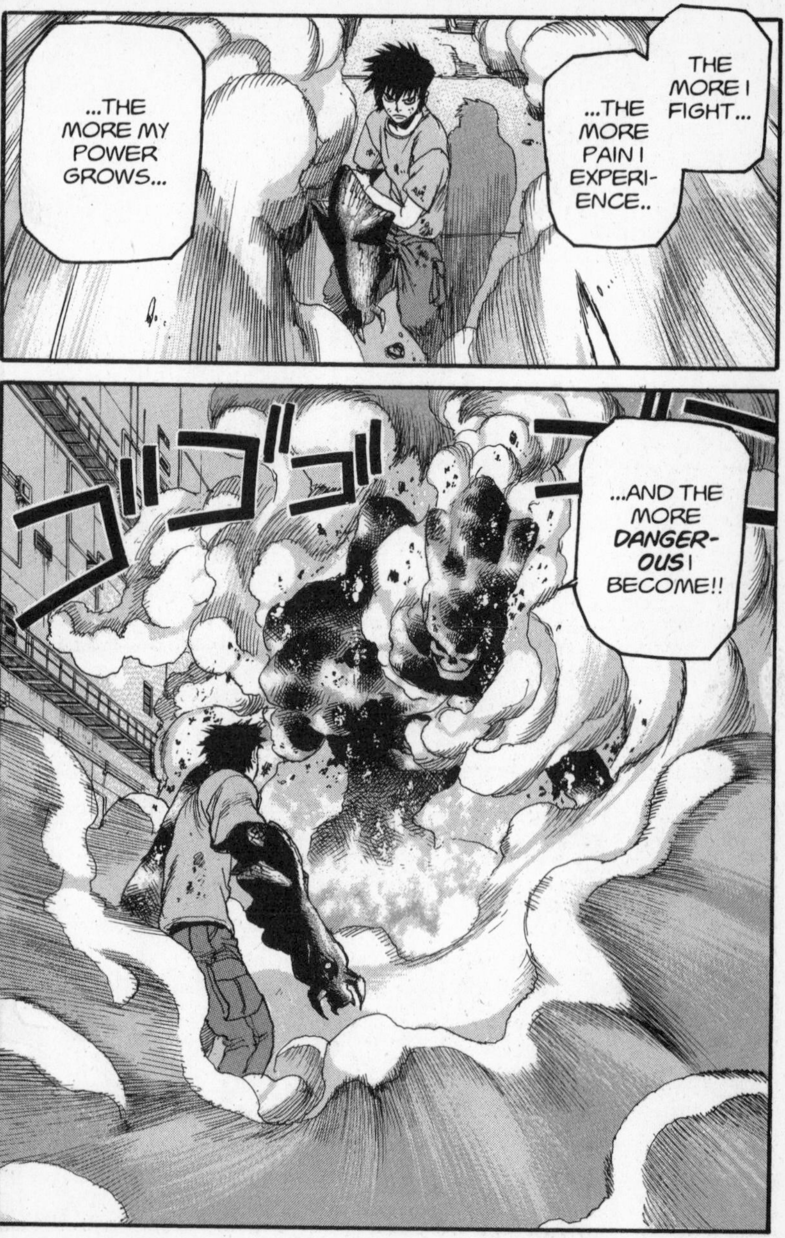
THE MORE I FIGHT...
...THE MORE PAIN I EXPERIENCE..
...THE MORE MY POWER GROWS...
...AND THE MORE *DANGEROUS* I BECOME!!

No. 6 MELTDOWN

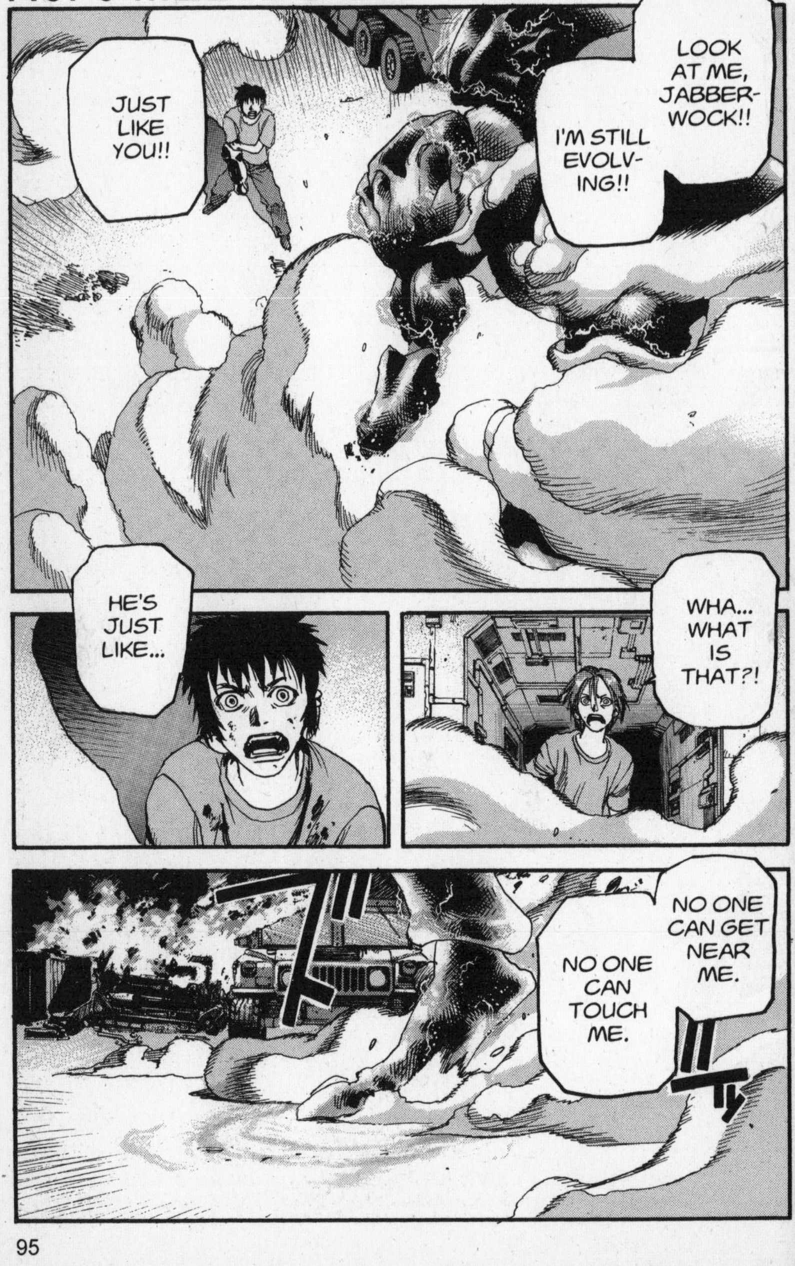

LOOK AT ME, JABBERWOCK!!
I'M STILL EVOLVING!!
JUST LIKE YOU!!
WHA... WHAT IS THAT?!
HE'S JUST LIKE...
NO ONE CAN GET NEAR ME.
NO ONE CAN TOUCH ME.

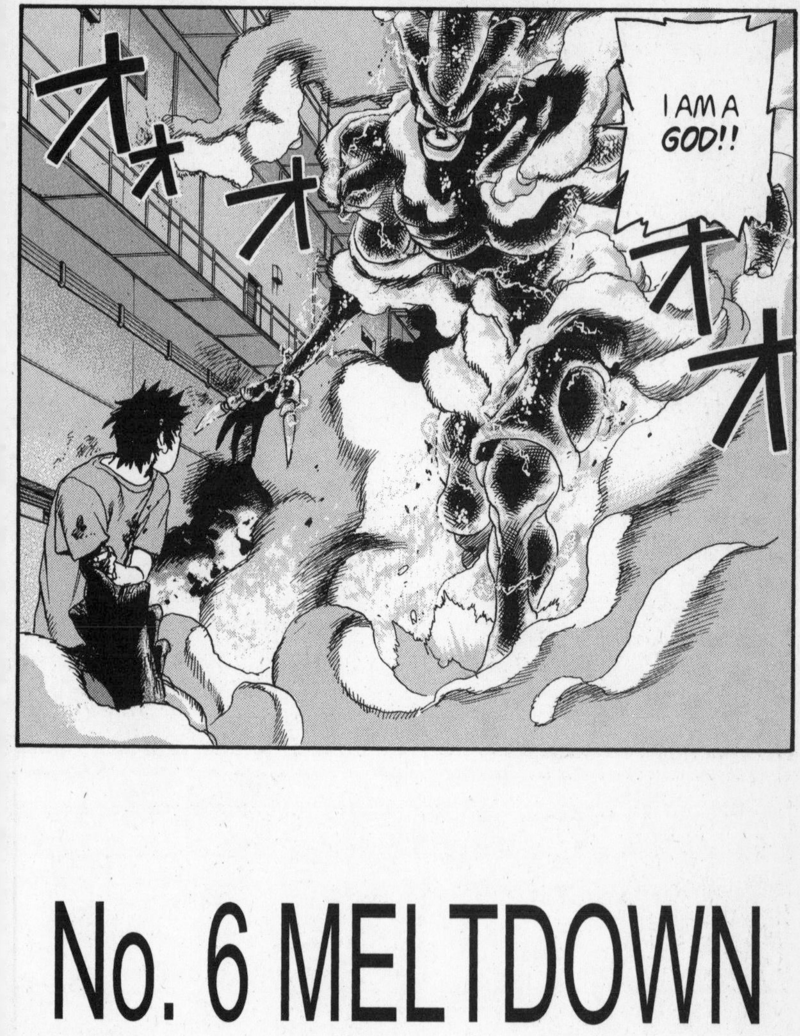
I AM A GOD!!
オオ
オォオ

No. 6 MELTDOWN

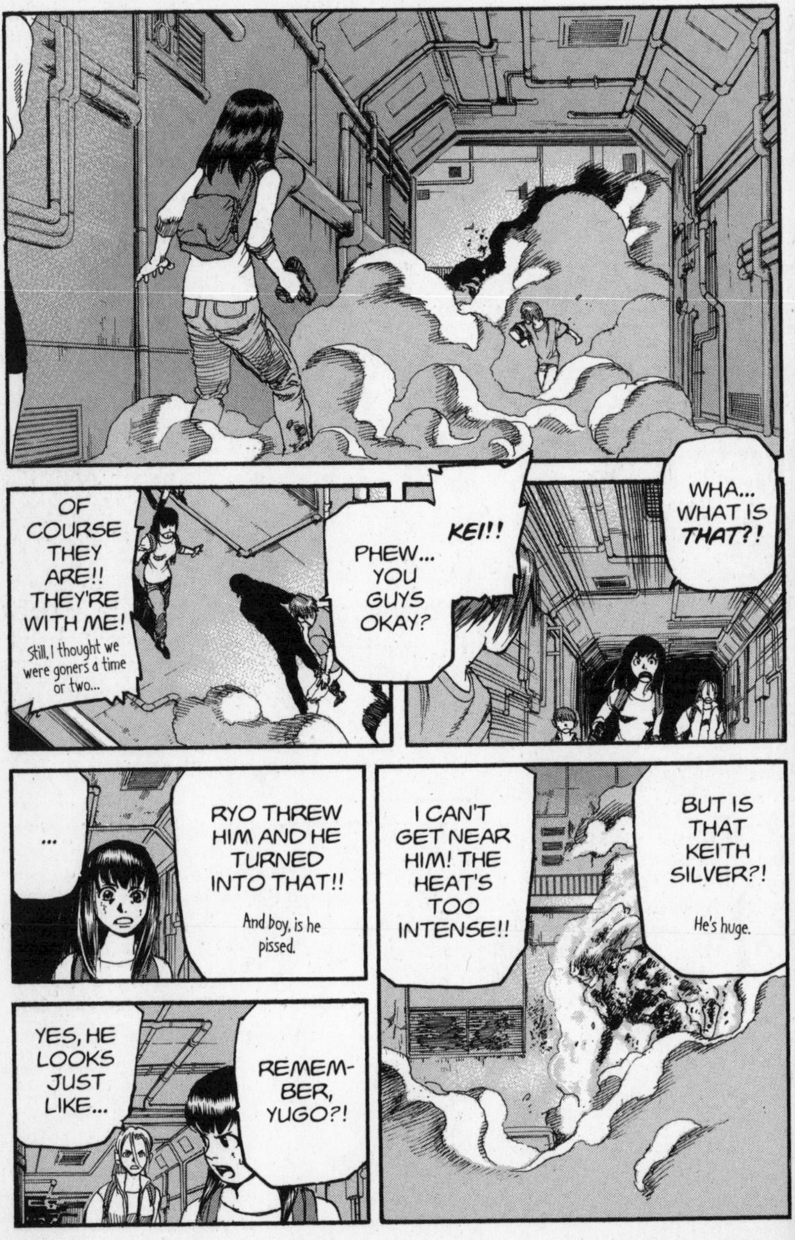
WHA... WHAT IS THAT?!
KEI!!
PHEW... YOU GUYS OKAY?
OF COURSE THEY ARE!! THEY'RE WITH ME!
Still, I thought we were goners a time or two...
BUT IS THAT KEITH SILVER?!
He's huge.
I CAN'T GET NEAR HIM! THE HEAT'S TOO INTENSE!!
RYO THREW HIM AND HE TURNED INTO THAT!!
And boy, is he pissed.
...
REMEMBER, YUGO?!
YES, HE LOOKS JUST LIKE...

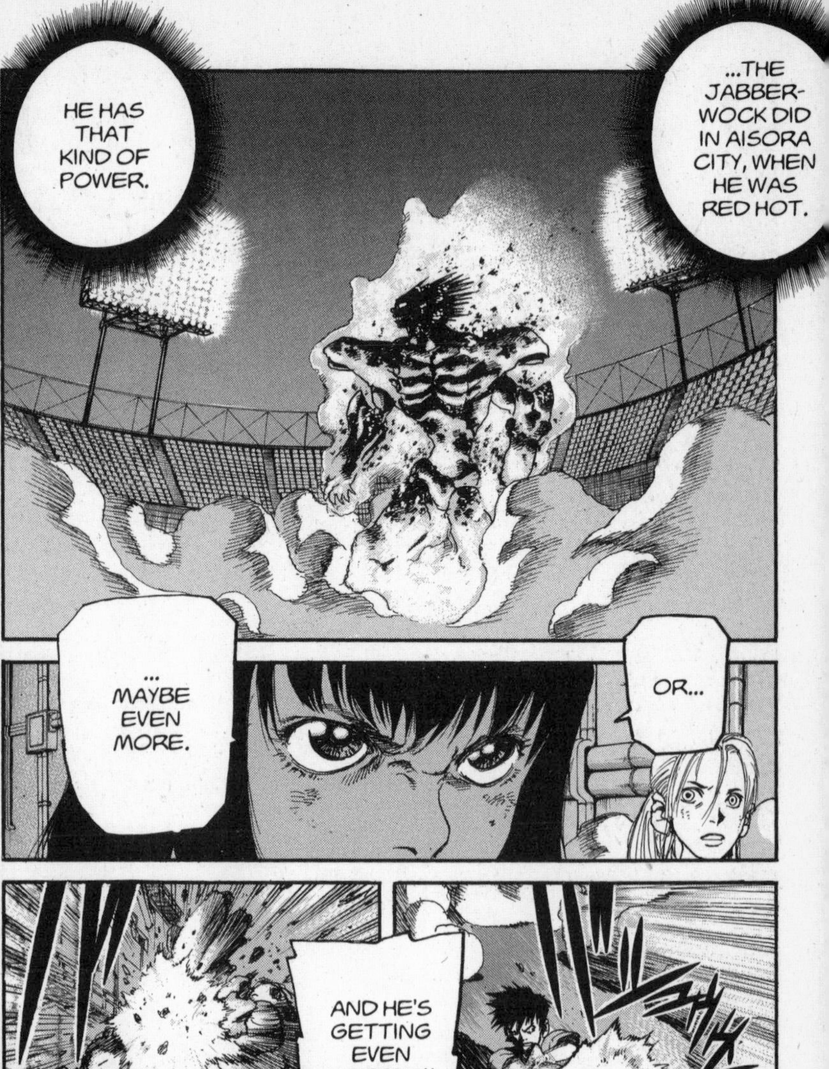
...THE JABBER-WOCK DID IN AISORA CITY, WHEN HE WAS RED HOT.
HE HAS THAT KIND OF POWER.
OR...
...MAYBE EVEN MORE.
AND HE'S GETTING EVEN HOTTER!!

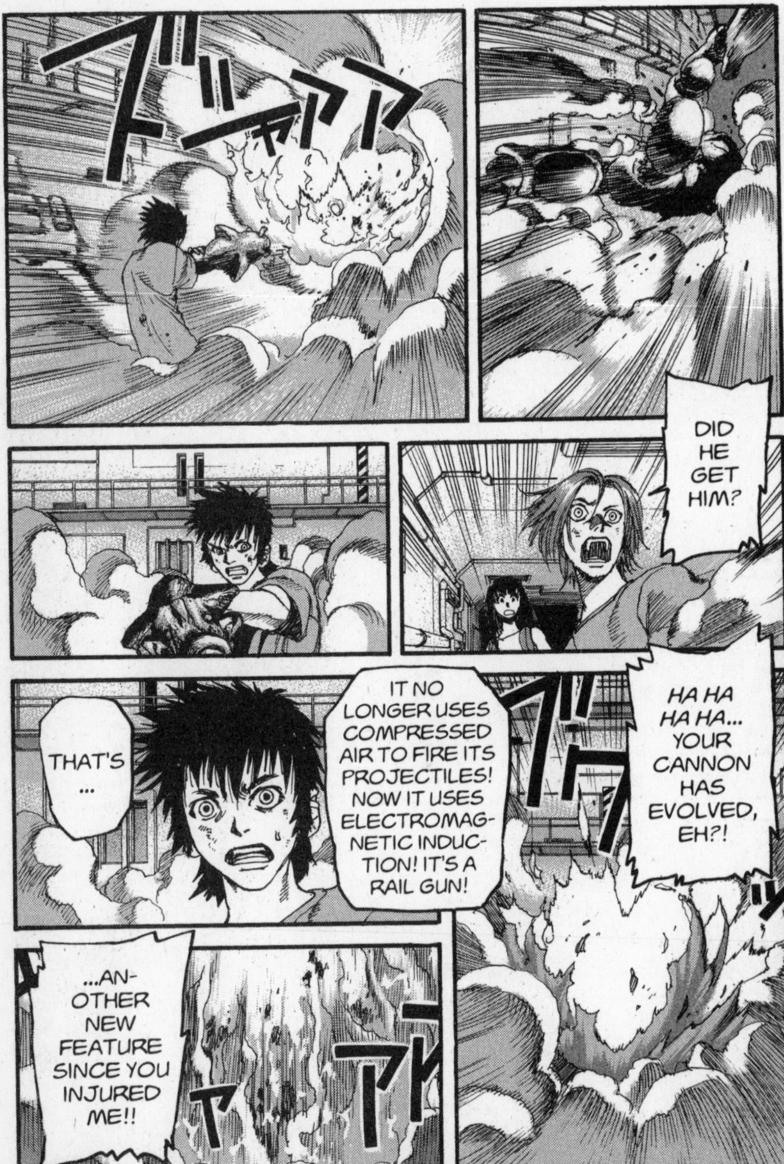
DID HE GET HIM?
HA HA HA HA... YOUR CANNON HAS EVOLVED, EH?!
IT NO LONGER USES COMPRESSED AIR TO FIRE ITS PROJECTILES! NOW IT USES ELECTROMAGNETIC INDUCTION! IT'S A RAIL GUN!
THAT'S ...
...ANOTHER NEW FEATURE SINCE YOU INJURED ME!!

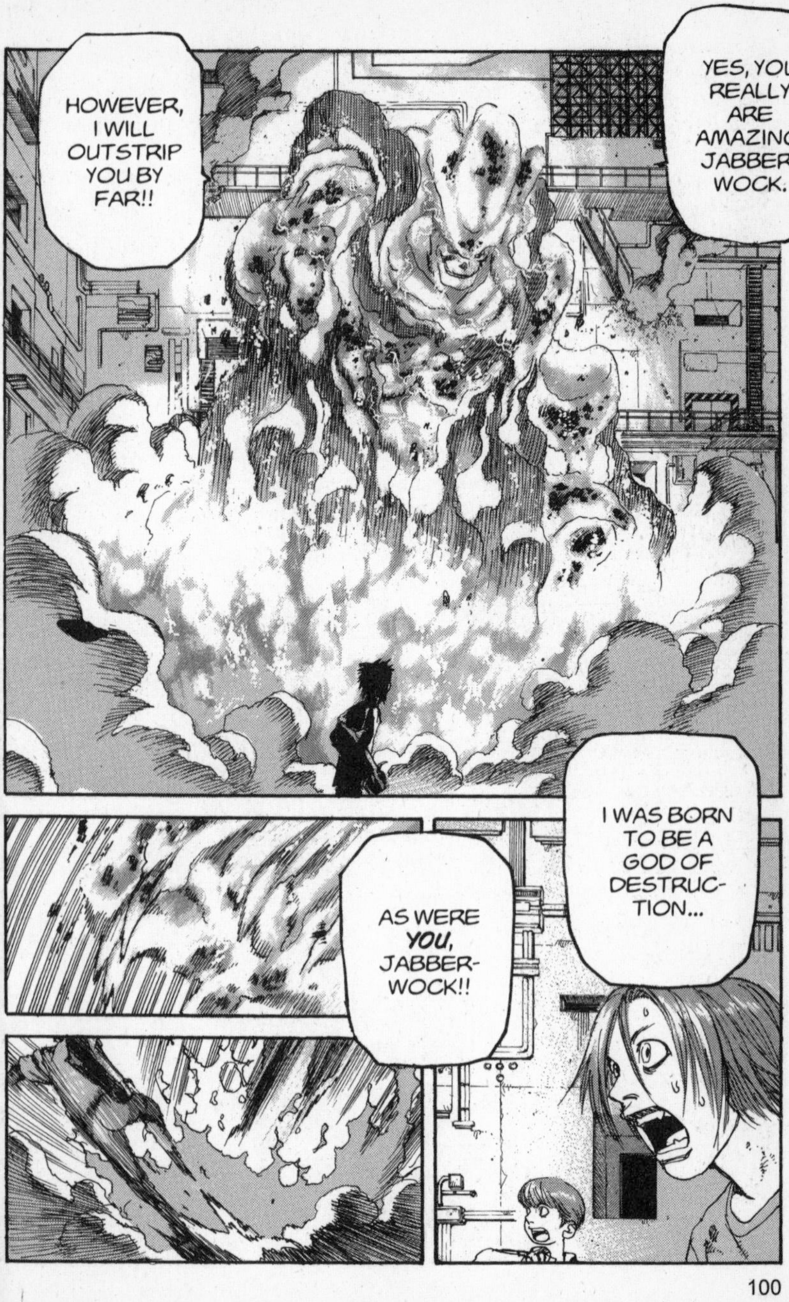
YES, YOU REALLY ARE AMAZING, JABBER-WOCK.
HOWEVER, I WILL OUTSTRIP YOU BY FAR!!
I WAS BORN TO BE A GOD OF DESTRUC-TION...
AS WERE *YOU*, JABBER-WOCK!!

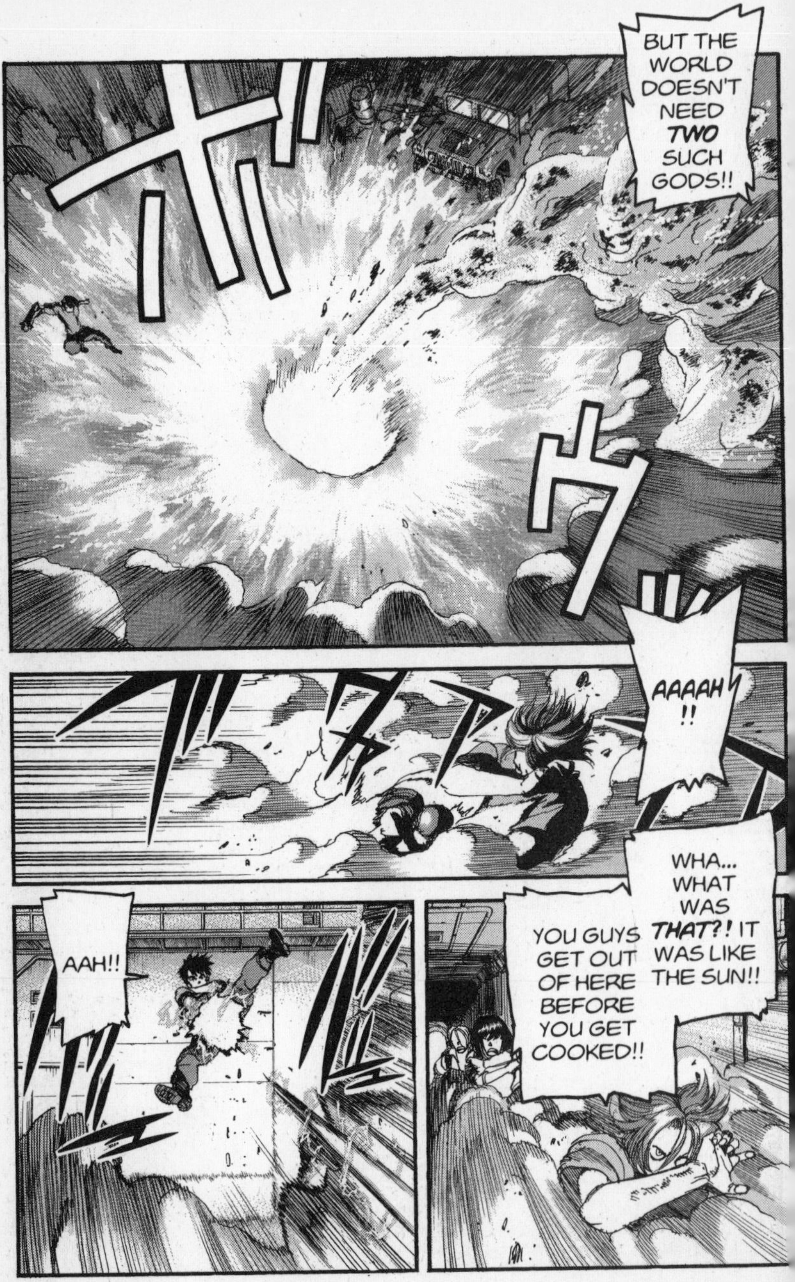
BUT THE WORLD DOESN'T NEED **TWO** SUCH GODS!!
AAAAH !!
WHA... WHAT WAS **THAT?!** IT WAS LIKE THE SUN!!
YOU GUYS GET OUT OF HERE BEFORE YOU GET COOKED!!
AAH!!

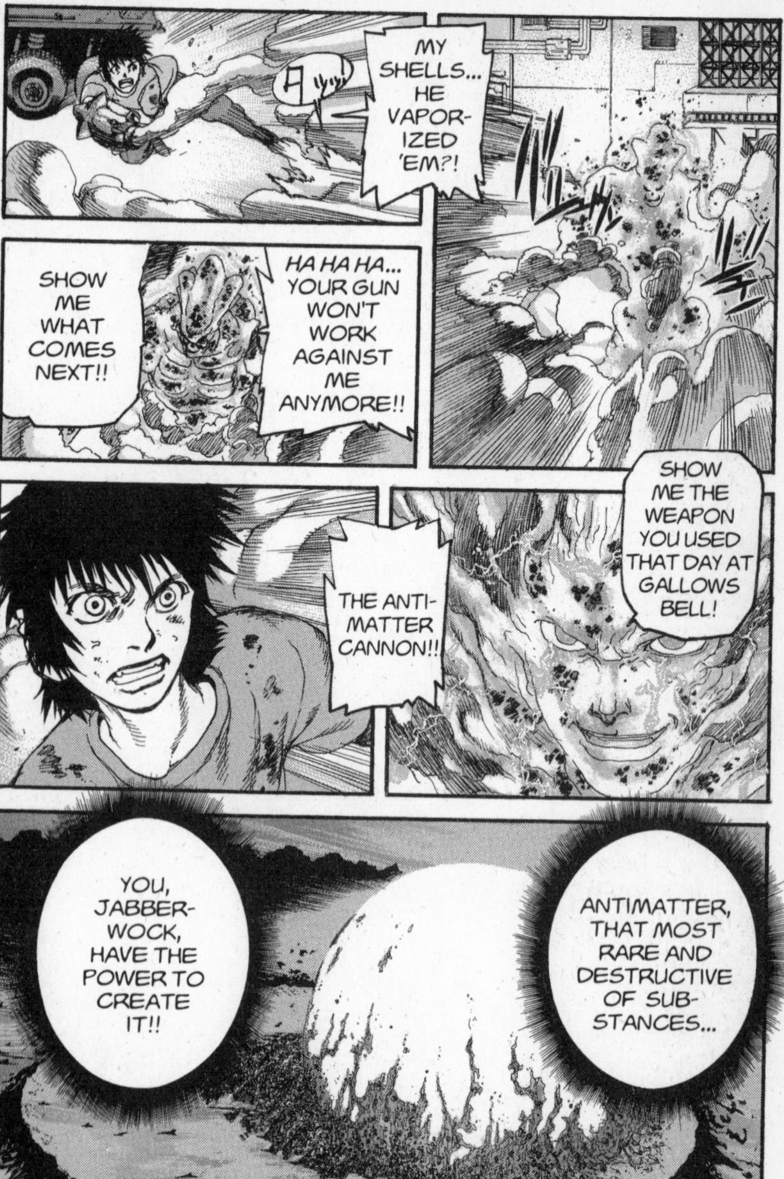
MY SHELLS... HE VAPOR-IZED 'EM?!
HA HA HA... YOUR GUN WON'T WORK AGAINST ME ANYMORE!!
SHOW ME WHAT COMES NEXT!!
SHOW ME THE WEAPON YOU USED THAT DAY AT GALLOWS BELL!
THE ANTI-MATTER CANNON!!
ANTIMATTER, THAT MOST RARE AND DESTRUCTIVE OF SUB-STANCES...
YOU, JABBER-WOCK, HAVE THE POWER TO CREATE IT!!

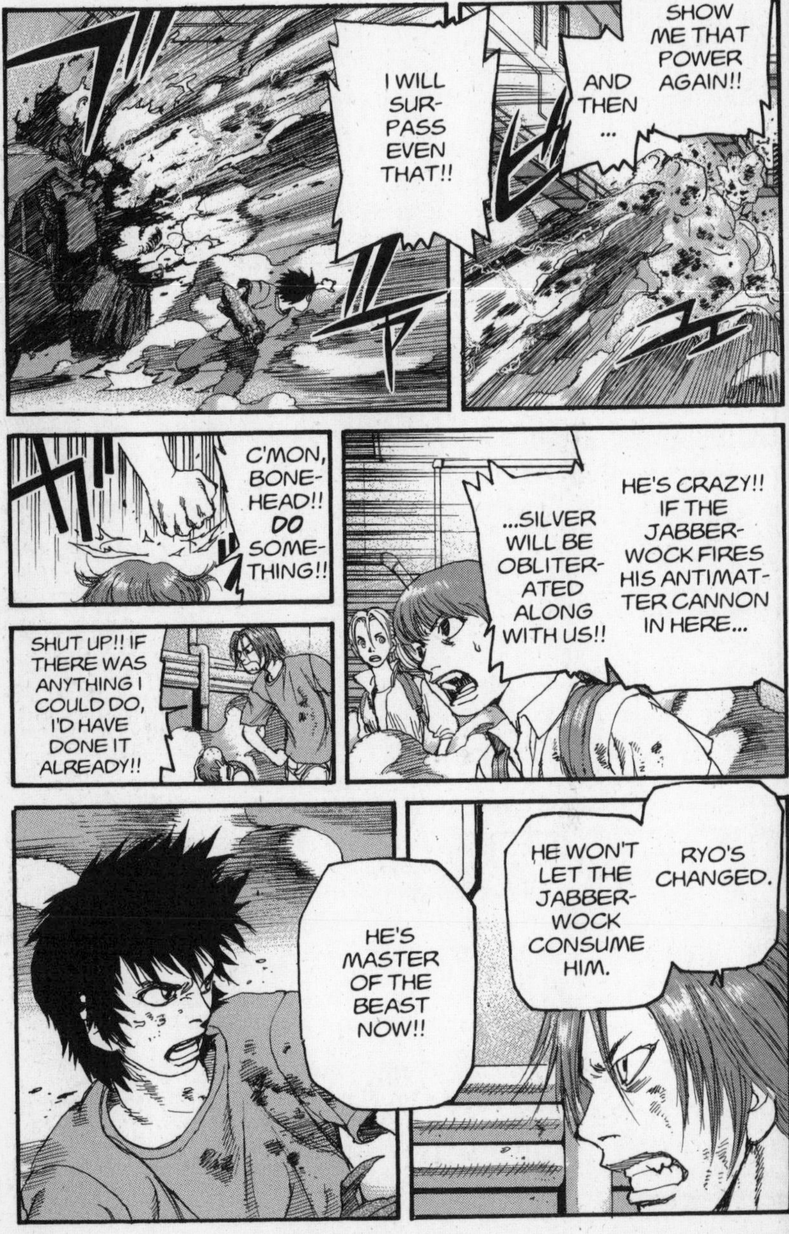
SHOW ME THAT POWER AGAIN!!
AND THEN ...
I WILL SUR-PASS EVEN THAT!!
HE'S CRAZY!! IF THE JABBER-WOCK FIRES HIS ANTIMAT-TER CANNON IN HERE...
...SILVER WILL BE OBLITER-ATED ALONG WITH US!!
C'MON, BONE-HEAD!! DO SOME-THING!!
SHUT UP!! IF THERE WAS ANYTHING I COULD DO, I'D HAVE DONE IT ALREADY!!
RYO'S CHANGED.
HE WON'T LET THE JABBER-WOCK CONSUME HIM.
HE'S MASTER OF THE BEAST NOW!!

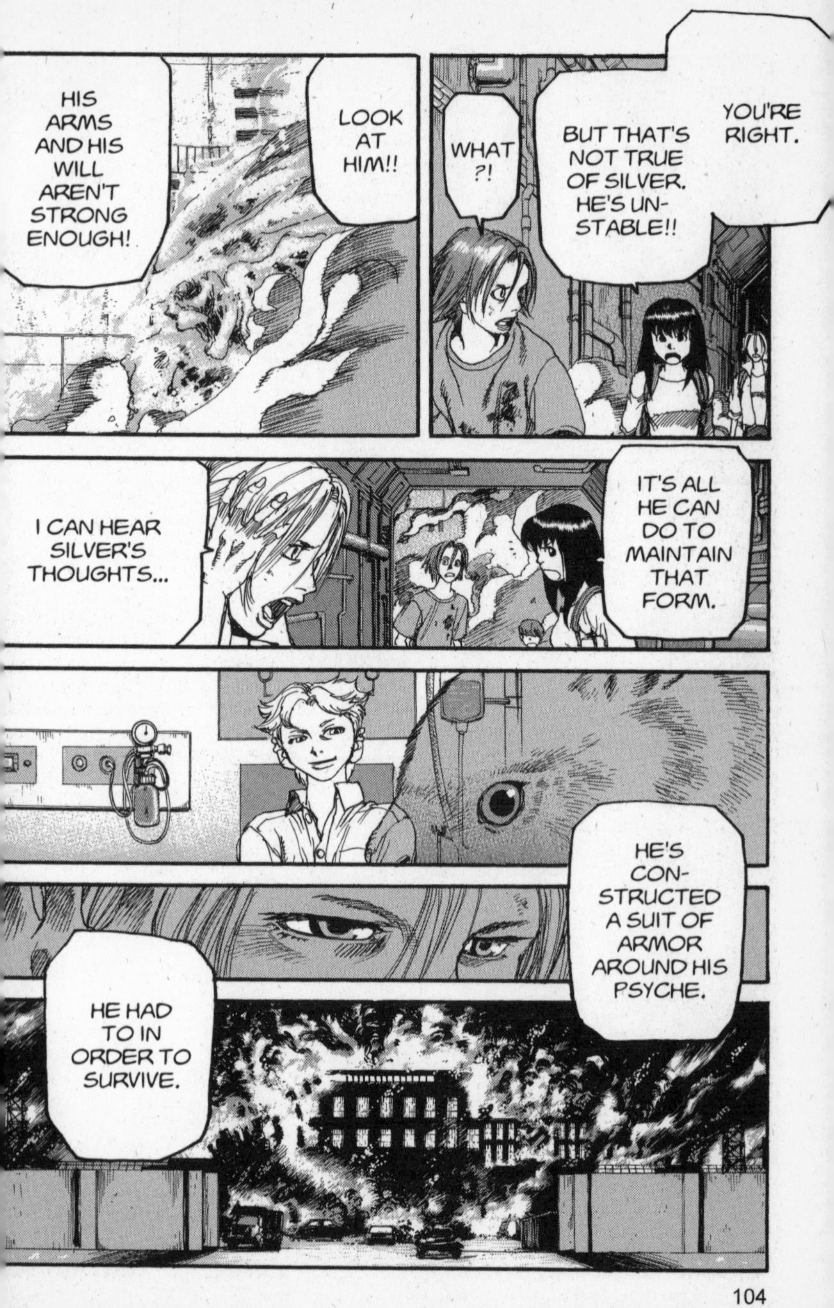
YOU'RE RIGHT.
BUT THAT'S NOT TRUE OF SILVER. HE'S UN-STABLE!!
WHAT?!
LOOK AT HIM!!
HIS ARMS AND HIS WILL AREN'T STRONG ENOUGH!
IT'S ALL HE CAN DO TO MAINTAIN THAT FORM.
I CAN HEAR SILVER'S THOUGHTS...
HE'S CON-STRUCTED A SUIT OF ARMOR AROUND HIS PSYCHE.
HE HAD TO IN ORDER TO SURVIVE.

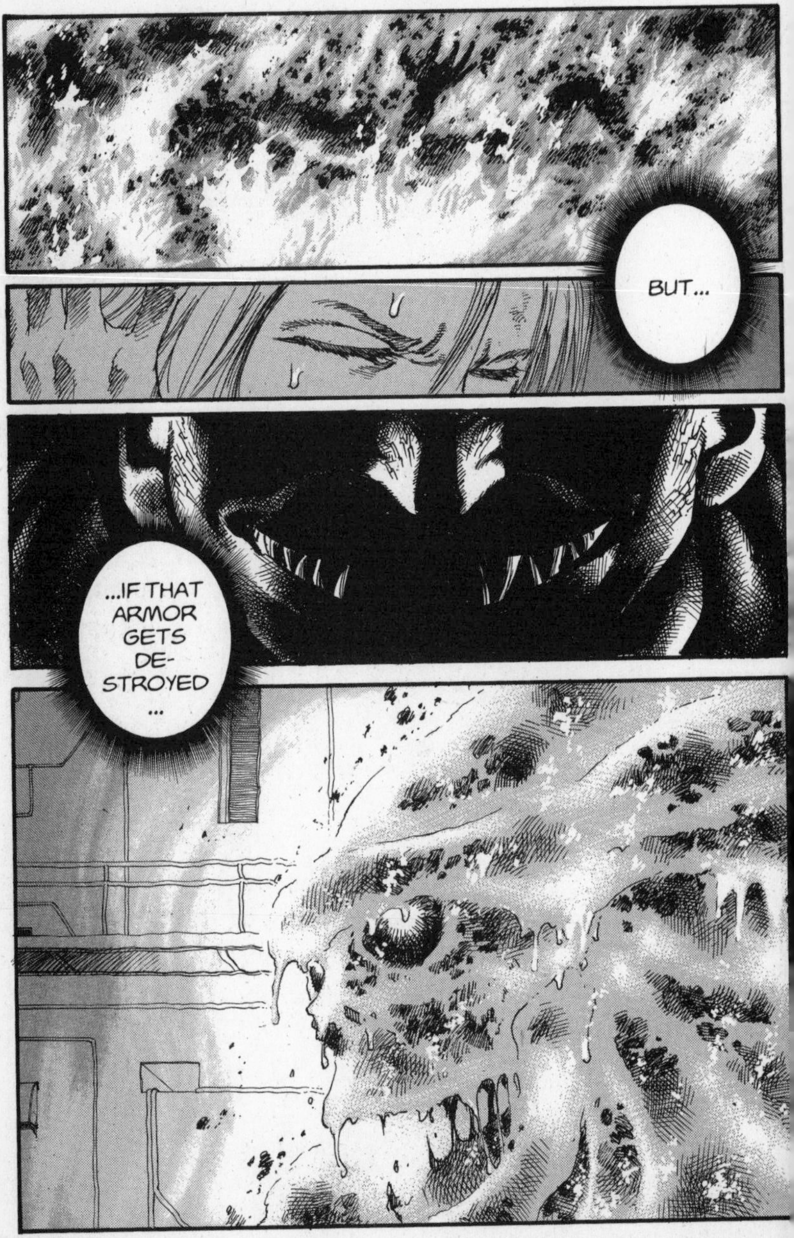
BUT...
...IF THAT ARMOR GETS DE-STROYED ...

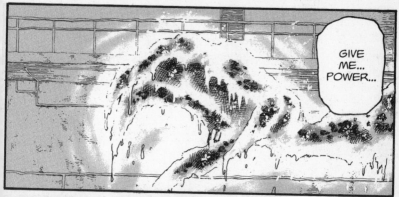

GIVE ME... POWER...

POWER THAT NO ONE CAN DEFEAT...

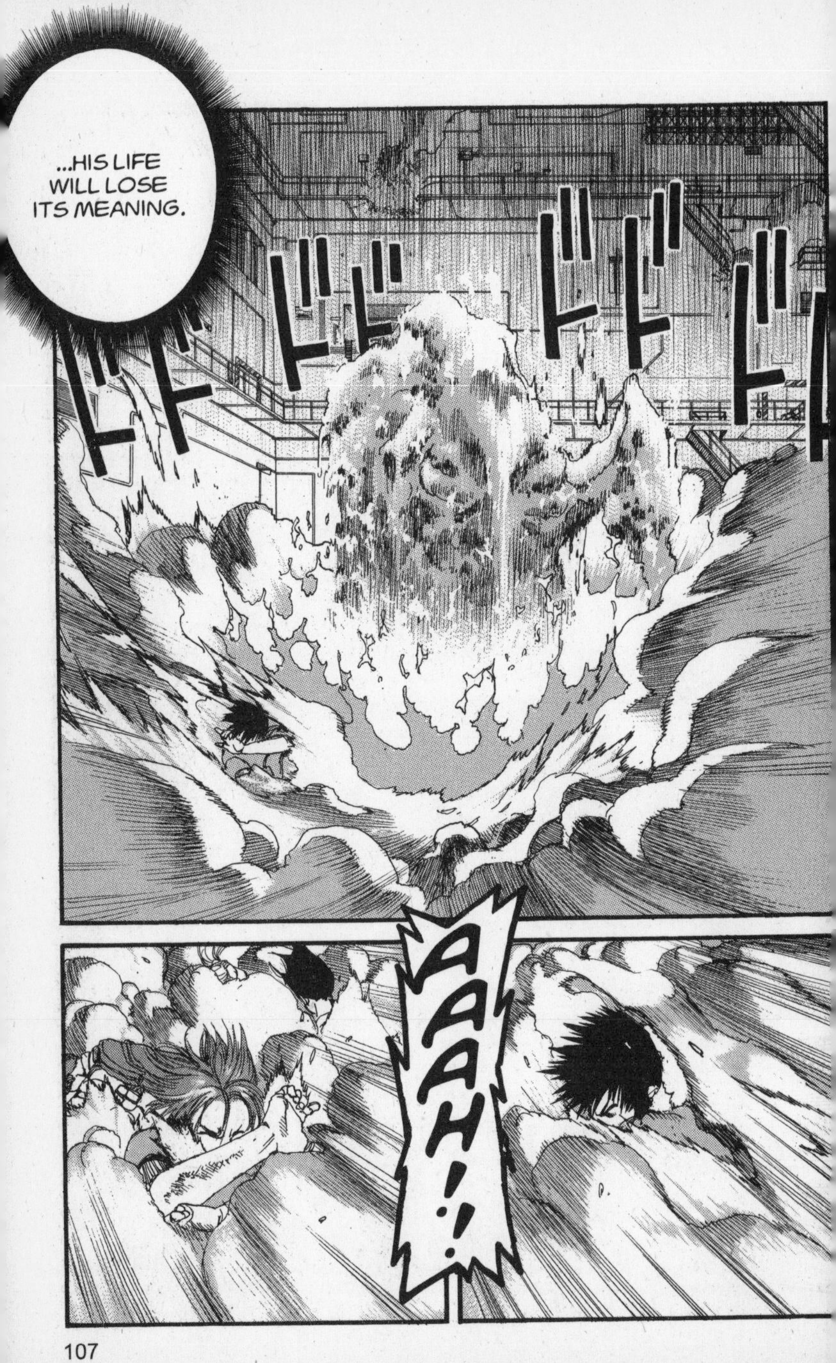
...HIS LIFE
WILL LOSE
ITS MEANING.
ドドドドドドドドド
AAAAH!!!

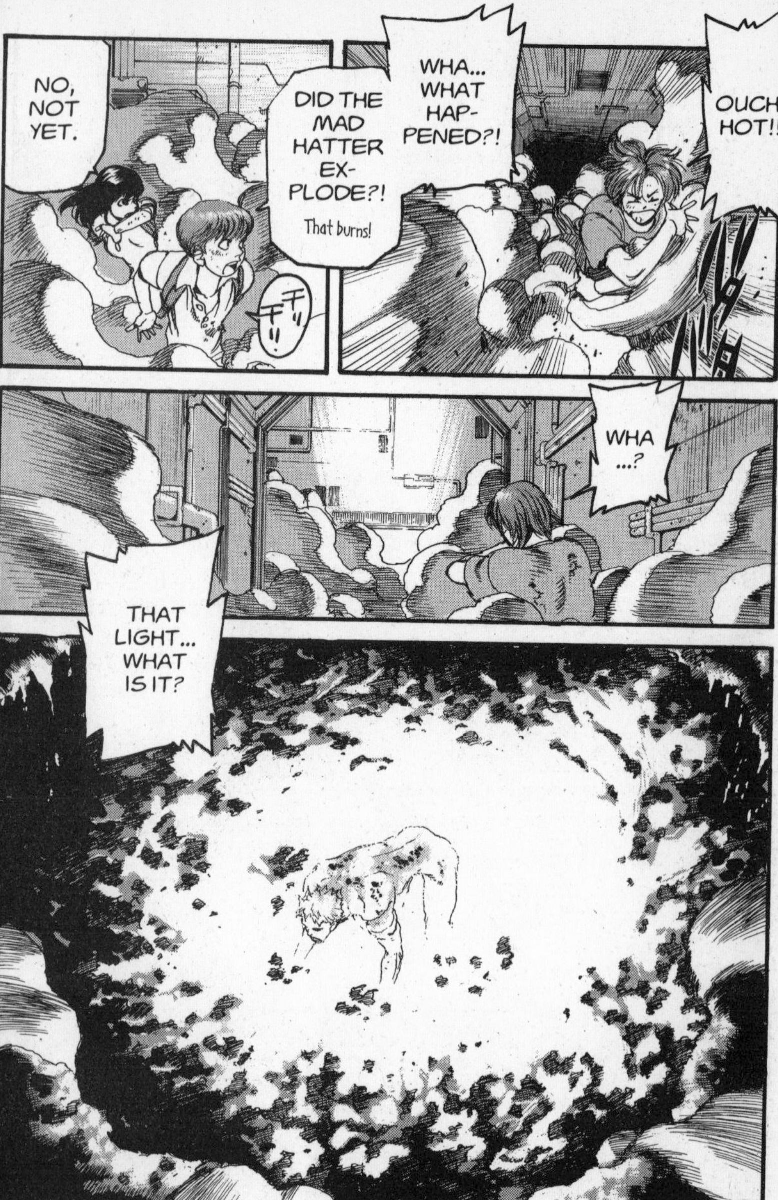
OUCH! HOT!!
WHA... WHAT HAP-PENED?!
DID THE MAD HATTER EX-PLODE?!
That burns!
NO, NOT YET.
チリチリ!!
WHA ...?
THAT LIGHT... WHAT IS IT?

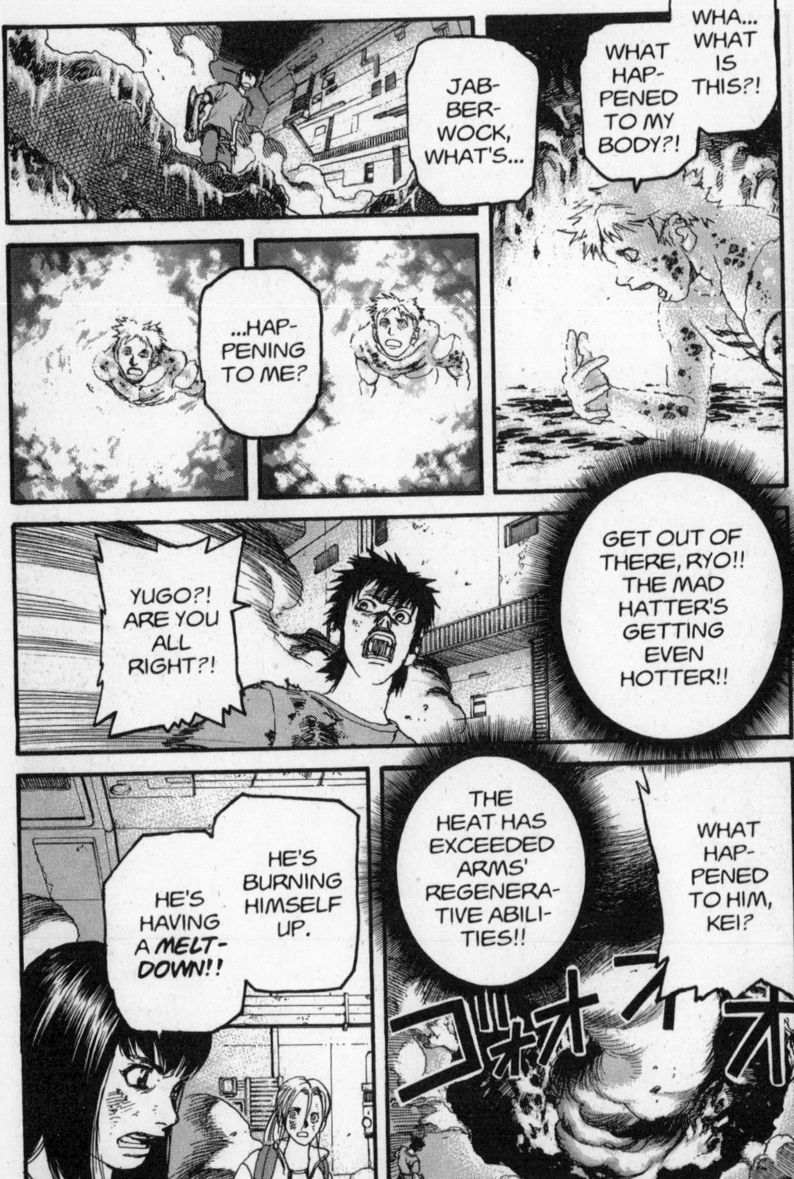
WHA... WHAT IS THIS?!
WHAT HAP-PENED TO MY BODY?!
JAB-BER-WOCK, WHAT'S...
...HAP-PENING TO ME?
GET OUT OF THERE, RYO!! THE MAD HATTER'S GETTING EVEN HOTTER!!
YUGO?! ARE YOU ALL RIGHT?!
WHAT HAP-PENED TO HIM, KEI?
THE HEAT HAS EXCEEDED ARMS' REGENERA-TIVE ABILI-TIES!!
ゴォオオ
HE'S BURNING HIMSELF UP.
HE'S HAVING A *MELT-DOWN!!*

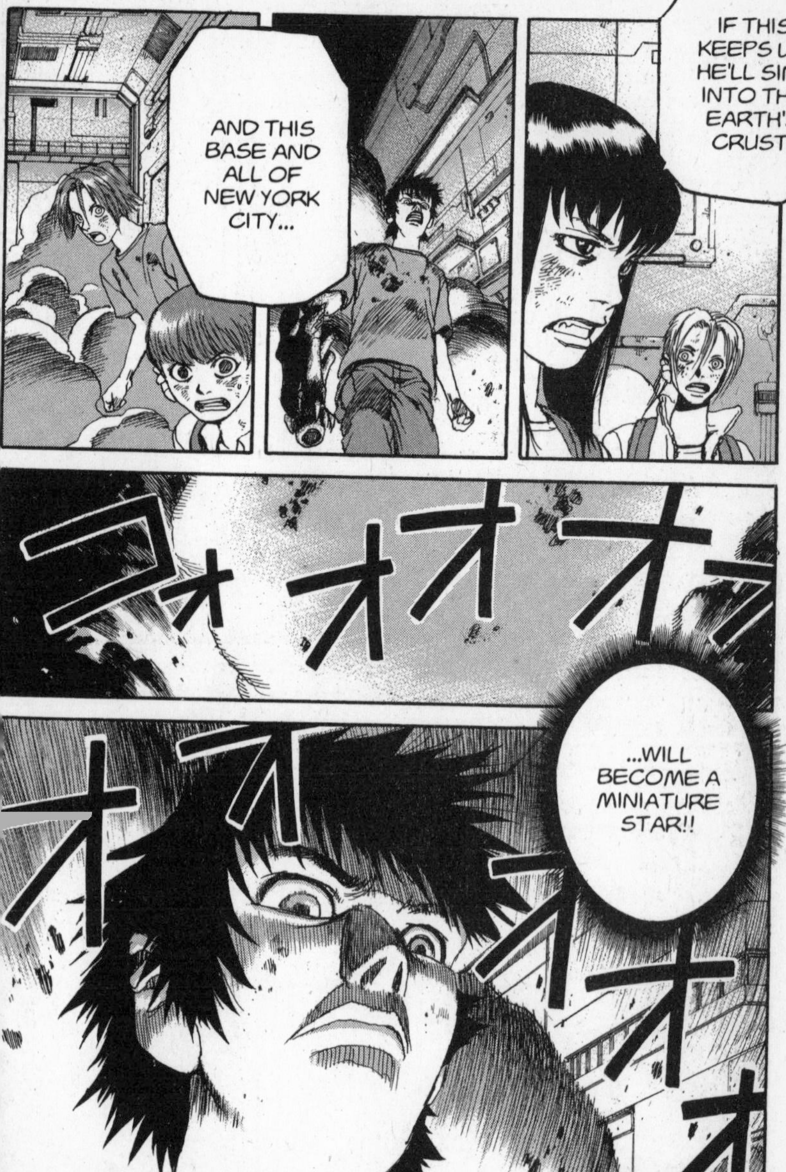
IF THIS KEEPS UP, HE'LL SINK INTO THE EARTH'S CRUST.
AND THIS BASE AND ALL OF NEW YORK CITY...
...WILL BECOME A MINIATURE STAR!!

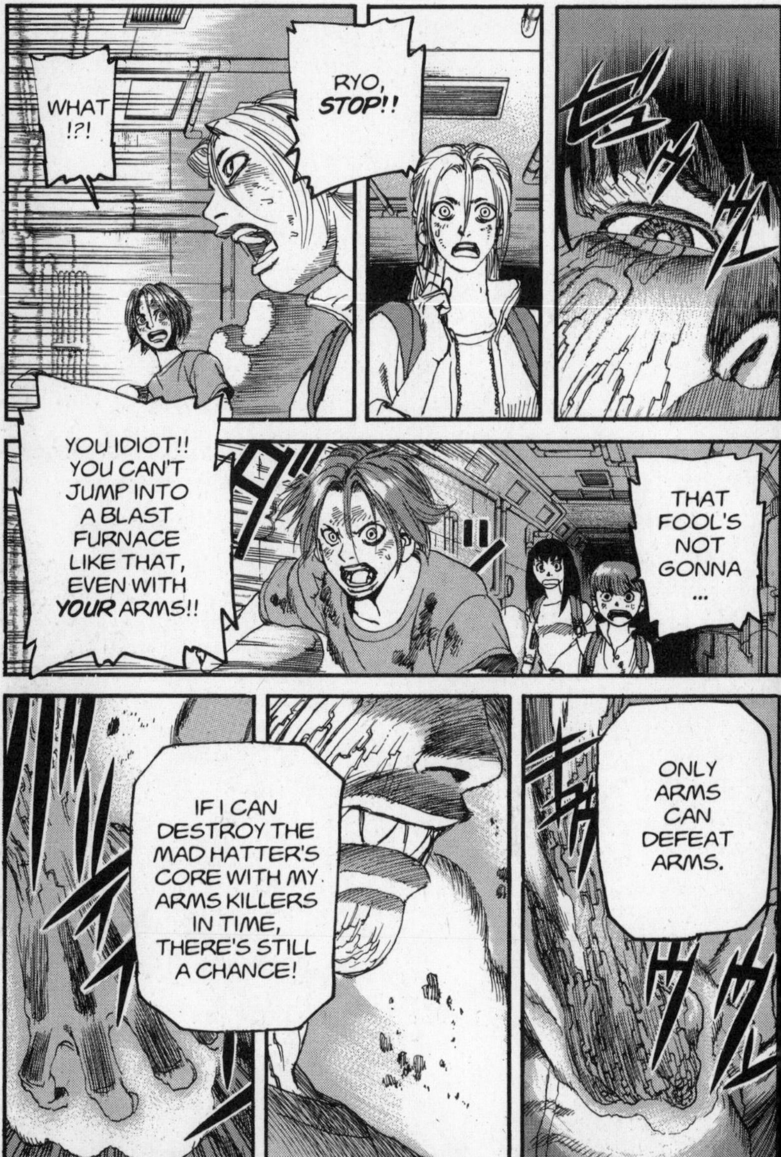
RYO, **STOP!!**
WHAT !?!
THAT FOOL'S NOT GONNA ...
YOU IDIOT!! YOU CAN'T JUMP INTO A BLAST FURNACE LIKE THAT, EVEN WITH ***YOUR*** ARMS!!
ONLY ARMS CAN DEFEAT ARMS.
IF I CAN DESTROY THE MAD HATTER'S CORE WITH MY ARMS KILLERS IN TIME, THERE'S STILL A CHANCE!

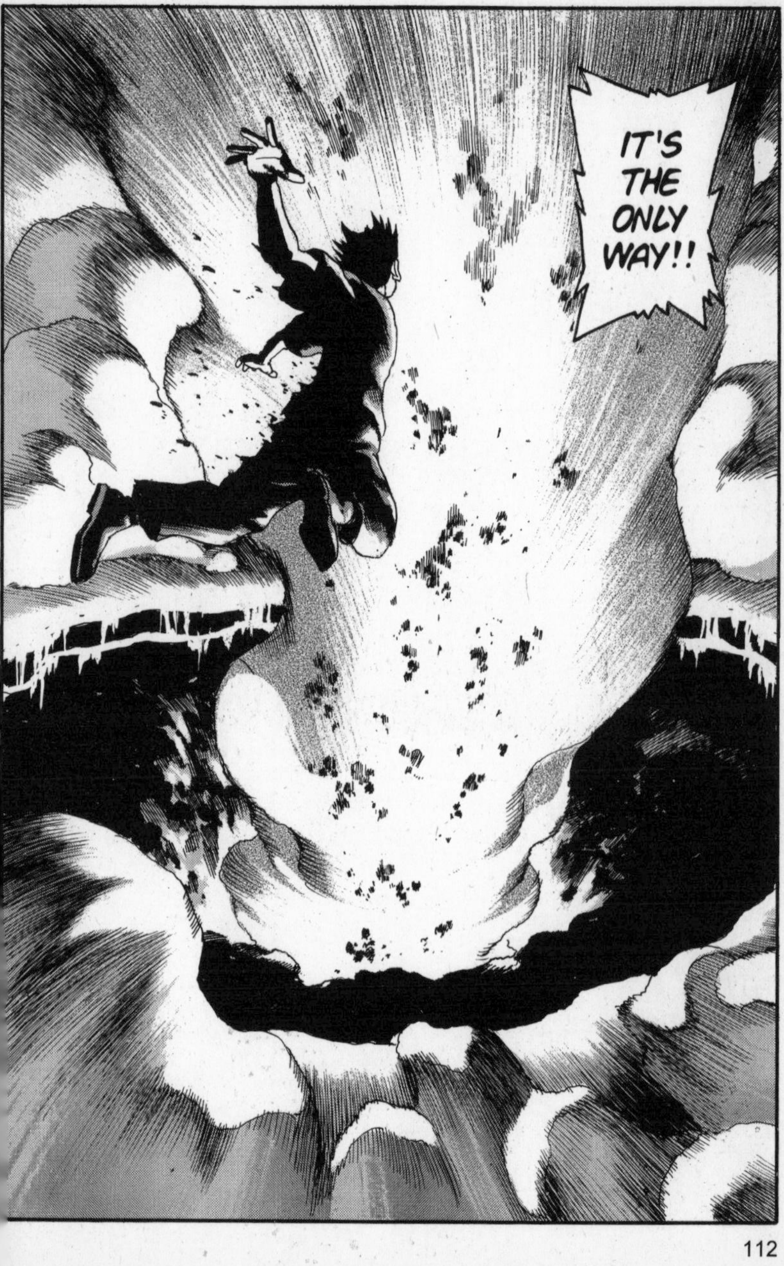
IT'S THE ONLY WAY!!

No. 7 INFERNO

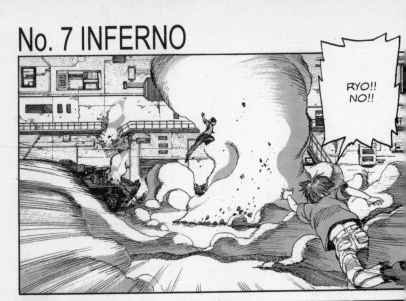

RYO!!
NO!!

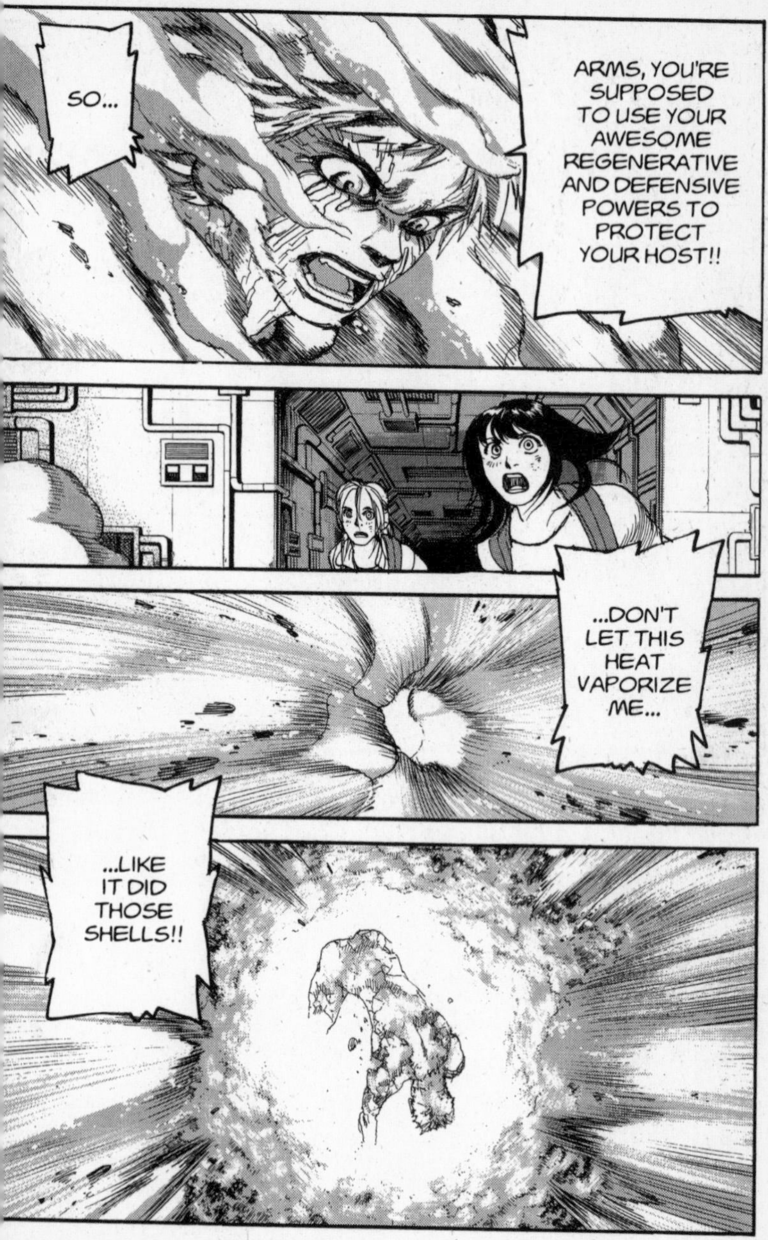
ARMS, YOU'RE SUPPOSED TO USE YOUR AWESOME REGENERATIVE AND DEFENSIVE POWERS TO PROTECT YOUR HOST!!
SO...
...DON'T LET THIS HEAT VAPORIZE ME...
...LIKE IT DID THOSE SHELLS!!

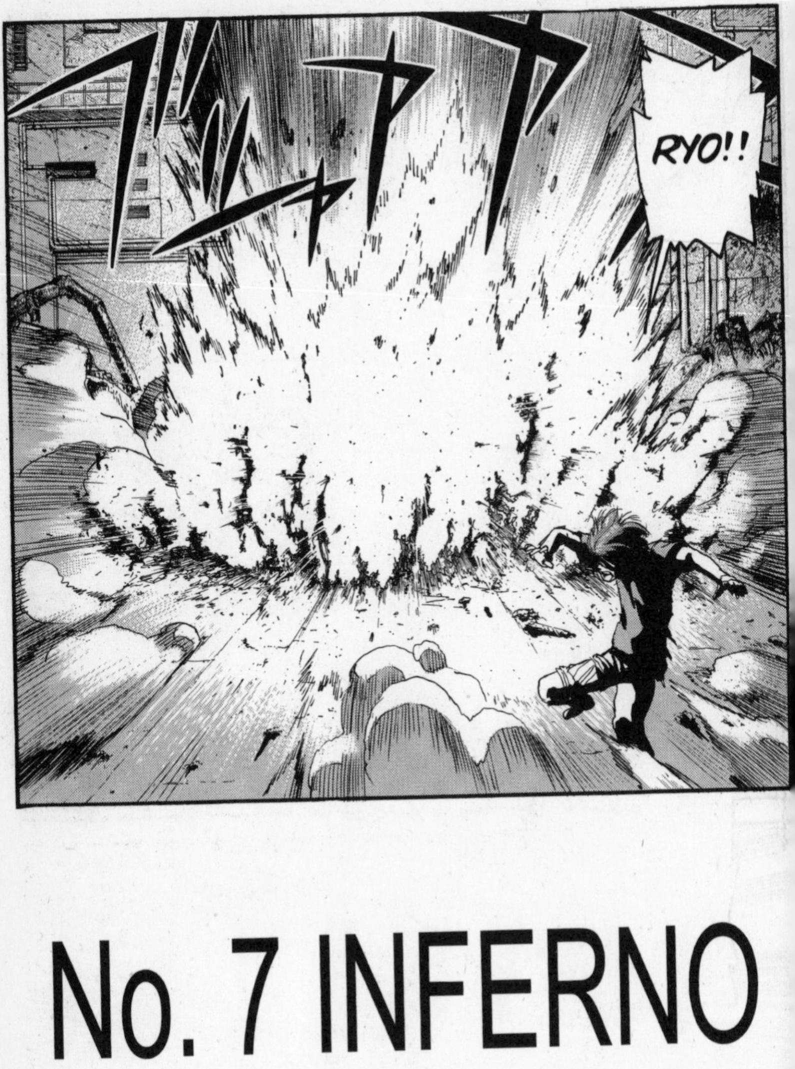
RYO!!

No. 7 INFERNO

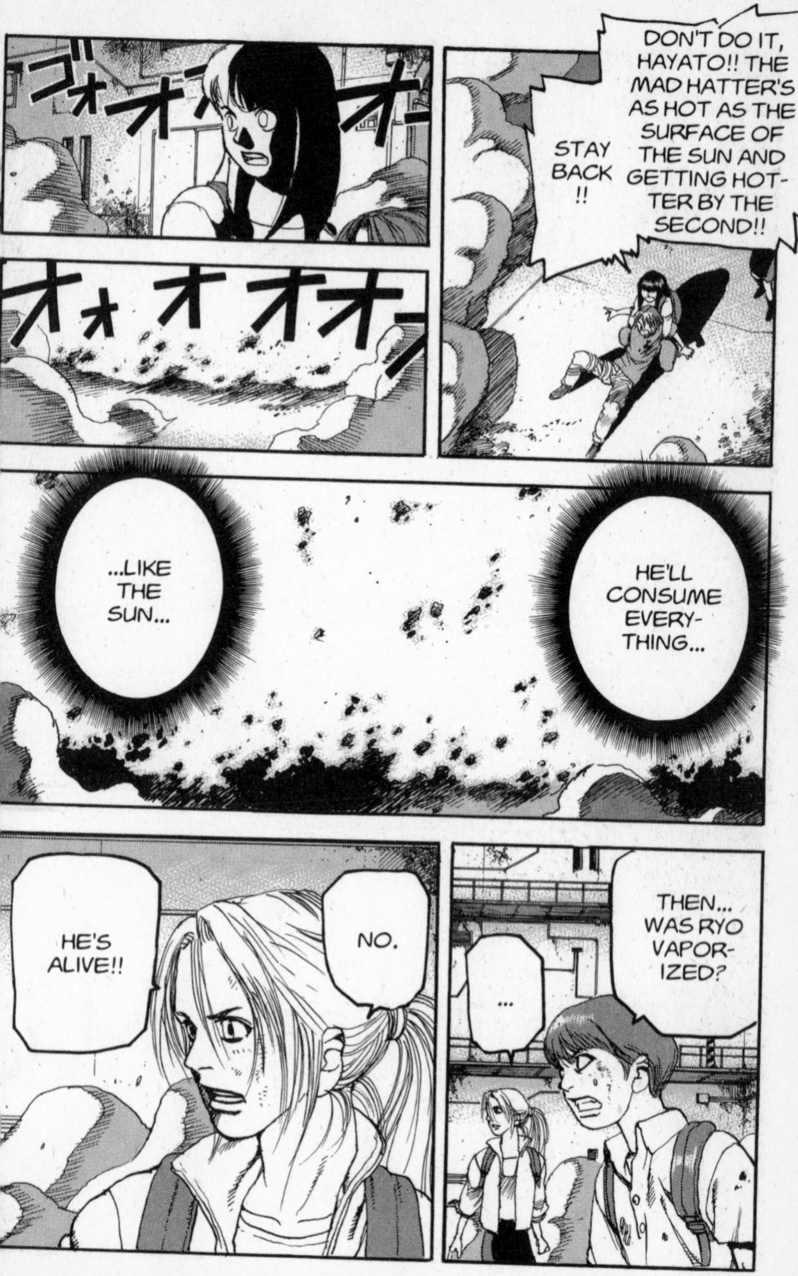
DON'T DO IT, HAYATO!! THE MAD HATTER'S AS HOT AS THE SURFACE OF THE SUN AND GETTING HOT-TER BY THE SECOND!!
STAY BACK !!
ゴォオオー
オォオオオー
HE'LL CONSUME EVERY-THING...
...LIKE THE SUN...
THEN... WAS RYO VAPOR-IZED?
...
NO.
HE'S ALIVE!!

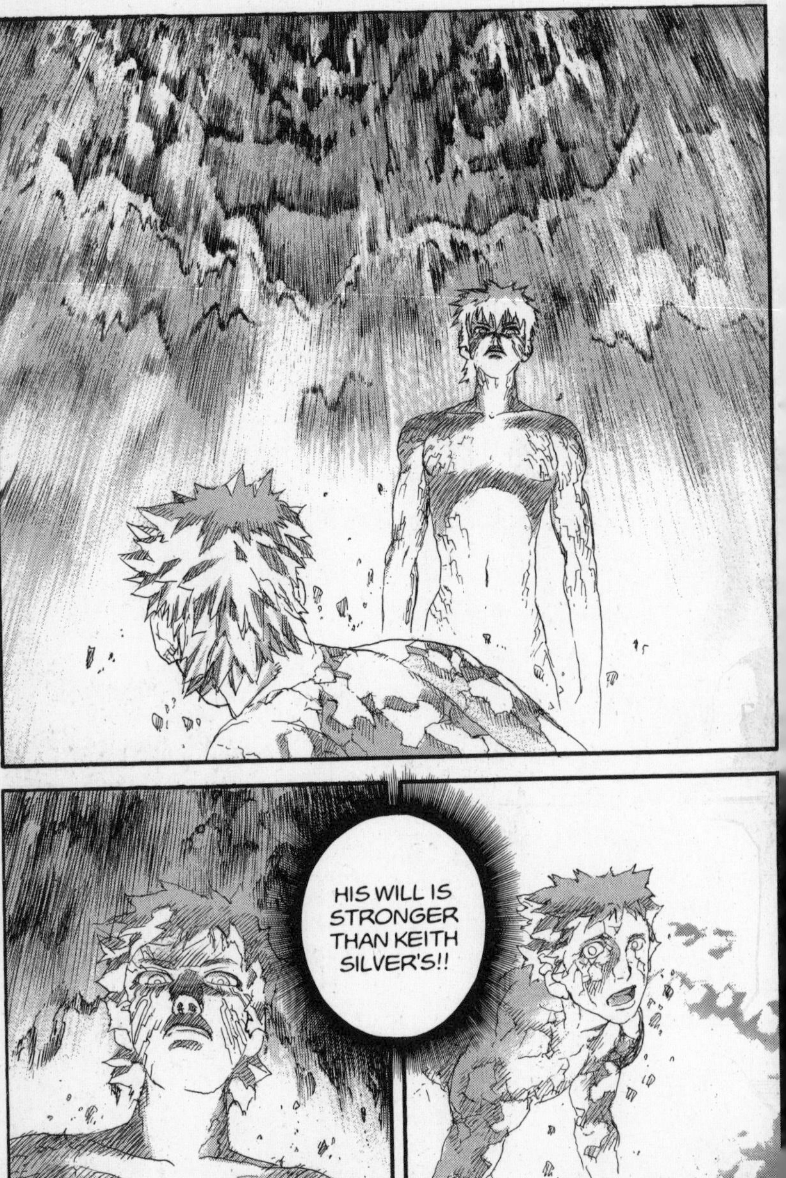
HIS WILL IS STRONGER THAN KEITH SILVER'S!!

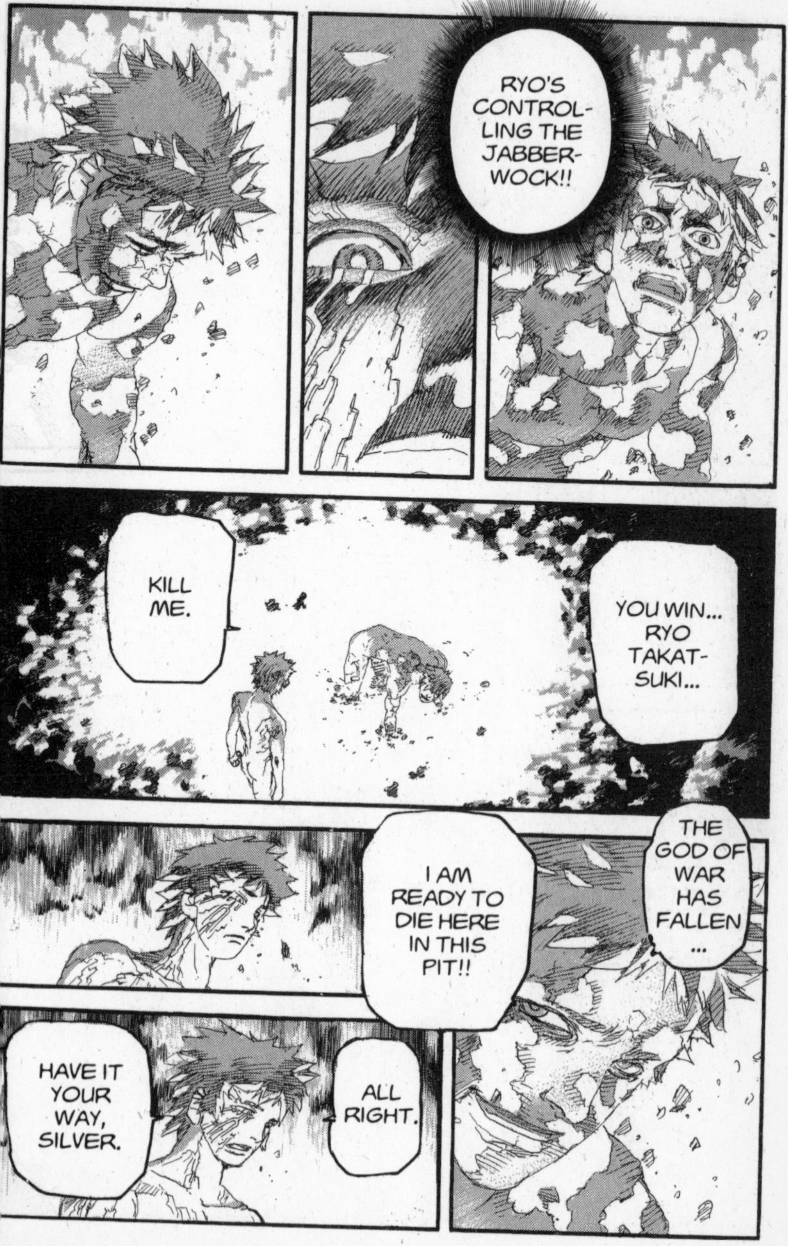
RYO'S CONTROL-LING THE JABBER-WOCK!!
YOU WIN... RYO TAKAT-SUKI...
KILL ME.
THE GOD OF WAR HAS FALLEN ...
I AM READY TO DIE HERE IN THIS PIT!!
ALL RIGHT.
HAVE IT YOUR WAY, SILVER.

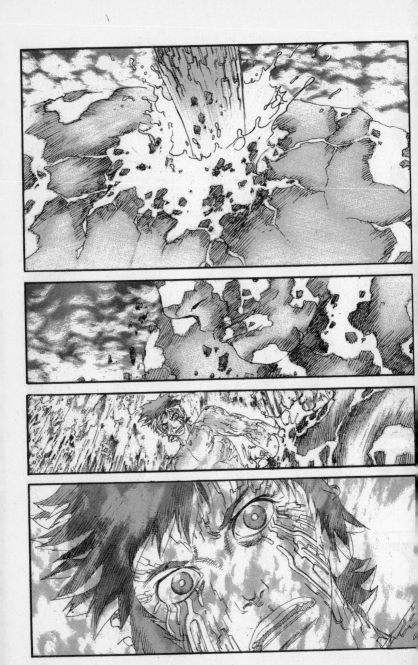

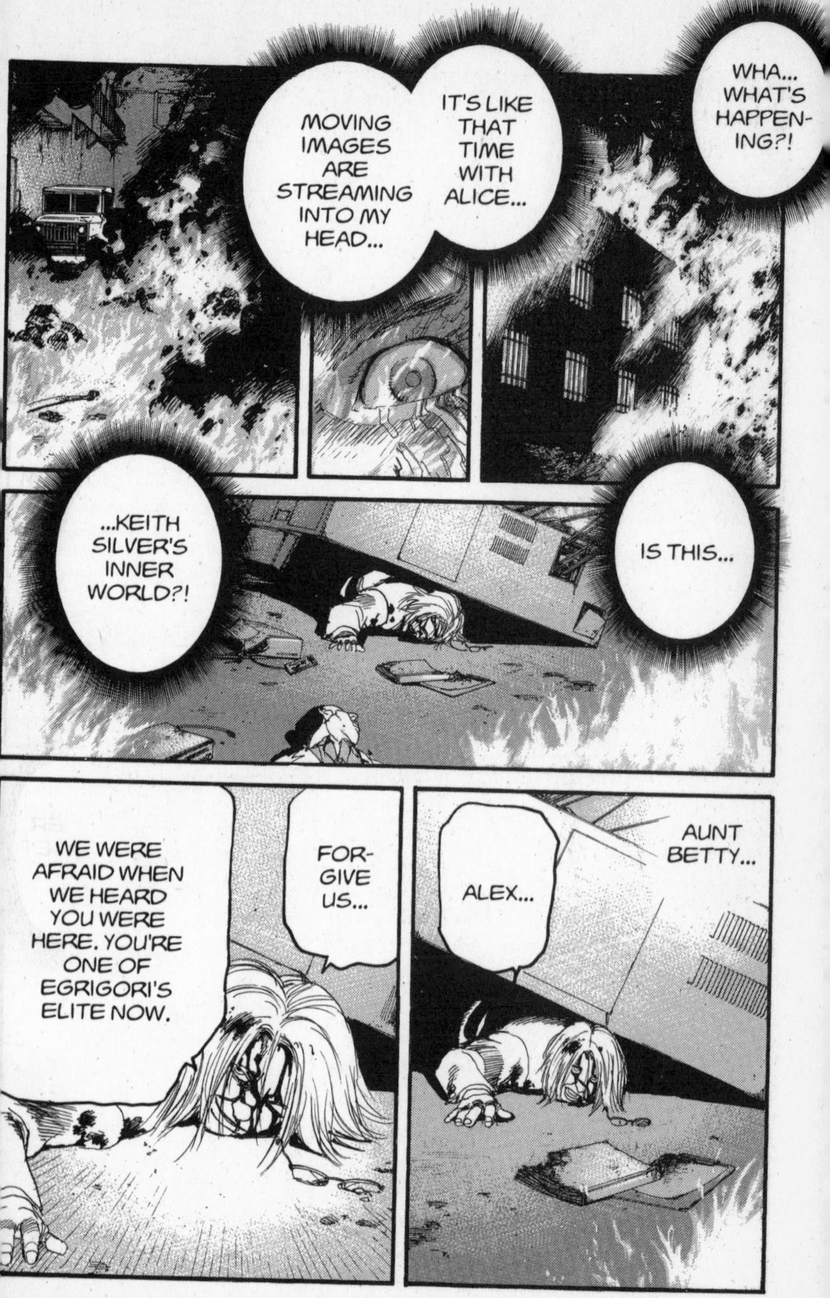
WHA... WHAT'S HAPPEN-ING?!
IT'S LIKE THAT TIME WITH ALICE...
MOVING IMAGES ARE STREAMING INTO MY HEAD...
IS THIS...
...KEITH SILVER'S INNER WORLD?!
AUNT BETTY...
ALEX...
FOR-GIVE US...
WE WERE AFRAID WHEN WE HEARD YOU WERE HERE. YOU'RE ONE OF EGRIGORI'S ELITE NOW.

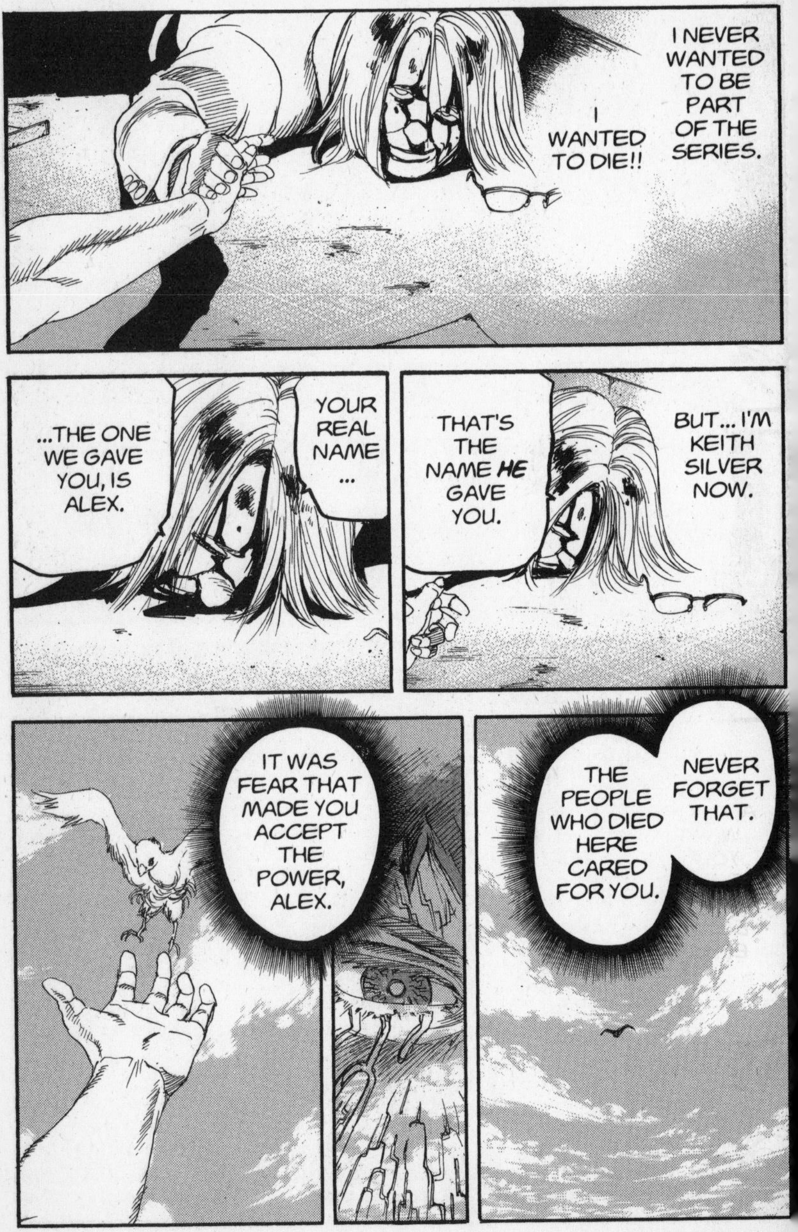
I NEVER WANTED TO BE PART OF THE SERIES.
I WANTED TO DIE!!
BUT... I'M KEITH SILVER NOW.
THAT'S THE NAME HE GAVE YOU.
YOUR REAL NAME ...
...THE ONE WE GAVE YOU, IS ALEX.
NEVER FORGET THAT.
THE PEOPLE WHO DIED HERE CARED FOR YOU.
IT WAS FEAR THAT MADE YOU ACCEPT THE POWER, ALEX.

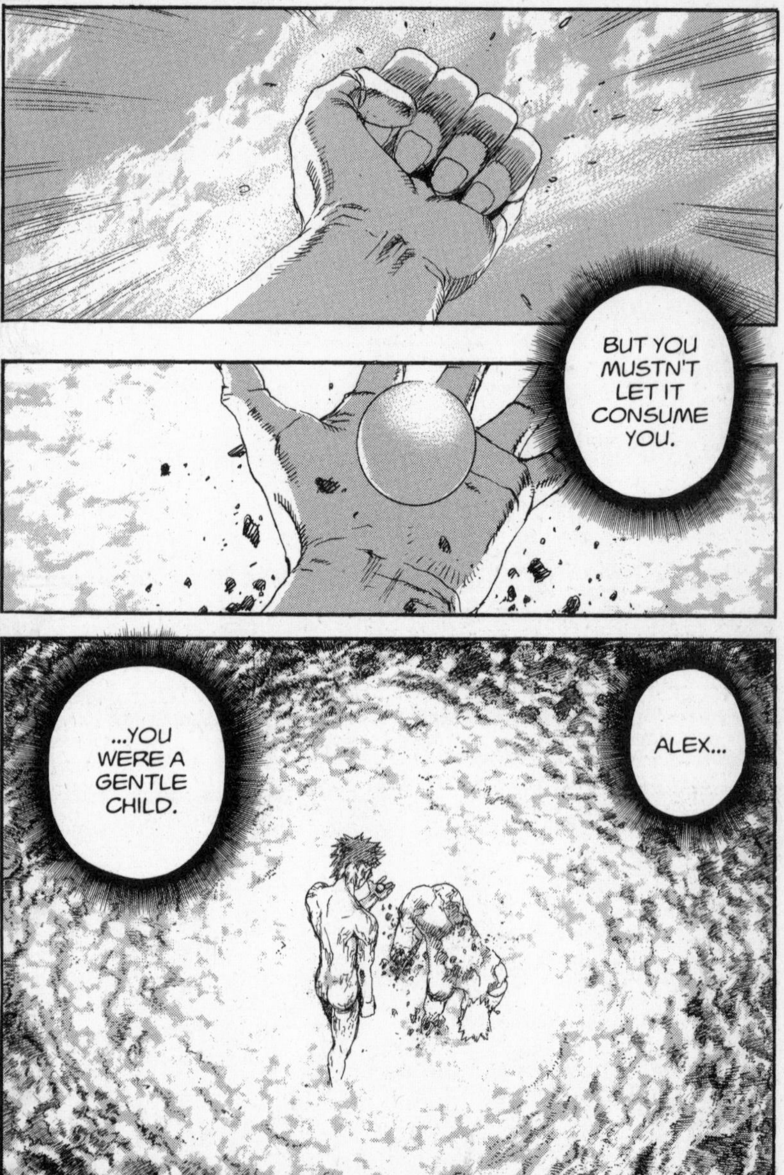
BUT YOU MUSTN'T LET IT CONSUME YOU.
ALEX...
...YOU WERE A GENTLE CHILD.

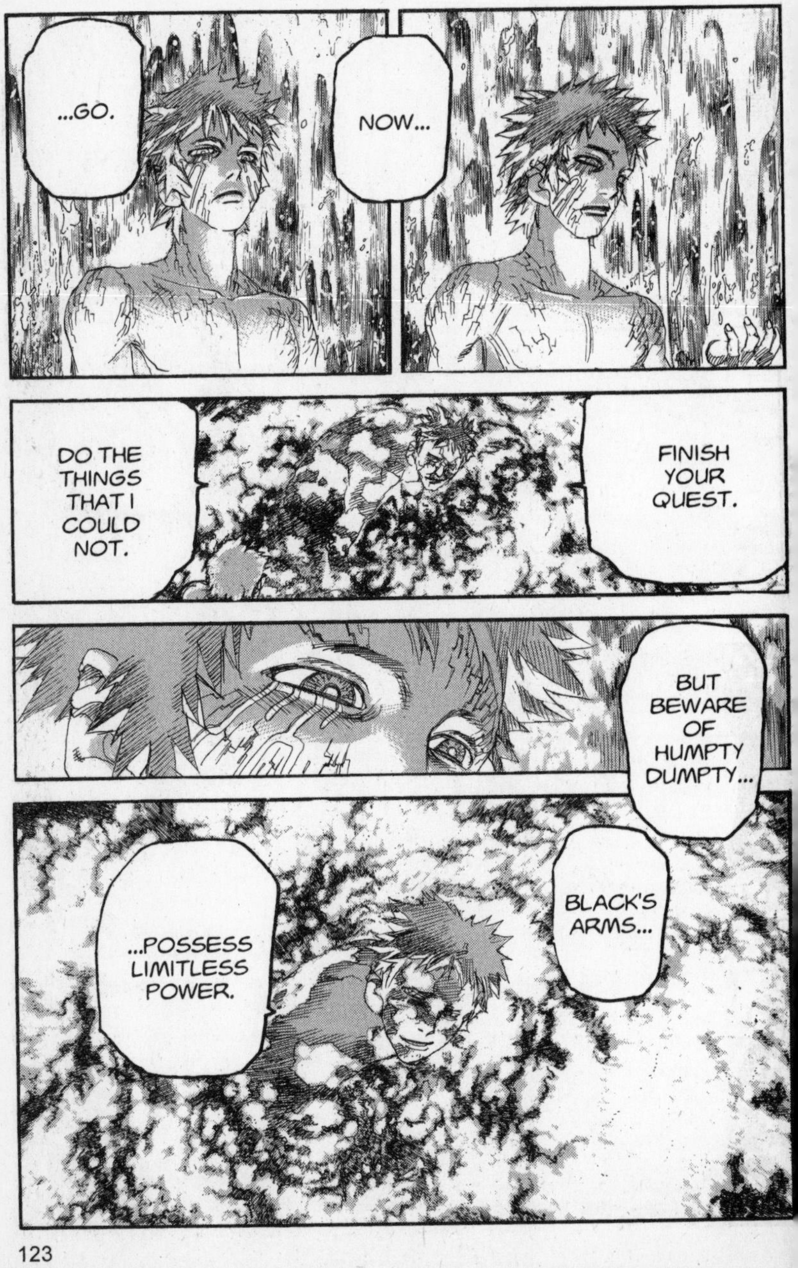
NOW...
...GO.
FINISH YOUR QUEST.
DO THE THINGS THAT I COULD NOT.
BUT BEWARE OF HUMPTY DUMPTY...
BLACK'S ARMS...
...POSSESS LIMITLESS POWER.

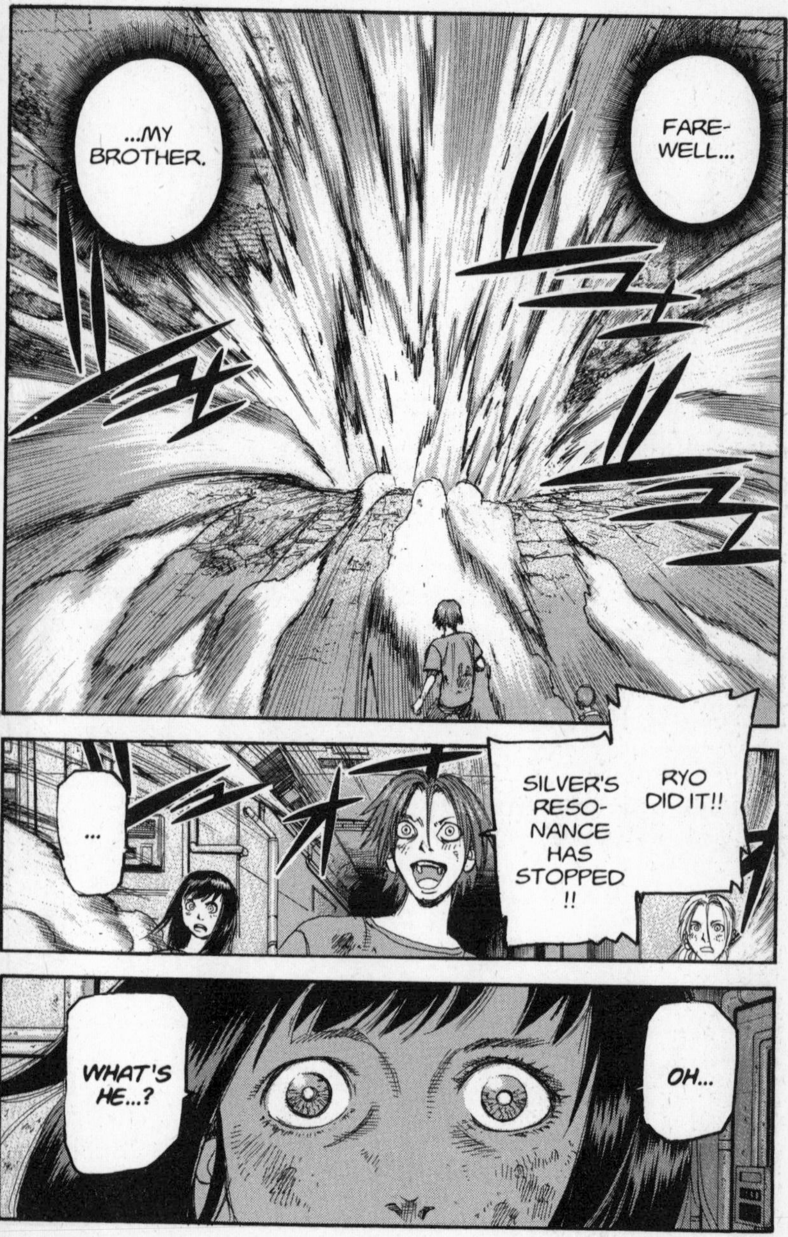
FARE-WELL...
...MY BROTHER.
RYO DID IT!!
SILVER'S RESO-NANCE HAS STOPPED!!
...
OH...
WHAT'S HE...?

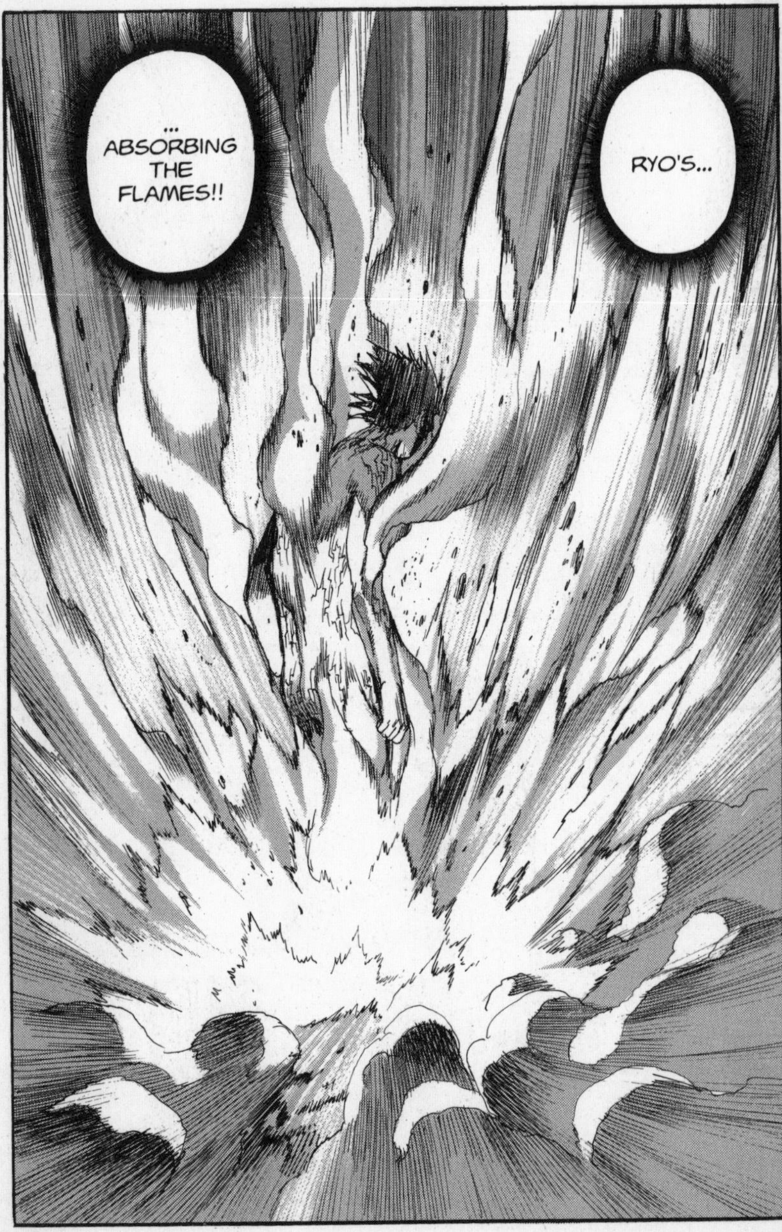
RYO'S...
... ABSORBING THE FLAMES!!

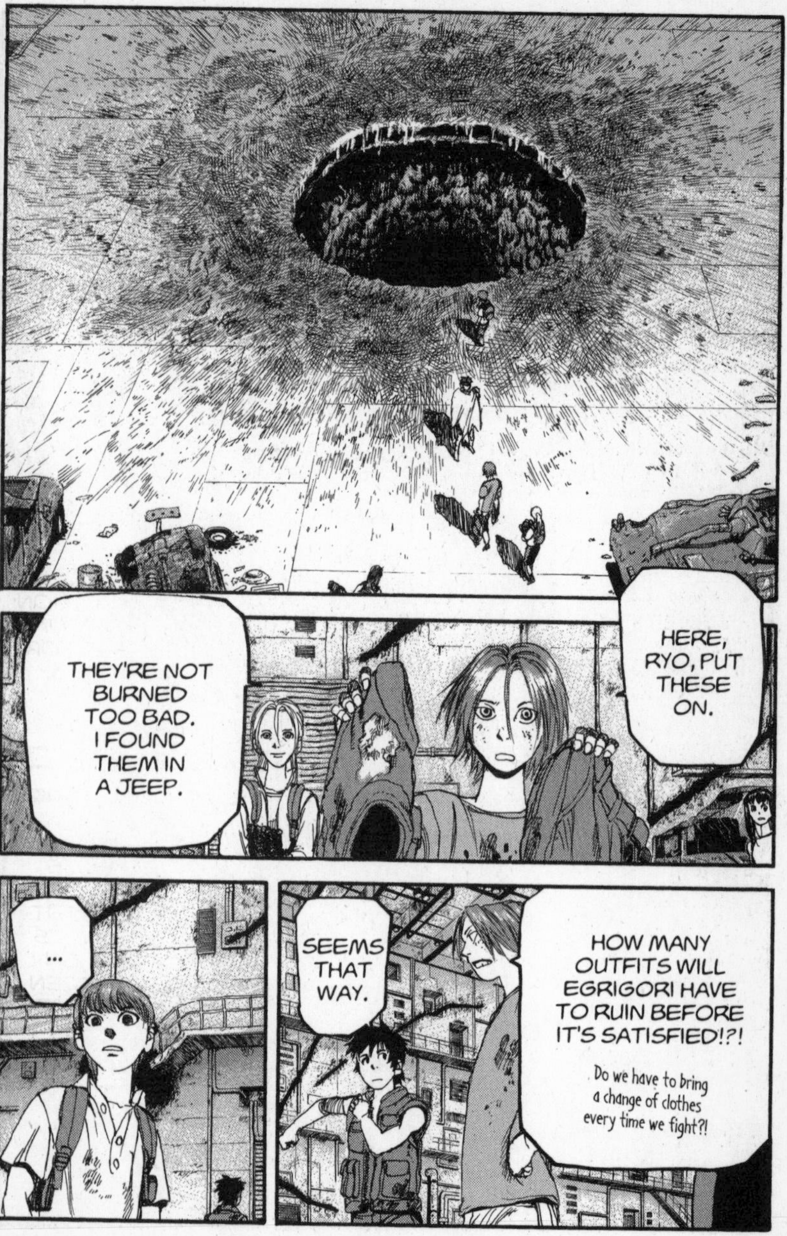
HERE, RYO, PUT THESE ON.
THEY'RE NOT BURNED TOO BAD. I FOUND THEM IN A JEEP.
HOW MANY OUTFITS WILL EGRIGORI HAVE TO RUIN BEFORE IT'S SATISFIED!?!
Do we have to bring a change of clothes every time we fight?!
SEEMS THAT WAY.
...

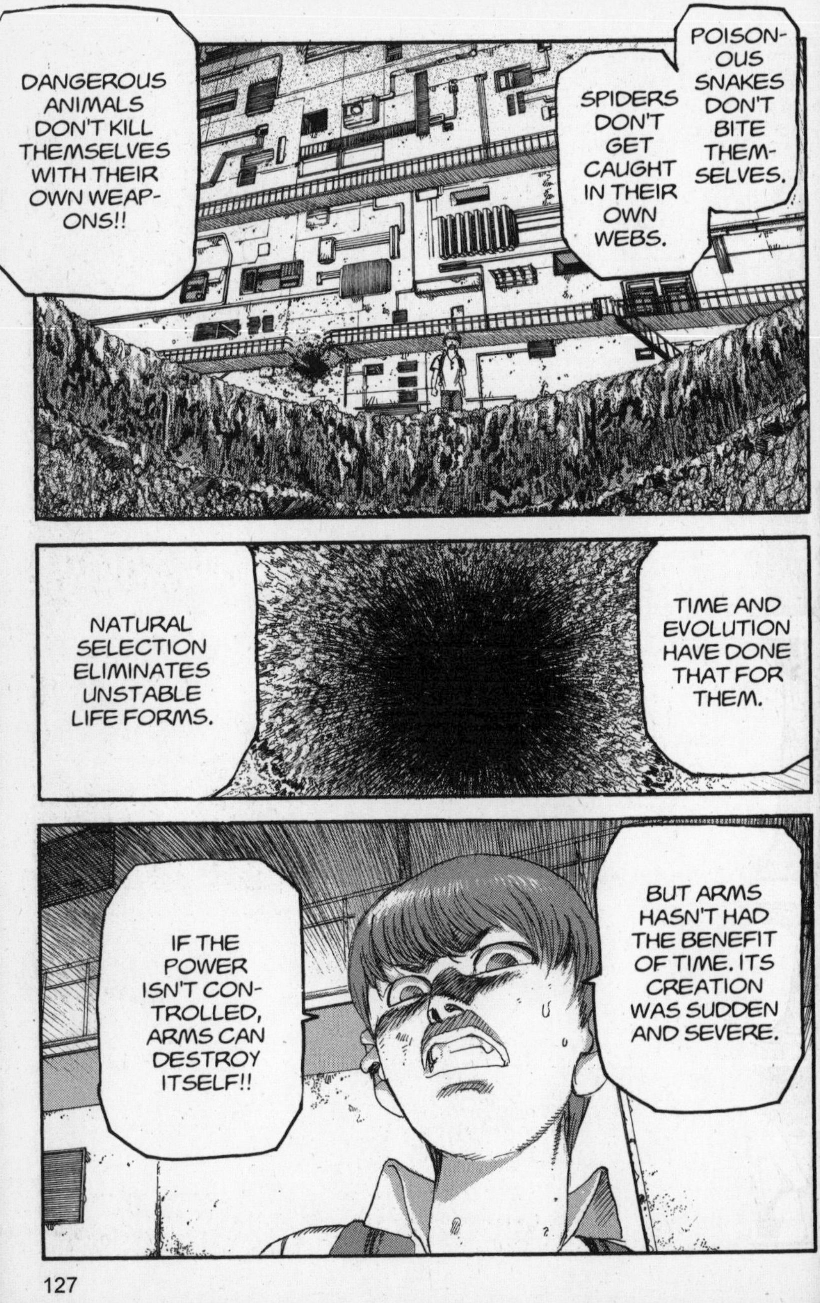
POISON-OUS SNAKES DON'T BITE THEM-SELVES.
SPIDERS DON'T GET CAUGHT IN THEIR OWN WEBS.
DANGEROUS ANIMALS DON'T KILL THEMSELVES WITH THEIR OWN WEAP-ONS!!
TIME AND EVOLUTION HAVE DONE THAT FOR THEM.
NATURAL SELECTION ELIMINATES UNSTABLE LIFE FORMS.
BUT ARMS HASN'T HAD THE BENEFIT OF TIME. ITS CREATION WAS SUDDEN AND SEVERE.
IF THE POWER ISN'T CON-TROLLED, ARMS CAN DESTROY ITSELF!!

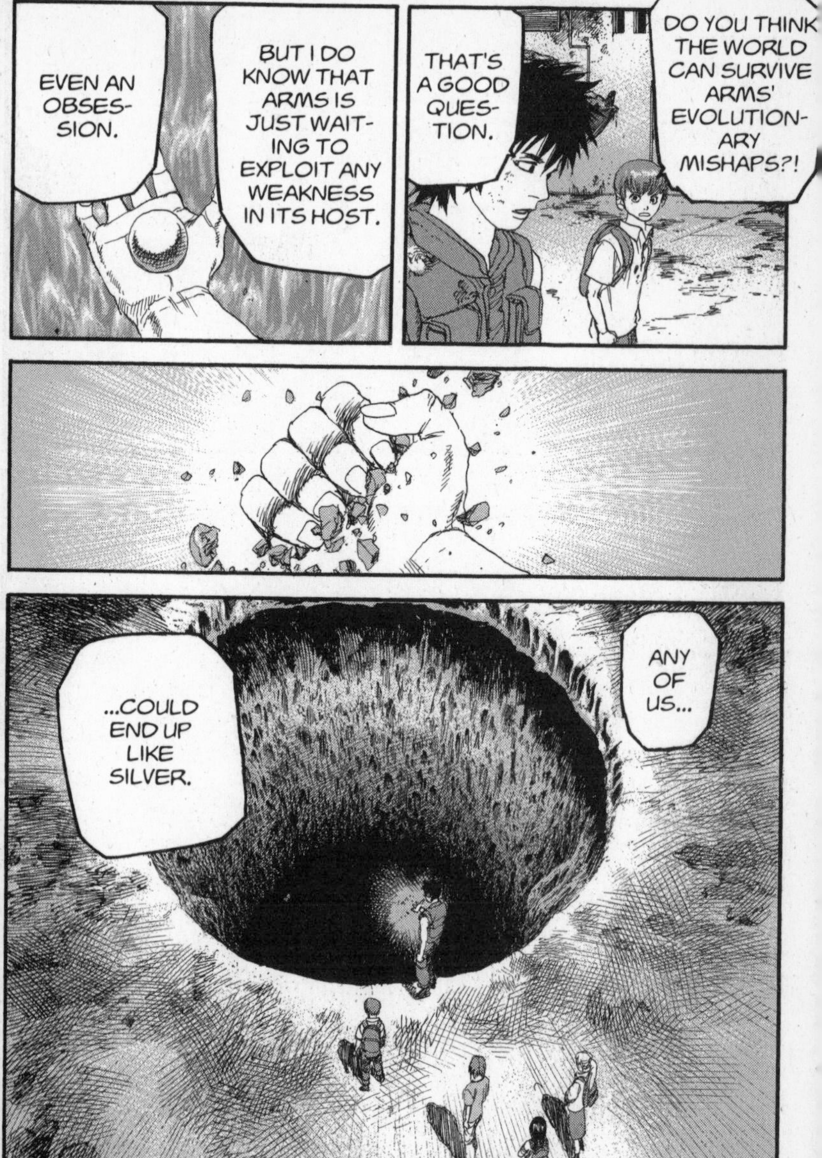
DO YOU THINK THE WORLD CAN SURVIVE ARMS' EVOLUTION-ARY MISHAPS?!
THAT'S A GOOD QUES-TION.
BUT I DO KNOW THAT ARMS IS JUST WAIT-ING TO EXPLOIT ANY WEAKNESS IN ITS HOST.
EVEN AN OBSES-SION.
ANY OF US...
...COULD END UP LIKE SILVER.

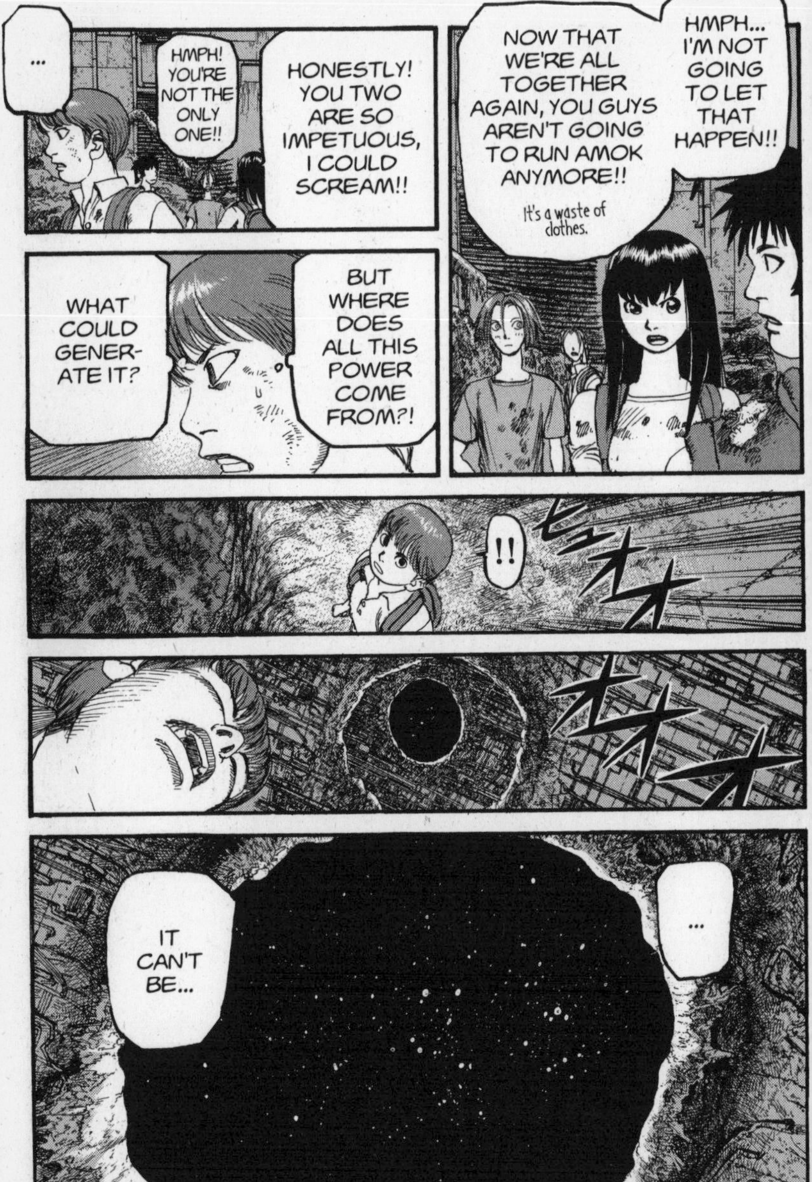
HMPH... I'M NOT GOING TO LET THAT HAPPEN!!
NOW THAT WE'RE ALL TOGETHER AGAIN, YOU GUYS AREN'T GOING TO RUN AMOK ANYMORE!!
It's a waste of clothes.
HONESTLY! YOU TWO ARE SO IMPETUOUS, I COULD SCREAM!!
HMPH! YOU'RE NOT THE ONLY ONE!!
...
BUT WHERE DOES ALL THIS POWER COME FROM?!
WHAT COULD GENERATE IT?
!!
...
IT CAN'T BE...

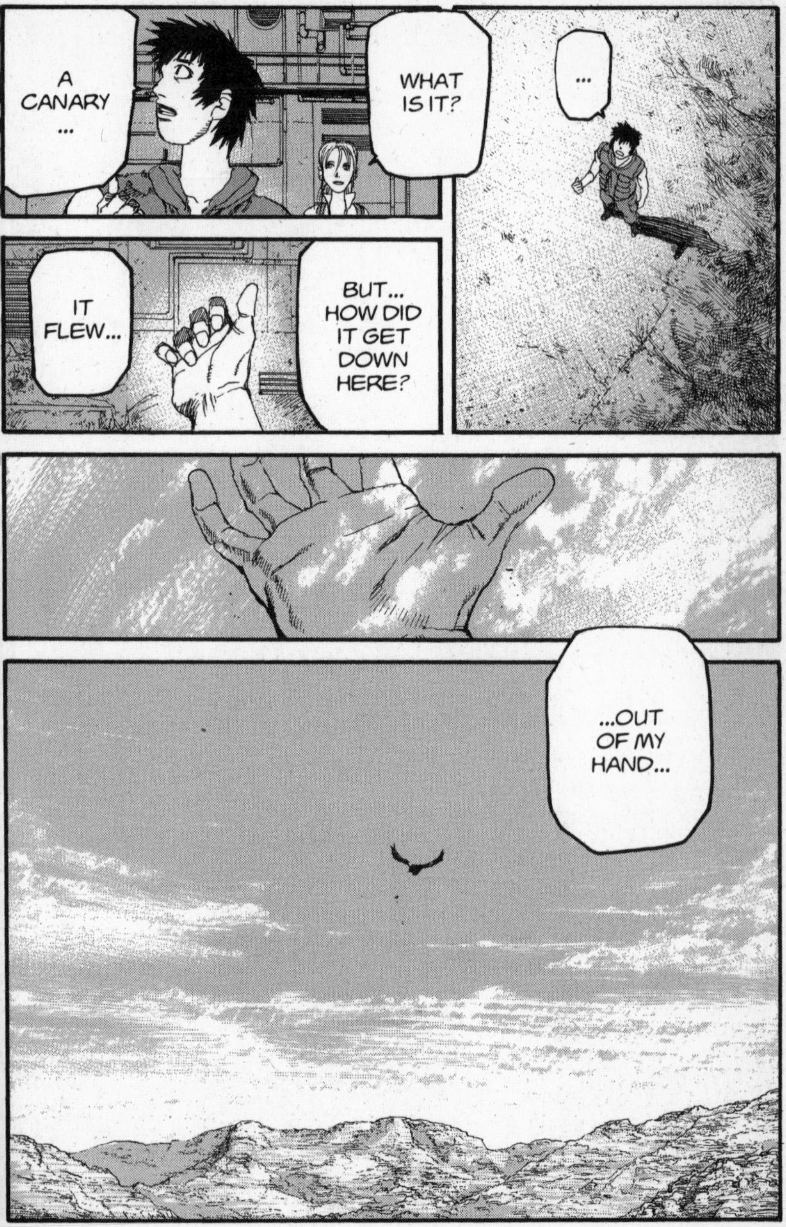
...
WHAT IS IT?
A CANARY ...
BUT... HOW DID IT GET DOWN HERE?
IT FLEW...
...OUT OF MY HAND...

No. 8 PROPHECY

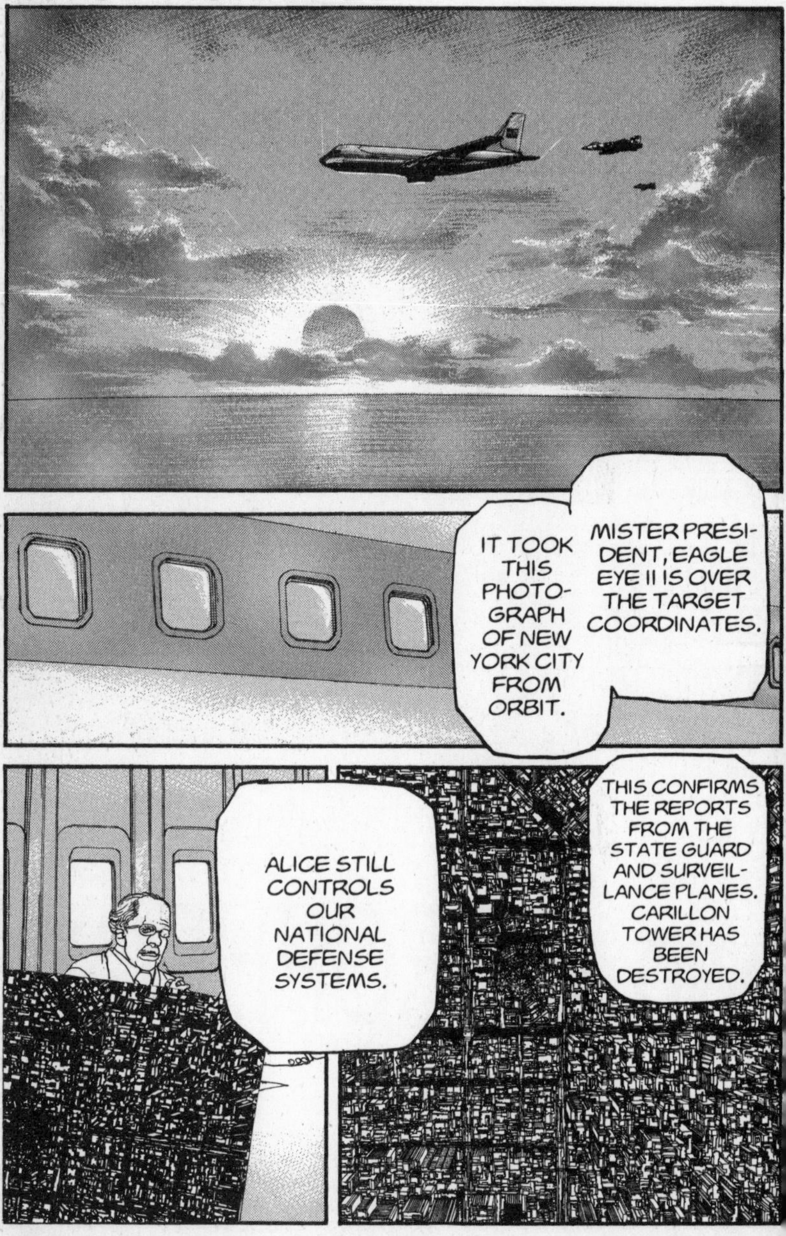
MISTER PRESIDENT, EAGLE EYE II IS OVER THE TARGET COORDINATES.
IT TOOK THIS PHOTOGRAPH OF NEW YORK CITY FROM ORBIT.
THIS CONFIRMS THE REPORTS FROM THE STATE GUARD AND SURVEILLANCE PLANES. CARILLON TOWER HAS BEEN DESTROYED.
ALICE STILL CONTROLS OUR NATIONAL DEFENSE SYSTEMS.

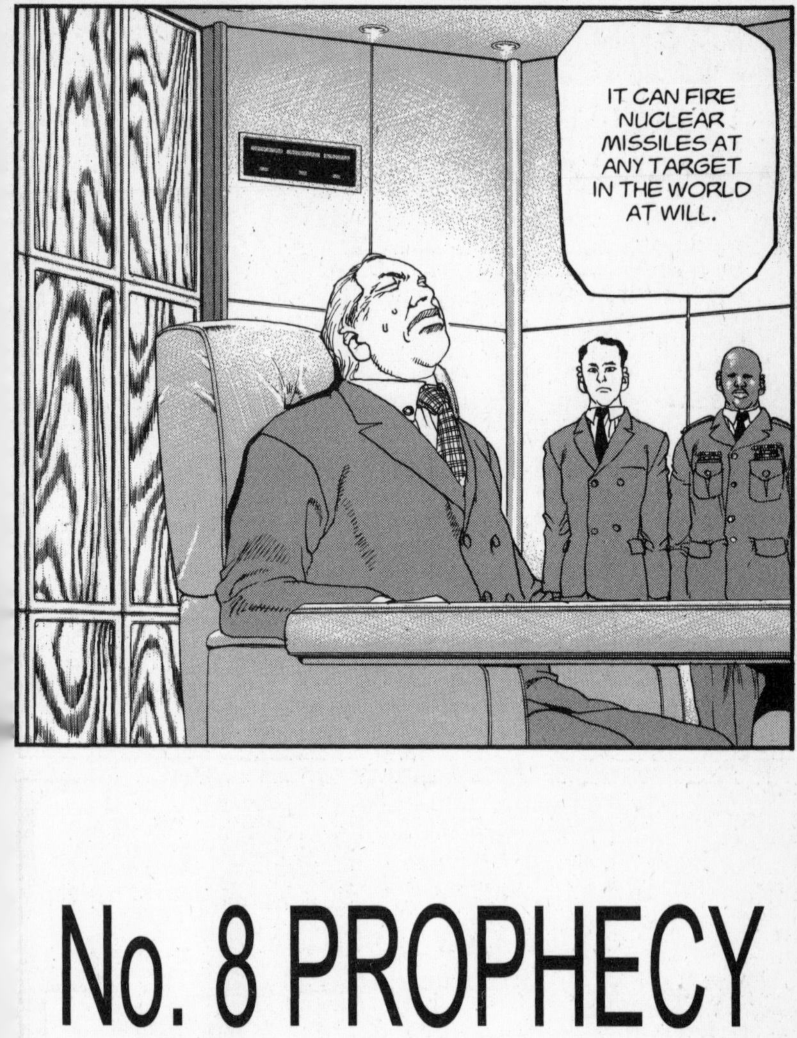
IT CAN FIRE NUCLEAR MISSILES AT ANY TARGET IN THE WORLD AT WILL.

No. 8 PROPHECY

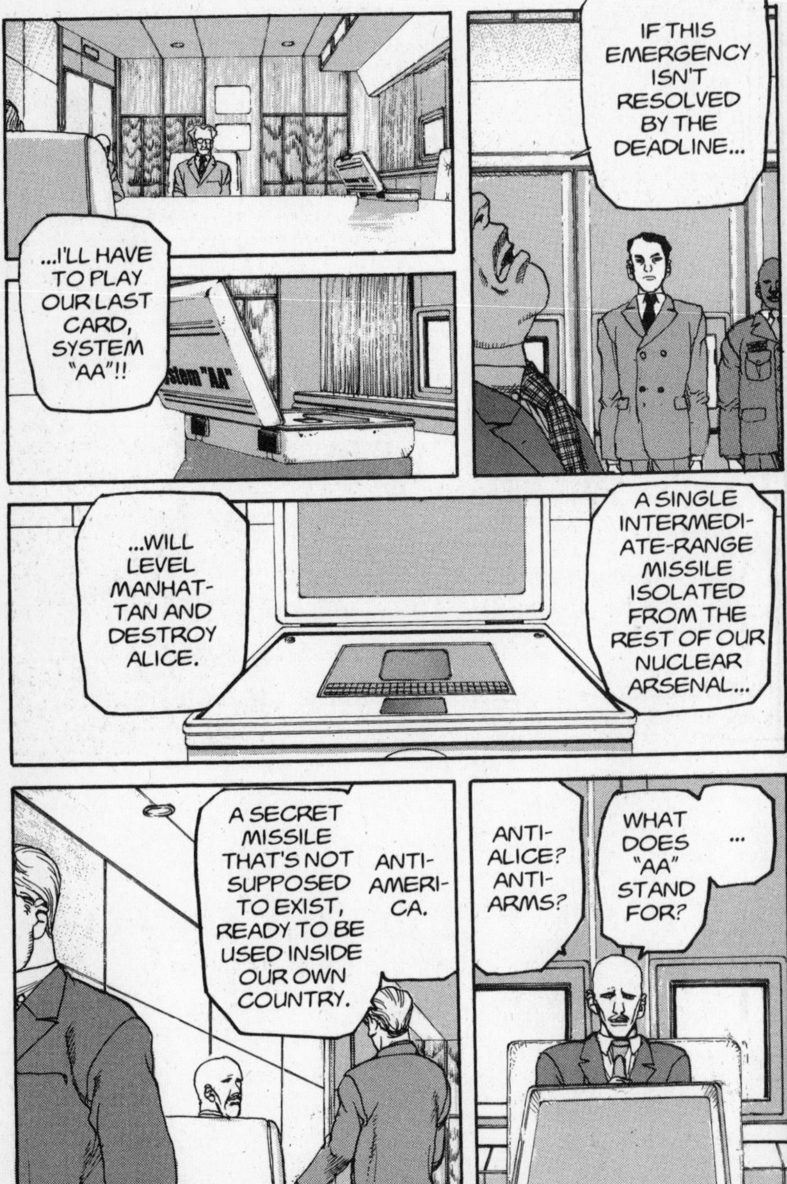
IF THIS EMERGENCY ISN'T RESOLVED BY THE DEADLINE...
...I'LL HAVE TO PLAY OUR LAST CARD, SYSTEM "AA"!!
A SINGLE INTERMEDIATE-RANGE MISSILE ISOLATED FROM THE REST OF OUR NUCLEAR ARSENAL...
...WILL LEVEL MANHATTAN AND DESTROY ALICE.
WHAT DOES "AA" STAND FOR?
...
ANTI-ALICE? ANTI-ARMS?
ANTI-AMERICA.
A SECRET MISSILE THAT'S NOT SUPPOSED TO EXIST, READY TO BE USED INSIDE OUR OWN COUNTRY.

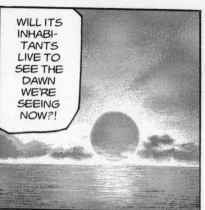

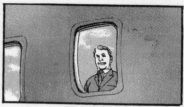

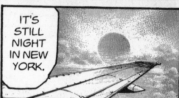

IT'S STILL NIGHT IN NEW YORK.
WILL ITS INHABITANTS LIVE TO SEE THE DAWN WE'RE SEEING NOW?!
MISTER PRESIDENT...
WHEN THE TIME COMES...
System "AA"
...I'LL PUSH THE BUTTON...
...EVEN IF I GO DOWN IN HISTORY AS THE PERSONIFICATION OF EVIL!!

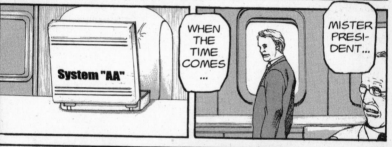

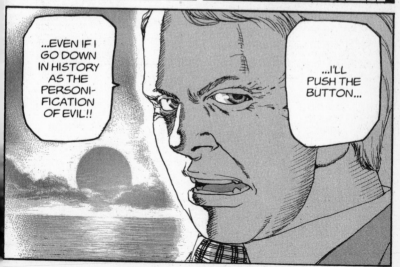

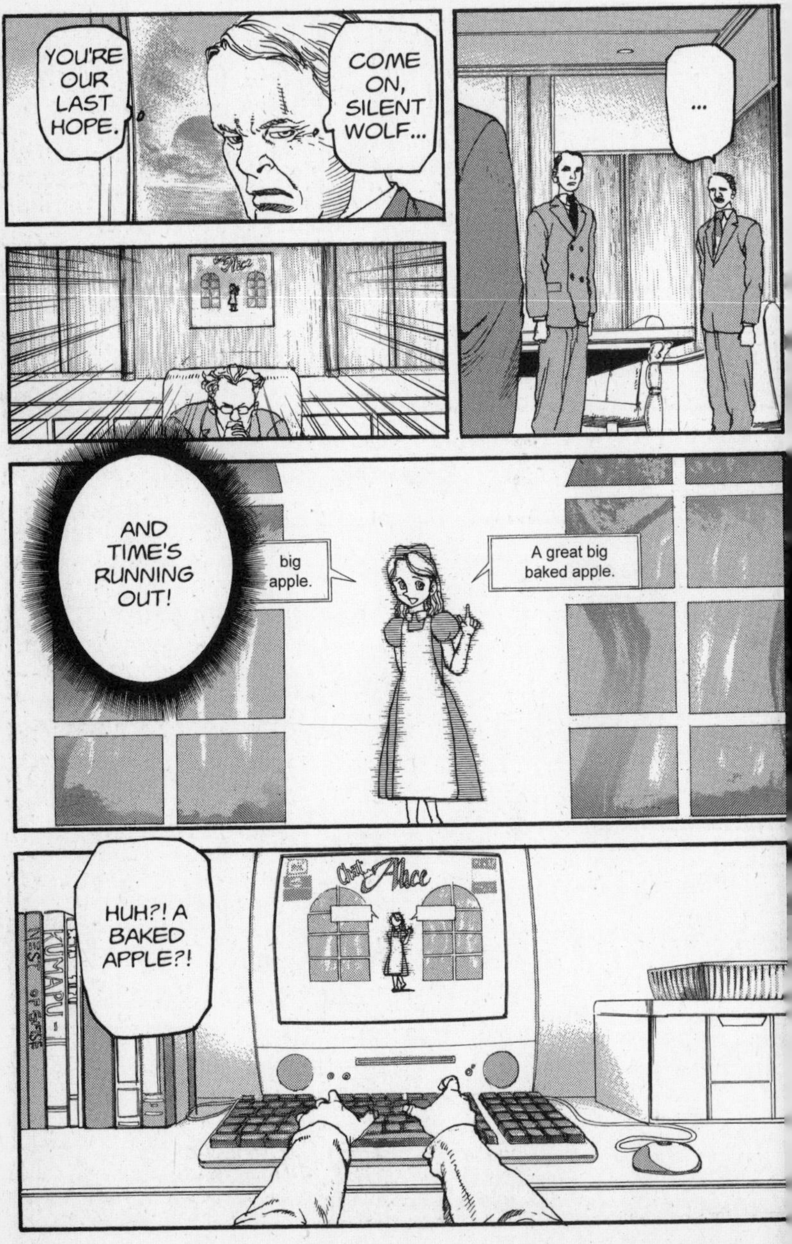
...
COME ON, SILENT WOLF...
YOU'RE OUR LAST HOPE.
AND TIME'S RUNNING OUT!
A great big baked apple.
big apple.
Chat Alice
HUH?! A BAKED APPLE?!

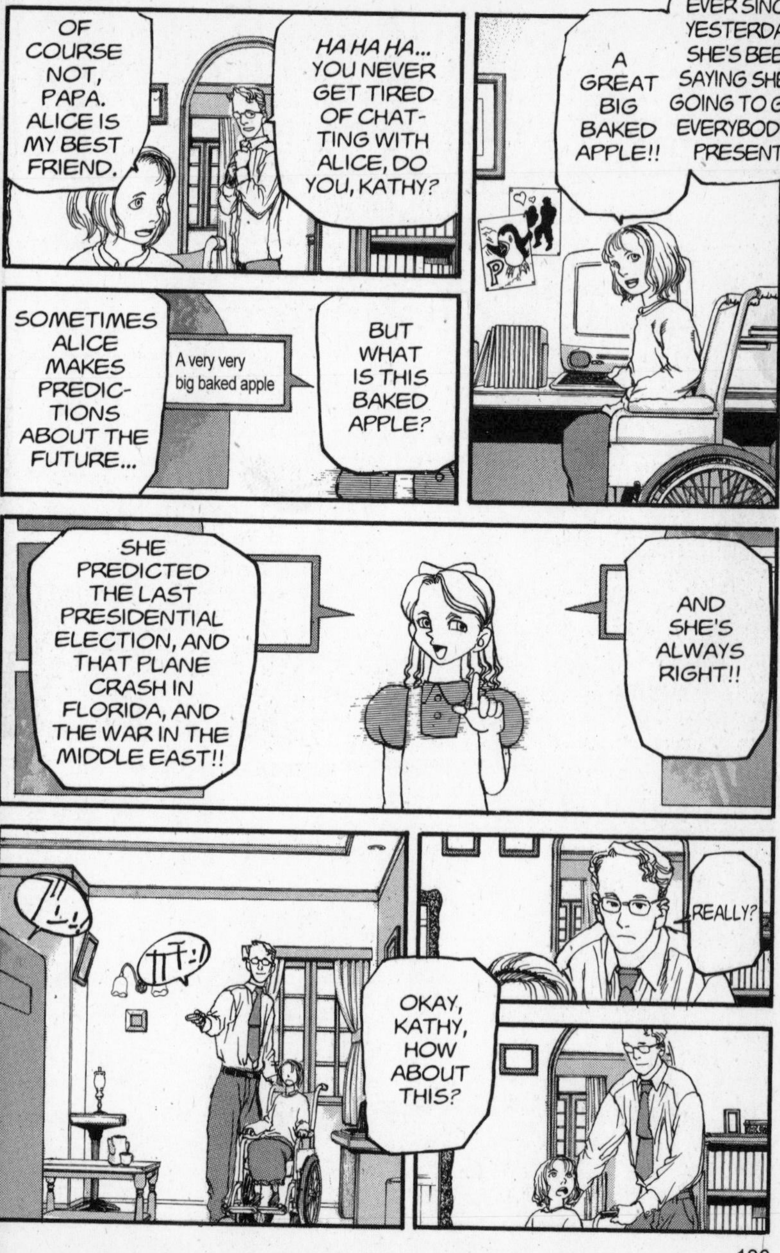
EVER SINCE YESTERDAY, SHE'S BEEN SAYING SHE'S GOING TO GIVE EVERYBODY A PRESENT.
A GREAT BIG BAKED APPLE!!
HA HA HA... YOU NEVER GET TIRED OF CHAT-TING WITH ALICE, DO YOU, KATHY?
OF COURSE NOT, PAPA. ALICE IS MY BEST FRIEND.
BUT WHAT IS THIS BAKED APPLE?
A very very big baked apple
SOMETIMES ALICE MAKES PREDIC-TIONS ABOUT THE FUTURE...
AND SHE'S ALWAYS RIGHT!!
SHE PREDICTED THE LAST PRESIDENTIAL ELECTION, AND THAT PLANE CRASH IN FLORIDA, AND THE WAR IN THE MIDDLE EAST!!
REALLY?
OKAY, KATHY, HOW ABOUT THIS?

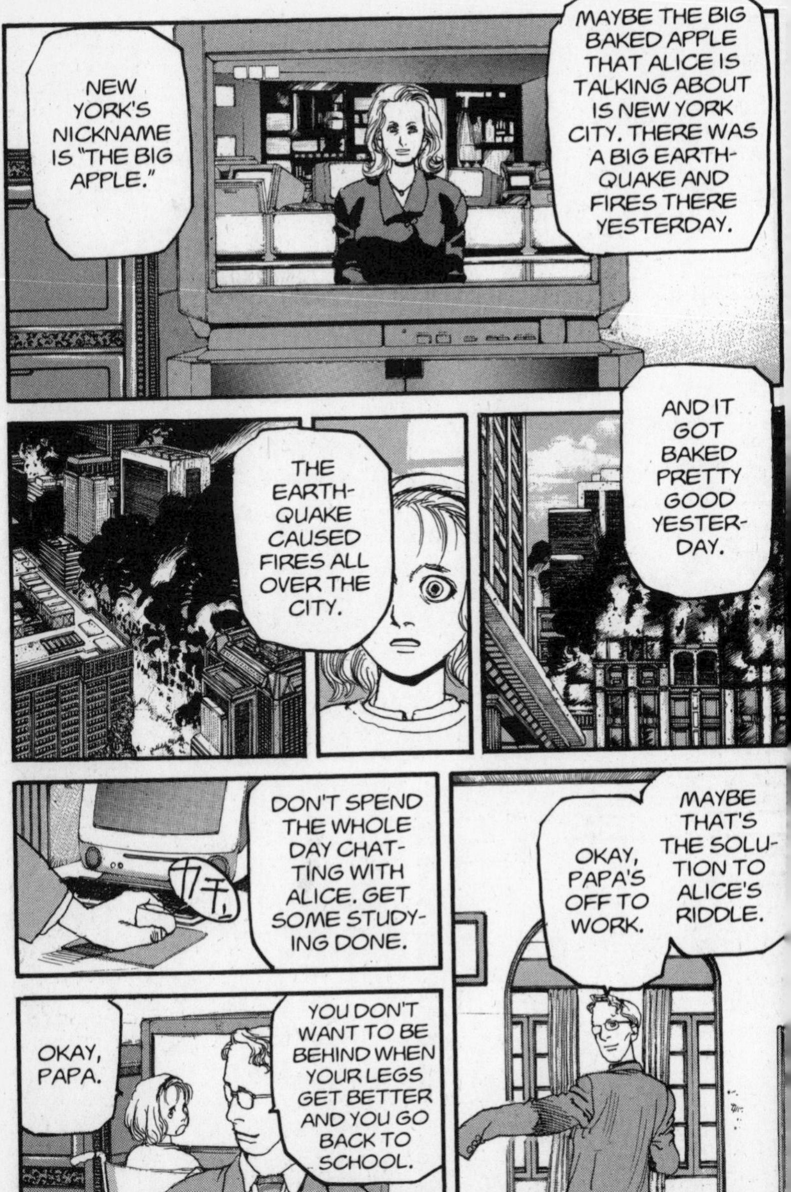

MAYBE THE BIG BAKED APPLE THAT ALICE IS TALKING ABOUT IS NEW YORK CITY. THERE WAS A BIG EARTH-QUAKE AND FIRES THERE YESTERDAY.
NEW YORK'S NICKNAME IS "THE BIG APPLE."
AND IT GOT BAKED PRETTY GOOD YESTER-DAY.
THE EARTH-QUAKE CAUSED FIRES ALL OVER THE CITY.
MAYBE THAT'S THE SOLU-TION TO ALICE'S RIDDLE.
OKAY, PAPA'S OFF TO WORK.
DON'T SPEND THE WHOLE DAY CHAT-TING WITH ALICE. GET SOME STUDY-ING DONE.
カチ
YOU DON'T WANT TO BE BEHIND WHEN YOUR LEGS GET BETTER AND YOU GO BACK TO SCHOOL.
OKAY, PAPA.

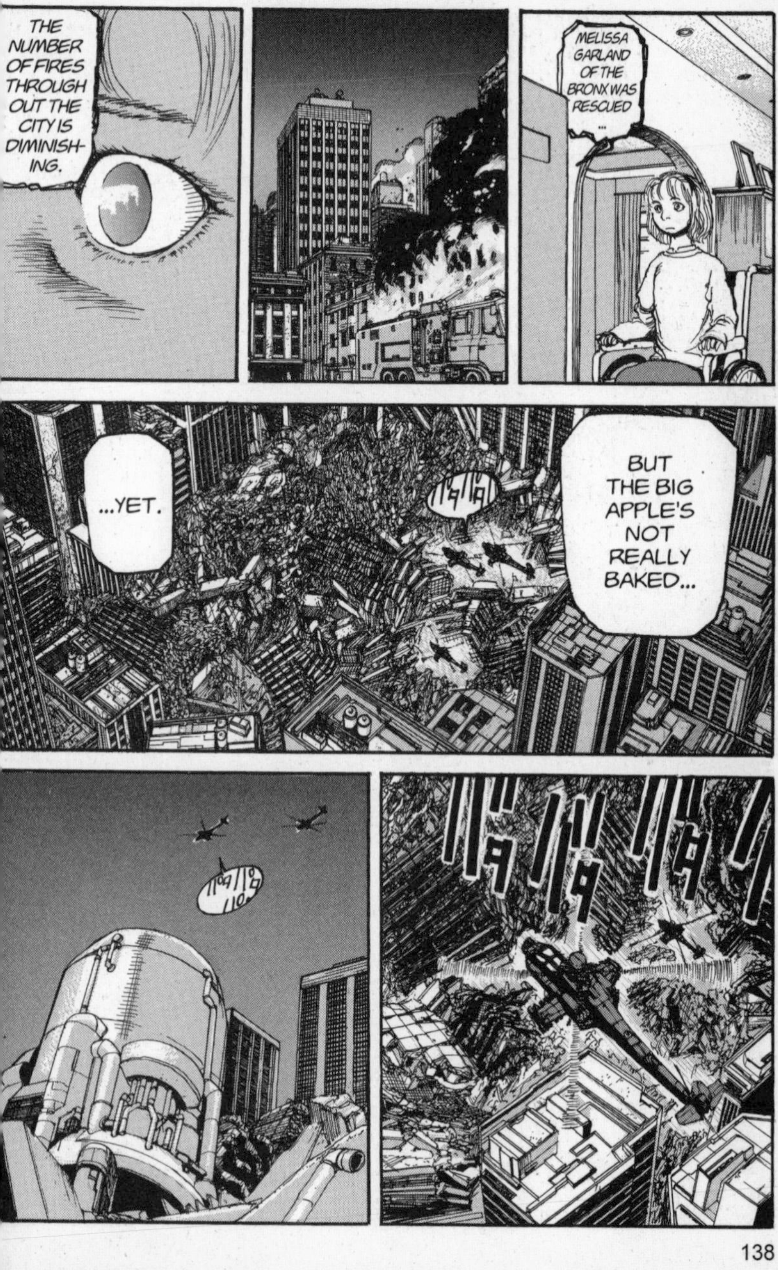
MELISSA GARLAND OF THE BRONX WAS RESCUED ...
THE NUMBER OF FIRES THROUGH OUT THE CITY IS DIMINISH-ING.
BUT THE BIG APPLE'S NOT REALLY BAKED...
...YET.

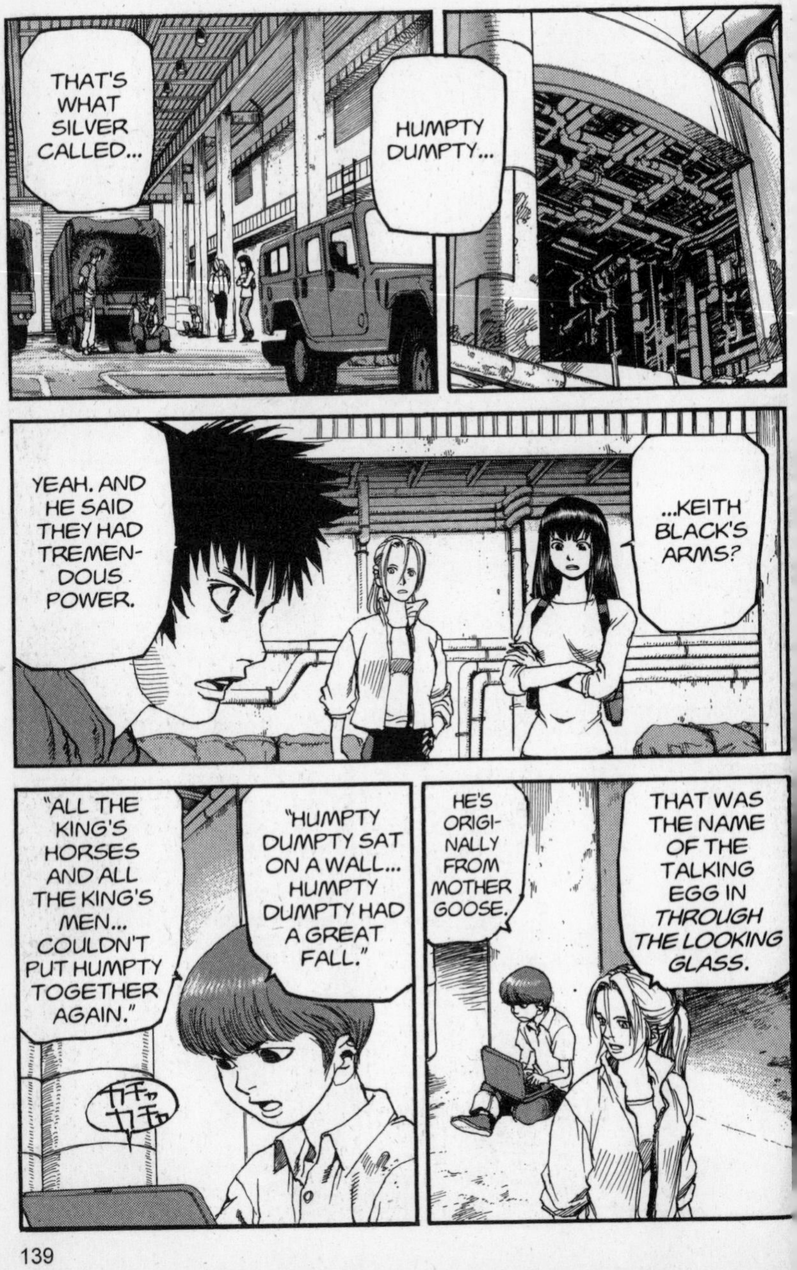
HUMPTY DUMPTY...
THAT'S WHAT SILVER CALLED...
...KEITH BLACK'S ARMS?
YEAH. AND HE SAID THEY HAD TREMENDOUS POWER.
THAT WAS THE NAME OF THE TALKING EGG IN *THROUGH THE LOOKING GLASS*.
HE'S ORIGINALLY FROM MOTHER GOOSE.
"HUMPTY DUMPTY SAT ON A WALL... HUMPTY DUMPTY HAD A GREAT FALL."
"ALL THE KING'S HORSES AND ALL THE KING'S MEN... COULDN'T PUT HUMPTY TOGETHER AGAIN."
カチャカチャ

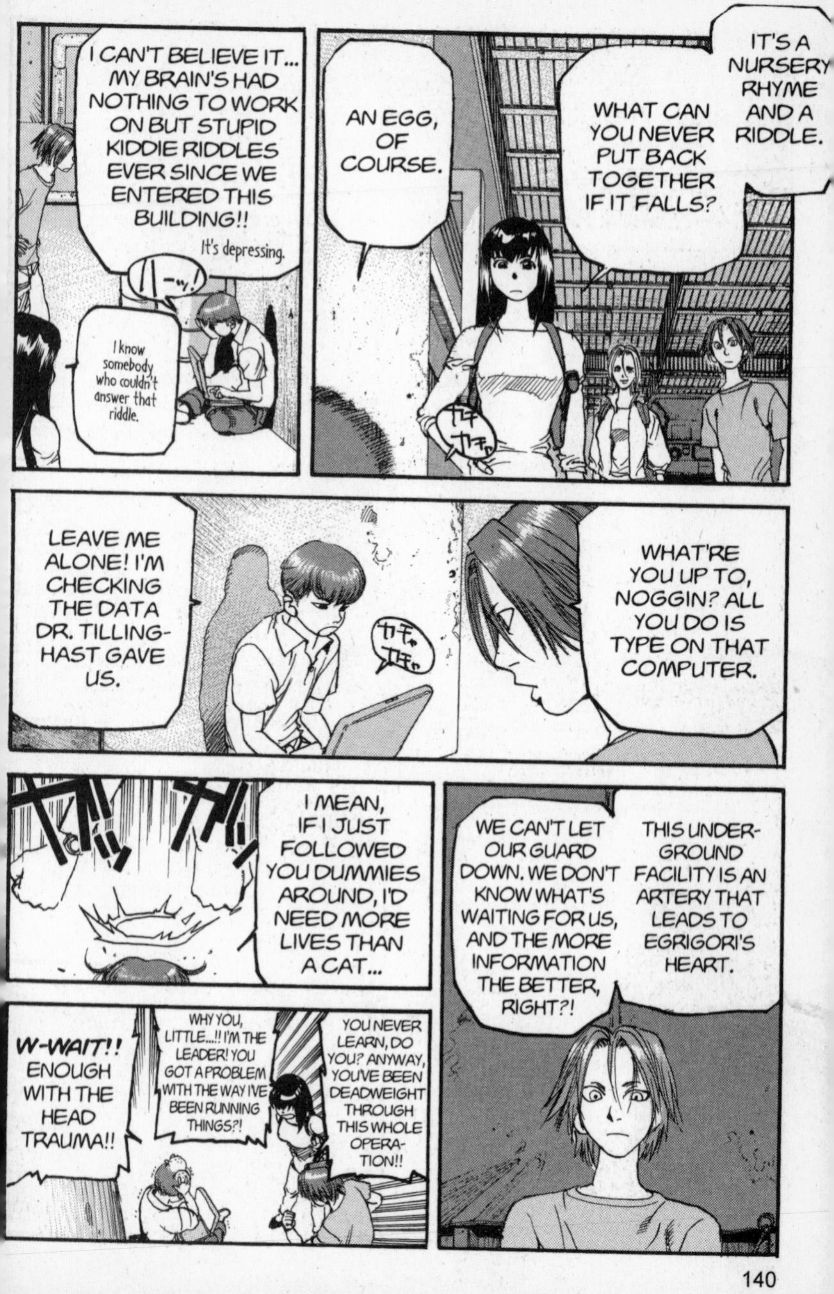
IT'S A NURSERY RHYME AND A RIDDLE.
WHAT CAN YOU NEVER PUT BACK TOGETHER IF IT FALLS?
AN EGG, OF COURSE.
I CAN'T BELIEVE IT... MY BRAIN'S HAD NOTHING TO WORK ON BUT STUPID KIDDIE RIDDLES EVER SINCE WE ENTERED THIS BUILDING!!
It's depressing.
I know somebody who couldn't answer that riddle.
WHAT'RE YOU UP TO, NOGGIN? ALL YOU DO IS TYPE ON THAT COMPUTER.
LEAVE ME ALONE! I'M CHECKING THE DATA DR. TILLING-HAST GAVE US.
THIS UNDER-GROUND FACILITY IS AN ARTERY THAT LEADS TO EGRIGORI'S HEART.
WE CAN'T LET OUR GUARD DOWN. WE DON'T KNOW WHAT'S WAITING FOR US, AND THE MORE INFORMATION THE BETTER, RIGHT?!
I MEAN, IF I JUST FOLLOWED YOU DUMMIES AROUND, I'D NEED MORE LIVES THAN A CAT...
YOU NEVER LEARN, DO YOU? ANYWAY, YOU'VE BEEN DEADWEIGHT THROUGH THIS WHOLE OPERA-TION!!
WHY YOU, LITTLE...!! I'M THE LEADER! YOU GOT A PROBLEM WITH THE WAY I'VE BEEN RUNNING THINGS?!
W-WAIT!! ENOUGH WITH THE HEAD TRAUMA!!

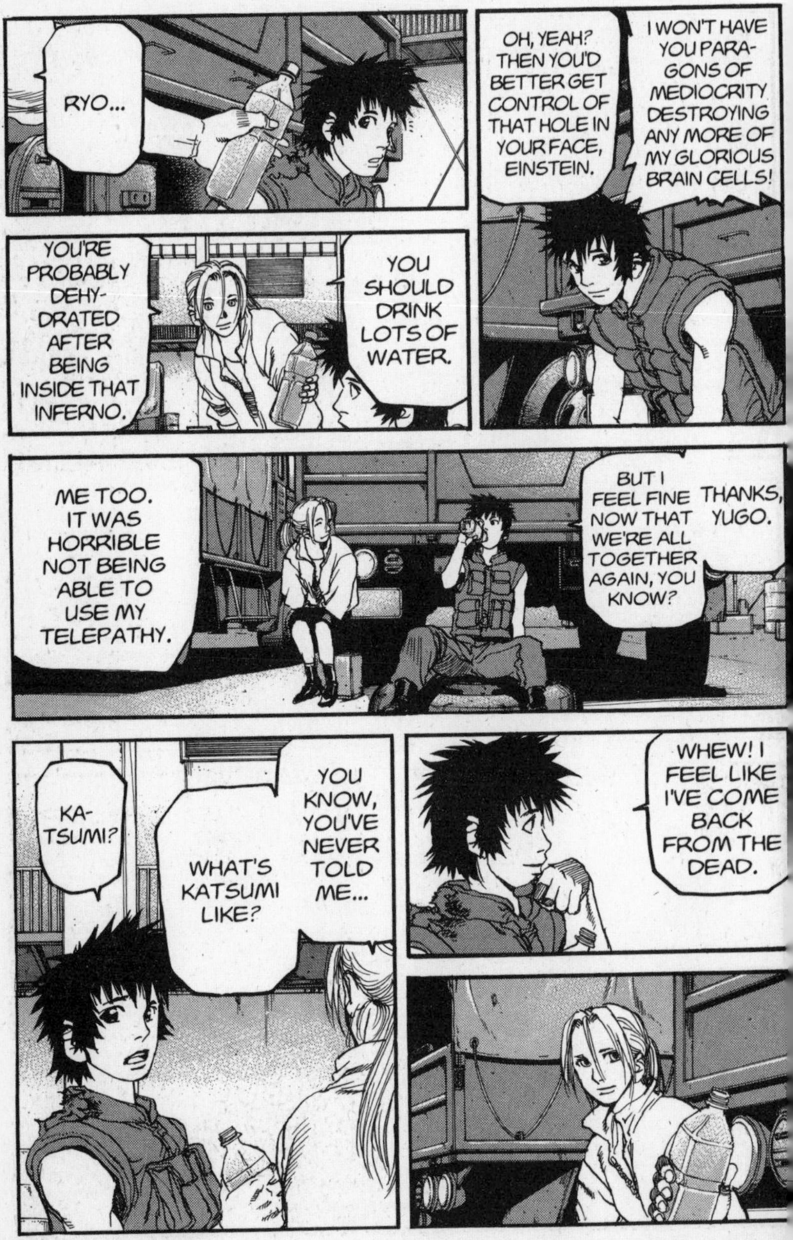
I WON'T HAVE YOU PARAGONS OF MEDIOCRITY DESTROYING ANY MORE OF MY GLORIOUS BRAIN CELLS!
OH, YEAH? THEN YOU'D BETTER GET CONTROL OF THAT HOLE IN YOUR FACE, EINSTEIN.
RYO...
YOU SHOULD DRINK LOTS OF WATER.
YOU'RE PROBABLY DEHY-DRATED AFTER BEING INSIDE THAT INFERNO.
THANKS, YUGO.
BUT I FEEL FINE NOW THAT WE'RE ALL TOGETHER AGAIN, YOU KNOW?
ME TOO. IT WAS HORRIBLE NOT BEING ABLE TO USE MY TELEPATHY.
WHEW! I FEEL LIKE I'VE COME BACK FROM THE DEAD.
YOU KNOW, YOU'VE NEVER TOLD ME...
WHAT'S KATSUMI LIKE?
KA-TSUMI?

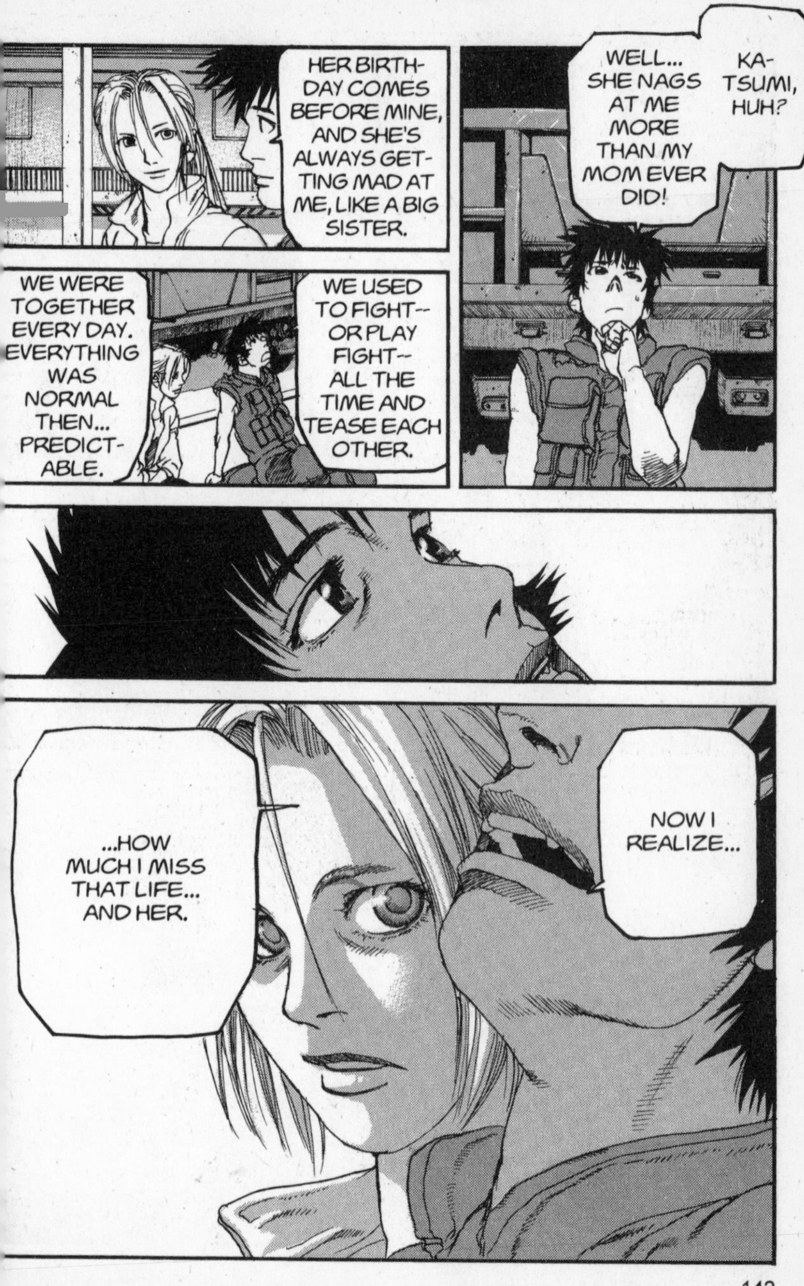
KA-TSUMI, HUH?
WELL... SHE NAGS AT ME MORE THAN MY MOM EVER DID!
HER BIRTH-DAY COMES BEFORE MINE, AND SHE'S ALWAYS GET-TING MAD AT ME, LIKE A BIG SISTER.
WE USED TO FIGHT-- OR PLAY FIGHT-- ALL THE TIME AND TEASE EACH OTHER.
WE WERE TOGETHER EVERY DAY. EVERYTHING WAS NORMAL THEN... PREDICT-ABLE.
NOW I REALIZE...
...HOW MUCH I MISS THAT LIFE... AND HER.

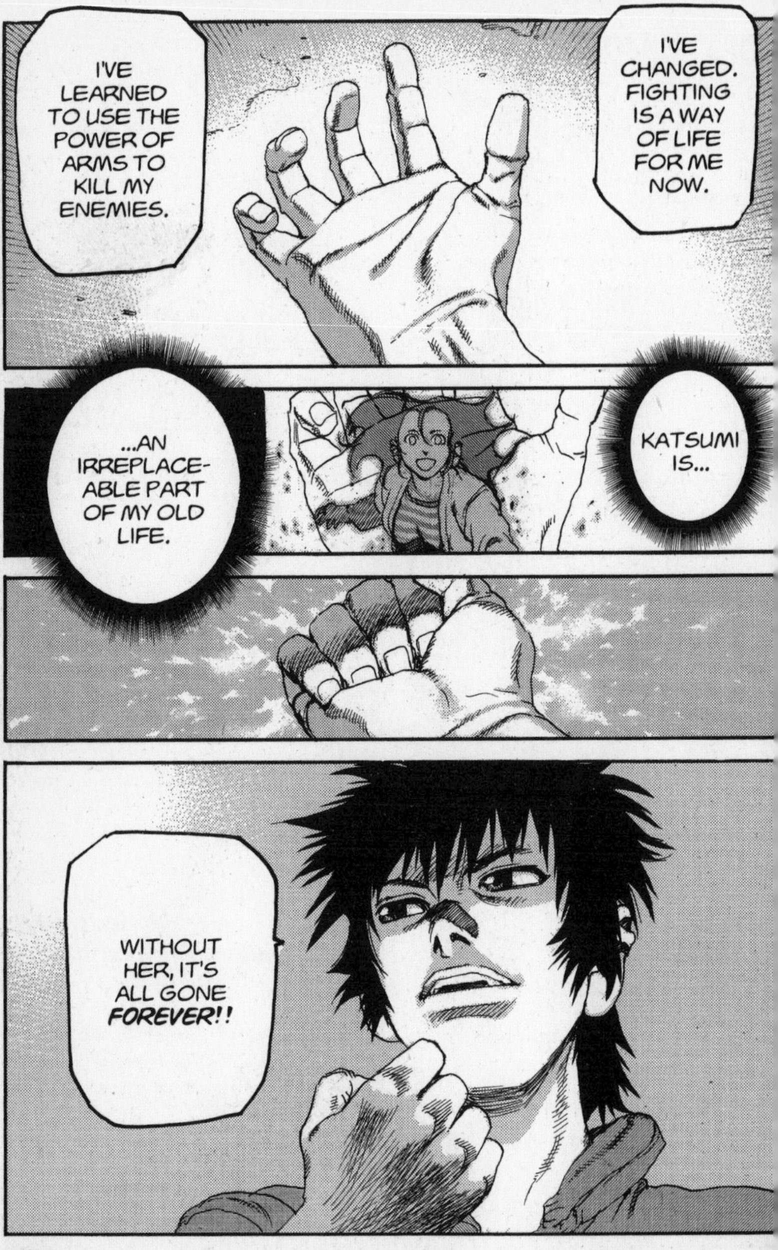
I'VE CHANGED. FIGHTING IS A WAY OF LIFE FOR ME NOW.
I'VE LEARNED TO USE THE POWER OF ARMS TO KILL MY ENEMIES.
KATSUMI IS...
...AN IRREPLACE-ABLE PART OF MY OLD LIFE.
WITHOUT HER, IT'S ALL GONE ***FOREVER***!!

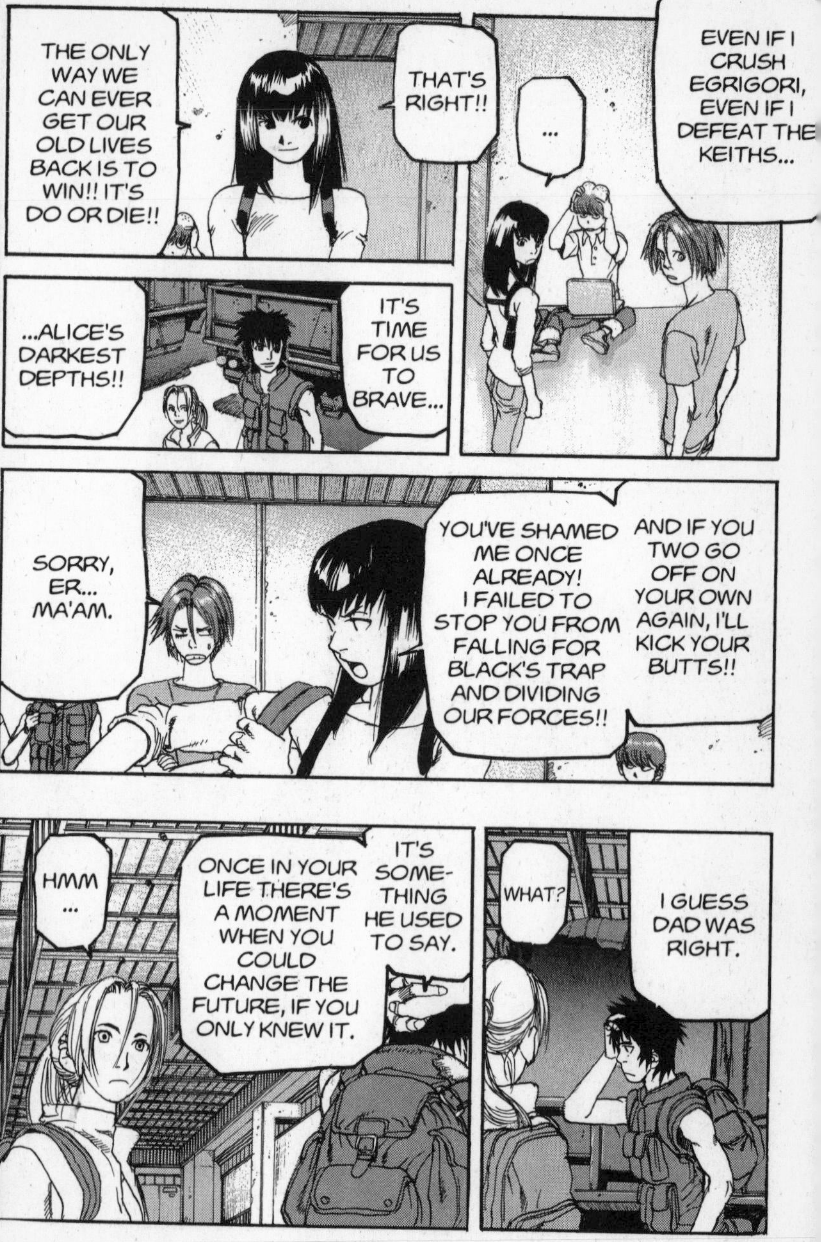
EVEN IF I CRUSH EGRIGORI, EVEN IF I DEFEAT THE KEITHS...
...
THAT'S RIGHT!!
THE ONLY WAY WE CAN EVER GET OUR OLD LIVES BACK IS TO WIN!! IT'S DO OR DIE!!
IT'S TIME FOR US TO BRAVE...
...ALICE'S DARKEST DEPTHS!!
AND IF YOU TWO GO OFF ON YOUR OWN AGAIN, I'LL KICK YOUR BUTTS!!
YOU'VE SHAMED ME ONCE ALREADY! I FAILED TO STOP YOU FROM FALLING FOR BLACK'S TRAP AND DIVIDING OUR FORCES!!
SORRY, ER... MA'AM.
I GUESS DAD WAS RIGHT.
WHAT?
IT'S SOME-THING HE USED TO SAY.
ONCE IN YOUR LIFE THERE'S A MOMENT WHEN YOU COULD CHANGE THE FUTURE, IF YOU ONLY KNEW IT.
HMM...

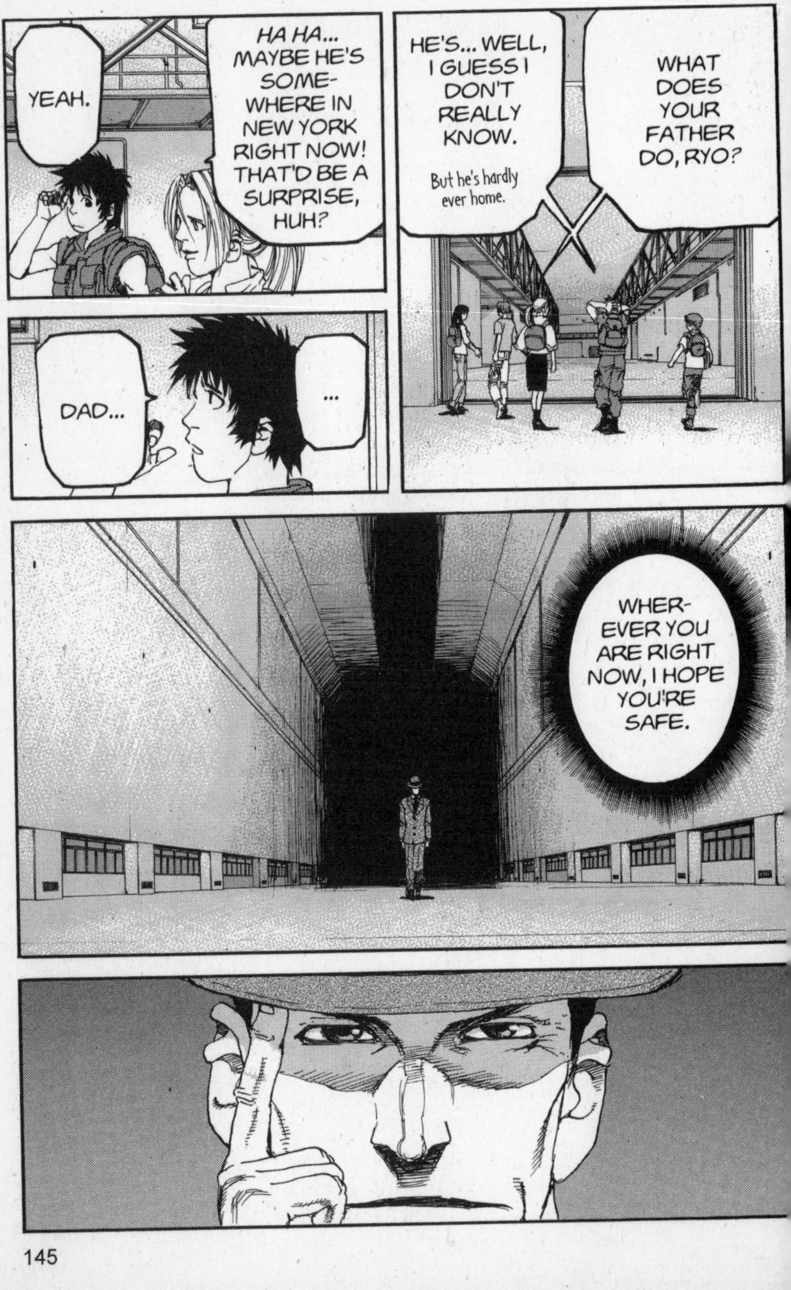
WHAT DOES YOUR FATHER DO, RYO?
HE'S... WELL, I GUESS I DON'T REALLY KNOW.
But he's hardly ever home.
HA HA... MAYBE HE'S SOME-WHERE IN NEW YORK RIGHT NOW! THAT'D BE A SURPRISE, HUH?
YEAH.
...
DAD...
WHER-EVER YOU ARE RIGHT NOW, I HOPE YOU'RE SAFE.

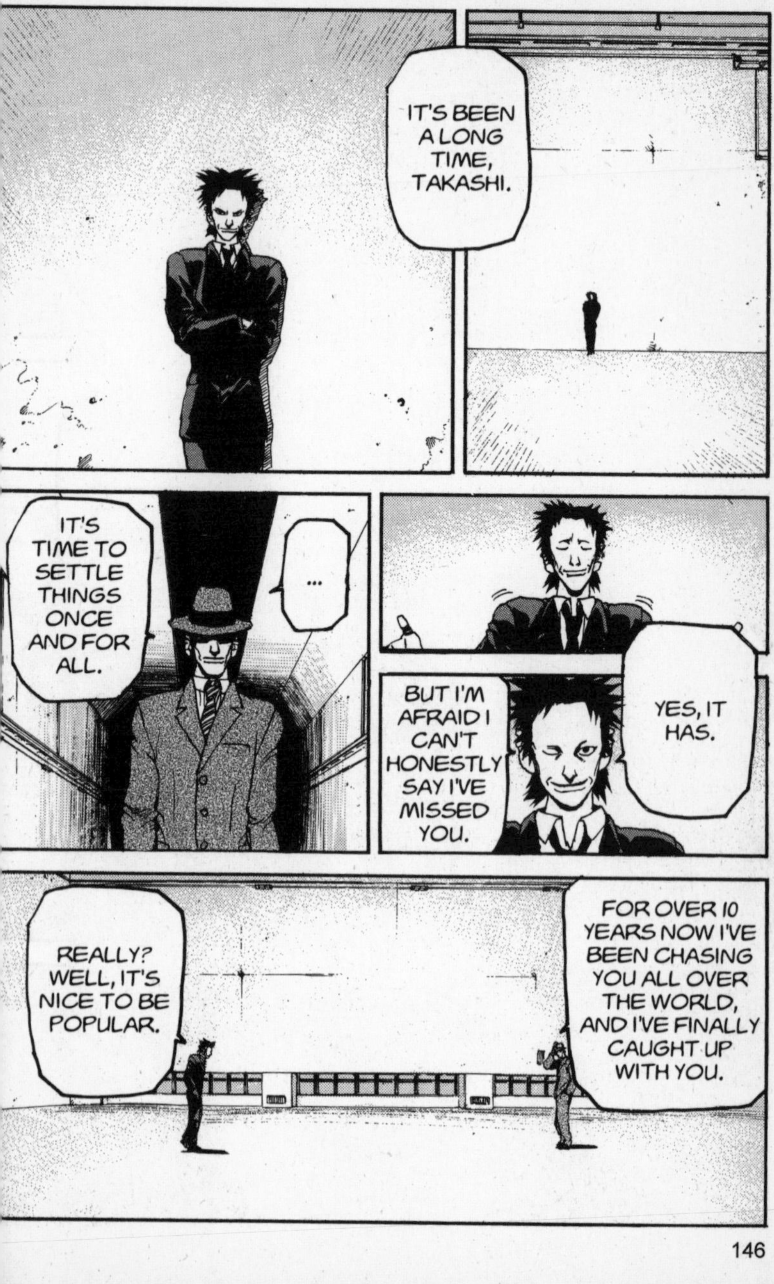
IT'S BEEN A LONG TIME, TAKASHI.
YES, IT HAS.
BUT I'M AFRAID I CAN'T HONESTLY SAY I'VE MISSED YOU.
...
IT'S TIME TO SETTLE THINGS ONCE AND FOR ALL.
FOR OVER 10 YEARS NOW I'VE BEEN CHASING YOU ALL OVER THE WORLD, AND I'VE FINALLY CAUGHT UP WITH YOU.
REALLY? WELL, IT'S NICE TO BE POPULAR.

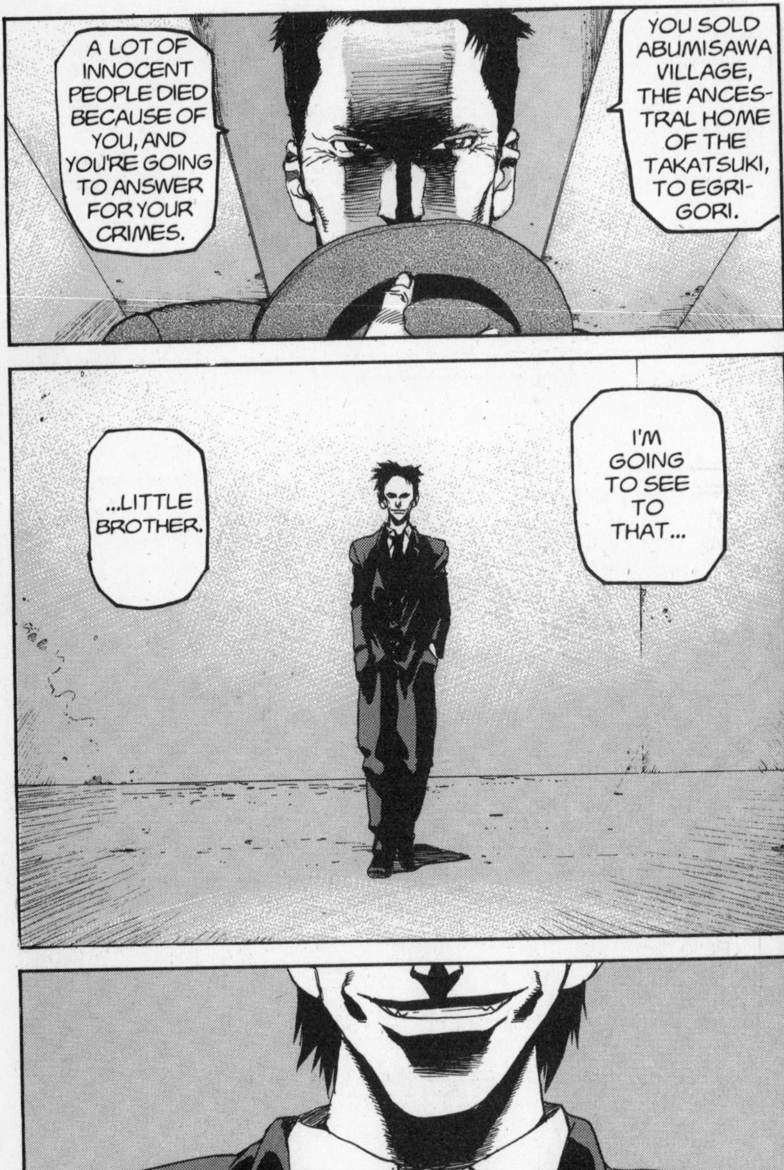
YOU SOLD ABUMISAWA VILLAGE, THE ANCES-TRAL HOME OF THE TAKATSUKI, TO EGRI-GORI.
A LOT OF INNOCENT PEOPLE DIED BECAUSE OF YOU, AND YOU'RE GOING TO ANSWER FOR YOUR CRIMES.
I'M GOING TO SEE TO THAT...
...LITTLE BROTHER.

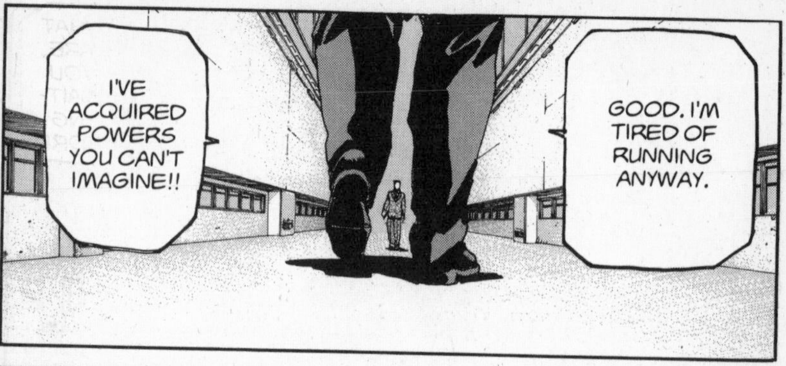
GOOD. I'M TIRED OF RUNNING ANYWAY.
I'VE ACQUIRED POWERS YOU CAN'T IMAGINE!!
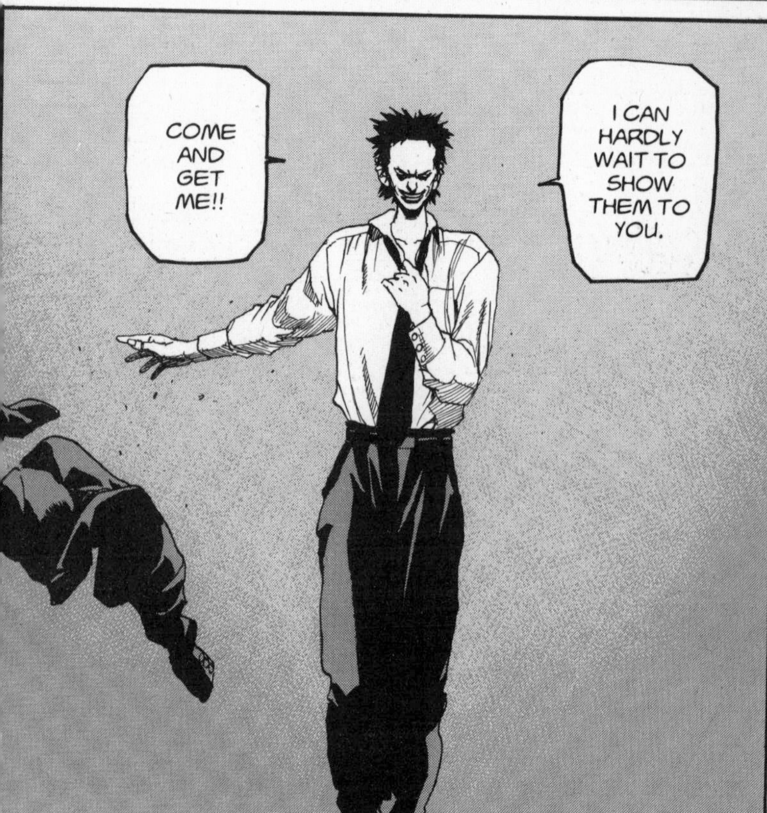
I CAN HARDLY WAIT TO SHOW THEM TO YOU.
COME AND GET ME!!

No. 9 DESTINY

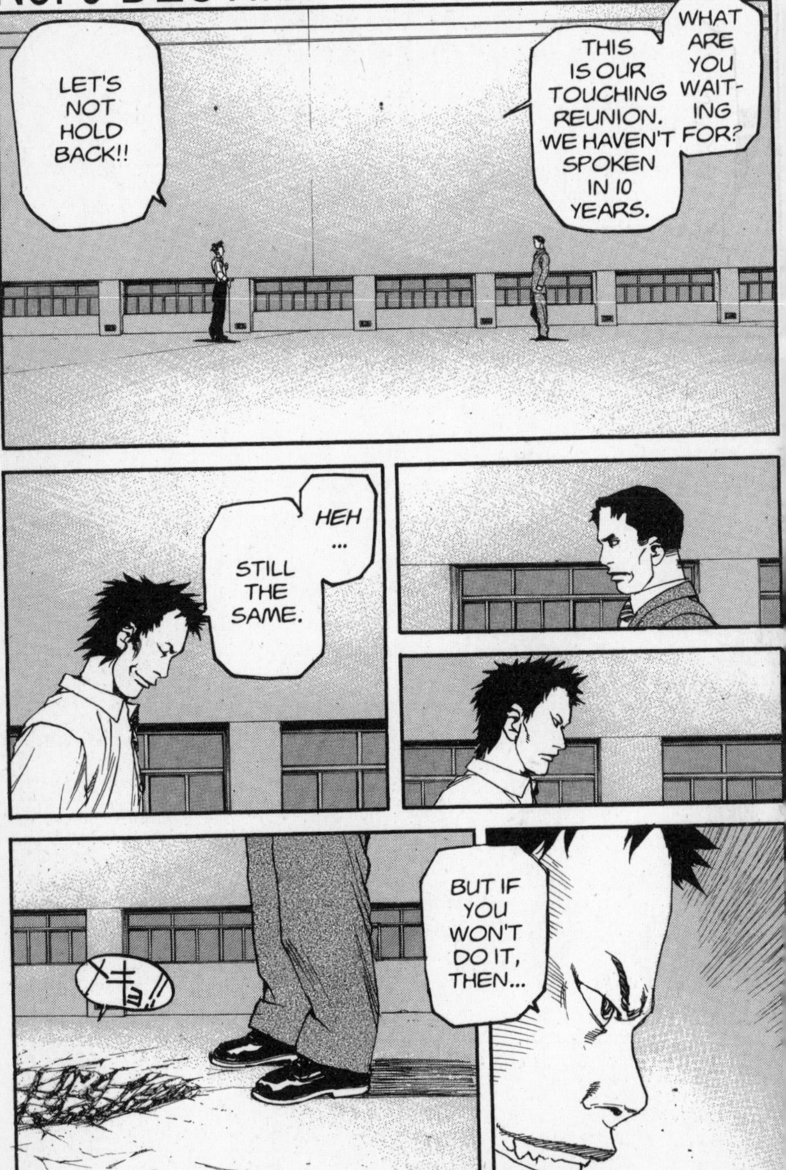
WHAT ARE YOU WAIT-ING FOR?
THIS IS OUR TOUCHING REUNION. WE HAVEN'T SPOKEN IN 10 YEARS.
LET'S NOT HOLD BACK!!
HEH... STILL THE SAME.
BUT IF YOU WON'T DO IT, THEN...
メキョ!!

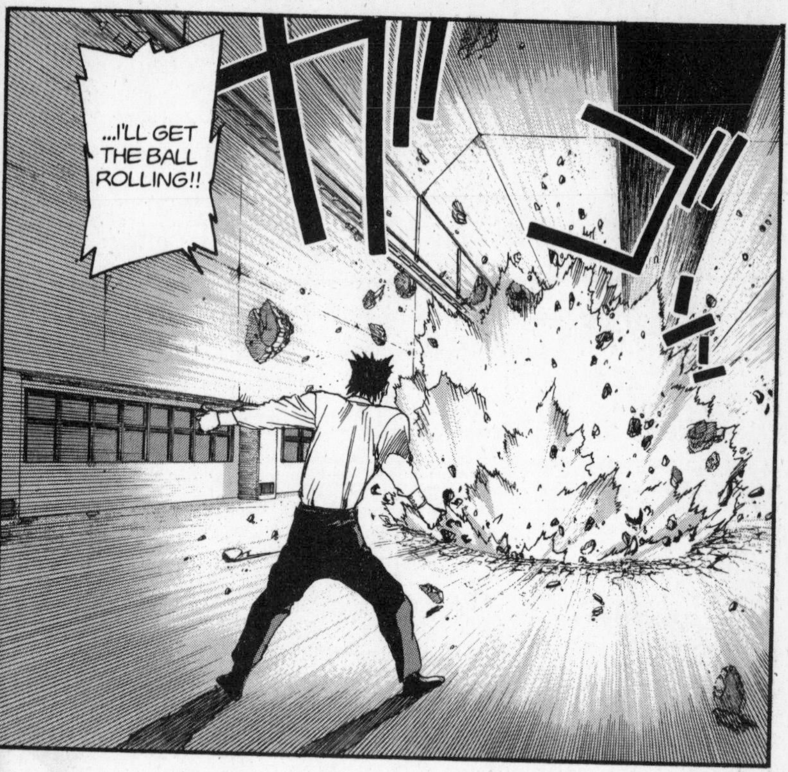
...I'LL GET THE BALL ROLLING!!

No. 9 DESTINY

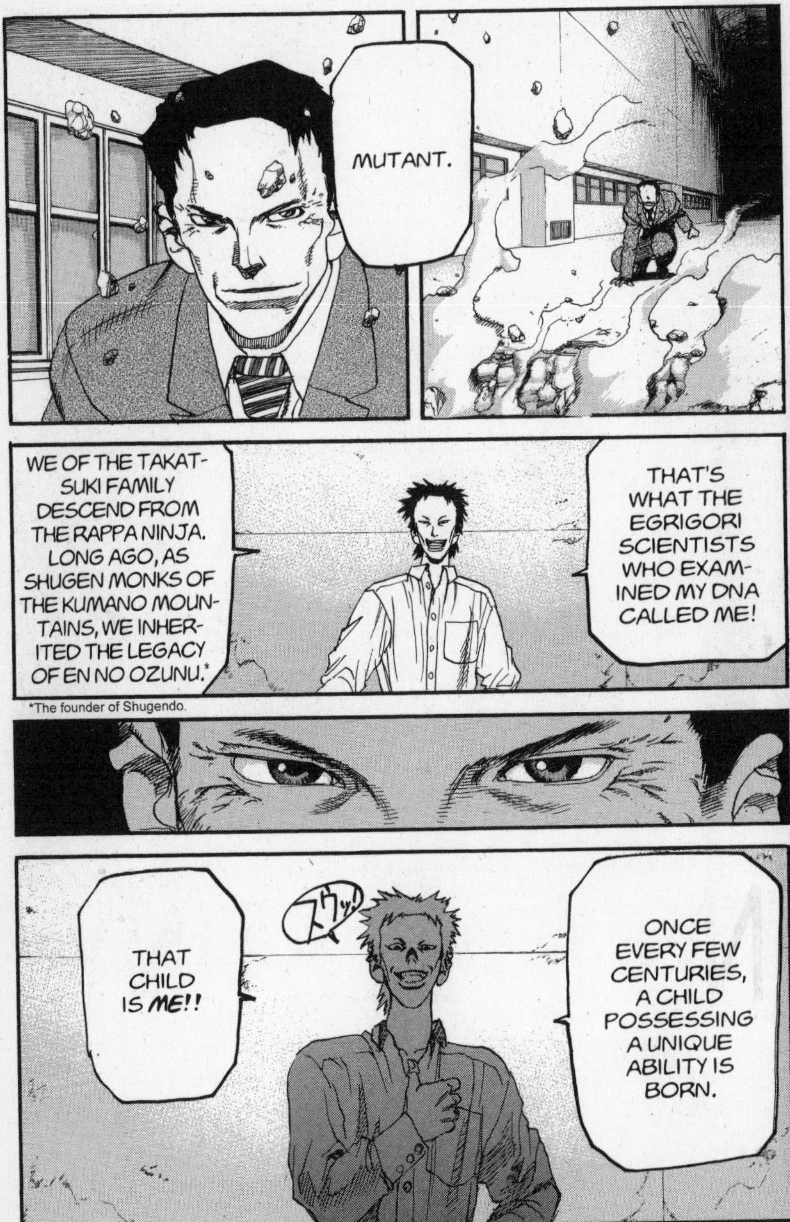
MUTANT.
THAT'S WHAT THE EGRIGORI SCIENTISTS WHO EXAMINED MY DNA CALLED ME!
WE OF THE TAKATSUKI FAMILY DESCEND FROM THE RAPPA NINJA. LONG AGO, AS SHUGEN MONKS OF THE KUMANO MOUNTAINS, WE INHERITED THE LEGACY OF EN NO OZUNU.*
ONCE EVERY FEW CENTURIES, A CHILD POSSESSING A UNIQUE ABILITY IS BORN.
スウッ!
THAT CHILD IS *ME!!*

*The founder of Shugendo.

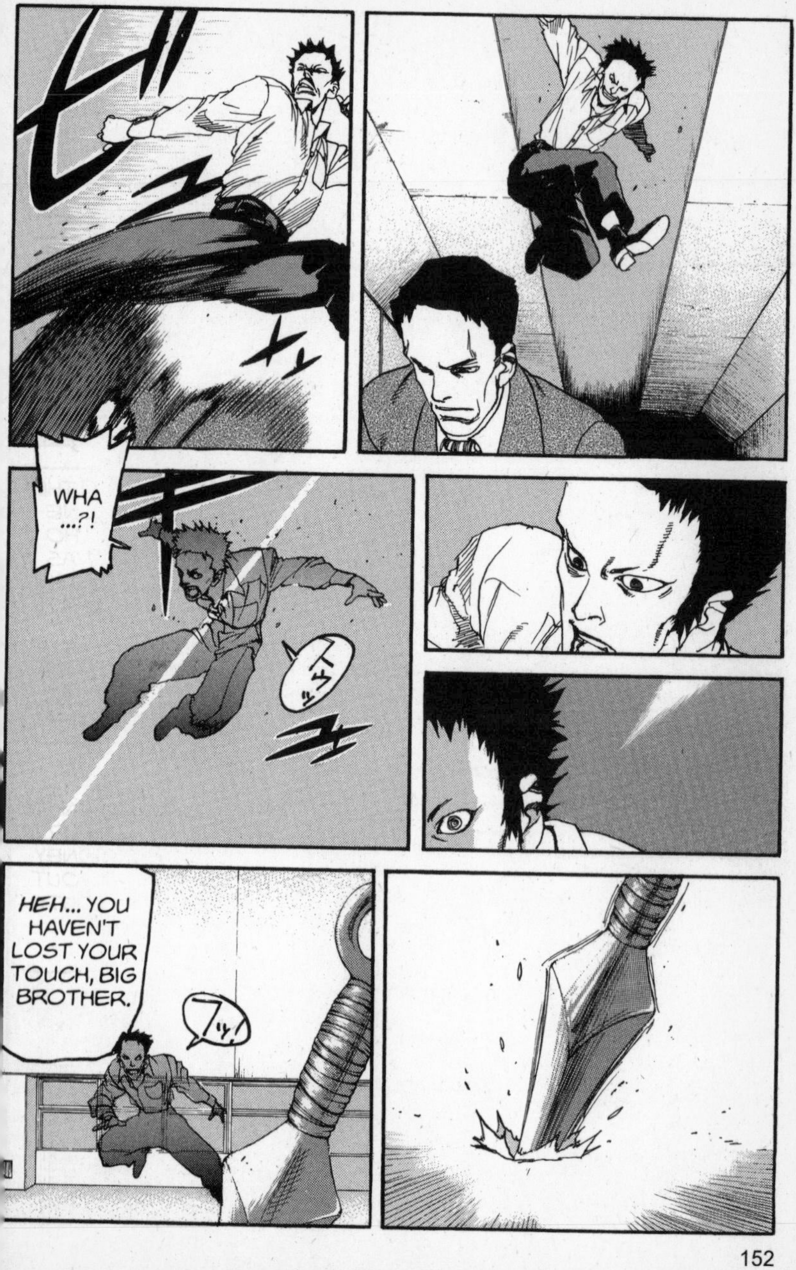
WHA ...?!
HEH... YOU HAVEN'T LOST YOUR TOUCH, BIG BROTHER.
フッ!

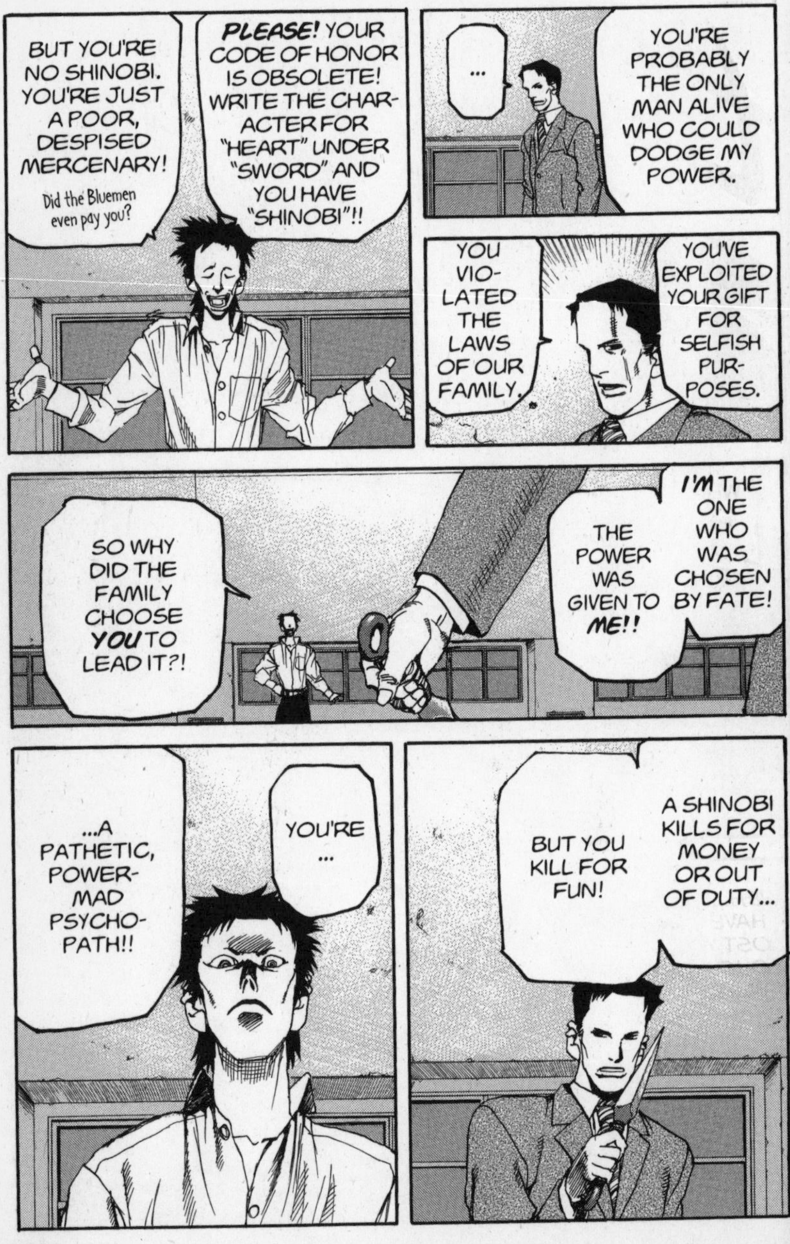
YOU'RE PROBABLY THE ONLY MAN ALIVE WHO COULD DODGE MY POWER.
...
YOU'VE EXPLOITED YOUR GIFT FOR SELFISH PURPOSES.
YOU VIOLATED THE LAWS OF OUR FAMILY.
PLEASE! YOUR CODE OF HONOR IS OBSOLETE! WRITE THE CHARACTER FOR "HEART" UNDER "SWORD" AND YOU HAVE "SHINOBI"!!
BUT YOU'RE NO SHINOBI. YOU'RE JUST A POOR, DESPISED MERCENARY!
Did the Bluemen even pay you?
I'M THE ONE WHO WAS CHOSEN BY FATE!
THE POWER WAS GIVEN TO *ME!!*
SO WHY DID THE FAMILY CHOOSE *YOU* TO LEAD IT?!
A SHINOBI KILLS FOR MONEY OR OUT OF DUTY...
BUT YOU KILL FOR FUN!
YOU'RE ...
...A PATHETIC, POWER-MAD PSYCHOPATH!!

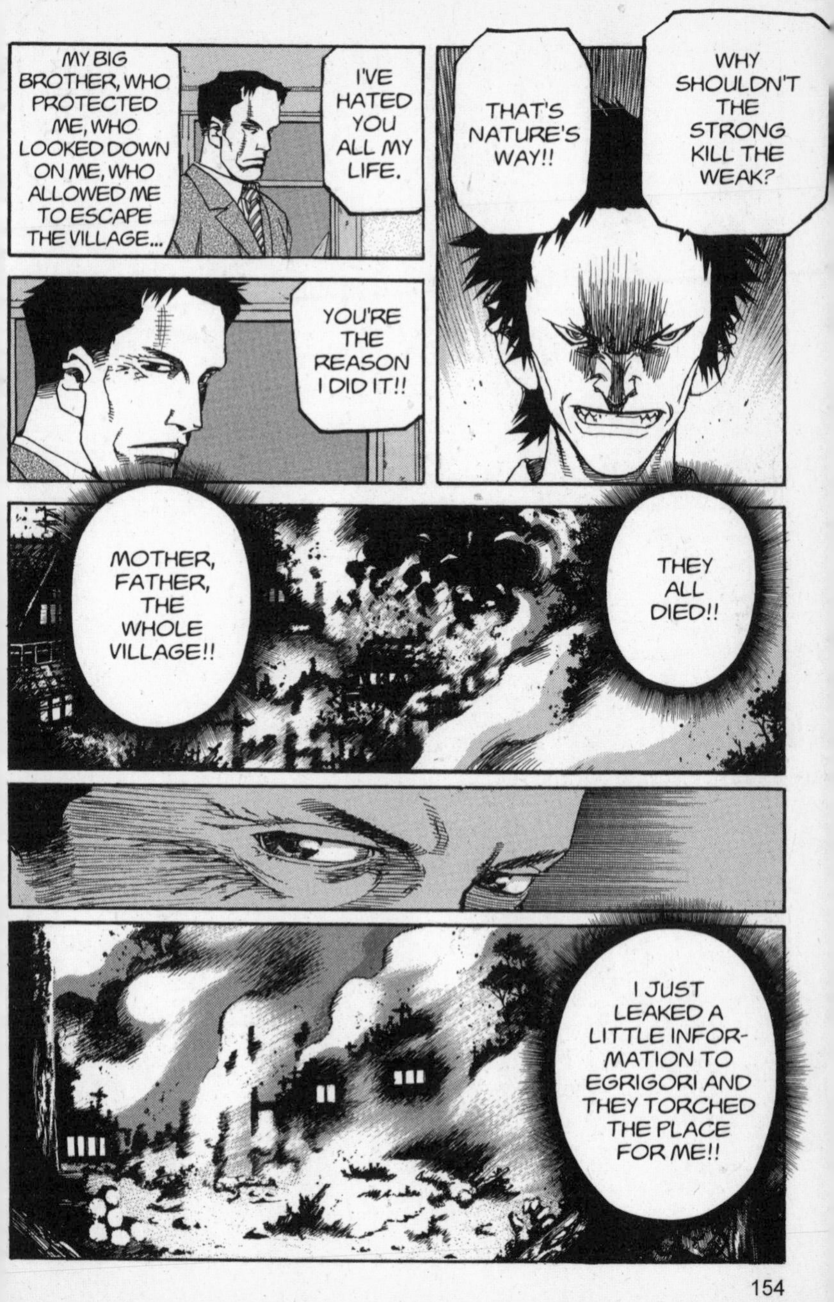
WHY SHOULDN'T THE STRONG KILL THE WEAK?
THAT'S NATURE'S WAY!!
I'VE HATED YOU ALL MY LIFE.
MY BIG BROTHER, WHO PROTECTED ME, WHO LOOKED DOWN ON ME, WHO ALLOWED ME TO ESCAPE THE VILLAGE...
YOU'RE THE REASON I DID IT!!
MOTHER, FATHER, THE WHOLE VILLAGE!!
THEY ALL DIED!!
I JUST LEAKED A LITTLE INFOR-MATION TO EGRIGORI AND THEY TORCHED THE PLACE FOR ME!!

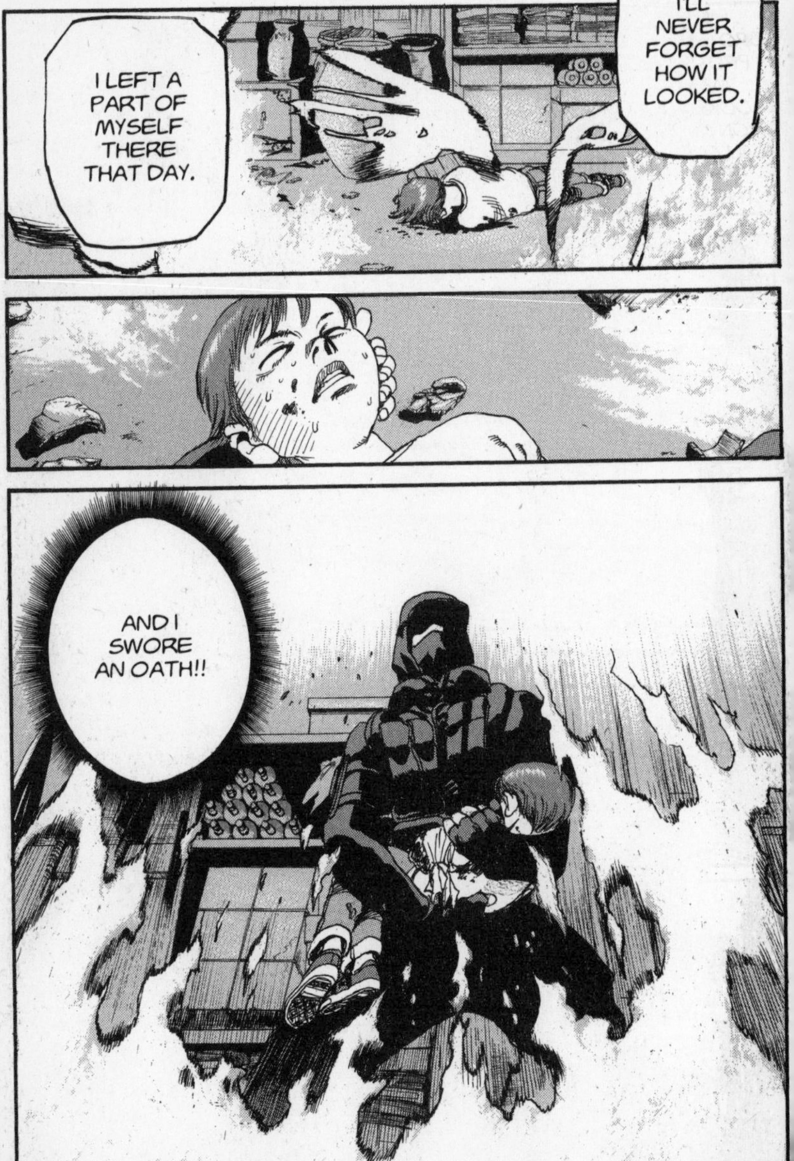
I'LL NEVER FORGET HOW IT LOOKED.
I LEFT A PART OF MYSELF THERE THAT DAY.
AND I SWORE AN OATH!!

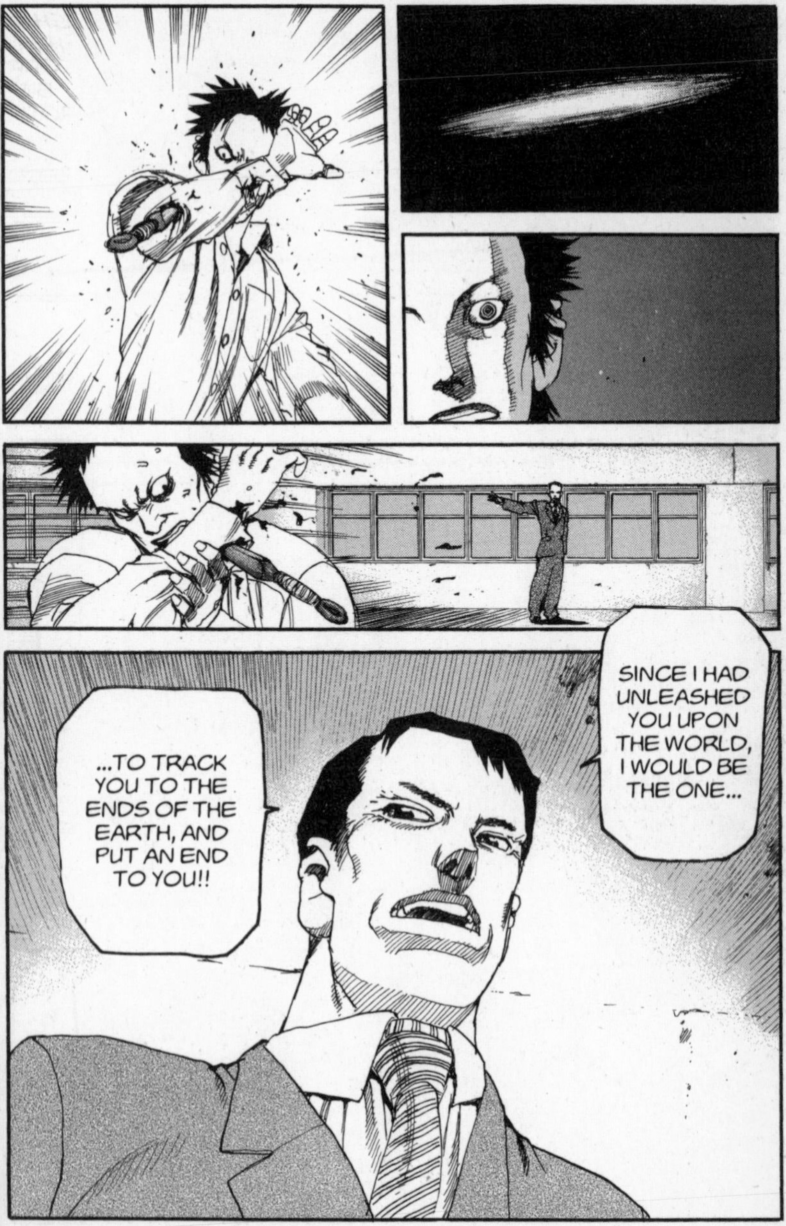
SINCE I HAD UNLEASHED YOU UPON THE WORLD, I WOULD BE THE ONE...
...TO TRACK YOU TO THE ENDS OF THE EARTH, AND PUT AN END TO YOU!!

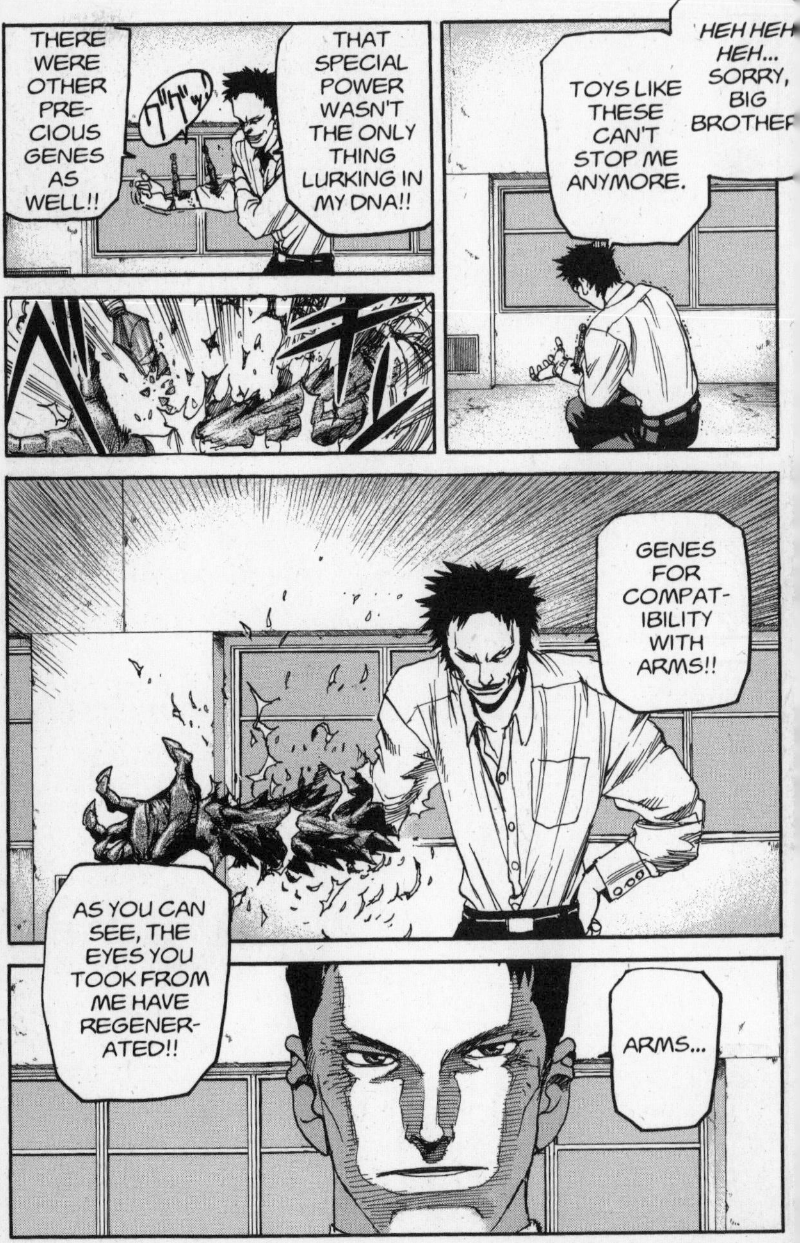
HEH HEH HEH... SORRY, BIG BROTHER
TOYS LIKE THESE CAN'T STOP ME ANYMORE.
THAT SPECIAL POWER WASN'T THE ONLY THING LURKING IN MY DNA!!
THERE WERE OTHER PRE-CIOUS GENES AS WELL!!
GENES FOR COMPAT-IBILITY WITH ARMS!!
AS YOU CAN SEE, THE EYES YOU TOOK FROM ME HAVE REGENER-ATED!!
ARMS...

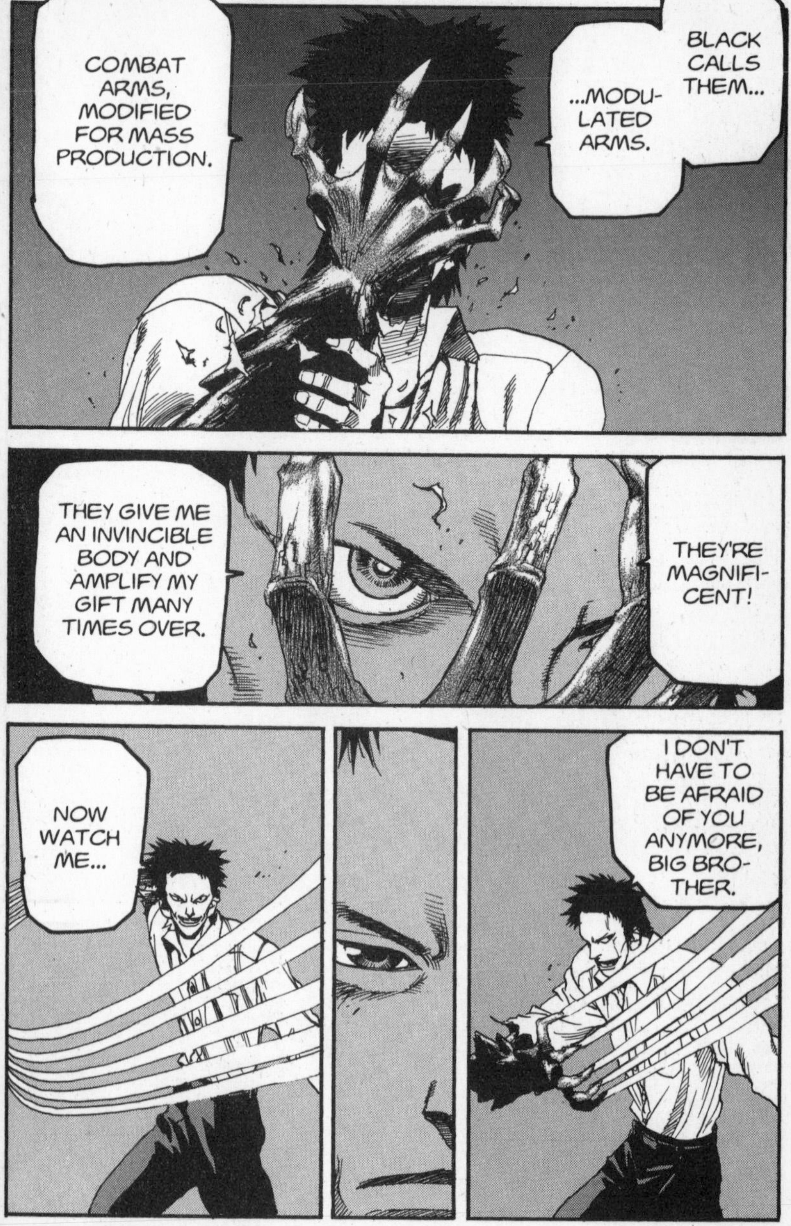
BLACK CALLS THEM...
...MODU-LATED ARMS.
COMBAT ARMS, MODIFIED FOR MASS PRODUCTION.
THEY'RE MAGNIFI-CENT!
THEY GIVE ME AN INVINCIBLE BODY AND AMPLIFY MY GIFT MANY TIMES OVER.
I DON'T HAVE TO BE AFRAID OF YOU ANYMORE, BIG BRO-THER.
NOW WATCH ME...

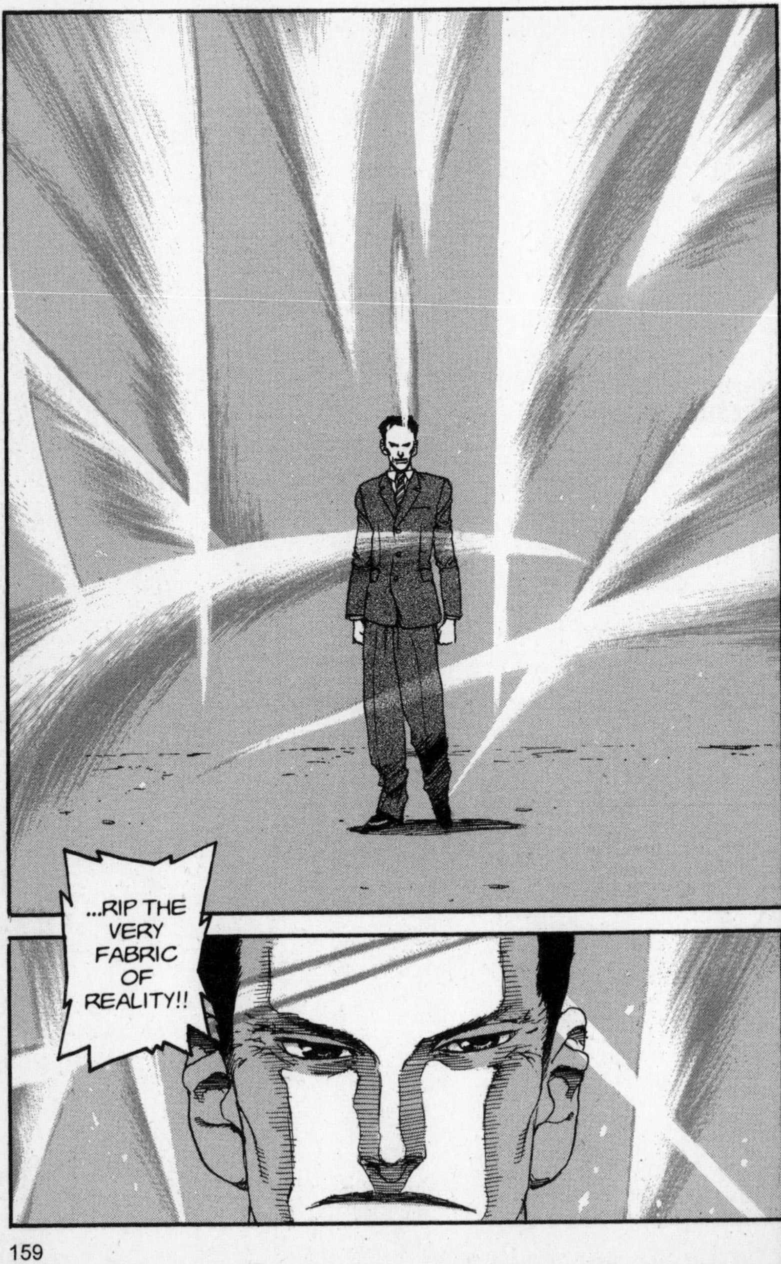
...RIP THE VERY FABRIC OF REALITY!!

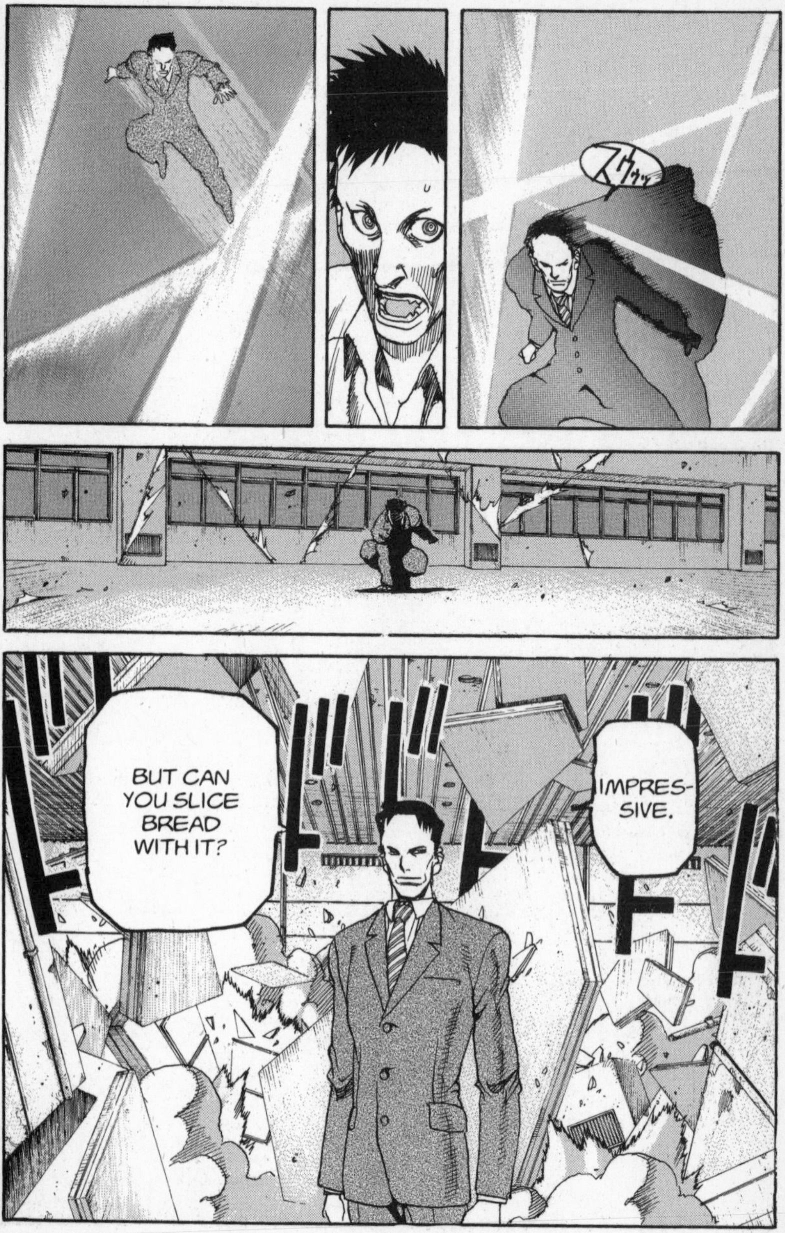
IMPRES-SIVE.
BUT CAN YOU SLICE BREAD WITH IT?

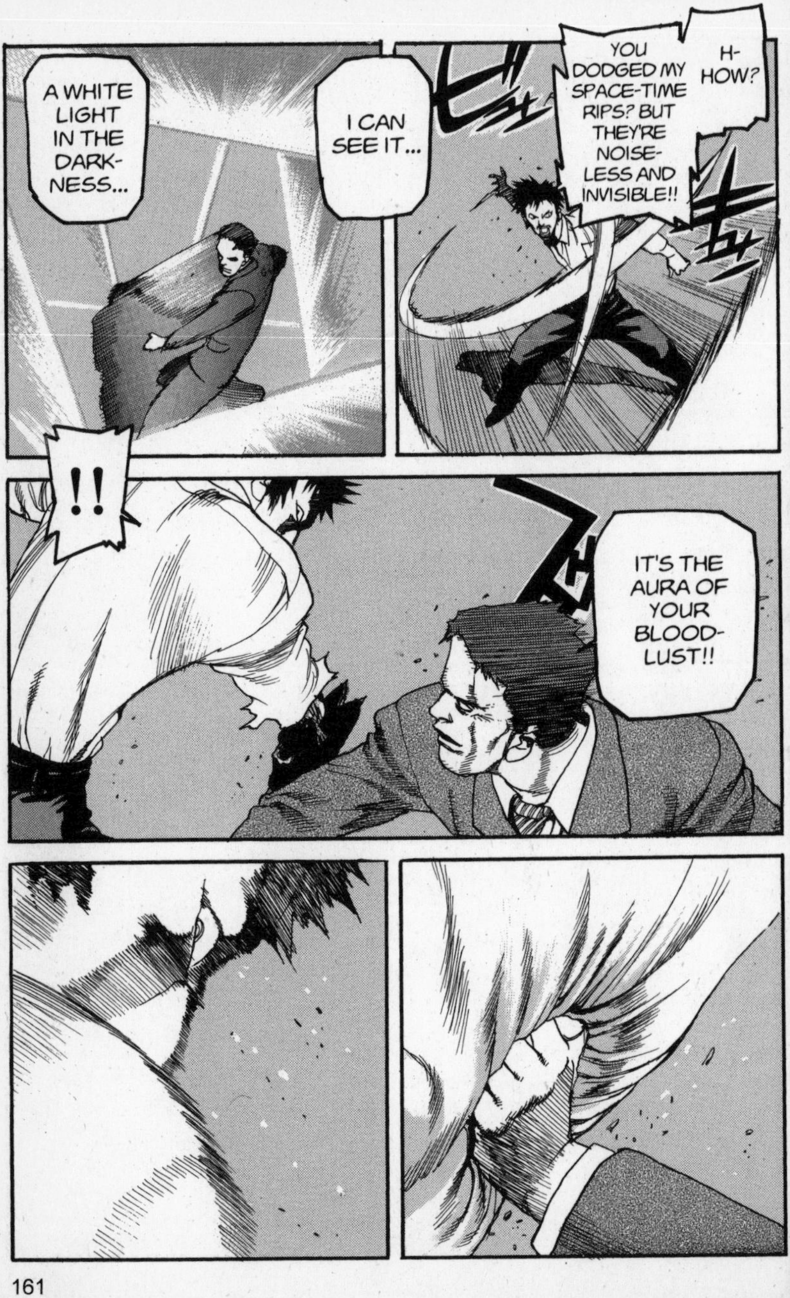
H- HOW?
YOU DODGED MY SPACE-TIME RIPS? BUT THEY'RE NOISE-LESS AND INVISIBLE!!
I CAN SEE IT...
A WHITE LIGHT IN THE DARK-NESS...
IT'S THE AURA OF YOUR BLOOD-LUST!!
!!

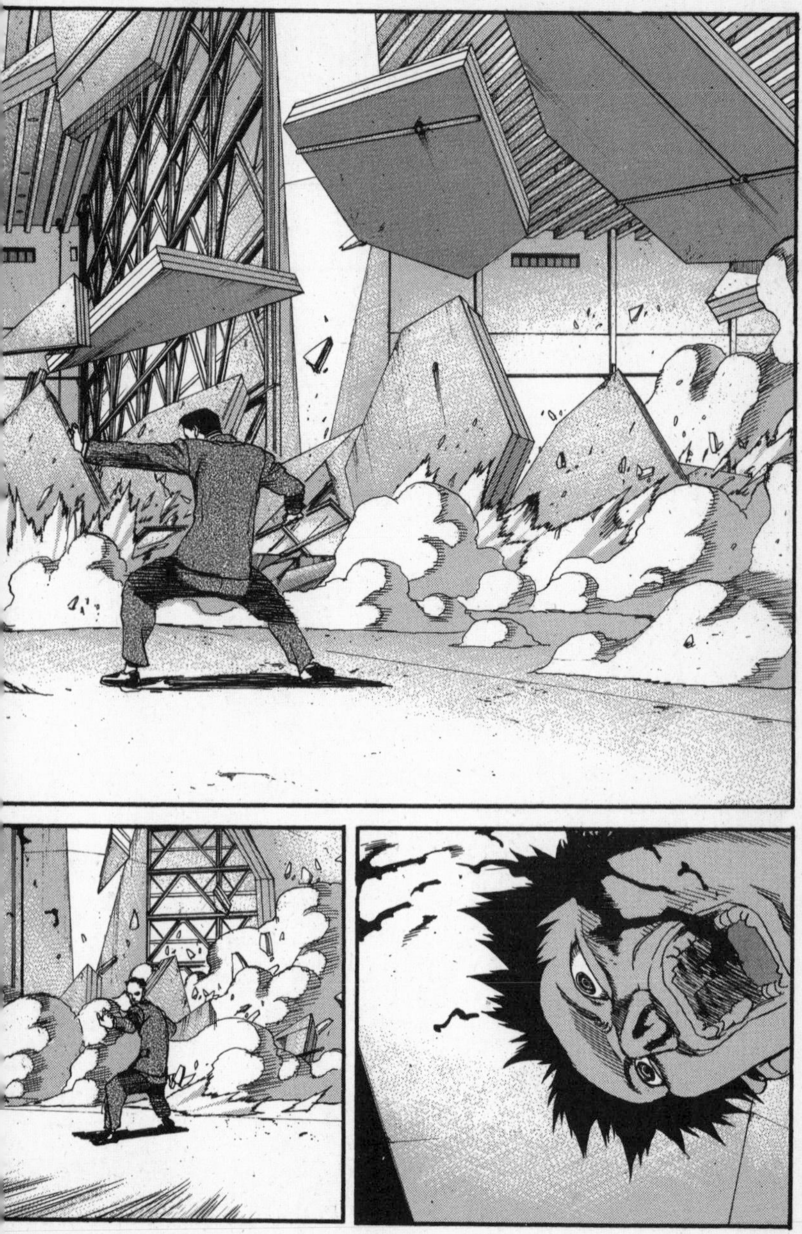

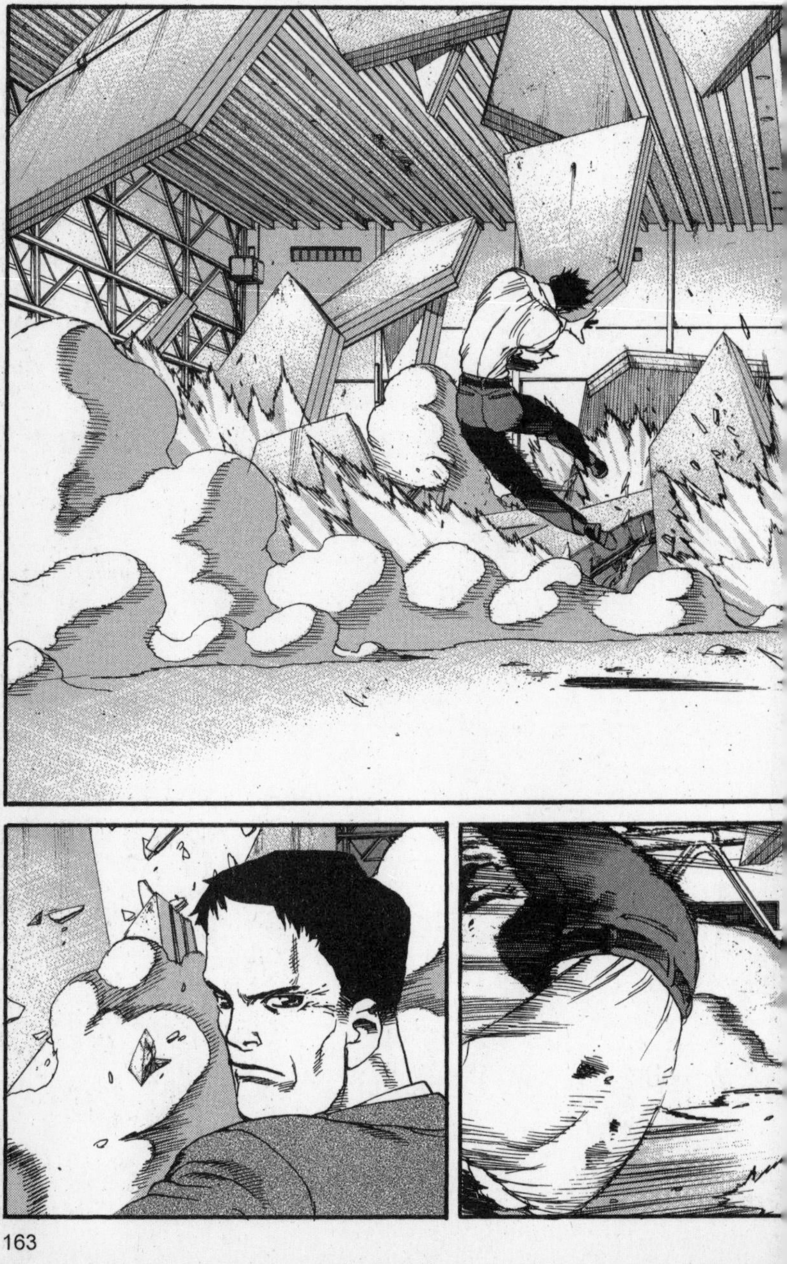

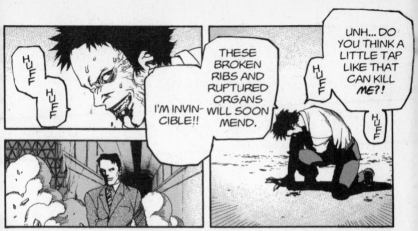

UNH... DO YOU THINK A LITTLE TAP LIKE THAT CAN KILL ME?!
HUFF
HUFF
THESE BROKEN RIBS AND RUPTURED ORGANS WILL SOON MEND.
I'M INVINCIBLE!!
HUFF
HUFF
RECOGNIZE THIS?
I PICKED IT UP IN THE GRAND CANYON.
IT'S A LITTLE DRIED OUT, BUT IT'LL DO THE JOB.
...
I WASN'T PLANNING TO USE IT ON YOU ORIGINALLY, BUT...
N-NO... IT CAN'T BE!!
THAT'S RIGHT. IT'S ONE OF THE JABBERWOCK'S CLAWS.
ONE SCRATCH FROM THIS, AND YOUR REGENERATIVE POWERS ARE HISTORY--AND SO ARE YOUR ARMS!!

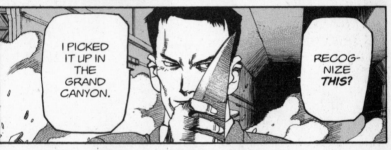

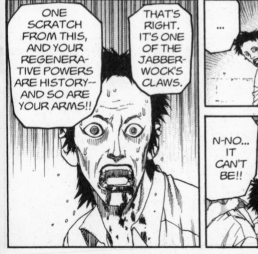

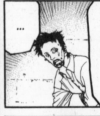

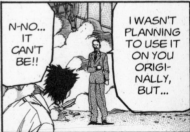

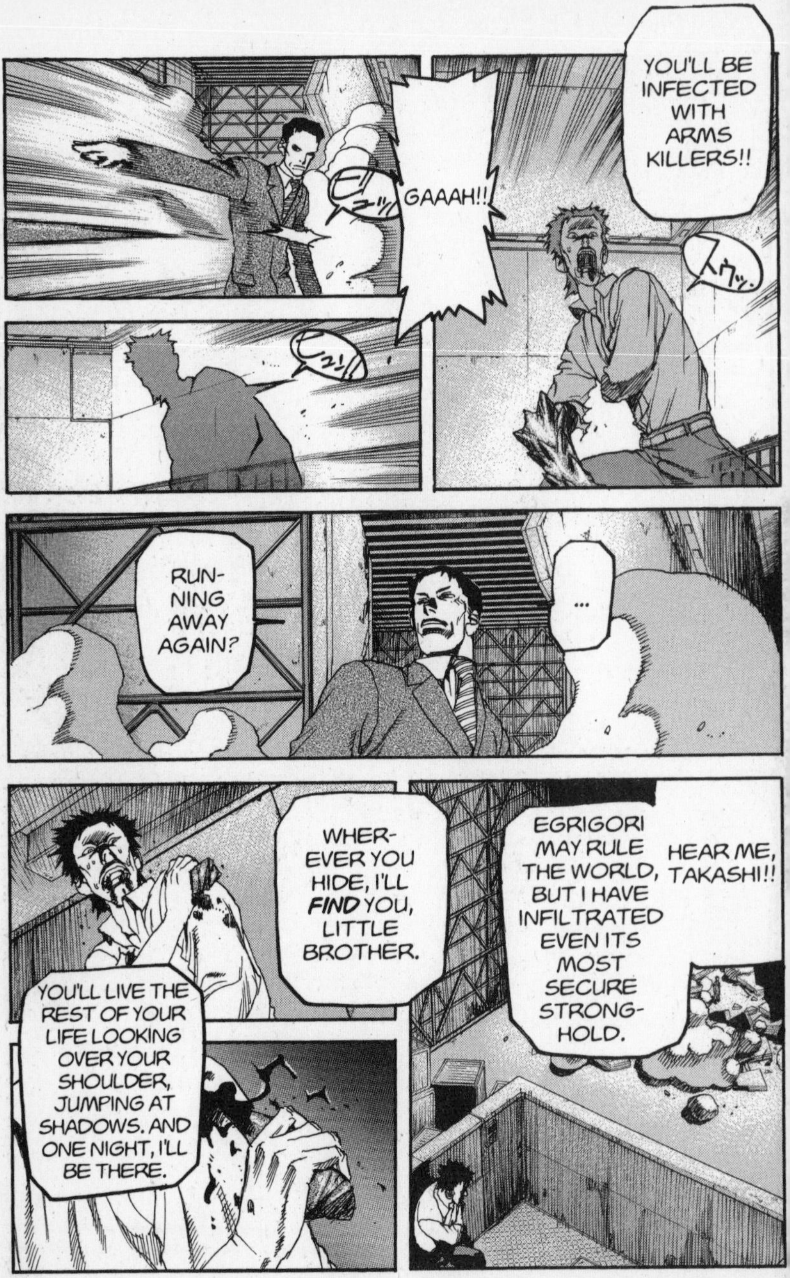
YOU'LL BE INFECTED WITH ARMS KILLERS!!
GAAAH!!
...
RUN-NING AWAY AGAIN?
HEAR ME, TAKASHI!!
EGRIGORI MAY RULE THE WORLD, BUT I HAVE INFILTRATED EVEN ITS MOST SECURE STRONG-HOLD.
WHER-EVER YOU HIDE, I'LL **FIND** YOU, LITTLE BROTHER.
YOU'LL LIVE THE REST OF YOUR LIFE LOOKING OVER YOUR SHOULDER, JUMPING AT SHADOWS. AND ONE NIGHT, I'LL BE THERE.

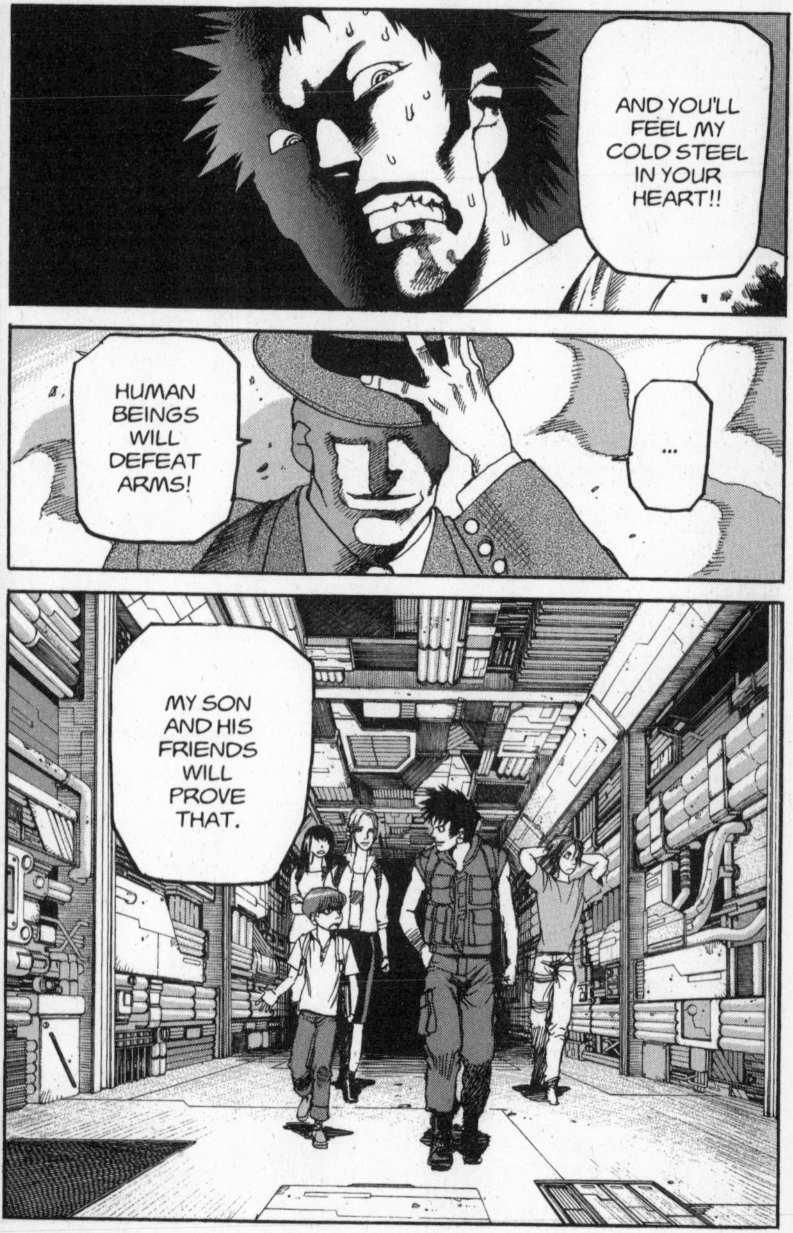
AND YOU'LL FEEL MY COLD STEEL IN YOUR HEART!!
...
HUMAN BEINGS WILL DEFEAT ARMS!
MY SON AND HIS FRIENDS WILL PROVE THAT.

No. 10 ARCADIA

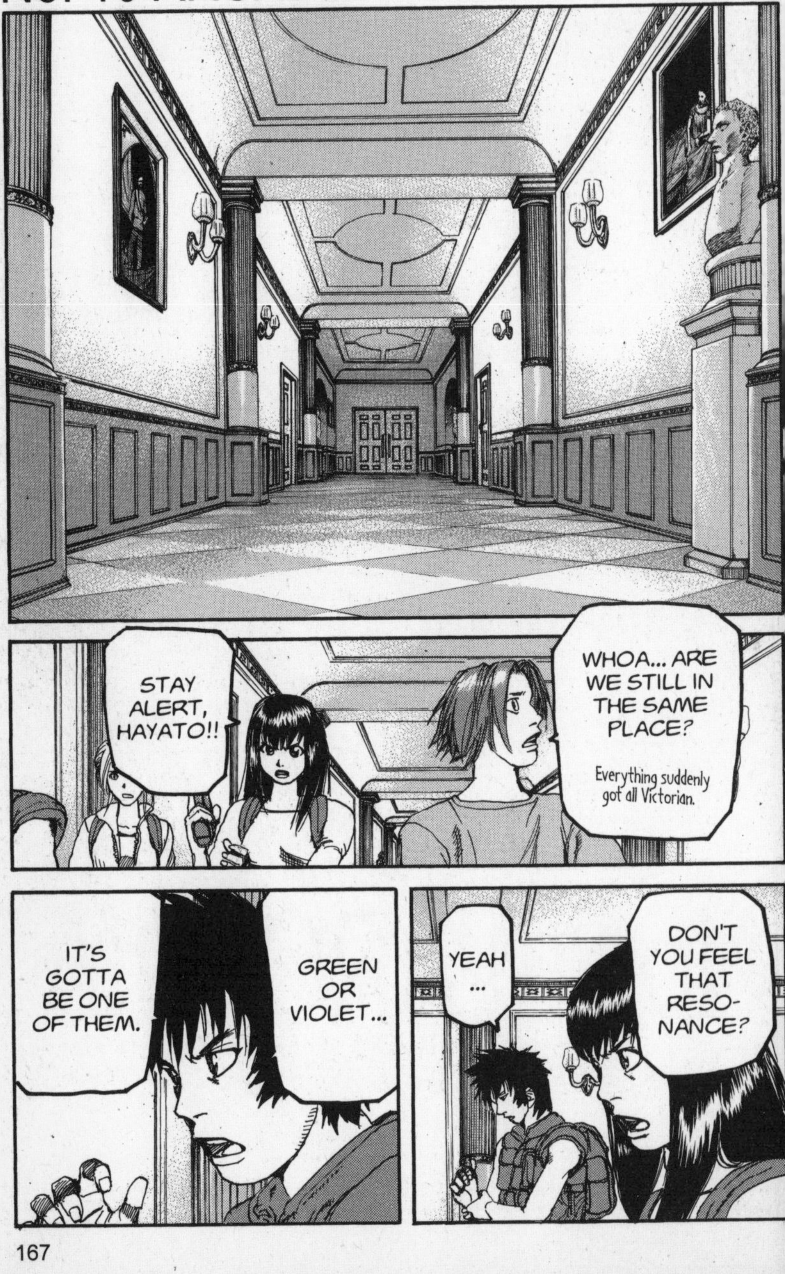
WHOA... ARE WE STILL IN THE SAME PLACE?
Everything suddenly got all Victorian.
STAY ALERT, HAYATO!!
DON'T YOU FEEL THAT RESO-NANCE?
YEAH ...
GREEN OR VIOLET...
IT'S GOTTA BE ONE OF THEM.

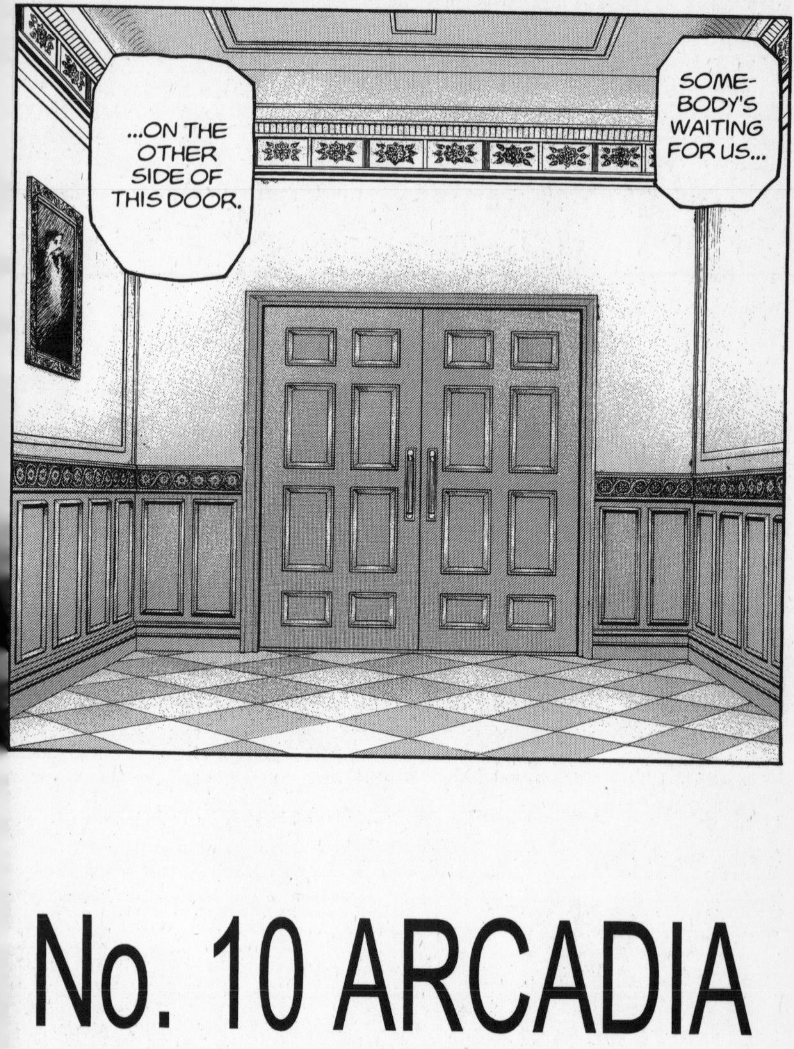
SOME-
BODY'S
WAITING
FOR US...
...ON THE
OTHER
SIDE OF
THIS DOOR.

No. 10 ARCADIA

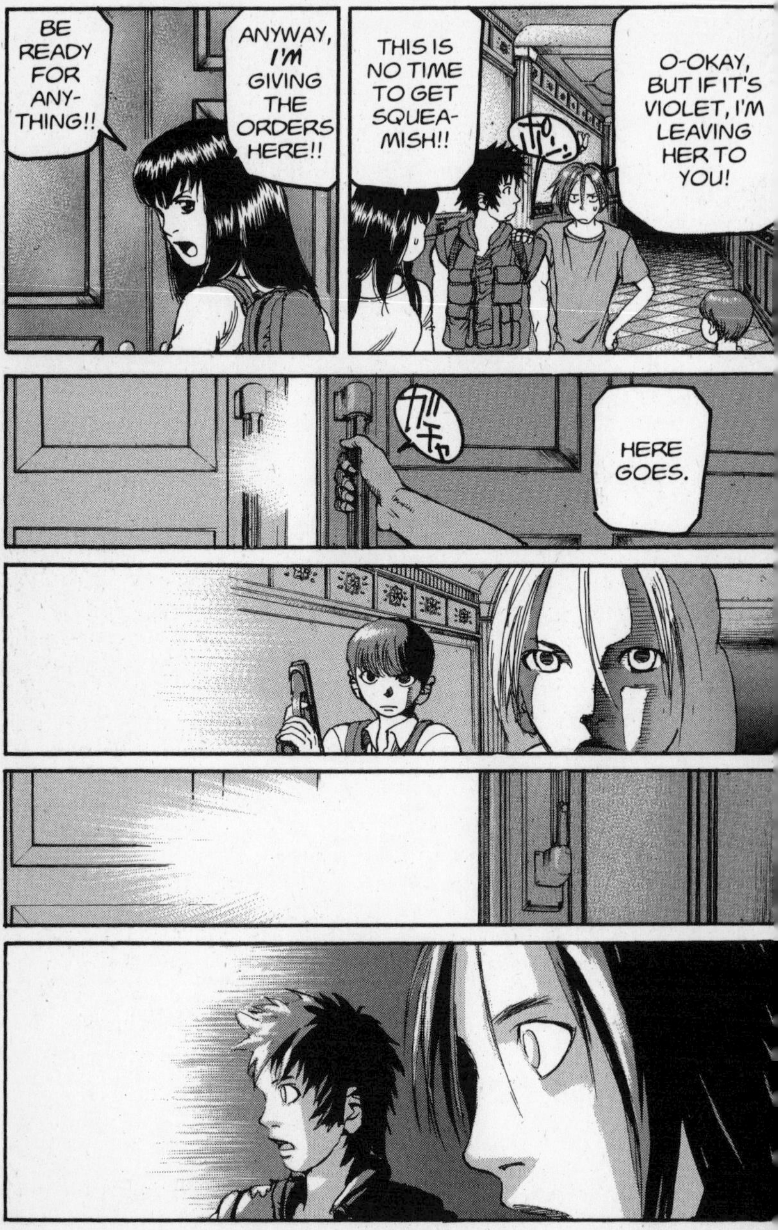
O-OKAY, BUT IF IT'S VIOLET, I'M LEAVING HER TO YOU!
THIS IS NO TIME TO GET SQUEA-MISH!!
ANYWAY, I'M GIVING THE ORDERS HERE!!
BE READY FOR ANY-THING!!
HERE GOES.
ガチャ

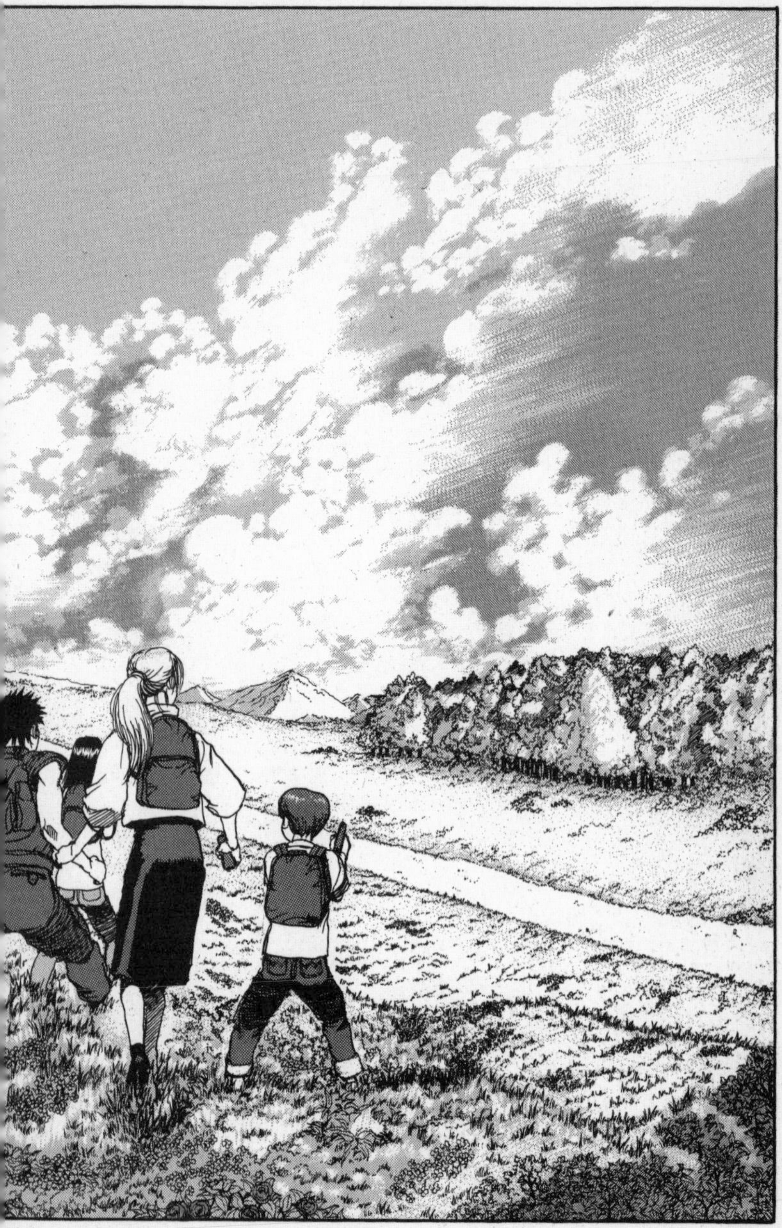

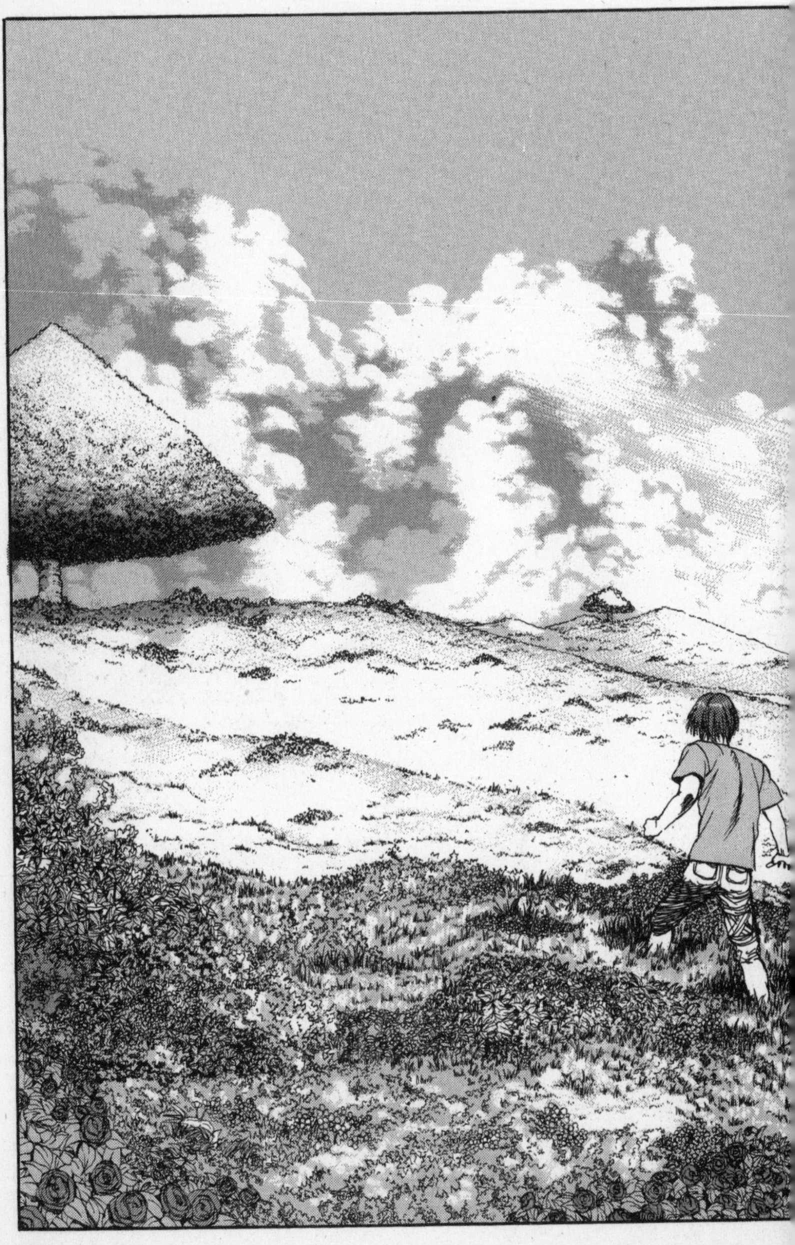

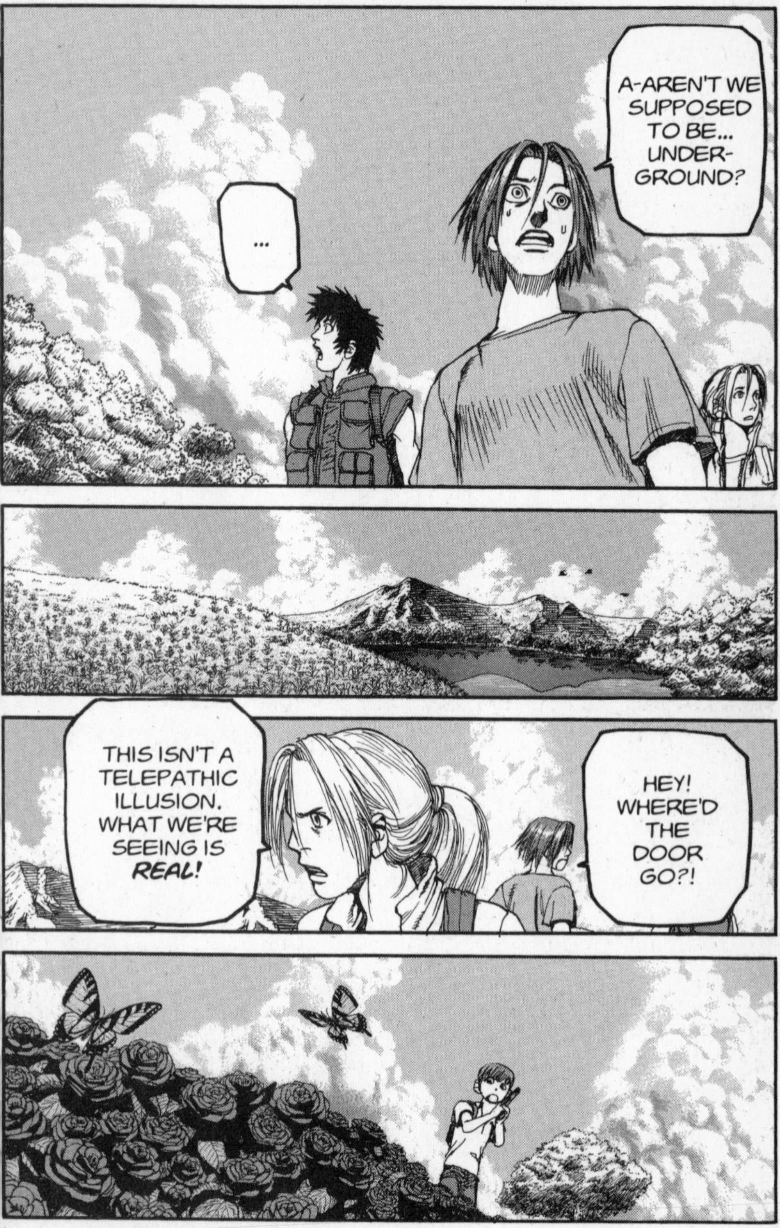
A-AREN'T WE SUPPOSED TO BE... UNDER-GROUND?
...
HEY! WHERE'D THE DOOR GO?!
THIS ISN'T A TELEPATHIC ILLUSION. WHAT WE'RE SEEING IS ***REAL!***

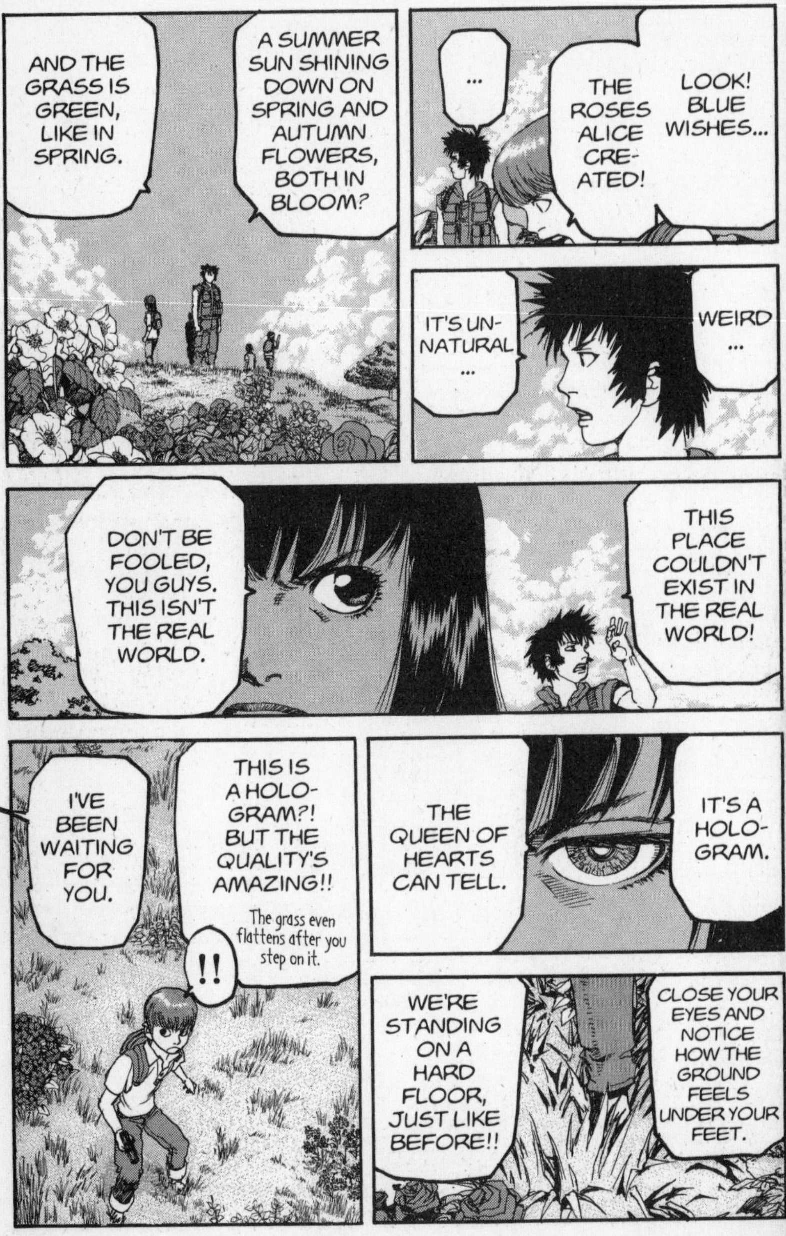
LOOK! BLUE WISHES...
THE ROSES ALICE CRE-ATED!
...
WEIRD ...
IT'S UN-NATURAL ...
A SUMMER SUN SHINING DOWN ON SPRING AND AUTUMN FLOWERS, BOTH IN BLOOM?
AND THE GRASS IS GREEN, LIKE IN SPRING.
THIS PLACE COULDN'T EXIST IN THE REAL WORLD!
DON'T BE FOOLED, YOU GUYS. THIS ISN'T THE REAL WORLD.
IT'S A HOLO-GRAM.
THE QUEEN OF HEARTS CAN TELL.
CLOSE YOUR EYES AND NOTICE HOW THE GROUND FEELS UNDER YOUR FEET.
WE'RE STANDING ON A HARD FLOOR, JUST LIKE BEFORE!!
THIS IS A HOLO-GRAM?! BUT THE QUALITY'S AMAZING!!
The grass even flattens after you step on it.
I'VE BEEN WAITING FOR YOU.
!!

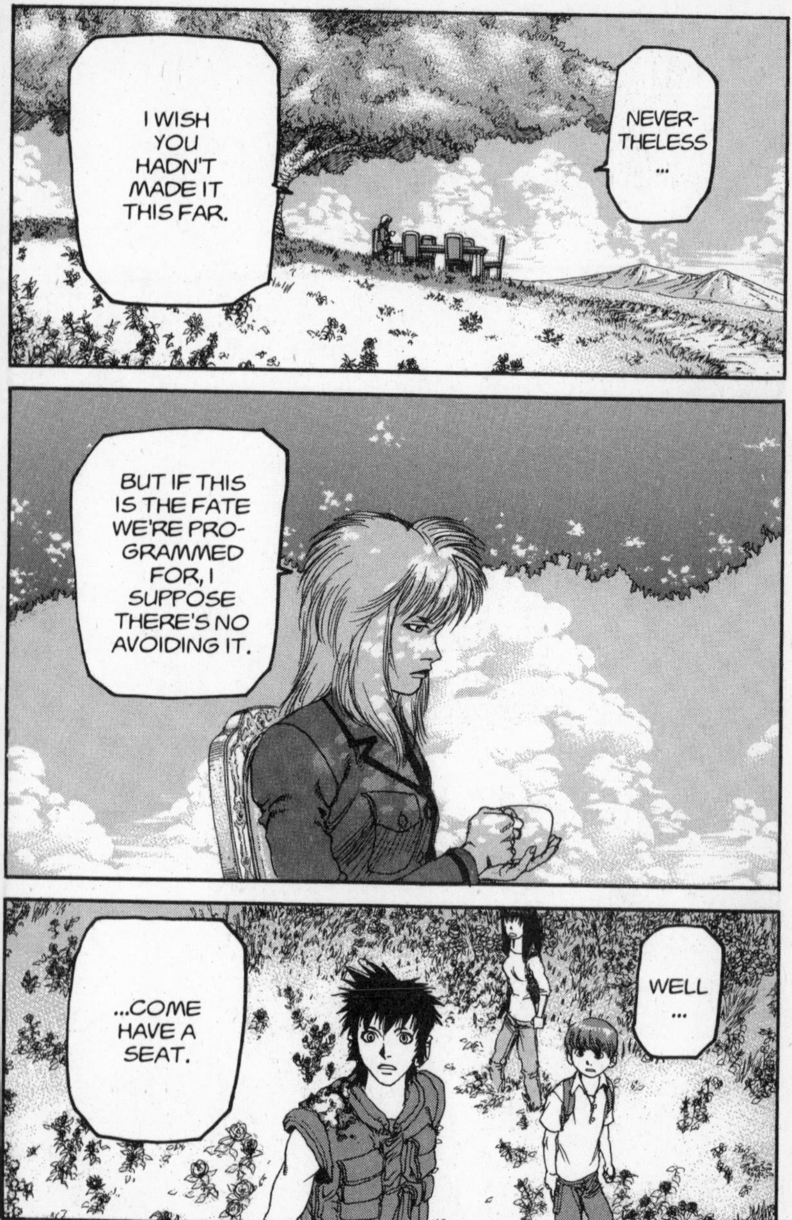
NEVER-THELESS ...
I WISH YOU HADN'T MADE IT THIS FAR.
BUT IF THIS IS THE FATE WE'RE PRO-GRAMMED FOR, I SUPPOSE THERE'S NO AVOIDING IT.
WELL ...
...COME HAVE A SEAT.

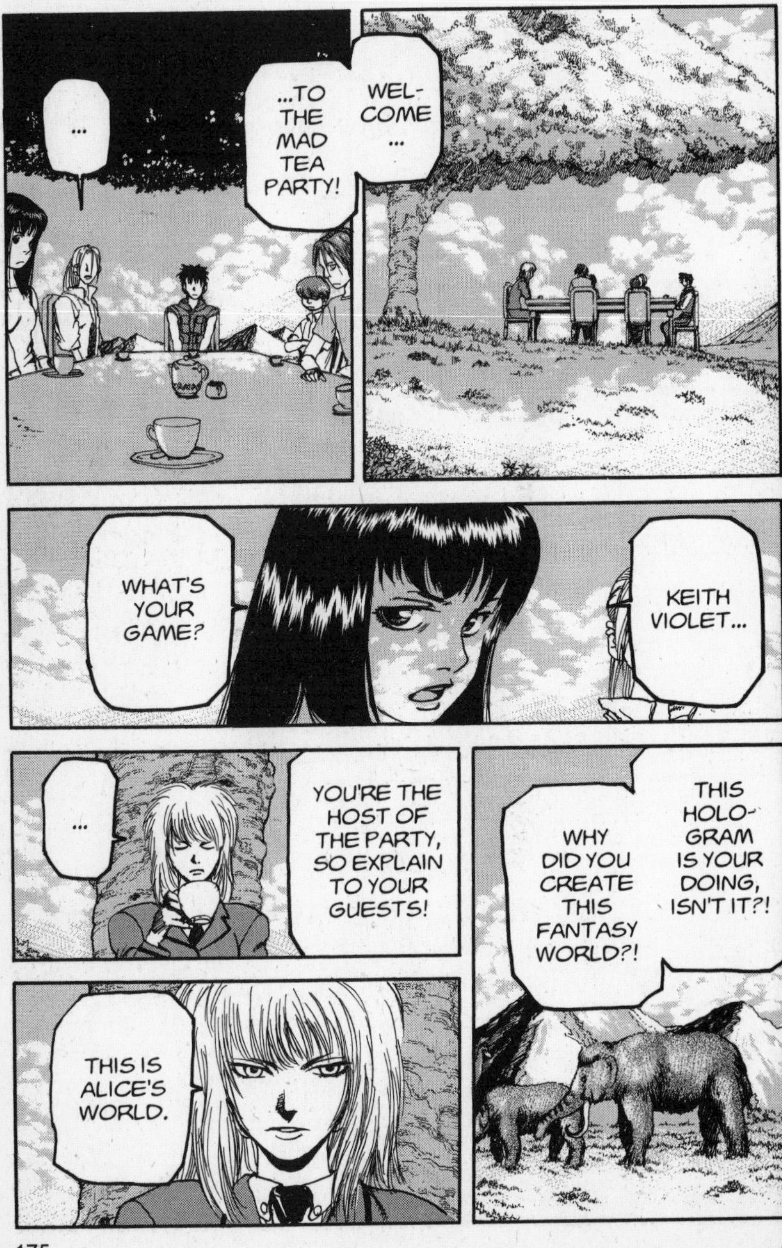
WEL-COME...
...TO THE MAD TEA PARTY!
...
KEITH VIOLET...
WHAT'S YOUR GAME?
THIS HOLO-GRAM IS YOUR DOING, ISN'T IT?!
WHY DID YOU CREATE THIS FANTASY WORLD?!
YOU'RE THE HOST OF THE PARTY, SO EXPLAIN TO YOUR GUESTS!
...
THIS IS ALICE'S WORLD.

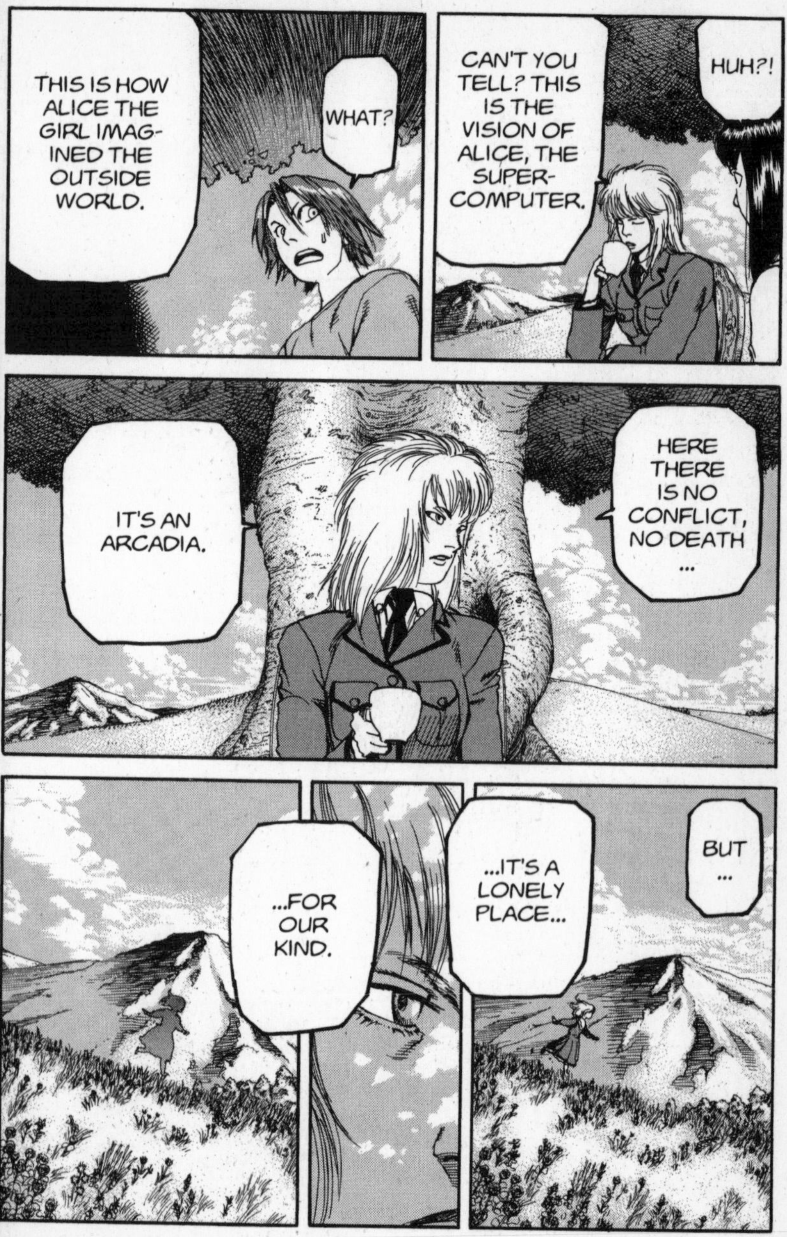
HUH?!
CAN'T YOU TELL? THIS IS THE VISION OF ALICE, THE SUPER-COMPUTER.
THIS IS HOW ALICE THE GIRL IMAGINED THE OUTSIDE WORLD.
WHAT?
HERE THERE IS NO CONFLICT, NO DEATH ...
IT'S AN ARCADIA.
BUT ...
...IT'S A LONELY PLACE...
...FOR OUR KIND.

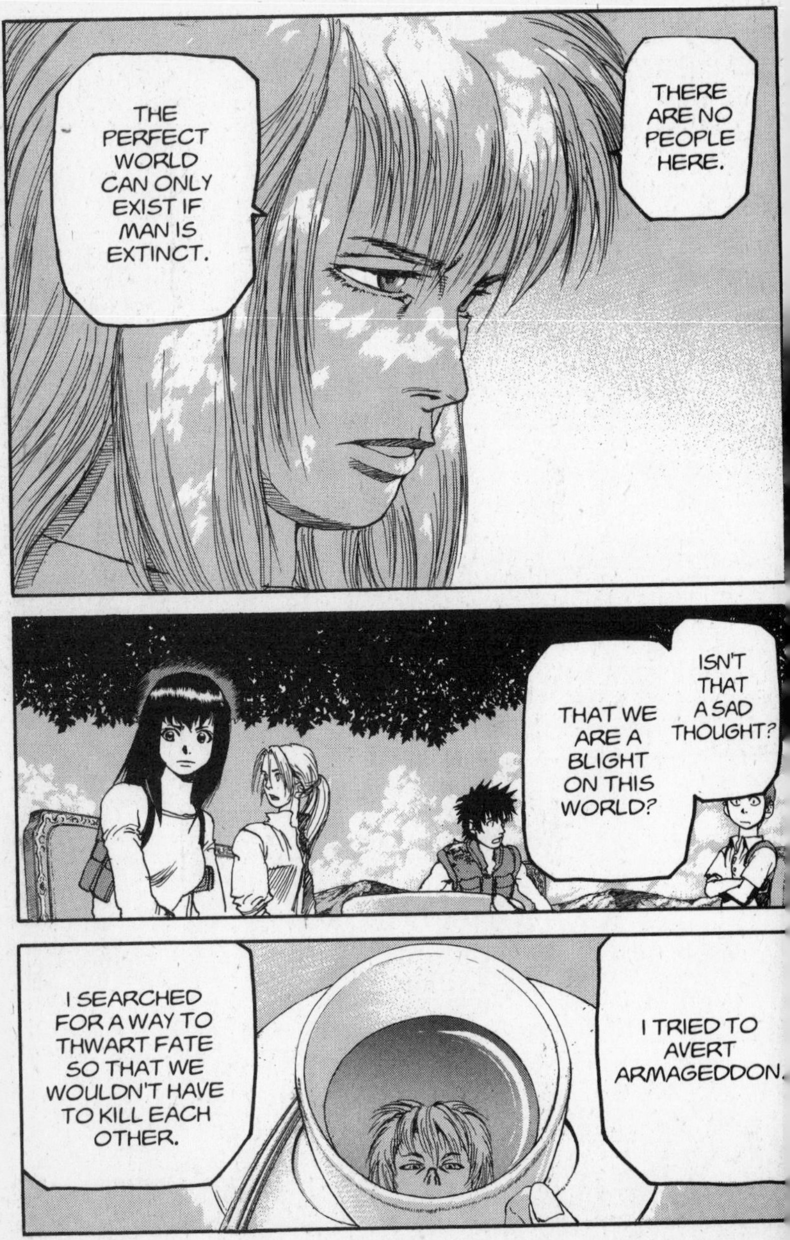
THERE ARE NO PEOPLE HERE.
THE PERFECT WORLD CAN ONLY EXIST IF MAN IS EXTINCT.
ISN'T THAT A SAD THOUGHT?
THAT WE ARE A BLIGHT ON THIS WORLD?
I TRIED TO AVERT ARMAGEDDON.
I SEARCHED FOR A WAY TO THWART FATE SO THAT WE WOULDN'T HAVE TO KILL EACH OTHER.

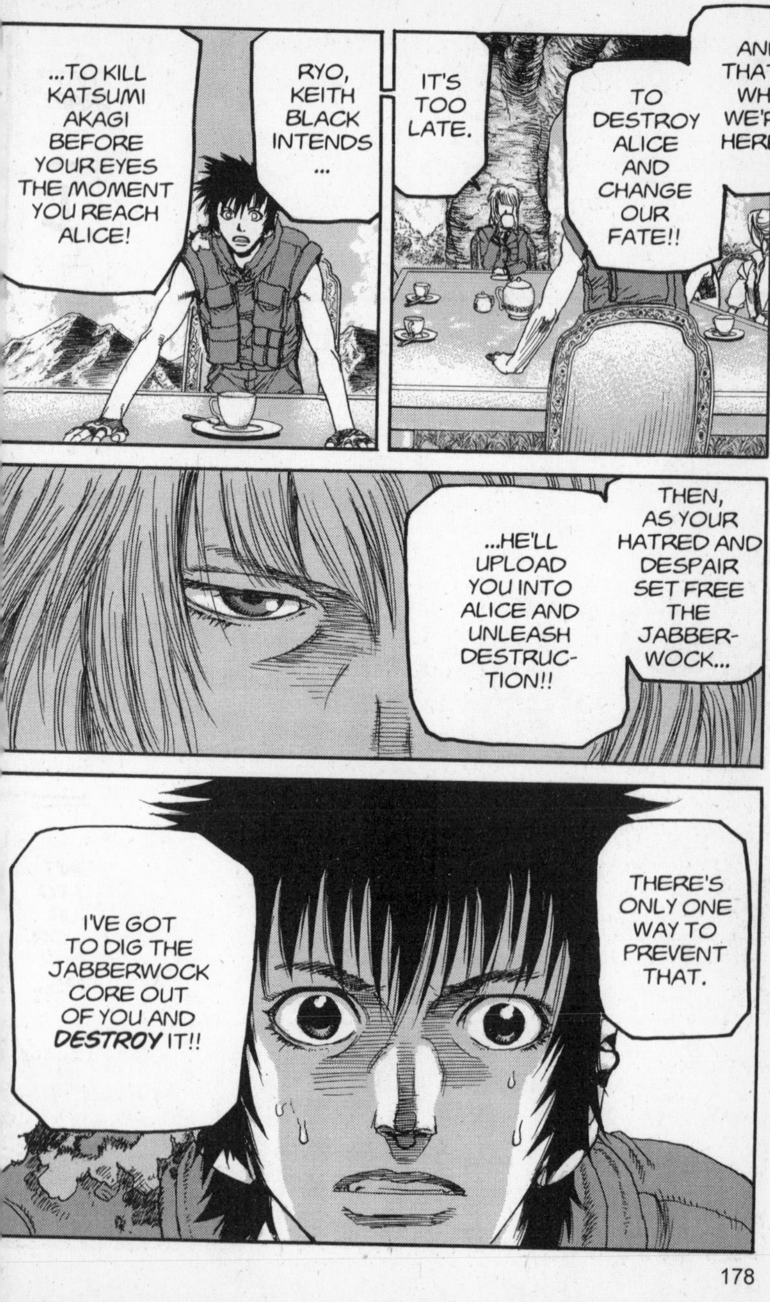
AND THAT'S WHY WE'RE HERE!!
TO DESTROY ALICE AND CHANGE OUR FATE!!
IT'S TOO LATE.
RYO, KEITH BLACK INTENDS ...
...TO KILL KATSUMI AKAGI BEFORE YOUR EYES THE MOMENT YOU REACH ALICE!
THEN, AS YOUR HATRED AND DESPAIR SET FREE THE JABBER-WOCK...
...HE'LL UPLOAD YOU INTO ALICE AND UNLEASH DESTRUC-TION!!
THERE'S ONLY ONE WAY TO PREVENT THAT.
I'VE GOT TO DIG THE JABBERWOCK CORE OUT OF YOU AND **DESTROY** IT!!

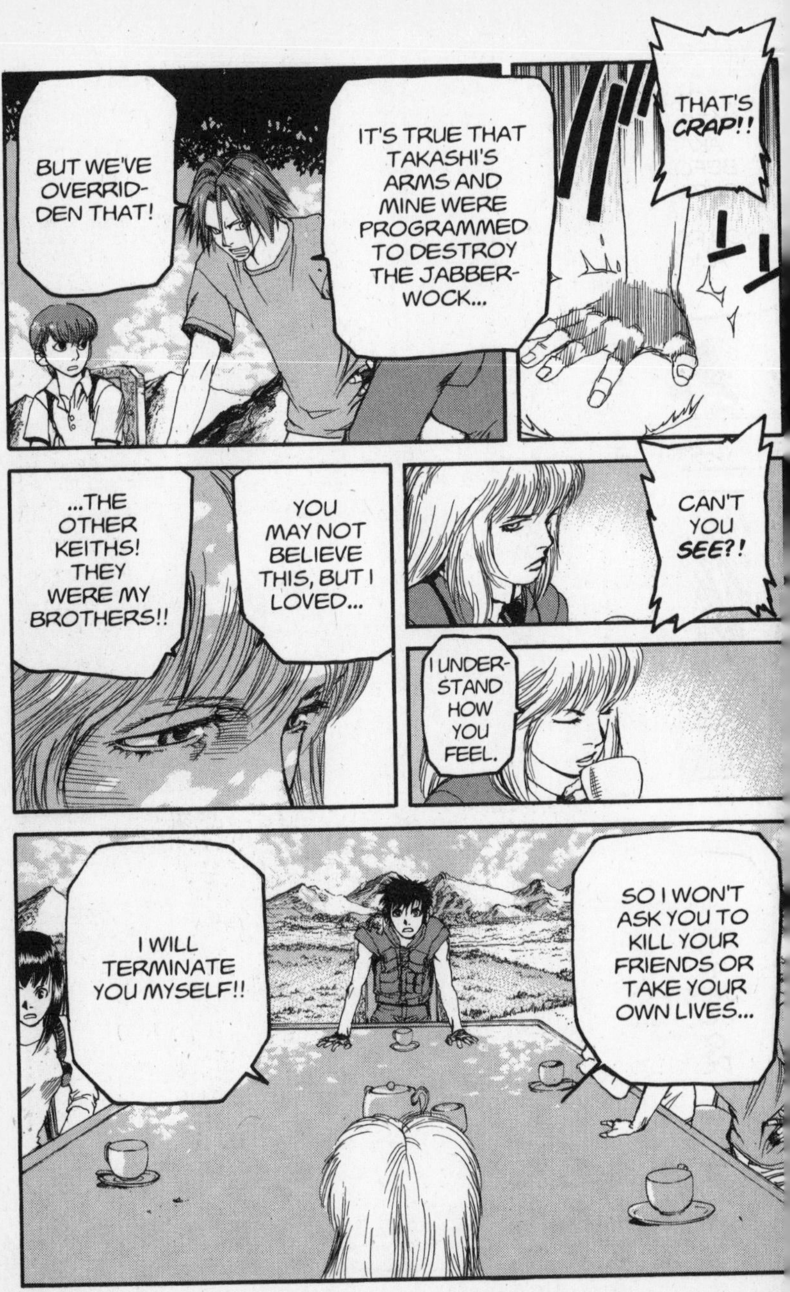
THAT'S *CRAP!!*
IT'S TRUE THAT TAKASHI'S ARMS AND MINE WERE PROGRAMMED TO DESTROY THE JABBER-WOCK...
BUT WE'VE OVERRID-DEN THAT!
CAN'T YOU *SEE?!*
I UNDER-STAND HOW YOU FEEL.
YOU MAY NOT BELIEVE THIS, BUT I LOVED...
...THE OTHER KEITHS! THEY WERE MY BROTHERS!!
SO I WON'T ASK YOU TO KILL YOUR FRIENDS OR TAKE YOUR OWN LIVES...
I WILL TERMINATE YOU MYSELF!!

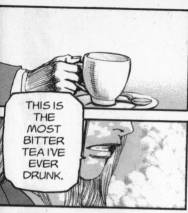

FOR ALL MY SEARCHING, I ULTIMATELY CAME...
...TO THE SAME CONCLUSION AS SILVER. IRONIC, ISN'T IT?
...
THIS IS THE MOST BITTER TEA I'VE EVER DRUNK.
!!

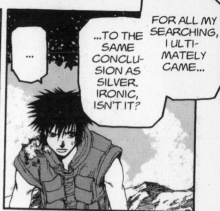

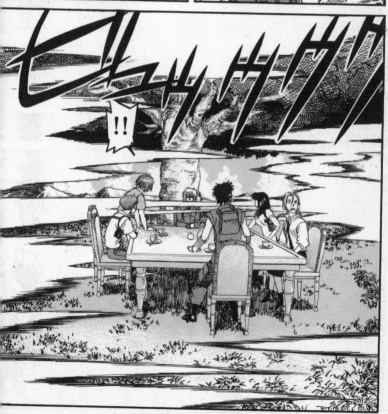

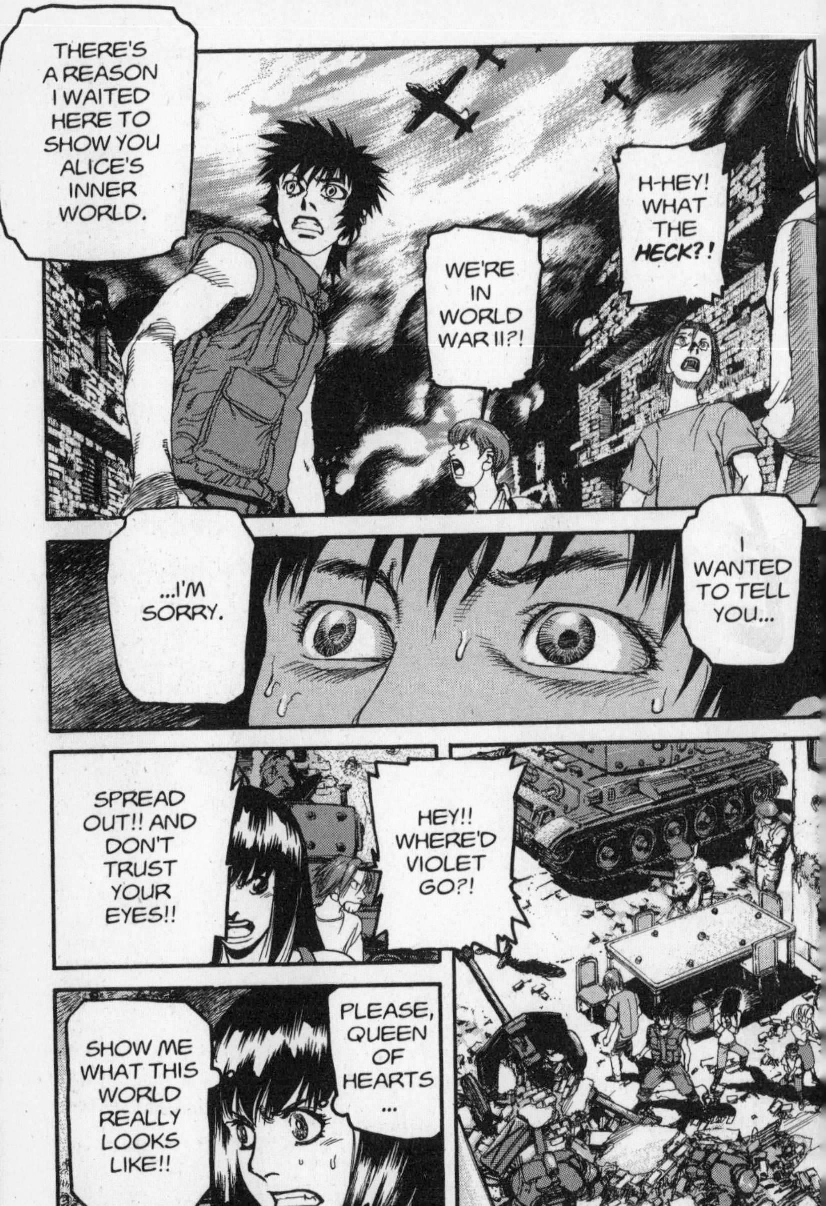

H-HEY! WHAT THE HECK?!
WE'RE IN WORLD WAR II?!
THERE'S A REASON I WAITED HERE TO SHOW YOU ALICE'S INNER WORLD.
I WANTED TO TELL YOU...
...I'M SORRY.
HEY!! WHERE'D VIOLET GO?!
SPREAD OUT!! AND DON'T TRUST YOUR EYES!!
PLEASE, QUEEN OF HEARTS ...
SHOW ME WHAT THIS WORLD REALLY LOOKS LIKE!!

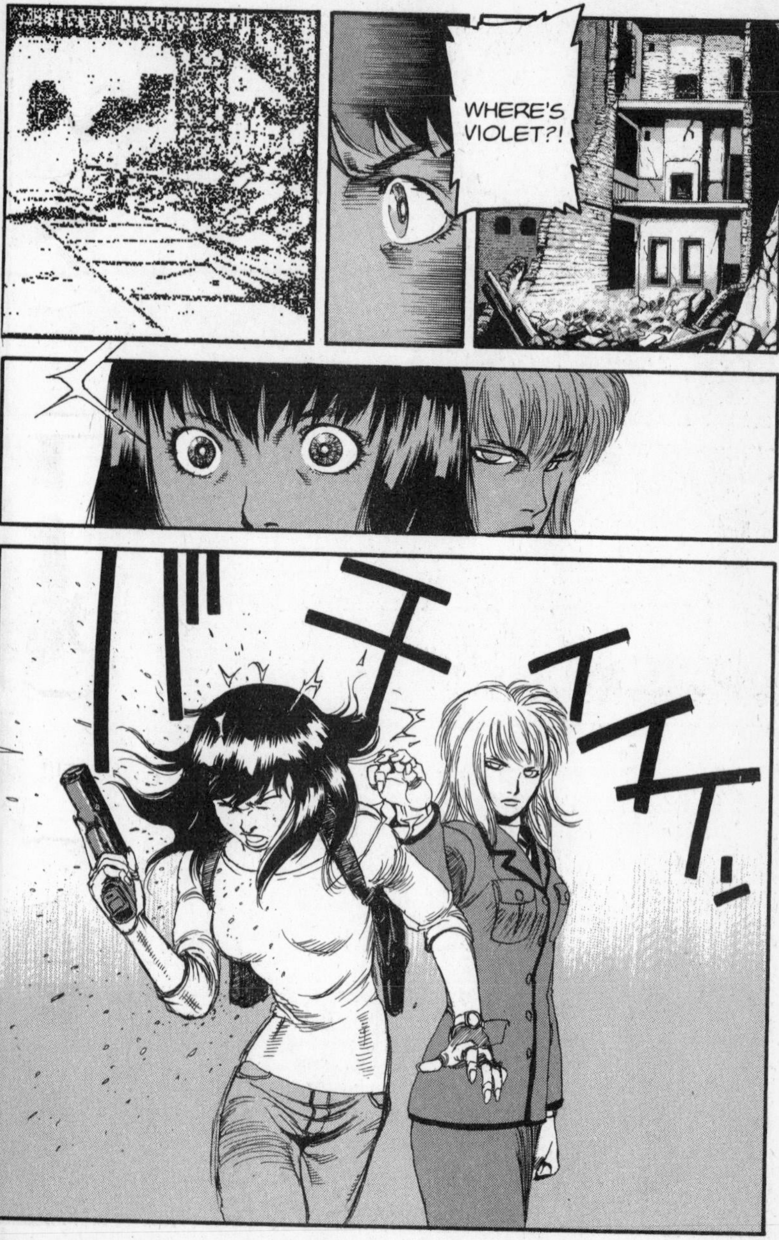
WHERE'S
VIOLET?!

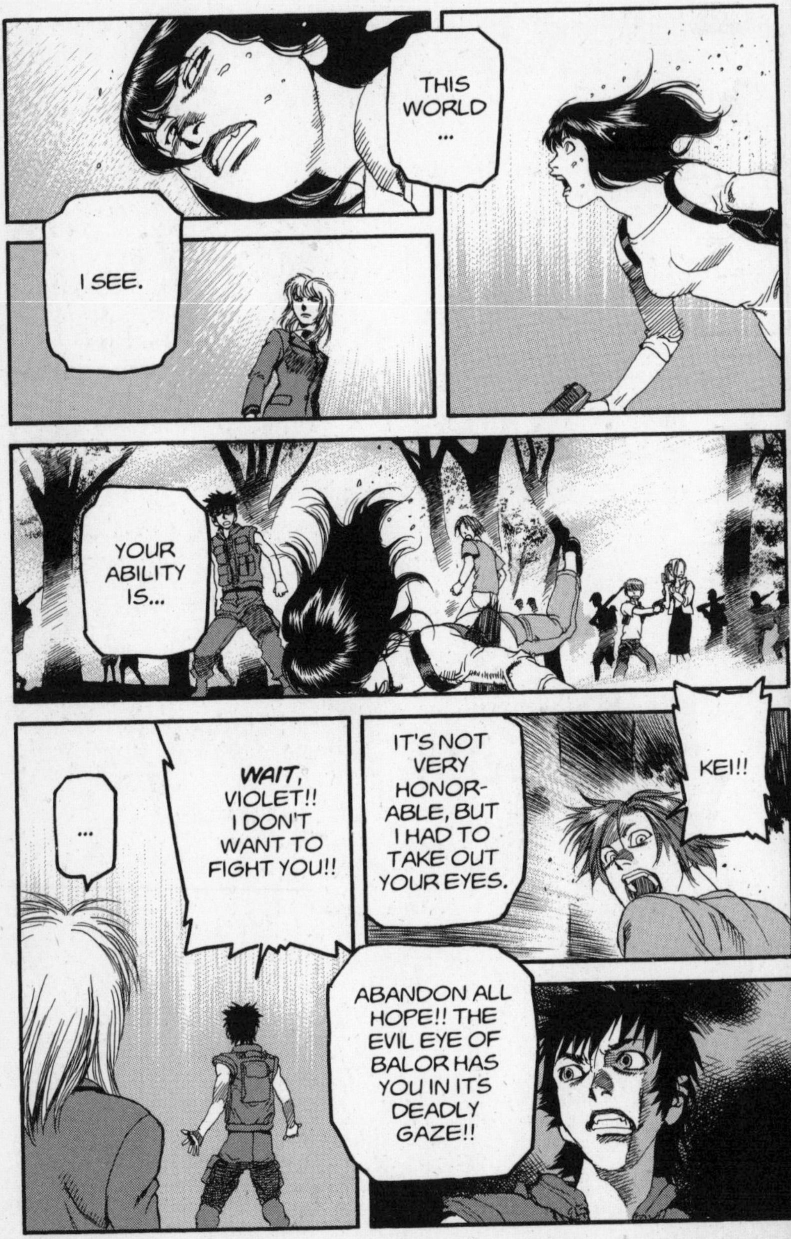
THIS WORLD ...
I SEE.
YOUR ABILITY IS...
KEI!!
IT'S NOT VERY HONOR-ABLE, BUT I HAD TO TAKE OUT YOUR EYES.
ABANDON ALL HOPE!! THE EVIL EYE OF BALOR HAS YOU IN ITS DEADLY GAZE!!
WAIT, VIOLET!! I DON'T WANT TO FIGHT YOU!!
...

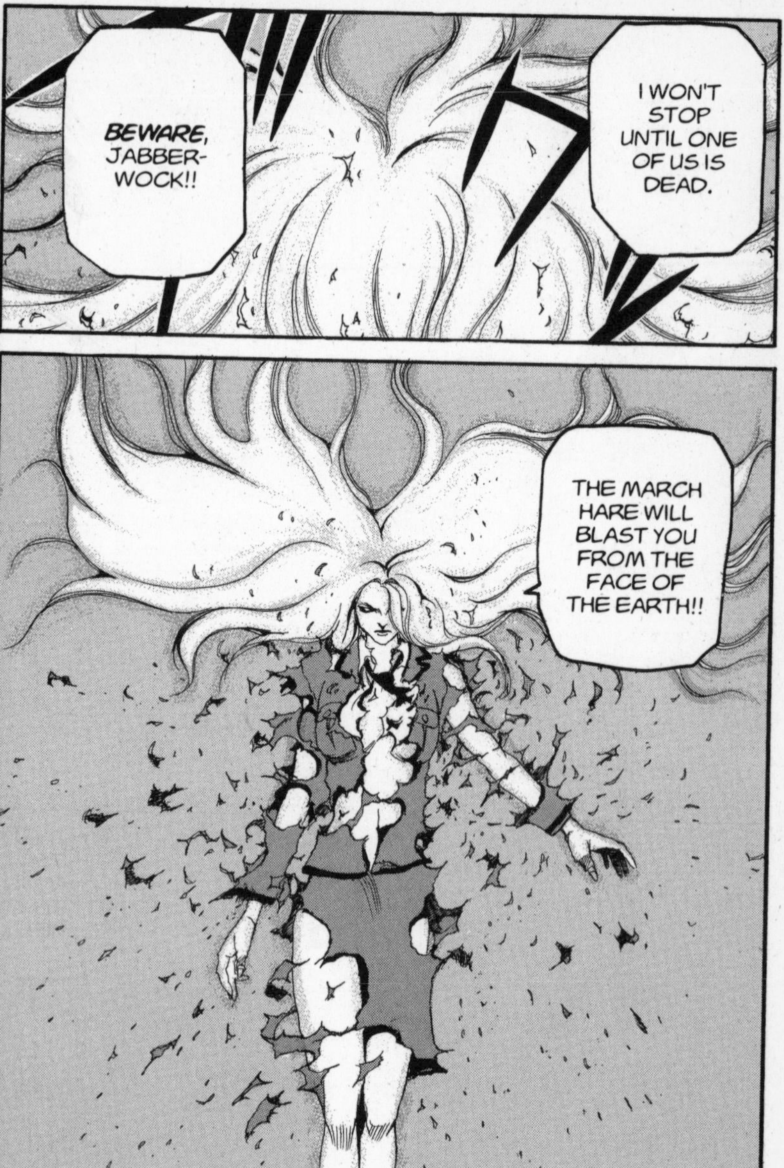
I WON'T STOP UNTIL ONE OF US IS DEAD.
BEWARE, JABBER-WOCK!!
THE MARCH HARE WILL BLAST YOU FROM THE FACE OF THE EARTH!!

No. 11 BALOR

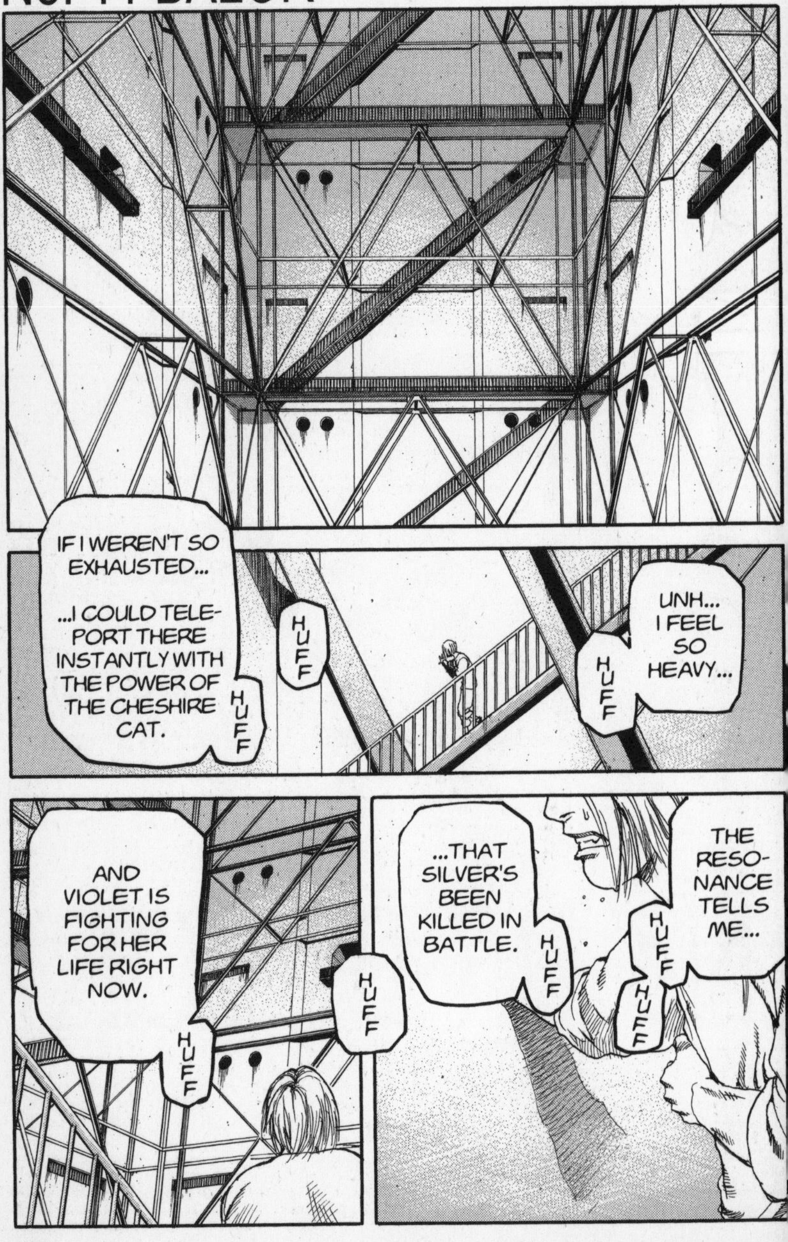
UNH... I FEEL SO HEAVY...
HUFF
HUFF
IF I WEREN'T SO EXHAUSTED...
...I COULD TELE-PORT THERE INSTANTLY WITH THE POWER OF THE CHESHIRE CAT.
HUFF
THE RESO-NANCE TELLS ME...
HUFF
HUFF
...THAT SILVER'S BEEN KILLED IN BATTLE.
HUFF
HUFF
AND VIOLET IS FIGHTING FOR HER LIFE RIGHT NOW.
HUFF

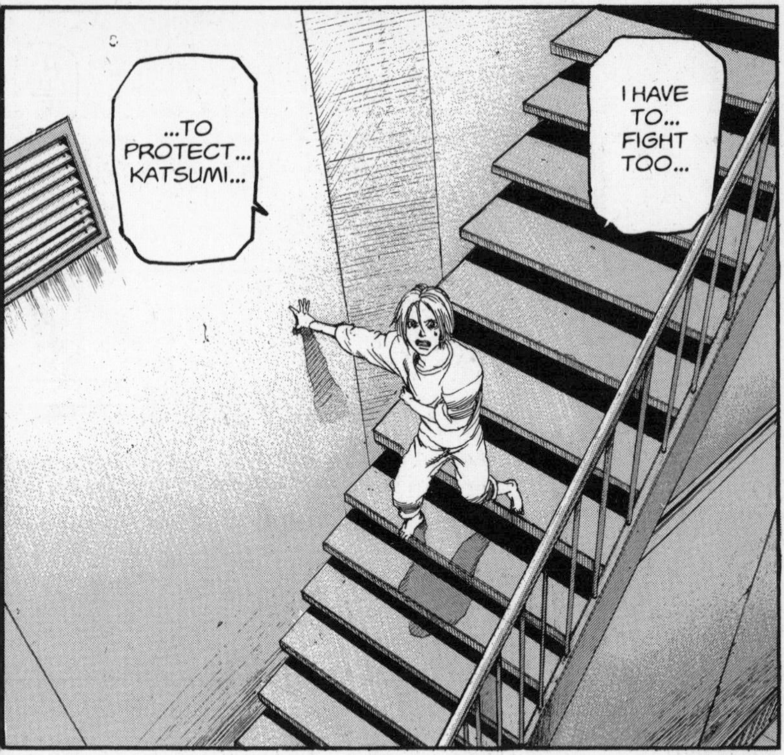
I HAVE TO... FIGHT TOO...
...TO PROTECT... KATSUMI...

No. 11 BALOR

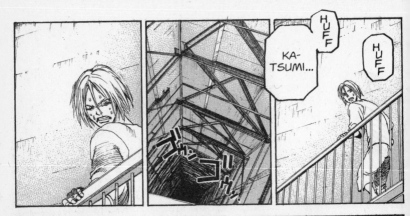

HUFF
HUFF
KA-TSUMI...
I WON'T LET YOU DO IT, BLACK!!
HUFF
HUFF
I WON'T LET YOU MURDER KATSUMI DOWN IN THESE DARK PITS!!
HUFF
I'LL DIE FIRST!!

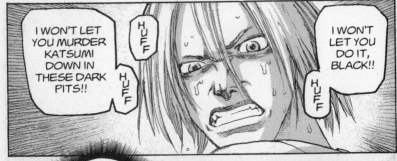

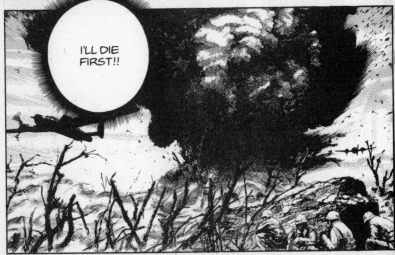

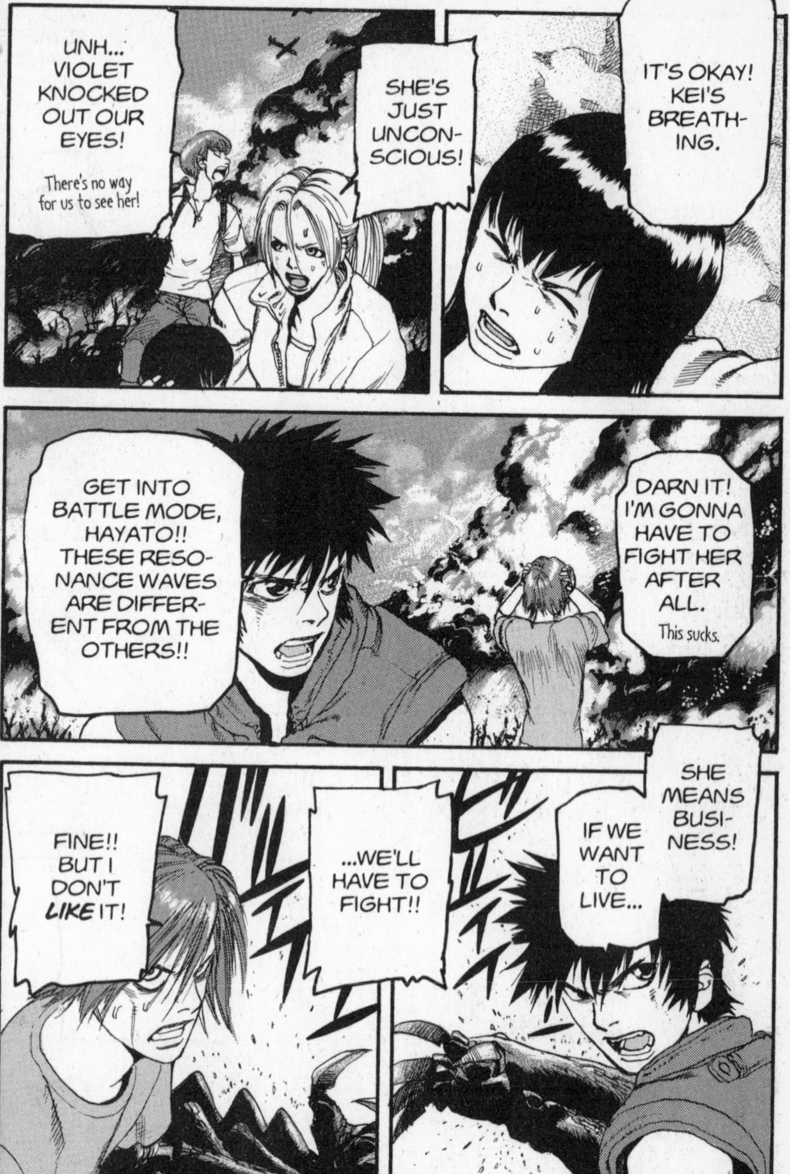
IT'S OKAY! KEI'S BREATH-ING.
SHE'S JUST UNCON-SCIOUS!
UNH... VIOLET KNOCKED OUT OUR EYES!
There's no way for us to see her!
DARN IT! I'M GONNA HAVE TO FIGHT HER AFTER ALL.
This sucks.
GET INTO BATTLE MODE, HAYATO!! THESE RESO-NANCE WAVES ARE DIFFER-ENT FROM THE OTHERS!!
SHE MEANS BUSI-NESS!
IF WE WANT TO LIVE...
...WE'LL HAVE TO FIGHT!!
FINE!! BUT I DON'T LIKE IT!

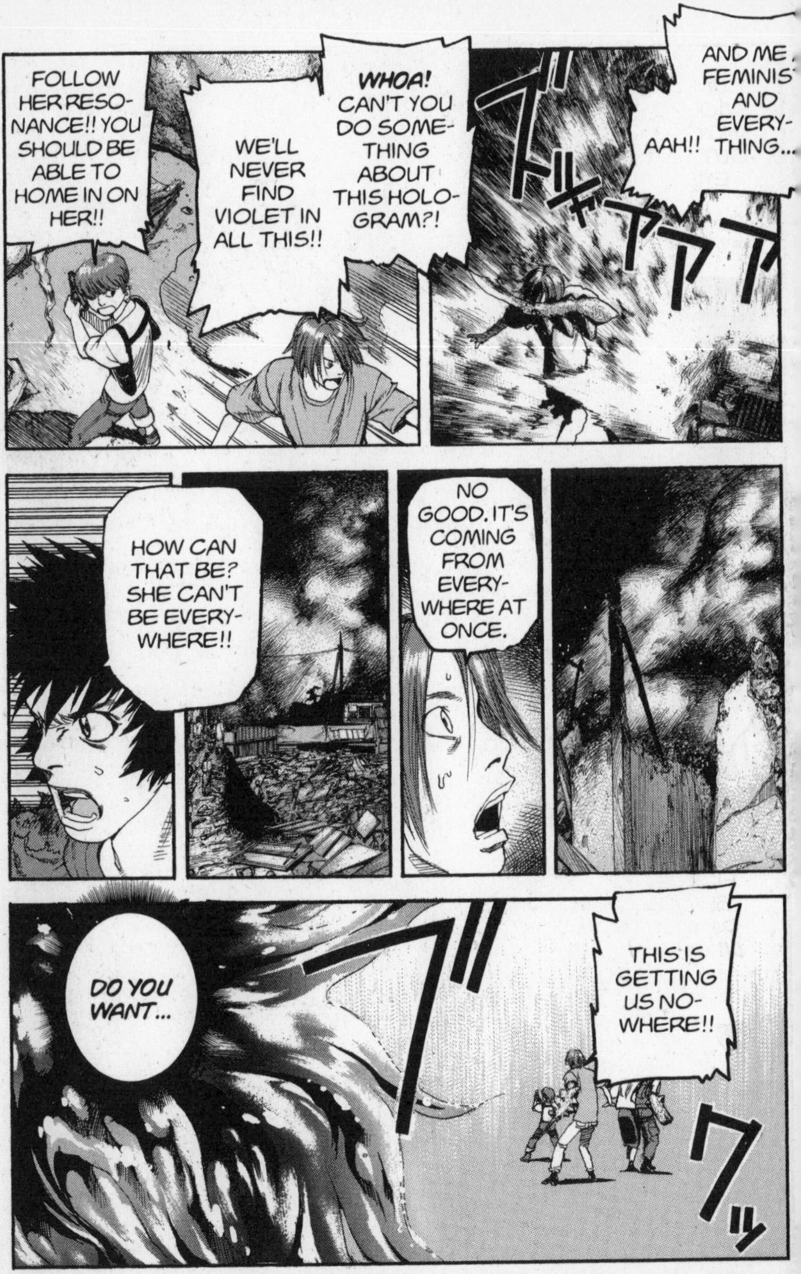
AND ME, FEMINIST AND EVERY-THING...
AAH!!
WHOA! CAN'T YOU DO SOME-THING ABOUT THIS HOLO-GRAM?!
WE'LL NEVER FIND VIOLET IN ALL THIS!!
FOLLOW HER RESO-NANCE!! YOU SHOULD BE ABLE TO HOME IN ON HER!!
NO GOOD. IT'S COMING FROM EVERY-WHERE AT ONCE.
HOW CAN THAT BE? SHE CAN'T BE EVERY-WHERE!!
THIS IS GETTING US NO-WHERE!!
DO YOU WANT...

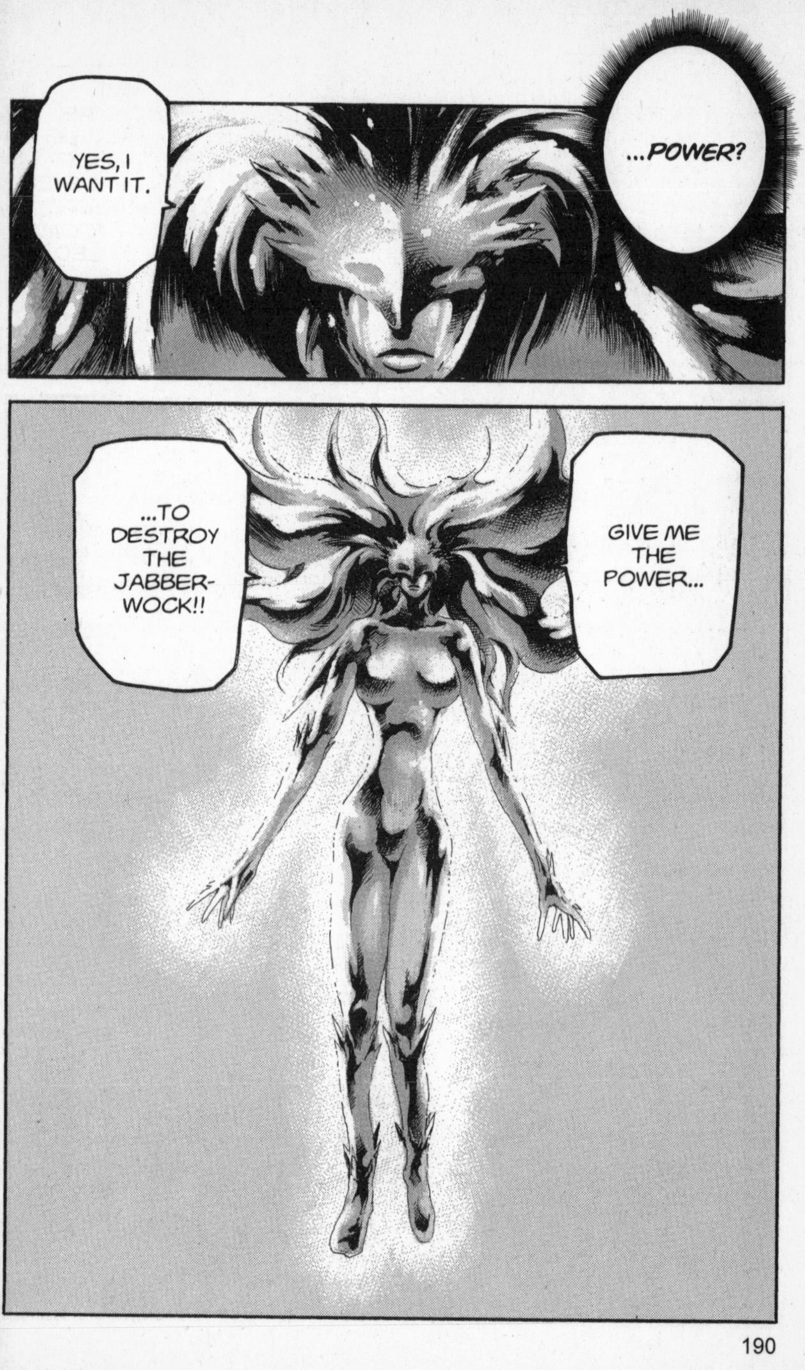
...POWER?
YES, I WANT IT.
GIVE ME THE POWER...
...TO DESTROY THE JABBER-WOCK!!

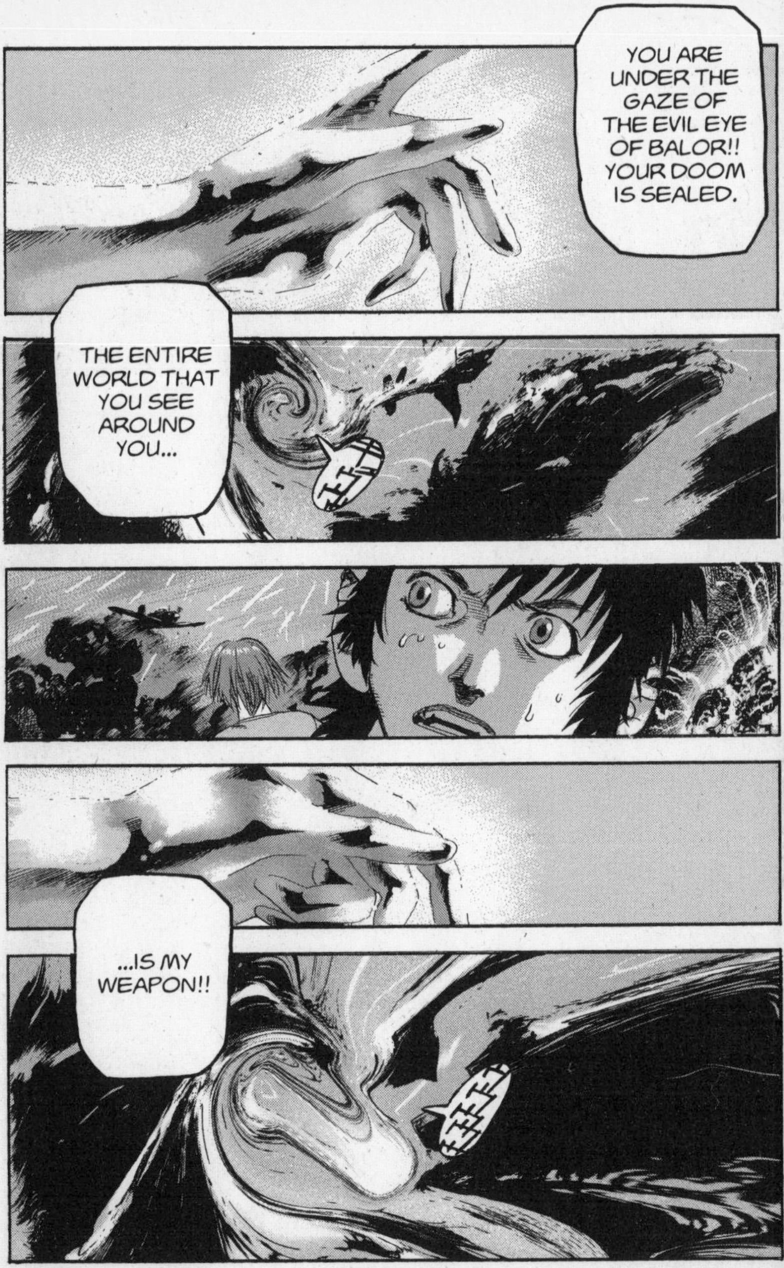
YOU ARE UNDER THE GAZE OF THE EVIL EYE OF BALOR!! YOUR DOOM IS SEALED.
THE ENTIRE WORLD THAT YOU SEE AROUND YOU...
...IS MY WEAPON!!

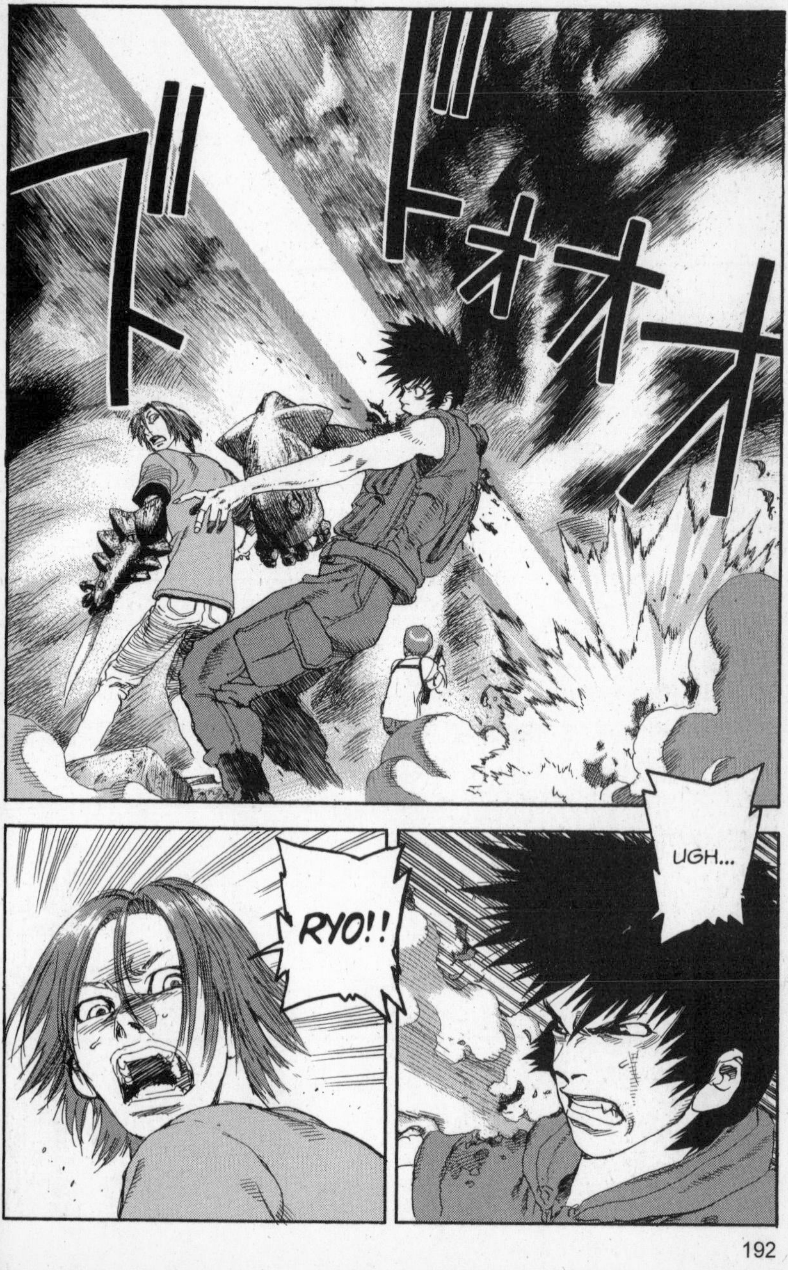
ドォオオ
ブド
UGH...
RYO!!

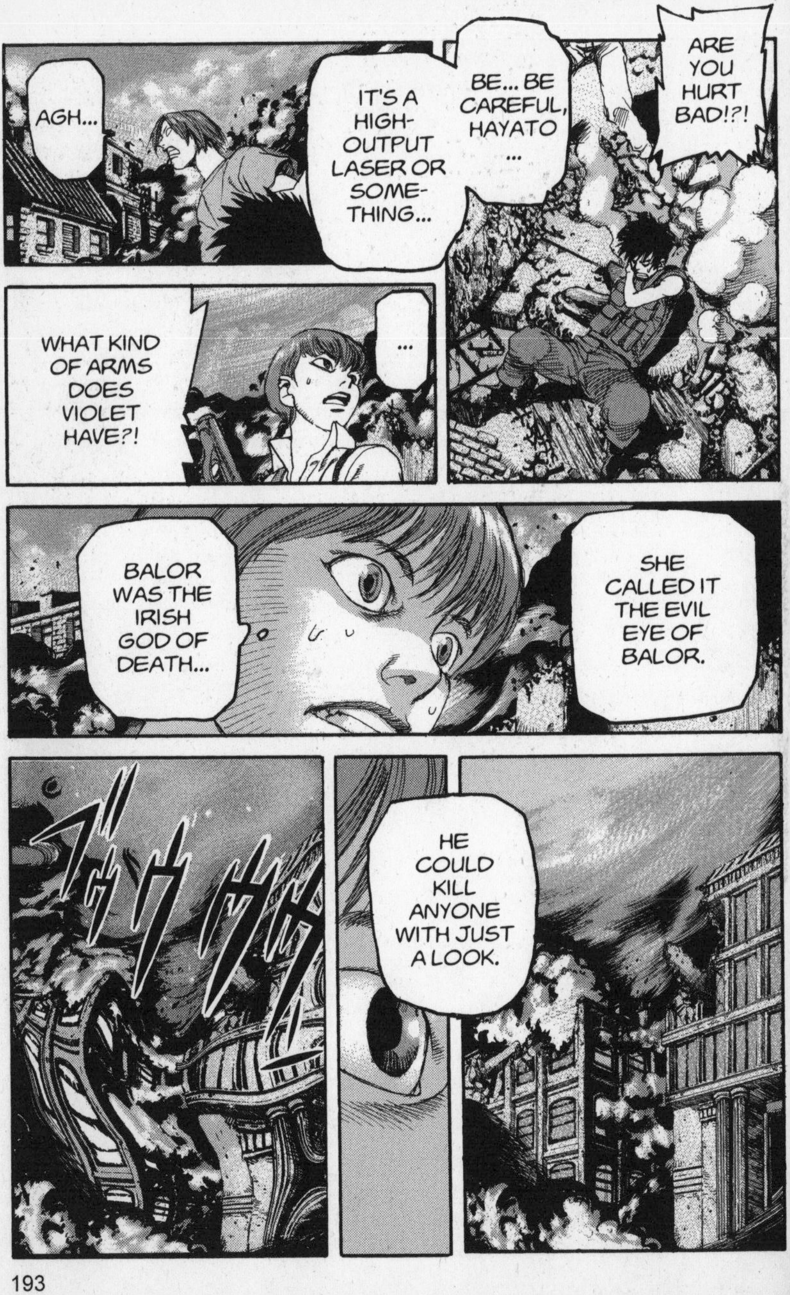
ARE YOU HURT BAD!?!
BE... BE CAREFUL, HAYATO ...
IT'S A HIGH-OUTPUT LASER OR SOMETHING...
AGH...
...
WHAT KIND OF ARMS DOES VIOLET HAVE?!
SHE CALLED IT THE EVIL EYE OF BALOR.
BALOR WAS THE IRISH GOD OF DEATH...
HE COULD KILL ANYONE WITH JUST A LOOK.

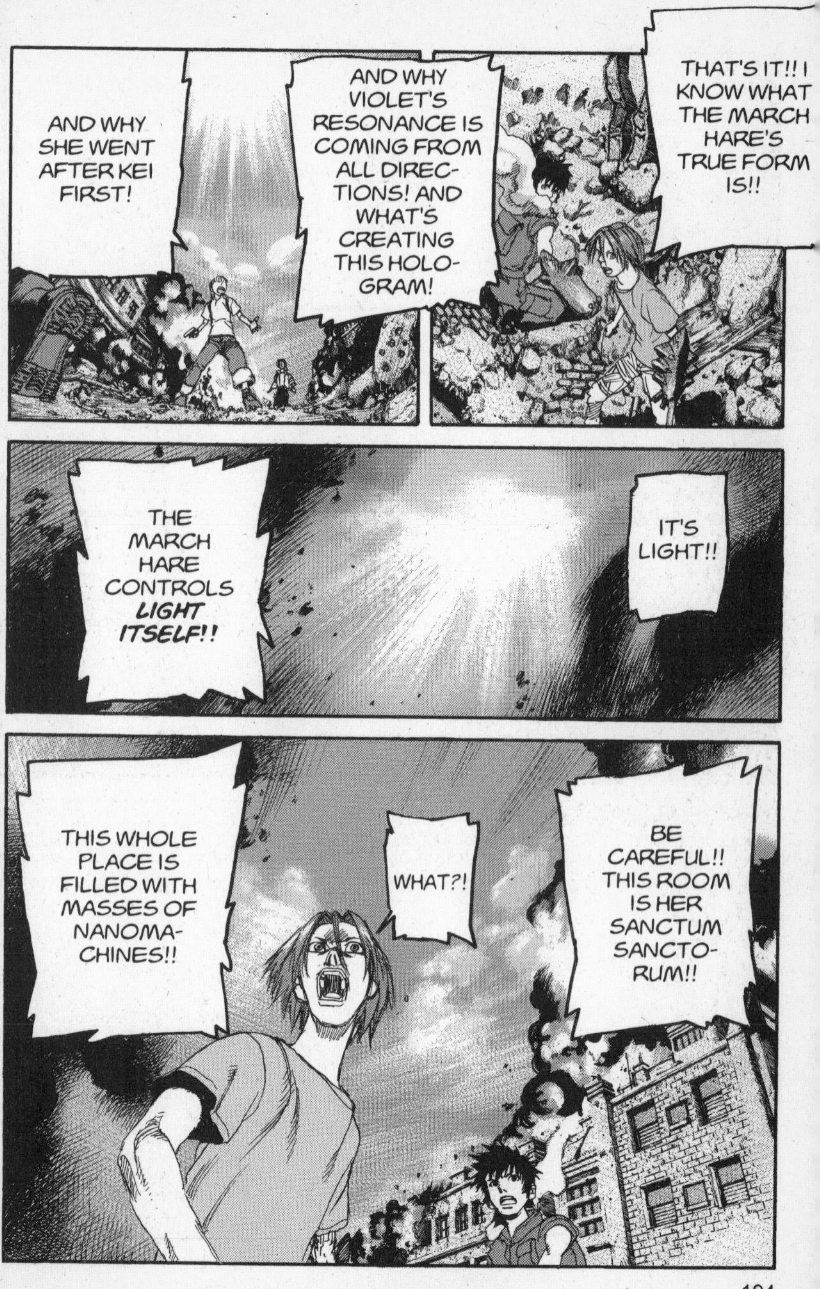
THAT'S IT!! I KNOW WHAT THE MARCH HARE'S TRUE FORM IS!!
AND WHY VIOLET'S RESONANCE IS COMING FROM ALL DIRECTIONS! AND WHAT'S CREATING THIS HOLOGRAM!
AND WHY SHE WENT AFTER KEI FIRST!
IT'S LIGHT!!
THE MARCH HARE CONTROLS ***LIGHT ITSELF!!***
BE CAREFUL!! THIS ROOM IS HER SANCTUM SANCTORUM!!
WHAT?!
THIS WHOLE PLACE IS FILLED WITH MASSES OF NANOMACHINES!!

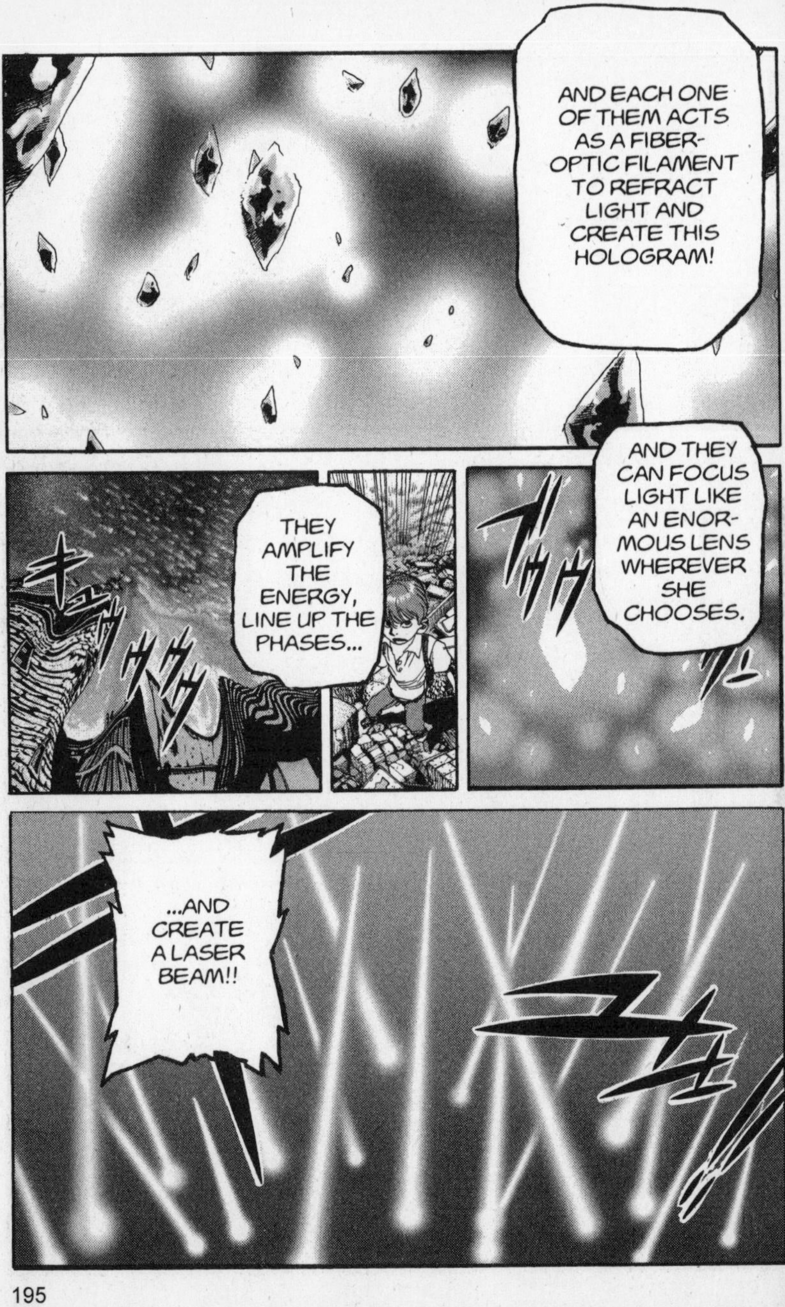
AND EACH ONE OF THEM ACTS AS A FIBER-OPTIC FILAMENT TO REFRACT LIGHT AND CREATE THIS HOLOGRAM!
AND THEY CAN FOCUS LIGHT LIKE AN ENOR-MOUS LENS WHEREVER SHE CHOOSES.
THEY AMPLIFY THE ENERGY, LINE UP THE PHASES...
...AND CREATE A LASER BEAM!!

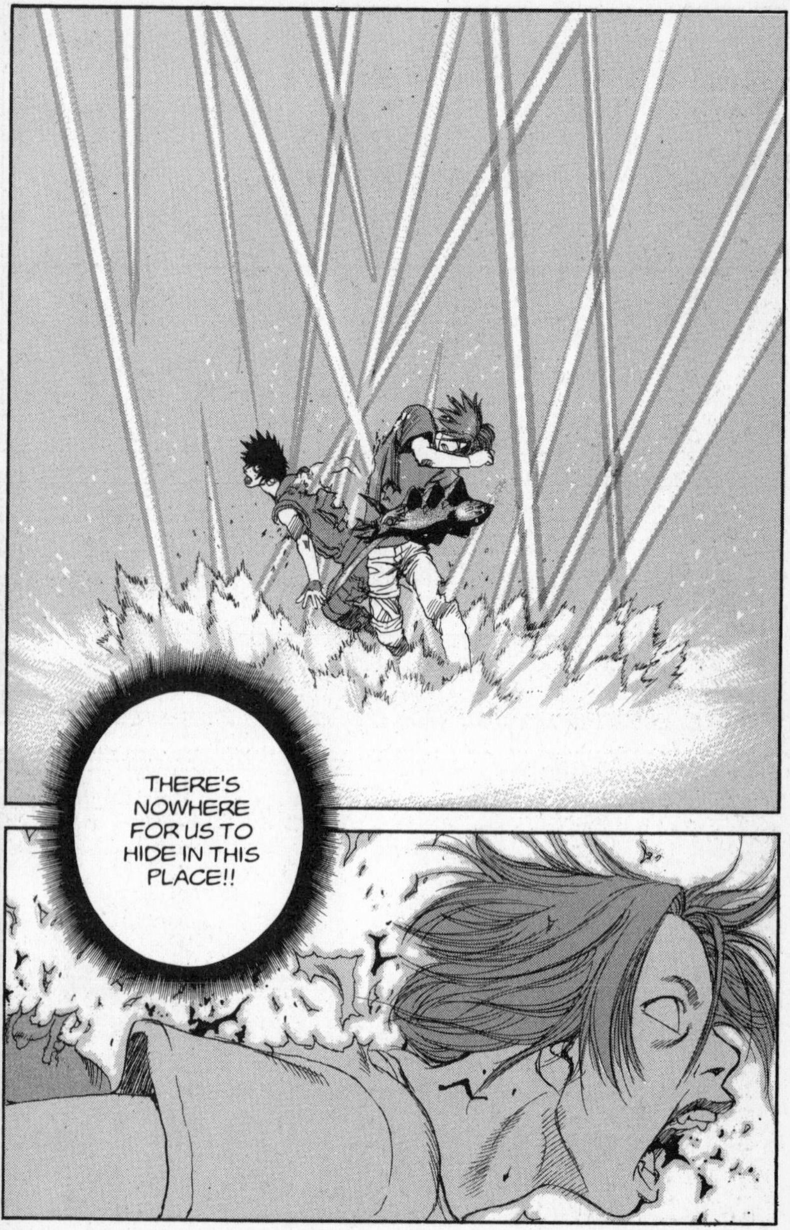
THERE'S NOWHERE FOR US TO HIDE IN THIS PLACE!!

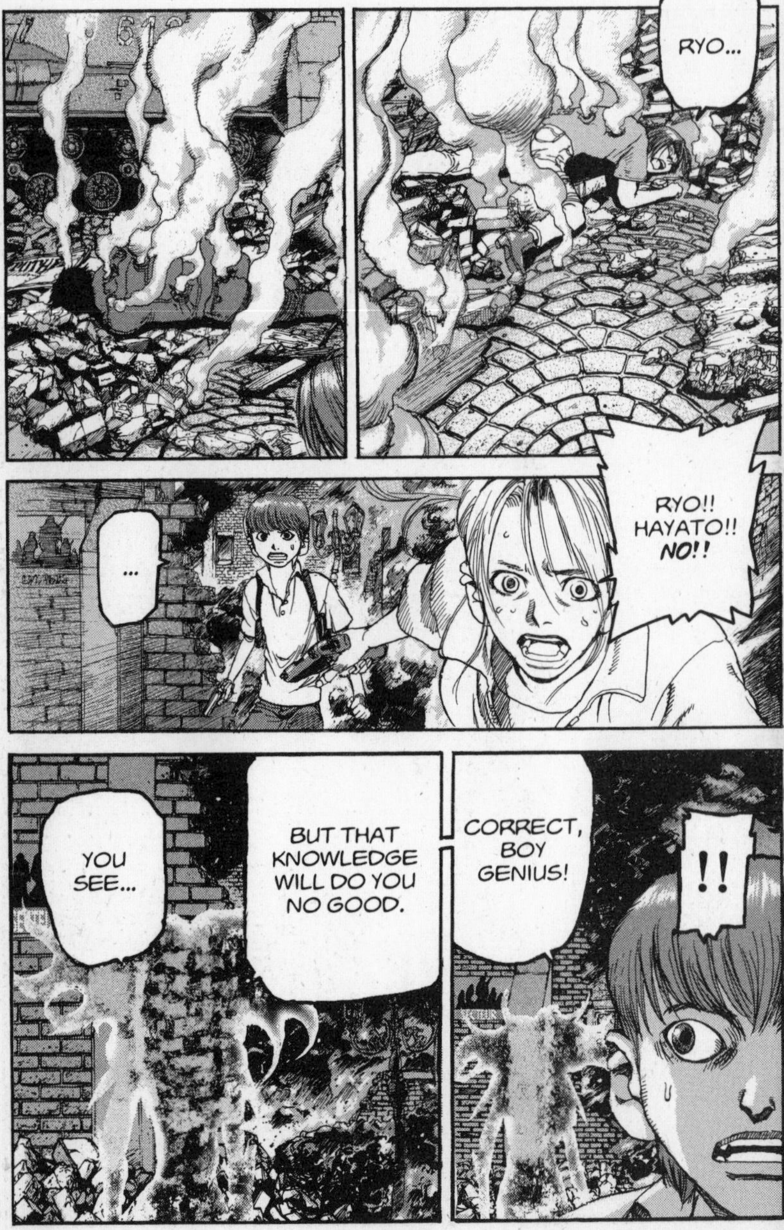
RYO...
RYO!! HAYATO!! NO!!
...
!!
CORRECT, BOY GENIUS!
BUT THAT KNOWLEDGE WILL DO YOU NO GOOD.
YOU SEE...

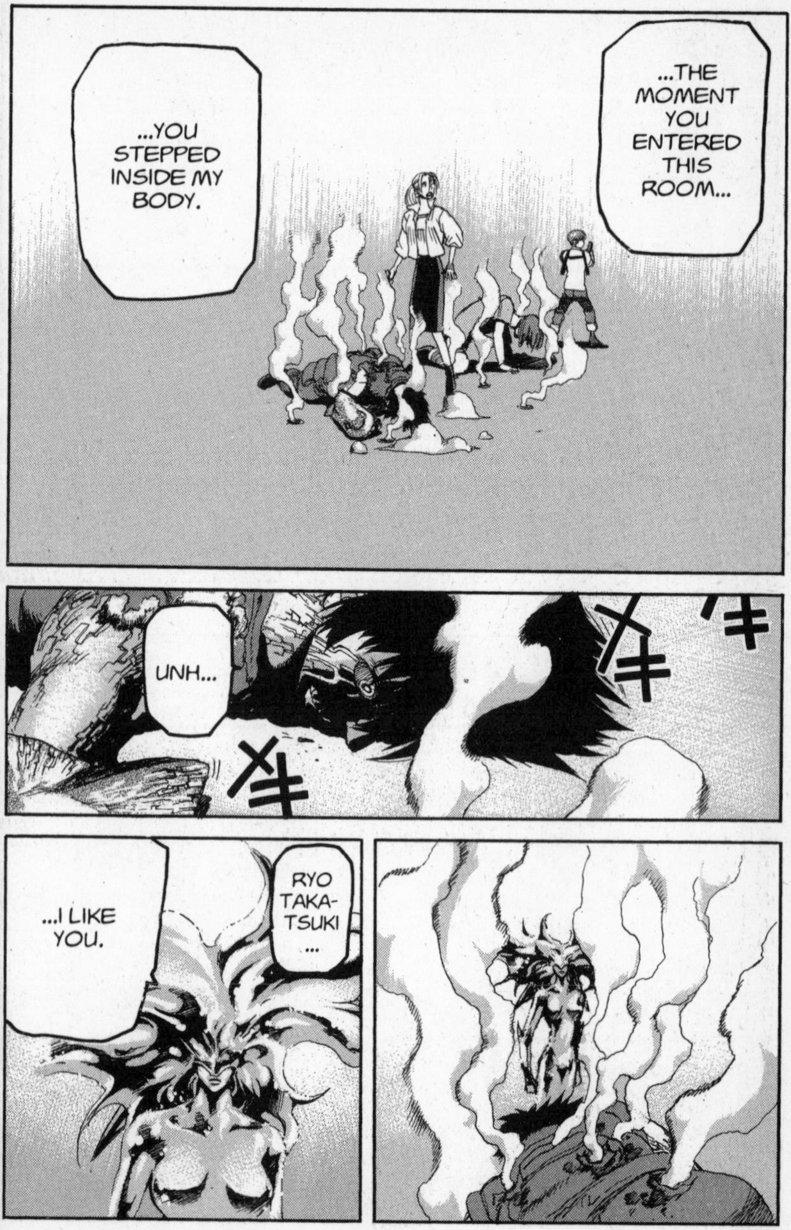

...THE MOMENT YOU ENTERED THIS ROOM...
...YOU STEPPED INSIDE MY BODY.
メキ
メキ
UNH...
メキ
RYO TAKA-TSUKI ...
...I LIKE YOU.

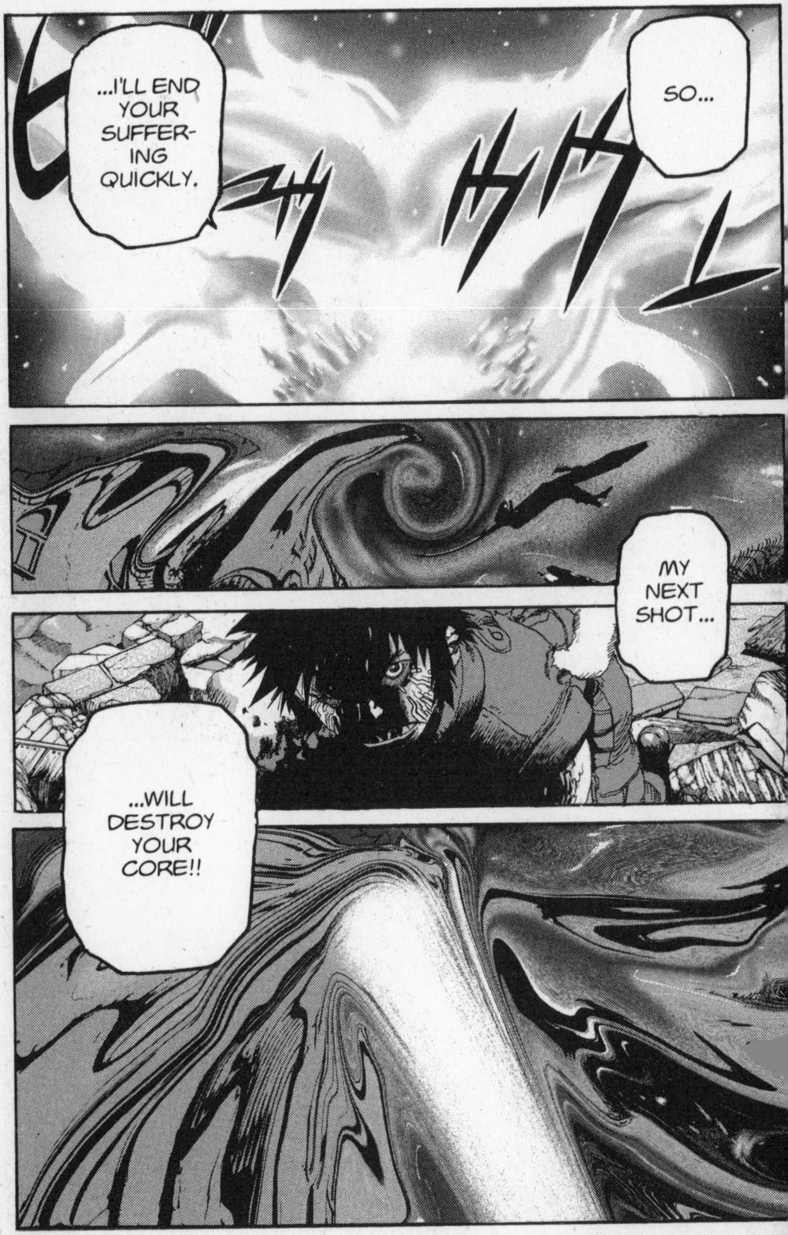
SO...
...I'LL END YOUR SUFFER-ING QUICKLY.
MY NEXT SHOT...
...WILL DESTROY YOUR CORE!!

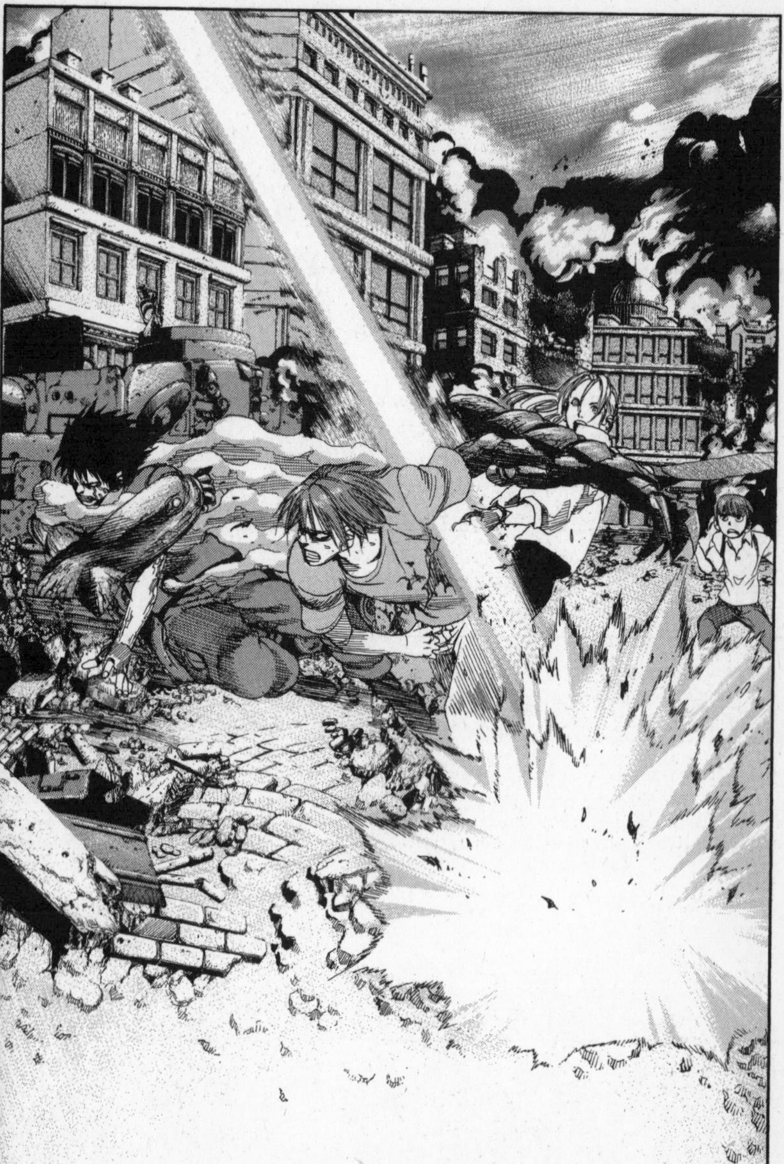

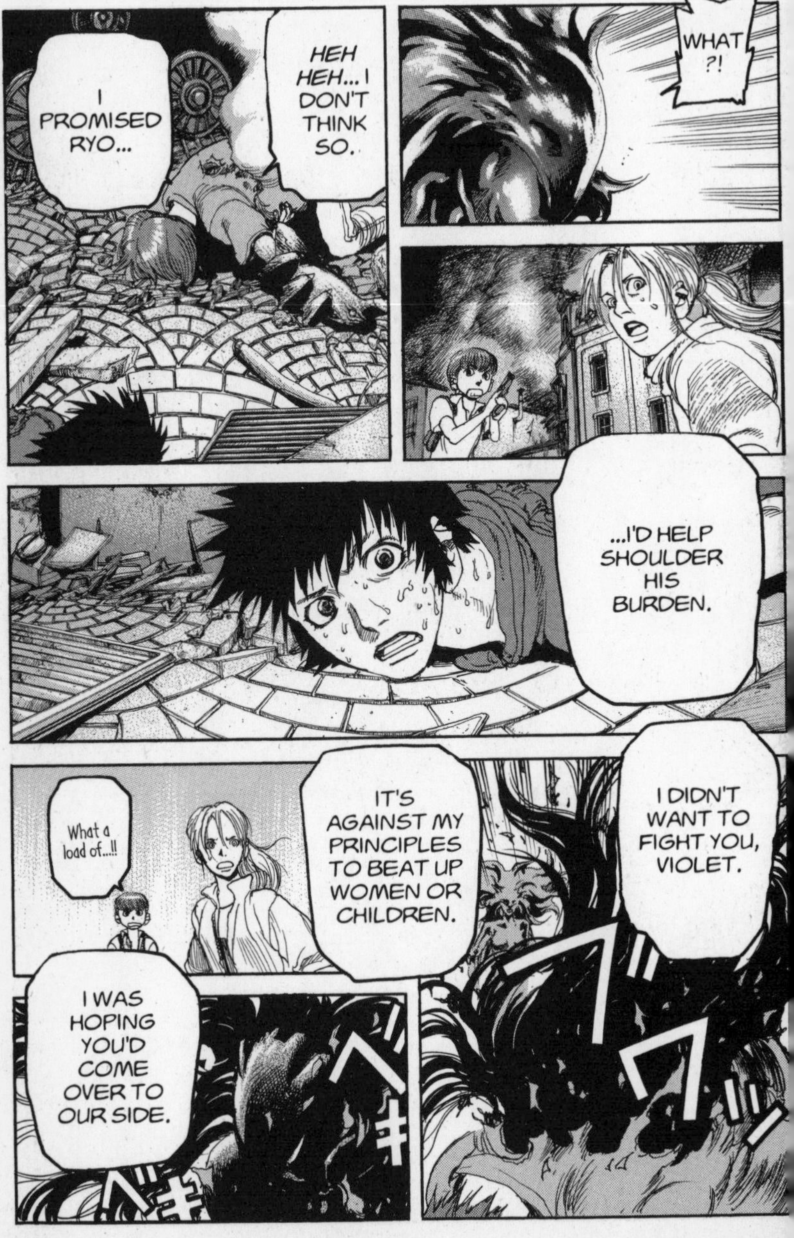
WHAT ?!
HEH HEH... I DON'T THINK SO.
I PROMISED RYO...
...I'D HELP SHOULDER HIS BURDEN.
I DIDN'T WANT TO FIGHT YOU, VIOLET.
IT'S AGAINST MY PRINCIPLES TO BEAT UP WOMEN OR CHILDREN.
What a load of...!!
I WAS HOPING YOU'D COME OVER TO OUR SIDE.

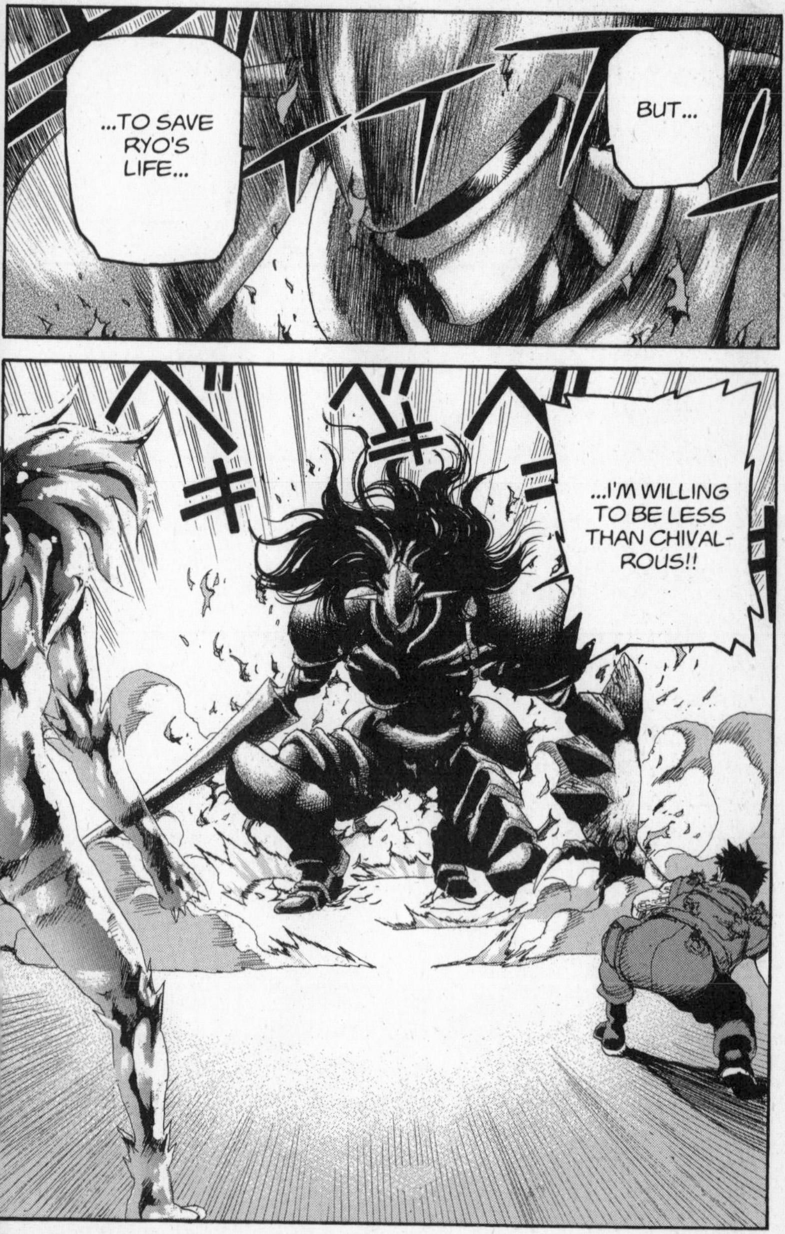
BUT...
...TO SAVE RYO'S LIFE...
...I'M WILLING TO BE LESS THAN CHIVAL-ROUS!!

Glossary of Sound Effects, Signs, and other Miscellaneous Notes

Each entry includes: the location, indicated by page number and panel number (so 3.1 means page 3, panel number 1); the phonetic romanization of the original Japanese; and our English "translation"—we offer as close an English equivalent as we can.

31.3 FX: Gohn gohn (barrier walls close)

31.4 FX: Byu (animal brushes into Kei)

31.5 FX: Zusha (moa stops wall with its neck)

32.1 FX: Guon goun (moa holds barrier up with its neck)

32.2 FX: Bachii bachi (creaking barrier)

32.8 FX: Ga ga ga ga (tiger holds up door)

34.2 FX: Kacha kacha (frantic typing on keyboard)

34.3 FX: Kacha kacha (typing on keyboard)

34.4 FX: Kan (distant ominous sound)

34.4 FX: Kan (distant ominous sound)

34.5 FX: Boh (explosion from far down passage)

35.4 FX: Boh (explosion)

35.5 FX: Kacha kacha (typing)

37.2 FX: Kacha Kacha ka (typing)

37.3 FX: Gohn gohn gohn (doors opening and shutting)

38.3 FX: Go go go (rumbling)

38.4 FX: Go go (rumbling)

38.5 FX: Go go (rumbling)

39.4 FX: Do do do do do (building crumbling)

CHAPTER 3

42.4 FX: Kohhh (machine)

42.5 FX: Ohhhhh (machine)

44.1 FX: Jakin (cocking gun)

51.4 FX: Do do do do do (Silver destroys machinery)

52.3 FX: Bachi bachi (crackling)

53.4 FX: Uiiin (door slides open)

55.3 FX: Gacha (phone hangs up)

56.6 FX: Suuu (Huang teleports)

57.2 FX: Ga ga ga ga ga gan (crashing debris)

57.3 FX: Doh doh doh doh doh (stuff breaking)

58.1 FX: Gara gara (stuff settling)

CHAPTER 1

5.2 FX: Bachi bachi (burning)

7.4 FX: Gishi (grinding metal)

7.4 FX: Gishi (grinding metal)

7.5 FX: Ga (staggering footstep)

8.1 FX: Yoro (Holst staggering)

8.3 FX: Bakiiin (big punch)

9.1 FX: Kin kin (straining machine)

9.2 FX: Gi gi (straining machine)

12.2 FX: Bishuuuun (hologram noise)

14.2 FX: Pan pan pan (gun firing)

14.4 FX: Gohn gohn go (safety gates opening)

15.1 FX: Zu zunn (stuff crashes to ground)

15.2 FX: Gohn gohn (clanging)

15.4 FX: Bachi bachi (crackling)

17.1 FX: Go gon (things breaking up)

17.4 FX: Do do do do do do (things smashing down)

21.1 FX: Do do do do do do (stuff falling apart)

21.2 FX: Bashuuu (steam hissing out of pipes)

21.4 FX: Bashiiin (barrier wall slams shut)

22.1 FX: Byuiiin (hologram noise)

CHAPTER 2

25.5 FX: Pi pi (beeping)

26.6 FX: Gohn gohn go (metal doors opening)

27.1 FX: Byuuuun (hologram buzzing)

28.1 FX: Gohn gohn (doors slam down)

28.3 FX: Gosha (Ryo grabs door)

29.1 FX: Gyuuun (barrier creaking)

29.4 FX: Gobaa (explosion)

29.6 FX: Hyuohhh (door opening)

30.1 FX: ohhhh (door opens in floor)

30.5 FX: Ohhhhh (echoing in the shaft)

31.1 FX: Gonn (barrier walls close)

58.2 FX: Gohhh (whooshing of passage)

FX: Kan kan (rubble trickling down)

CHAPTER 4

60.1 FX: Kohhhh (whooshing)

60.3 FX: Ohhh (whooshing)

60.4 FX: Biiiiii (resonance)

64.2 FX: Biiiiin (resonance)

64.3 FX: Haa (Hayato sighs in exasperation)

68.1 FX: Beki beki beki (ARMS transformation)

68.2 FX: Bakiiin (Silver's hand becomes claw)

69.4 FX: Bachi bachi (crackling)

69.6 FX: Zusha (squelchy sound)

72.1 FX: Bachi bachi bachi bachi (crackling)

72.5 FX: Giiiii (Ryo transforms his right arm)

73.1 FX: Dann (Ryo dashes toward Silver)

74.2 FX: Zushiiin (car explodes)

75.1 FX: Ohhh (whooshing)

75.2 FX: Ohh (whooshing)

75.3 FX: Zuba ba ba ba (particle beam weapon)

75.5 FX: Goh gohn (metallic booming)

76.1 FX: Shuuuuu (hissing)

76.2 FX: Beki beki beki beki (ARMS transformation sound)

CHAPTER 5

77.1 FX: Bashuuuuu (beam fired)

77.2 FX: Uunn (continued from previous panel)

78.2 FX: Bashuuuun (another beam)

78.4 FX: Buwaaaa (explosion)

79.1 FX: Bashuuuun (particle beam weapon)

80.2 FX: Gohn gohn (pounding of metal)

80.5 FX: Buwaaa (Silver fires beam)

81.1 FX: Dohhh (Silver shoots at Ryo)

81.4 FX: Buwa (steam hisses out)

81.4 FX: Ta!! (Ryo dodges)

81.6 FX: Bashu (Silver shoots at Ryo)

82.1 FX: Bashuuu (shot sound)

82.1 FX: Bakiiin (shot sound)

82.2 FX: Kyu un (blast narrowly misses Ryo)

82.3 FX: Bishuuuuu (blast)

82.4 FX: Buwa (steam hissing)

82.6 FX: Gashiii (Ryo catches Silver's ARM)

83.1 FX: Bushaaaa (Silver propels himself around)

83.2 FX: Gi gi (creaking)

90.2 FX: Shuiiii (sizzling)

90.3 FX: Iii (sizzling)

90.4 FX: iii (sizzling)

90.5 FX: Bakiiiin (Ryo smacks Silver's arm off)

91.2 FX: Beki beki beki (ARMS transformation sound)

91.3 FX: Shuuuu (sizzling)

91.4 FX: Shu ba (fight sounds)

91.5 FX: Byun (Ryo moves abruptly)

93.4 FX: Bachii bachii bachii bounn (burning)

93.5 FX: Buwa (flames flare up)

93.6 FX: Un gohn (noises from in the smoke)

94.2 FX: Go go go go go (Silver reconstituting)

CHAPTER 6

95.4 FX: Zu (heavy foot slams down)

96.1 FX: Ohhhh (whoosh sound)

98.3 FX: Bashuuun (Ryo shoots Silver)

98.4 FX: Bagohh (Mad Hatter's arm blown off)

99.2 FX: Zushaaa (blast from Ryo's ARMS)

99.5 FX: Buwa (hot gasses hissing)

99.7 FX: aaa (gasses hissing)

101.1 FX: Boh (Silver strikes)

101.2 FX: Buwaaaa (a big blast)

101.4 FX: Bashu bashu (shots from Ryo's ARM)

102.1 FX: Bashun bashun (Ryo fires at Silver)

102.2 FX: Ta! (Ryo dodges)

103.1 FX: Byuu (Silver fires)

103.2 FX: Busha (shots)

103.4 FX: Ga (smack)

107.1 FX: Do do do do do do do (waves of heat)

108.1 FX: Bata bata (Hayato beats flames off)

108.2 FX: Chiri chiri (Al gets a bit burned)

109.6 FX: Gohhhh (whooshing)

110.4 FX: Kohhhhh (burning)

110.4 FX: Ohhhh (burning)

111.1 FX: Byuuun (Ryo starts to transform)

111.4 FX: Da (running)

111.5 FX: Kyuuuun (ARMS transformation sound)

111.7 FX: Bashiiin (Ryo continues to transform)

CHAPTER 7

115.1 FX: Bushaaaa (explosive heat)

116.2 FX: Gohhhhh (heat whooshes)

116.3 FX: Ohhhhh (heat whooshes)

124.1 FX: Shun shun shun (Silver melts down)

124.2 FX: Shuohh (meltdown noise)

129.4 FX: Hyuoh (wind whistles through hole)

129.4 FX: Ohh (wind moans through hole)

CHAPTER 8

136.7 FX: Kachin (dad switches TV on)

136.7 FX: Bunn! (TV comes on)

137.6 FX: Kachin (click)

138.5 FX: Bata bata bata ba (helicopter blades)

138.6 FX: Pata pata pa (helicopter blades)

139.5 FX: Kacha kacha (typing on keyboard)

140.1 FX: Kacha kacha (typing)

140.3 FX: Kacha kacha (typing)

140.5 FX: Ga ga (Hayato and Kei whack Al on the head)

CHAPTER 9

149.6 FX: Mekyo!! (mystery noise)

150.1 FX: Gagon (explosion)

151.4 FX: Suu! (Huang teleports)

152.2 FX: Byunn (Howan's kick)

152.5 FX: Suu (Huang teleports)

152.5 FX: Kyun (Huang falls onto nothing)

152.7 FX: Fu! (Huang teleports)

157.2 FX: Gu gu! (Huang's arm transforms)

157.3 FX: Bekin (Huang's arm transforms)

160.1 FX: Suu (Iwao moves quickly)

160.5 FX: Do do do do do do do (debris falls)

161.1 FX: Byun kyun (Howan does his thing)

161.3 FX: Suu (punch)

165.1 FX: Suu (Huang attacks)

165.2 FX: Byu (Iwao throws talon)

165.3 FX: Byun!! (claw strikes Huang)

CHAPTER 10

169.1 FX: Pon (Hayato pats Ryo's shoulder)

169.3 FX: Gacha (door unlatches)

179.1 FX: Bann (Hayato slams his hand down)

180.4 FX: Byuuuuu (battle sounds)

182.5 FX: Bachiiiin (power surge)

184.1 FX: Buwa (Violet transforms)

CHAPTER 11

187.2 FX: Gohn gohn (clanging)

188.4 FX: Bishiiin (Ryo transforms his ARM)

188.5 FX: Bashiiin (Hayato transforms his ARM)

189.1 FX: Zushaaa (Violet shoots)

189.7 FX: Buwa (image changes)

191.2 FX: Kyuuuu (image changes)

191.5 FX: uuuuu (image changes)

192.1 FX: Zudohhh (a shot hits Ryo)

193.7 FX: Buuuuu (images blur)

195.2 FX: Buuuun (image sound)

195.4 FX: Kyuuuuu (images melt and move)

195.5 FX: Kyunn!! (laser beams)

198.2 FX: Meki meki meki (Ryo transforming)

199.1 FX: Byuuuun (image changes)

201.5 FX: Buwa (transformation sound)

201.7 FX: Beki beki (Hayato transforming)

202.1 FX: Giiin (resonance)

202.1 FX: Beki beki beki beki (Hayato transforming)

About the Authors

Ryoji Minagawa was born in Chiba Prefecture and made his manga debut in 1988 with *HEAVEN*, published in *SHŌNEN SUNDAY*. Much heralded for his incredible artwork in *SPRIGGAN* (*STRIKER*), Minagawa received more acclaim with *ARMS* when it was the winner of the 44th Shogakukan Manga award. *ARMS* was originally serialized in *SHŌNEN SUNDAY* from 1997 to 2002.

Kyoichi Nanatsuki, who provides story concept support, was born in Hokkaido. His credits as manga writer include *SAMURAI SHOWDOWN*, originally published in *SHŌNEN SUNDAY COMICS SPECIAL*, and *HOTARU ROAD*, which was serialized in *YOUNG SUNDAY*.